Pevensey Castle, Sussex

Excavations in the Roman Fort and Medieval Keep, 1993–95

By
Michael Fulford and Stephen Rippon

Pevensey Castle, Sussex

Excavations in the Roman Fort and Medieval Keep, 1993–95

By
Michael Fulford and Stephen Rippon

with contributions by
Denise Allen, S.J. Allen, Edward Carpenter, Johan Linderholm, Richard I. Macphail, Adrienne Powell, Richard Reece, David Richards†, Mark Robinson, N. Al Shaikhley, Dale Serjeantson, Ruth Shaffrey, E.M. Somerville, Jane Timby, Ian Tyers, Alan Vince†, and D.F. Williams

and illustrations by
Mike Rouillard, Sue Rouillard, Jane Timby, and S.J. Allen

Wessex Archaeology Report No. 26

Wessex Archaeology and University of Reading 2011

Published 2011 by Wessex Archaeology Ltd
Portway House, Old Sarum Park, Salisbury, SP4 6EB
http://www.wessexarch.co.uk/

British Library Cataloguing in Publication Data
A catalogue record for this book is available from the British Library

ISBN 978-1-874350-55-2

Edited by Philippa Bradley
Designed and produced by Kenneth Lymer
Cover design by Kenneth Lymer

Printed by Henry Ling (Dorset Press) Ltd, Dorchester

Cover photographs
Front: Pevensey Castle from the south (NMR 23375/04, 24th January 2004; © English Heritage, NMR)
Back: Pevensey Castle from the west, with the village of Pevensey beyond (NMR 23316/16, 24th January 2004; © English Heritage, NMR)

Wessex Archaeology Ltd is a registered charity No. 287786

Contents

List of Figures

List of Plates

List of Tables

Acknowledgements

This programme of survey and excavation would not have been possible without the help of the following: Elizabeth Wild, Jenny Compton, and Marilyn Day for supervising the finds processing; Tim Eaton and Sophie Hay for their supervision in the field, along with their assistants Nuwal Al Shaikhley, Stephen Benfield, Elaine Ingelson, Jason Lowe, Sarah Monks, Jamie Preston, Anthony Sibthorpe, David Slade, and Jason Walker; David Horniblow and Jason Lowe for their catering; and the English Heritage works teams at Tonbridge, Dover and Pevensey itself, in particular Jonathan Coad, Fred Powell, Danny Elliott, and Alison Moir. We are also grateful to the Ancient Monuments Laboratory for their prompt stabilisation of the coins, and the Sheffield Dendrochronology Laboratory for their report on the Roman timbers. Sue and Mike Rouillard have done an excellent job in preparing the drawings, and we are also grateful to English Heritage and the Sussex Archaeological Society for permission to reproduce material from their archives. We also thank Grenville Astill and Ann Curry for their discussions of both the archaeological and documentary evidence.

Steve Allen and Nuwal Al Shaikhley wish to acknowledge the advice offered during the preparation and execution of the standing building survey by Professor Grenville Astill and Professor Michael Fulford (both of the Department of Archaeology, University of Reading), and of Mr D. Elliott of English Heritage.

Richard Macphail acknowledges funding by English Heritage to complete his report, and thanks Michael Fulford and Stephen Rippon for the information they supplied. Sandra Bond (UCL), Ian Dormor, Johan Linderholm (Umeå University, Sweden), Kevin Reeves (UCL), Spectrum Petrographics, Stirling University and P. E. J. Wiltshire, are thanked for their contributions to this study.

The late David Richards wished to thank Paul Cannon of Newbury Museum and John Cherry of the British Museum who examined and kindly commented on the Tournai jeton and the gold ring respectively. Also Dr Martin Henig who examined several copper alloy objects and as usual gave much useful advice. Margaret Brooks formerly of Wiltshire Conservation Laboratory, Salisbury, carried out X-ray photography on the metalwork from the 1995 excavation as well as some initial conservation. The late Professor Perce Allen (University of Reading) is thanked for confirming the identification of the pieces of Wealden iron-ore and gave useful guidance into the literature of the Sussex iron industry. Professor John Allen (University of Reading) kindly examined samples of the slag and identified the late post-medieval blast furnace material.

E. M. Somerville would like to thank Polly Snowden, David Yates and John Bonnell for their work on the marine molluscs.

Jane Timby is grateful to Luke Barber (South-Eastern Archaeological Services), Dr Malcolm Lyne, Dr Paul Tyers, and the late Dr Alan Vince, for their invaluable assistance in identifying various wares.

Ian Tyers thanks Professor Michael Fulford and Steve Allen for the provision of information about the site and the timbers.

Finally, we must thank Wessex Archaeology for their work in editing and typesetting the report. The editing was undertaken by Pippa Bradley; Linda Coleman scanned the original artwork and provided advice on the drawings. The report was typeset by Kenneth Lymer, and Julie Gardiner managed the production of this volume.

Abstract

A programme of excavations on and around the Keep of Pevensey Castle (East Sussex) in 1993–95 established that the fort wall of the late Roman 'Saxon Shore' fort was constructed on the evidence of dendrochronology to AD 280–300, very possibly during the usurpation of Allectus (293–6). A deep sequence of 'dark earth' built up against the inside of the Roman fort wall during the Roman and early medieval periods, before and after the establishment of William I's Castle after 1066. The monumental, masonry phase began with the construction of a substantial stone Keep with projecting D-shaped towers on the inside of and against the surviving Roman fort wall, and above occupation containing ceramics broadly dated to the 11th to 13th century and probably around 1200. Close similarities in building style suggest that the gatehouse and postern to the Inner Bailey were constructed at about the same time. The excavation recovered traces of a tower on the outside of the Roman fort wall to protect the north-eastern corner of the Keep. Evidence was also recovered of substantial later repairs to the eastern side of the Keep, including the addition of a further tower against the outer face of the (collapsing) Roman wall, the construction of a garderobe chamber and the re-building of the north-east tower. Although these repairs were also later than occupation containing 11th to 13th century pottery, they are probably to be connected with a series of documented repairs of the early 14th century and occupation outside the Keep dated broadly by ceramics to the 13th to 15th century. The base of the now ruinous Keep was filled with clay after the 16th to 17th century, very possibly as an emergency measure in response to the survey of 1587, to provide a foundation for cannon to defend the Castle against possible Armada invasion in 1588. Robbing of the external towers during the 18th century destabilised the eastern side of the Keep which had then completely collapsed by the later 19th century.

Resumé

En 1993–95, un programme de fouilles dans et autour du donjon du château de Pevensey (East Sussex) a établi que la muraille de la forteresse de bord de mer saxonne de la période romaine tardive avait, selon les résultats des études dendrochronologiques, été construite vers 280–300 ap.J.C., très probablement pendant l'usurpation d'Allectus (293–6). Une profonde séquence de 'terre noire' s'était accumulée contre l'intérieur de la muraille du fort romain pendant la période romaine et au début du moyen-âge, avant et après la construction du château de Guillaume1^{er} après 1066. La phase de maçonnerie, monumentale, commença avec la construction d'un substantiel donjon de pierre avec des tours saillantes en forme de D à l'intérieur et contre la muraille du fort romain restante et au-dessus d'une occupation contenant des céramiques datant, en gros, du XIème au XIIème siècle et probablement vers 1200. De fortes ressemblances dans le style des bâtiments donnent à penser que le corps de garde et la poterne d'Inner Bailey avaient été construits à peu près à la même époque. Les fouilles mirent au jour les traces d'une tour à l'extérieur de la muraille du fort romain pour protéger le coin nord-est du donjon. On a également découvert des témoignages confirmant que plus tard d'importantes réparations avaient été effectuées sur le côté est du donjon, y compris l'adjonction d'une tour supplémentaire contre la face extérieure de la muraille romaine (qui s'écroulait), la construction d'une chambre garde robe et la reconstruction de la tour nord-est. Bien que ces réparations aient aussi eu lieu après l'occupation contenant de la poterie du XIème au XIIème siècle, elles avaient probablement un lien avec une série de réparations documentées du début du XIVème siècle et une occupation à l'extérieur du donjon datée grosso modo par des céramiques du XIIIème au XVème siècle. La base du donjon, maintenant en ruines, fut remplie d'argile après le XVIème ou XVIIème siècle, très probablement comme mesure d'urgence suite à l'étude de 1587, pour fournir un emplacement à canons pour défendre le château contre une éventuelle invasion de l'Armada en 1588. Le pillage des tours extérieures au XVIIIème siècle déstabilisa le côté est du donjon qui s'était complétement écroulé d'ici la deuxième moitié du XIXème siècle.

Traduction: Annie Pritchard

Zusammenfasung

Zwischen 1993 und 1995 konnte anhand von Ausgrabungen im Innen- und Außenbereich des Keeps (Wohn- und Wehrturm) von Pevensey Castle in der Grafschaft East Sussex gezeigt werden, dass die Umfassungsmauer des spätrömischen Kastells nach Ausweis dendrochronologischer Datierungen zwischen 280 und 300 n. Chr. errichtet wurde, sehr wahrscheinlich während der Usurpation des Allectus (293–296 n. Chr.). Das Kastell war Teil der spätrömischen Küstenbefestigung der britischen „Sachsenküste" (*limes saxonicum*). Eine tiefgründige Abfolge sogenannter „dark earth" Besiedlungs-schichten römischer und frühmittelalter-licher Zeitstellung lagerte sich entlang der Innenseite der römischen Kastellmauer ab, sowohl vor als auch nach der Errichtung der Burg Wilhelms des Eroberers nach 1066. Die monumentale Steinbauphase begann mit der Errrichtung eines massiven steinernen Keeps mit aus dem Maurring hervorkragenden D-förmigen Türmen. Der Keep wurde innerhalb und teilweise entlang der römischen Kastellmauer auf Siedlungsschichten errichtet, deren keramisches Fundmaterial grob in das 11. bis 13. Jh. und wahrscheinlich um 1200 datiert werden kann. Die große Ähnlichkeit der Baustile des Torhauses und der Pforte zur Vorburg legt nahe, dass beide in etwa zeitgleich errichtet wurden. Im Zuge der Ausgrabungen wurden Spuren eines Turmes außerhalb der römischen Kastellmauer gefunden, der wahrscheinlich der Sicherung der Nordost-Ecke des Keeps diente. Es fanden sich auch Hinweise auf umfangreiche spätere Ausbesserungen der Ostseite des Keeps, darunter der Anbau eines weiteren Turms an der Außenseite der (mittlerweile einstürzenden) römischen Kastellmauer, die Errichtung eines Aborterkers und der Wiederaufbau des Nordost-Turms. Obwohl diese Ausbesserungen ebenfalls später als die Besiedlungsschichten mit Keramik des 11. bis 13. Jhs. datieren, sind sie wahrscheinlich mit einer Reihe von urkundlich belegten Maßnahmen des frühen 14. Jhs. und der Besiedlung außerhalb des Keeps zu verbinden, die anhand von Keramikfunden dem 13. bis 15. Jh. zugewiesen werden können. Sehr wahrscheinlich als eine Notmaßnahme in Reaktion auf die Bestandsaufnahme von 1587 wurde das Fundament des mittlerweile baufälligen Keeps nach dem 16.–17. Jh. mit Ton verfüllt, vermutlich, um als Basis für Kanonen zur Verteidigung der Burg gegen die mögliche Invasion der Armada im Jahre 1588 zu dienen. Die Beraubung der äußeren Wehrtürme während des 18. Jhs. destabilisierten die Ostseite des Keeps, der dann spätestens im späten 19. Jh. vollständig verfallen war.

Übersetzung: Jörn Schuster

Preface

The excavations reported here were undertaken by the Department of Archaeology of the University of Reading at the invitation of English Heritage which has guardianship of Pevensey Castle. The aim was to investigate the eastern side of the Keep which now comprises fallen masses of Roman fort wall into which concrete pill-boxes constructed at the beginning of the Second World War have been inserted. Only the south-east tower of the Keep, which made use of an existing D-shaped bastion of the late Roman fort, survives more or less intact. The difficulty in interpreting these remains was compounded by the plan evidence presented in the English Heritage guidebook to the Castle which was in print in the early 1990s. This English Heritage Handbook, *Pevensey Castle Sussex*, was written by Sir Charles Peers and first published in 1953. In it the plan of the Keep shows with broken lines the outline of two, D-shaped towers projecting eastward beyond the lines of the Roman wall and the east wall of the Keep. There is no further information about these aspects of the Castle and, while the conjectured plan of the northern of the two makes sense as a tower to protect the north-east corner of the Keep, the function of its immediate neighbour is less clear. While the Roman fort has an imposing west gate flanked by two D-shaped towers, the East Gate is represented only by a narrow entrance without flanking towers. One possibility, therefore, was that the two indicated towers on the plan on the east side of the Keep originated as a more imposing East Gate to the Roman fort. The excavations were carried out over two, month-long seasons in 1993 and 1995 and one of three months duration in 1994 to complete the deep trench inside the Keep. With the exception of Ian Tyers report (1995) on the dendrochronology, all the specialist reports were completed between 1998 and 2002. However, Richard Reece revised his report on the coins in 2010 in the light of Malcolm Lyne's (2009) publication of the coins from earlier excavations. English Heritage grant aided both the excavation and post-excavation analysis. The archive is currently held by English Heritage at Fort Brockhurst, Gosport, Hampshire.

Michael Fulford
University of Reading

Stephen Rippon
University of Exeter
May 2010

Chapter 1
Introduction

Pevensey (TV 645 047) lies just inland from the present-day coast of East Sussex, 6 km to the north-east of Eastbourne and 17 km to the south-west of Hastings (Fig. 1.1). Formerly accessible by sea, the castle lies at the eastern end of a long narrow peninsula of land that projects into the Pevensey Levels, an area of drained coastal marshland now largely sheltered behind a shingle barrier which represents the present coastline. The Roman and medieval landscape context of Pevensey has been recently discussed by Pearson (2002, 118–9) and Rippon (2000, 157, 187–90).

The earliest visible remains at Pevensey relate to a late Roman fort, recorded in the *Notitia Dignitatum* (ch xxviii) as *Anderidos* or *Anderitos*, properly *Anderitum* (Rivet and Smith 1979, 250–1) as belonging to a series of forts under the control of the 'Count of the Saxon Shore' (Fig. 1.2, Pl. 1.1). Before the present programme of work it was unclear when the fort at Pevensey was constructed, though, notwithstanding a record of a number of late 3rd century coin finds, a date of *c.* 340 had become accepted based upon the discovery of a coin of 330–335 'in a beam-hole beneath one of the bastions which are of the same date of the wall... The end of the hole was open, but it is difficult to believe that the coin could have found its way 3 or 4 ft. under the thickness of the wall after the beam had decayed' (Bushe-Fox 1932, 67; Johnson 1976, 56–9; Pearson 2002, 59–60). The possibility of earlier occupation is indicated by the discovery by Salzmann of two brick stamps of the *classis Britannica* (*RIB* 2481.7; 2481.103). Bricks stamped with HON AVG ANDRIA, apparently referring to the emperor Honorius (395–423) and thought to indicate refurbishment of the defences in his reign, have since been shown to be modern forgeries (Peacock 1973; *RIB* 2484.1).

Reference to the Roman fort is made in the Anglo-Saxon Chronicle for the year 491 when it is stated that 'Aelle and Cissa besieged Andredesceaster, and killed all who lived in there; there was not even one Briton left' (Swanton 1996, 15). The Chronicle also records the events of 1066 when 'Earl William came from Normandy into Pevensey, on the eve of the Feast of St Michael [28 September], and as soon as they were fit, made a castle at Hastings market-town' (Swanton 1996, 199). Pevensey was granted to William's half-brother, Robert, Count of Mortain, who founded a small borough outside the old Roman fort and is likely to have established a castle within it. A castle is first documented in *Domesday* (Folio 20V: Sussex), when Alvred and William were the warders (Williams and Martin 1992, 48), and in 1088 the Anglo-Saxon

Plate 1.1 Aerial view of Pevensey Castle from the west with the Roman fortress wall and West Gate in the foreground. This formed the Outer Bailey of the medieval castle, the Inner Bailey of which lay to the east (top centre). Pevensey village lies beyond the castle (to the east) at the top of the photograph (NMR 23375/03, 24th January 2004; © English Heritage, NMR)

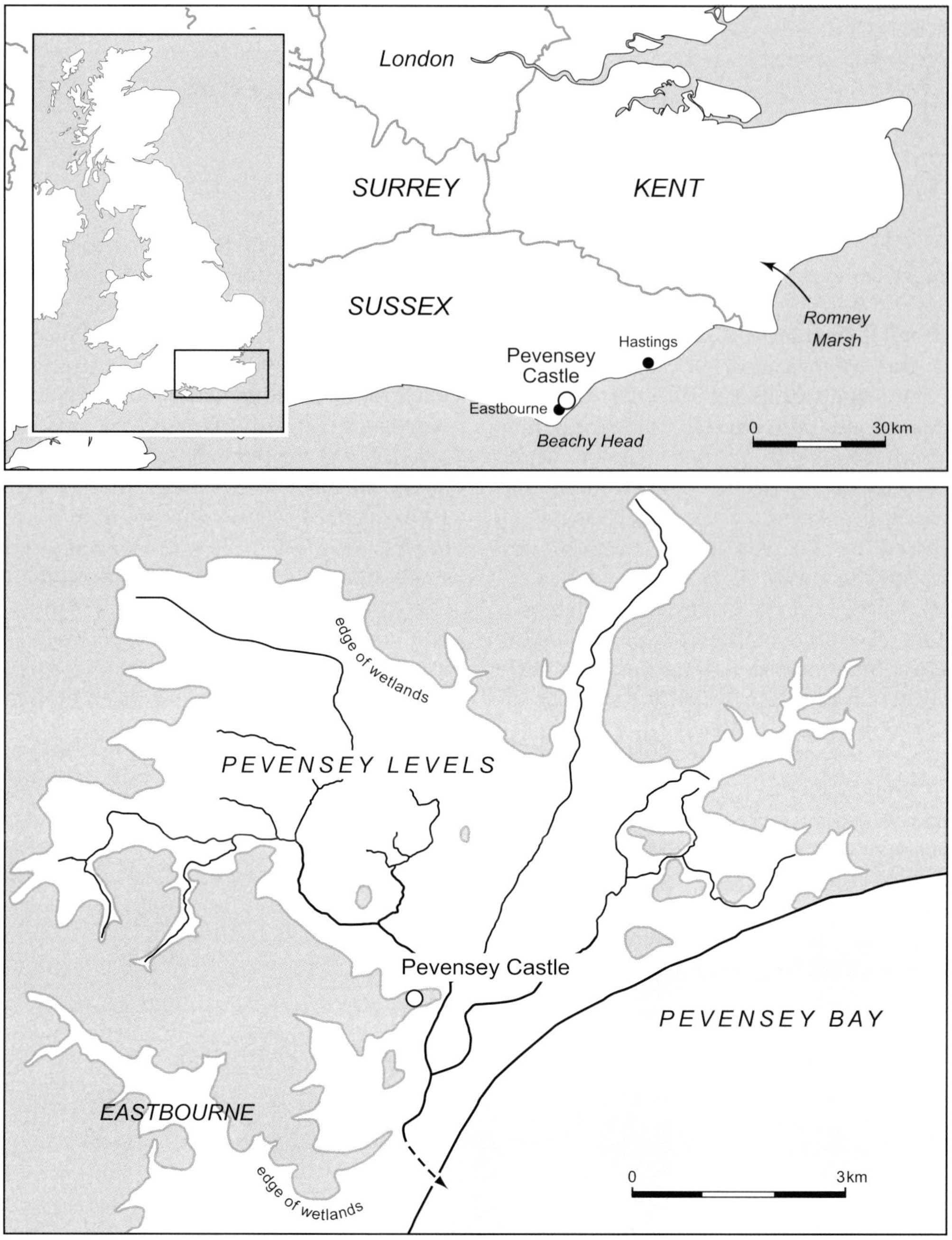

Figure 1.1 Location plan

Chronicle records that the king besieged Robert's son, Odo, Bishop of Bayeux (Swanton 1996, 224). In 1101 William, Count of Mortain, unsuccessfully rebelled against Henry I and the family finally forfeited Pevensey to the Crown. From 1101 the castle was held by a number of families who passed in and out of royal favour, though from 1264 it was usually in royal hands (Peers 1953, 6–11).

The medieval castle lay in the eastern part of the Roman fort so creating an inner and outer bailey (Fig. 1.2, Pls 1.1–1.2). The earliest medieval defensive work is likely to have been a banked and ditched enclosure and regular services of 'heckage' due from local manors suggests a substantial palisade which is explicitly referred to in 1188 (Table 1.1, Salzmann 1906, 3–4). The impressive gatehouse into the Inner Bailey is traditionally thought to have been built around 1190–1220 as the first stage in replacing the earthen and timber defences of the Inner Bailey (Fig. 1.2, Pl. 1.2). For a short while it may have been a free-standing masonry tower within this earthen embankment and timber palisade before the latter were replaced by the present stone curtain-wall and towers in the mid-13th century (Peers 1953, 21). In 1254 the Lord of Pevensey, Peter of Savoy, commuted the heckage services to cash payments

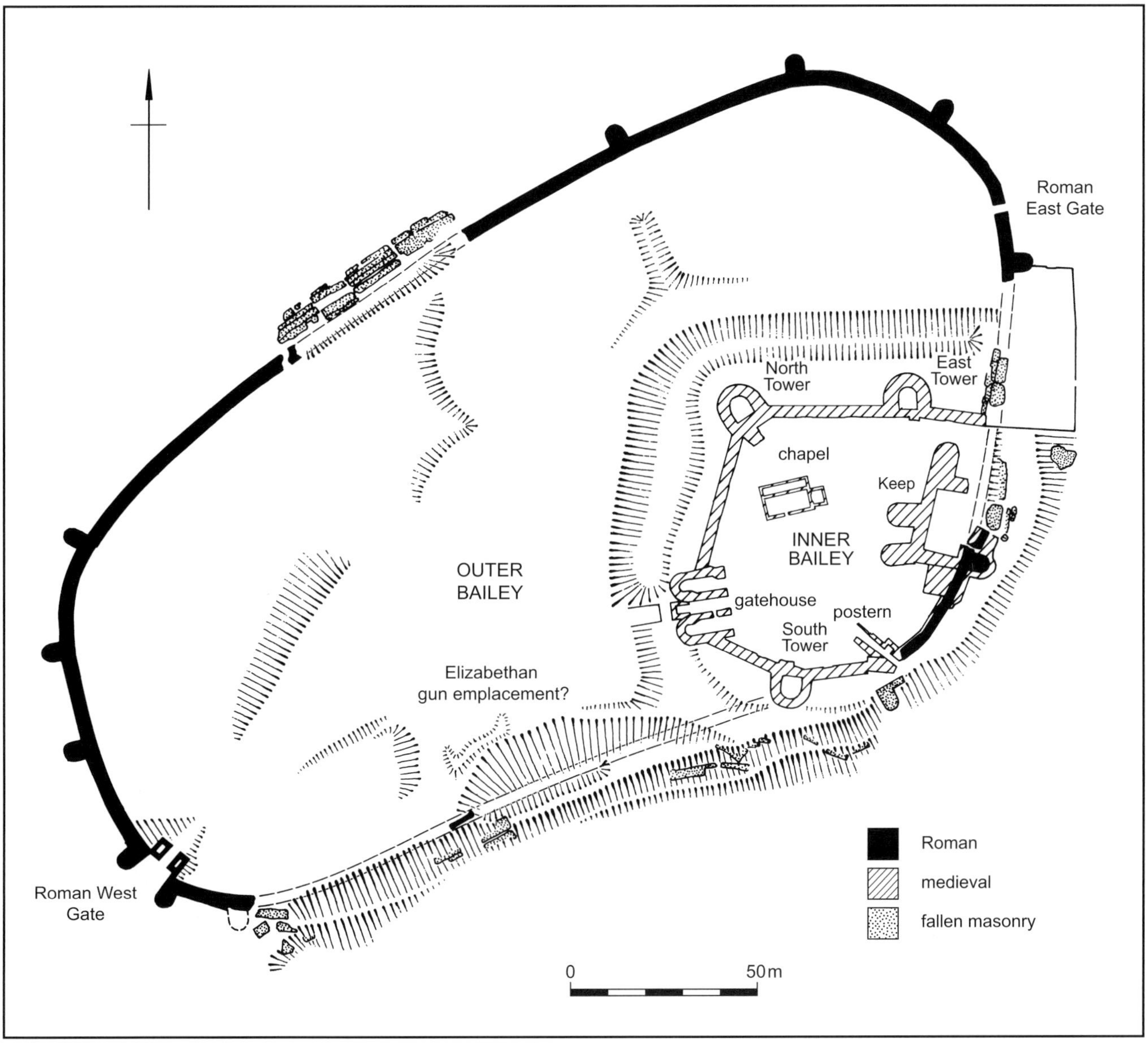

Figure 1.2 Plan of Pevensey Castle showing the medieval castle located in the south-east part of the Roman fort

suggesting that the defences had been rebuilt in stone by that date. A recent structural survey by Chapman (2007) has confirmed that the lower storey of the gatehouse is indeed earlier than the curtain wall and probably dates to the last decade of the 12th century, though the upper parts of both structures may have been contemporary.

Where the construction of the masonry Keep with its distinctive apsidal projections, the development of which is a major focus of the research reported here, fits into the development of the castle is far from clear. Peers was inclined to date the initial construction of the Keep to the late 11th or early 12th century, noting the reference to the documented existence of a *turris* de Penvesel in 1130 (Peers 1953, 19; Salzmann 1906, 2). In a subsequent, detailed consideration of the surviving Keep and its architecture Renn (1971) was sceptical of the identification of the *turris* with the Keep and of a date for it as early as that suggested by Peers. However, his detailed survey of the surviving fabric of the Keep suggested that the apsidal projections were a later addition, perhaps of the later 12th century, to a pre-existing, rectangular core, which in his view could well have dated from the late 11th century (Renn 1971, 61). If further repairs to the *domorum turris* in 1180–1 and *in operatione turris et fossati* in 1193 can be equated with repairs of the Keep, these events at least provide a possible *terminus ante quem* for some phase of its construction (Renn 1971, 63). About one hundred years later, from the mid-1280s through to the beginning of the 1300s, documents show through successive years of expenditure evidence of extensive alterations and repairs to the Keep and other parts of the castle (Salzmann 1906, 9–17; Table 1.1).

Table 1.1 Documented building work at Pevensey Castle (from Salzmann 1906)

Date	*Cost*	*Works*	
1161	£3 6s 6d		
1167	£5 10s 5d		
1188	£5 18s 4d	repairs to palisade	
1283	19s	repairs to Queens Chamber, a barn and other minor repairs	
1284		repairs to pigeon house, bridge and 20d for the Keep's windows	
1285		repairs to chapel, hall, Queens Chamber and stable	
1286		repairs to North and South Towers, chapel, bridge and gatehouse	
1287		repairs to Queens Chamber	
1288	£25 3s 3d	building work, including repairs to the wall thrown down in 1264	
1289/90	£42 18 1d	repairs to Queens Chamber, North Tower and Great Tower	
1290/91	£43 3s 4d	repairs to gate, hall and Queens Chamber and Great Tower	
1300/01	£6 10s 9d	rebuilding of chapel and other works	
1301/02	£3 12s 6d	repairs to Great Tower and granary tower	
1302/03	18s	repairs to Great Tower	
	£1 6s 5d	repairs to gatehouse	
	£2 2s 10d	repairs to fallen wall in inner bailey	
1306	estimates for repairs	Great Gate	£48
		barn	£14
		pigeon house	£2
		hall	£12
		Queens Chamber	£20
		Keep, four towers and other works	£1000
1318	estimates for repairs	Keep	£120
		Great Gate	£40
		North Tower	£100
		breach in Inner Bailey wall	£40 to rebuild
		two small towers	£50 to rebuild
		inner bailey walls	£20
		postern	£5
		hall	£12
		bridge	£2
		outer bailey wall (20 perches)	£1000
		barn	£3 7s
1318-21	£146 8s 8d	unspecified works	
1322		repairs	
1367	£4 8s 0d	repairs to bridge, Keep and gatehouse	
1371	£26 13s 5d	repairs to Keep	
1396	£1 15s 0d	repairs to gatehouse	
1407	£20 3s 2d	repairs to Keep, tower called Dameydeynestor, and gatehouse	
1440	£12 0s 3d	repairs	
1444	£7 17s 3d	repairs on various buildings	
1446	£1 15s 2d	repairs	
1452	£7	repairs	
1485	£1 8s 4d	repairs	

Plate 1.2 Aerial view of the Inner Bailey from the south-west with the gatehouse, built around 1190–1220, in the foreground. The excavations reported here lay to the east of the Keep (top centre) (NMR 4779/72, 29th July 1992; © Crown Copyright, NMR)

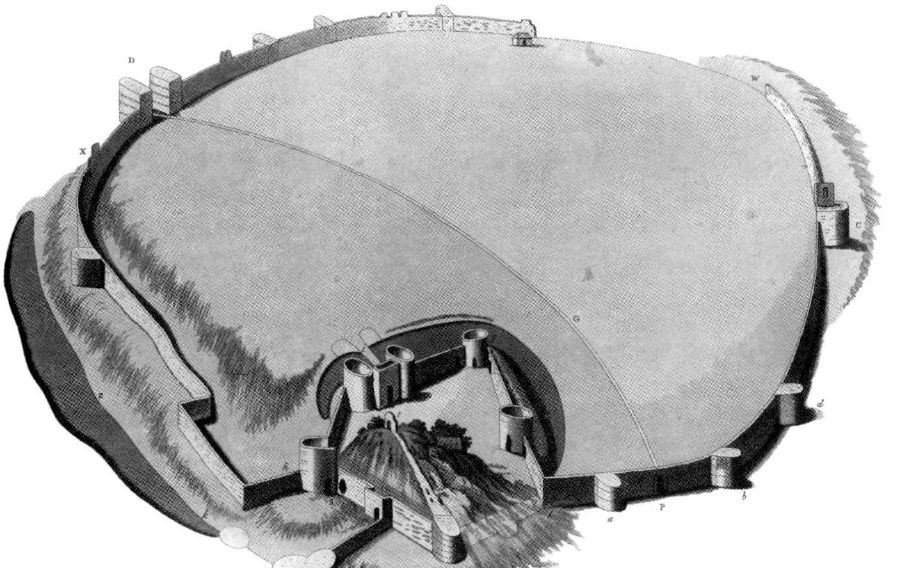

Plate 1.3 'Birdseye view of Pevensey Castle', engraved by Richardson for inclusion in Edward King's Munimenta antiqua; or, Observations on antient castles, *published in 1801, but based on an original painting of* c.*1780–85 by Samuel Hieronymus Grimm (1733–1794) and which is now part of the Burrell Collection in the British Library. This engraving clearly shows the Keep covered by a substantial mound (© Sussex Archaeological Society)*

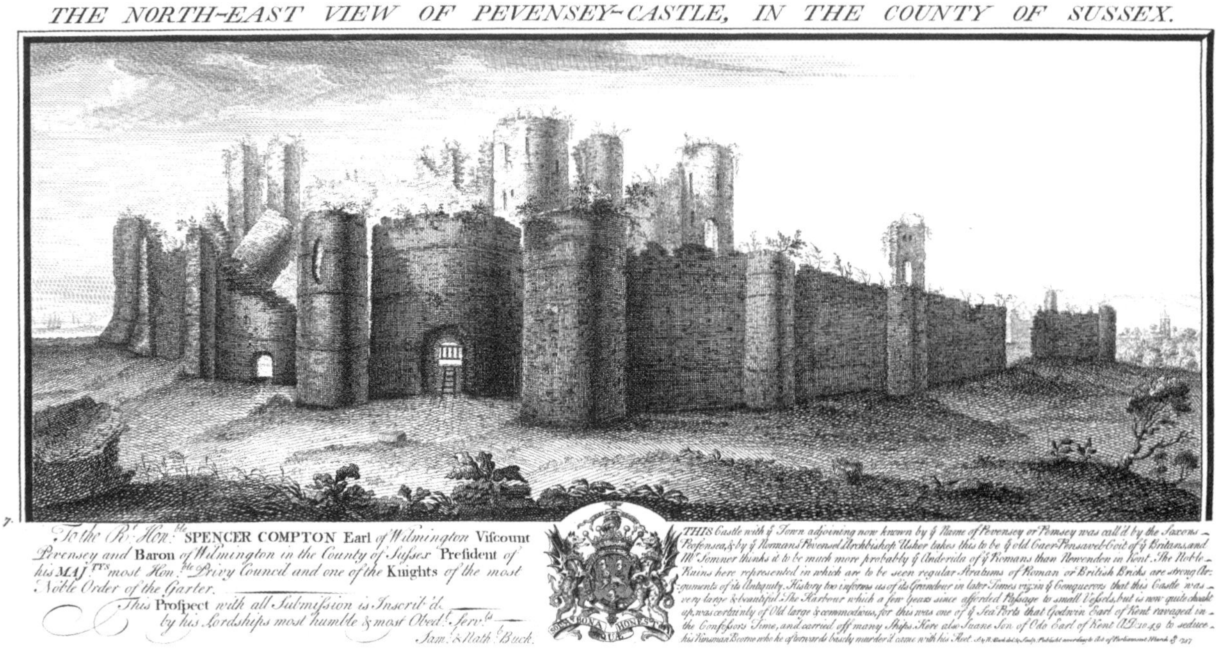

Plate 1.4 Engraving of Pevensey Castle, from the North East, by Samuel and Nathaniel Buck, in 1737. The Roman East Gate lies at the centre, with the Inner Bailey and Keep behind, the latter covered by a substantial mound (© English Heritage)

Plate 1.5 Photograph of Pevensey Castle from the south east, taken c. *1930, following the removal of the mound that covered the Keep by the Ministry of Works, revealing the interior of the Keep. The South Tower and postern gate of the Inner Bailey lies on the far left, and the East Tower on the far right. The Roman bastion at the centre of the photograph was used as the Keep's South East Tower, to the north (right) of which the Roman fortress/medieval keep wall has collapsed (© Crown Copyright, NMR)*

Further major repairs to the Keep were undertaken at the beginning of the 15th century and then, again, in the 1440s (Salzmann 1906, 23–6). By the 16th century, however, the castle was in a state of considerable decay. In 1573, a survey of the fabric took the view that it was not worth the expense of repairing; indeed lead and stone were being removed from the castle at this time (Salzmann 1906, 27–9). However, due to the threat from Spain in 1587, two small cannon were located in the castle, probably in a small earthwork emplacement on the southern side of the Outer Bailey (Fig. 1.2; Peers 1953, 9,12). Alternatively, one or both may have been located on a mound of clay that was deposited over the ruins of the Keep sometime in the late-medieval/early post-medieval period. This smothering of the Keep is shown in an 18th century aquatint by S. H. Grimm with material running over and covering the eastern side (Pl. 1.3). The mound is also, but less clearly, visible in the engraving of Pevensey Castle by Samuel and Nathaniel Buck dated to 1737 (Pl. 1.4). While the latter shows the castle in a very ruinous state, the fabric of the eastern side of the Keep still appears to be standing. During the Second World War (1939–45) the castle was pressed into military service for the last time, being used by British, American and Canadian

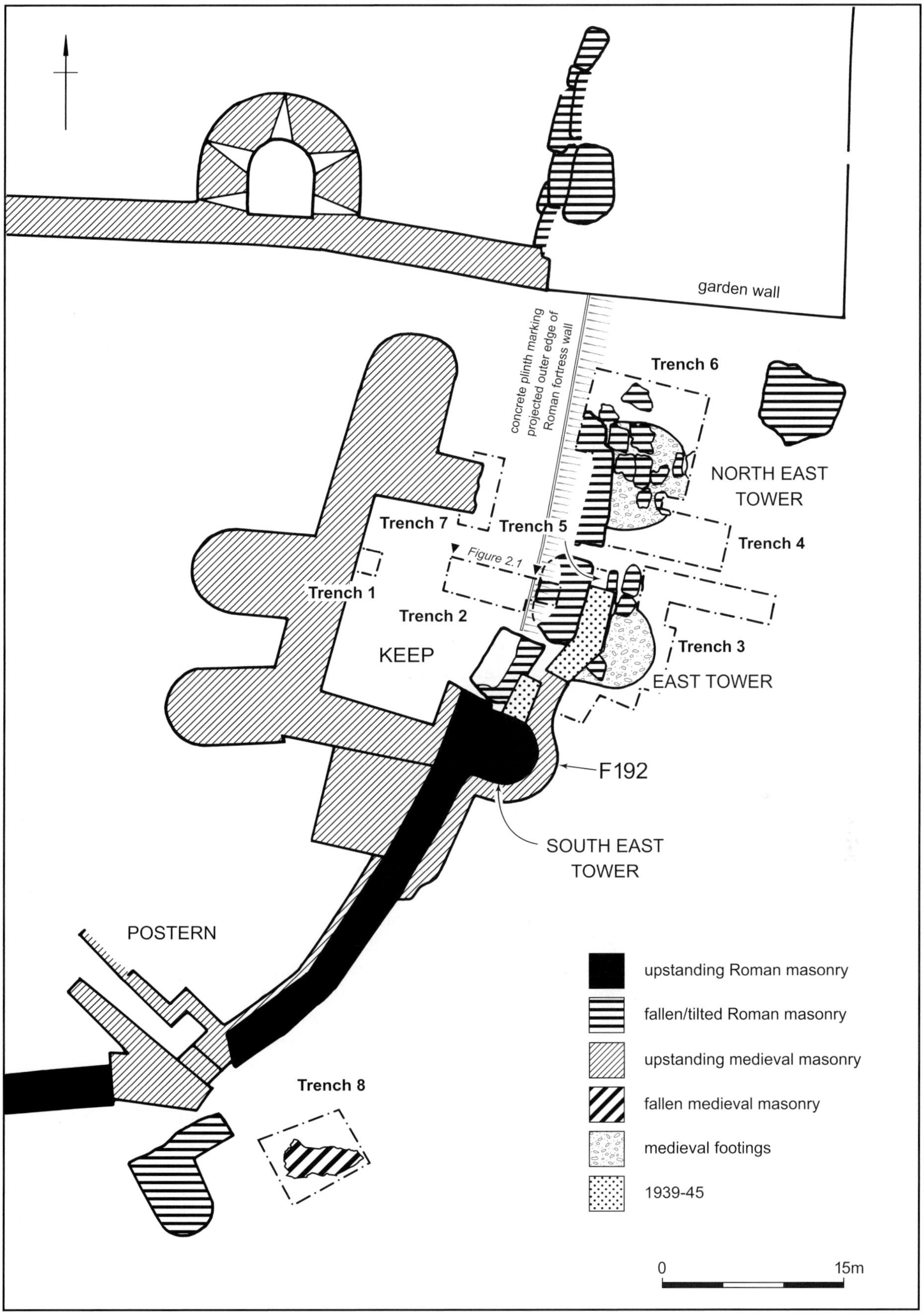

Figure 1.3 Plan of eastern part of the medieval Inner Bailey including the Keep, Postern Gate and excavations carried out between 1993–95

troops, and the Home Guard. By this time the eastern side of the Keep with its fallen masonry was certainly pretty much in its present condition before the modifications were made to defend it and accommodate soldiers between 1939 and 1945 (Peers 1953, 12).

The castle at Pevensey has seen a long, though not very illustrious, history of archaeological investigation. The earliest work was carried out in 1853 by Lower and Roach-Smith (Lower 1853; Roach-Smith 1858), while the first, rather inaccurate, description of the castle was made several decades later (Clarke 1882; 1884); the first accurate plan appears to have been drawn by W. Figg (appearing in Lower 1853). In 1906/7 the first proper excavations were carried out by Salzmann and Ray (1906/7; and see Dunning 1958) in the central and western part of the Roman fort, with further work carried out by Sands a year later (1908) on a substantial mound of yellow clay inside the medieval inner bailey that it is now known to have sealed the Keep. In 1925 the castle was given to the nation, and the then Office of Works carried out a programme of clearance which included completely removing the mound of clay that sealed the Keep (Pl. 1.5). Important excavations were undertaken within the enceinte of the Roman fort, but outside of the inner bailey of the medieval castle, between 1936 and 1939, most informatively by Frank Cotterill, but also by Arthur Burgess and B. W. Pearce. These have just been published by Lyne (2009). The findings from Cotterill's trench (XIII) against the north wall of the fort, in particular, are important to some of our results reported here. Finally, excavations, not yet published, were undertaken by Stuart Rigold in the 1960s (Wilson and Hurst 1962, 323–4; Wilson and Hurst 1965, 192), on behalf of the Ancient Monuments Section of the Ministry of Public Works. One of Rigold's excavations (1964) was located inside the medieval postern gate, an area also investigated by Sands (1908, 29). It is briefly reported on by Lyne (2009, 61).

The 1993–95 programme of work

The programme of fieldwork reported here was carried out between 1993 and 1995 under the auspices of the University of Reading (Fig. 1.3), in advance of conservation work by English Heritage on the site of the Keep (Fulford 1993; Fulford and Rippon 1994; 1995). Excavations concentrated on the eastern side of the medieval Keep where it formerly abutted the inside of the Roman fort wall. With the exception of the Keep's South East tower, which re-used a Roman bastion, both the eastern Keep wall and the associated stretch of Roman fort wall have collapsed leaving a jumbled mass of masonry that was partly exposed by the Ministry of Works during the 1930s (Pl. 1.5). That programme of work also found evidence for a D-shaped tower on the eastern side of the Keep which has appeared on subsequent site plans. Later plans also show the dashed outline of a second, D-shaped tower immediately to the north. In the absence of further information about the character and date of these remains, it was unclear whether these were exclusively medieval, or modifications of late Roman towers. If the latter, the positioning of the towers is suggestive of a gate, perhaps a sea-gate to give access to the adjacent tidal creek. The situation on the eastern side of the Keep is further complicated by the insertion of pill boxes among the fallen masonry in the 1940s.

The programme of excavations in 1993–95 was designed to investigate whether there was indeed evidence for any towers here and, if there was, to establish the character and date of the remains. The results would enhance our understanding of the structural history of the Keep as a whole, while at the same time, the collapse of the Roman fort wall at this point also gave the opportunity for the excavation of its foundations in the hope of establishing a more secure date of its construction. Subsidiary tasks included the clearing of the garderobe at the south-east corner of the Keep, the entrance to which had been largely obstructed by the construction of a Second World War pill box, and the re-investigation of a mass of masonry adjacent to the medieval postern gate.

Chapter 2
The Excavation

Introduction

A total of eight trenches were excavated in three locations in and around the Keep over about 16 weeks between September 1993 and the end of July 1995 (Fig. 1.3). In addition an assessment of the masonry of the Keep and part of the adjacent curtain wall was undertaken in March 1994 (see Appendix 1).

1. Three trenches were located inside the Keep: Trench 1 against the inside of the Keep's west wall; Trench 2 at right angles to and abutting the line of the Keep's east wall where it ran inside the Roman fort wall; and Trench 7 across the line of the Keep's north wall. Of these, Trench 2, commenced at the outset of the project, was the most significant. It was designed to explore the sequence down to the construction of the Roman fort wall. As the extent of the collapse of the wall and the stratigraphy originally retained by it was such that it obscured the relationship of the construction of the Keep with the stratigraphic sequence, Trenches 1 and 3 were opened in order to clarify that relationship.

2. Four trenches were excavated on the lower ground below the collapsed fort/Keep wall in order to locate and characterise the towers recorded on the plan of the castle. Trench 3, opened in 1993, focused on the D-shaped tower on the eastern side of the Keep recorded in the 1930s, with Trenches 4 and 6 located over the area of the hypothetical tower to the north and excavated in the following seasons, 1994–5. The small Trench 5 was located within the tumbled masonry blocks of the Roman fort wall.

The results of the above seven trenches in and around the Keep revealed a sequence of events relating to the defence and occupation of Pevensey Castle stretching from the late 3rd through to the 20th centuries and the Second World War. Fifteen phases can be identified:

1. Pre-fort Roman horizons inside the Roman enceinte
2. Roman fort construction (late 3rd century)
3. Sequence of late Roman to medieval occupation inside the Roman fort wall (late 3rd to 11th/13th century). This can be divided into three sub-phases:
   3.1 Roman
   3.2 Post-Roman/early medieval
   3.3 Norman
4. Horizons outside the fort pre-dating the 11th/13th century slumping
5. Slumping outside the Keep and levelling of the area with dumped clay (11th/13th century)
6. Construction of the Keep (11th/13th century)
7. Robbing of the Keep's North East Tower (11th/13th century)
8. Remodelling of the Keep's eastern side (11th/13th century)
9. Addition of garderobe chamber on the eastern side of the Keep (12th/13th century)
10. Activity to the east of the Keep, including the digging of refuse pits (14th–15th century)
11. Dumping of yellow/brown clay inside the Keep
12. Demolition and partial robbing of the Keep's eastern towers
13. Collapse of the eastern wall of the Keep and slumping of material inside Keep (late 18th century?)
14. Further robbing of eastern side of Keep (late 18th–19th century)
15. Ministry of Works and Second World War activity (20th century)

3. Trench 8 was excavated to explore an isolated block of collapsed masonry outside the postern gate 30 m to the south of the Keep (Fig. 1.3, Pls 2.7–2.8). This structure might be the fallen, possible baffle-wall investigated by Rigold in 1964. The sequence established in Trench 8 cannot be related to the above scheme of phasing (see below).

Phase 1: Pre-fort activity (Trench 2)

The earliest stratified deposits were located at the western end of Trench 2, inside the Keep (Fig. 2.1). The natural bedrock comprised intercalated grey clays and grey silt/silty sands, the top 0.3 m of which were slightly oxidised giving rise to an orange mottling (layer 72). Overlying this was a mottled orange/brown clay, 0.15 m thick (layer 71) which immediately pre-dates the construction of the Roman fort (demonstrated by the overlying upcast from the foundation trench: Phase 2, layers 63/67 below). A small amount of pottery cannot be more closely dated than to *c.* 240–400.

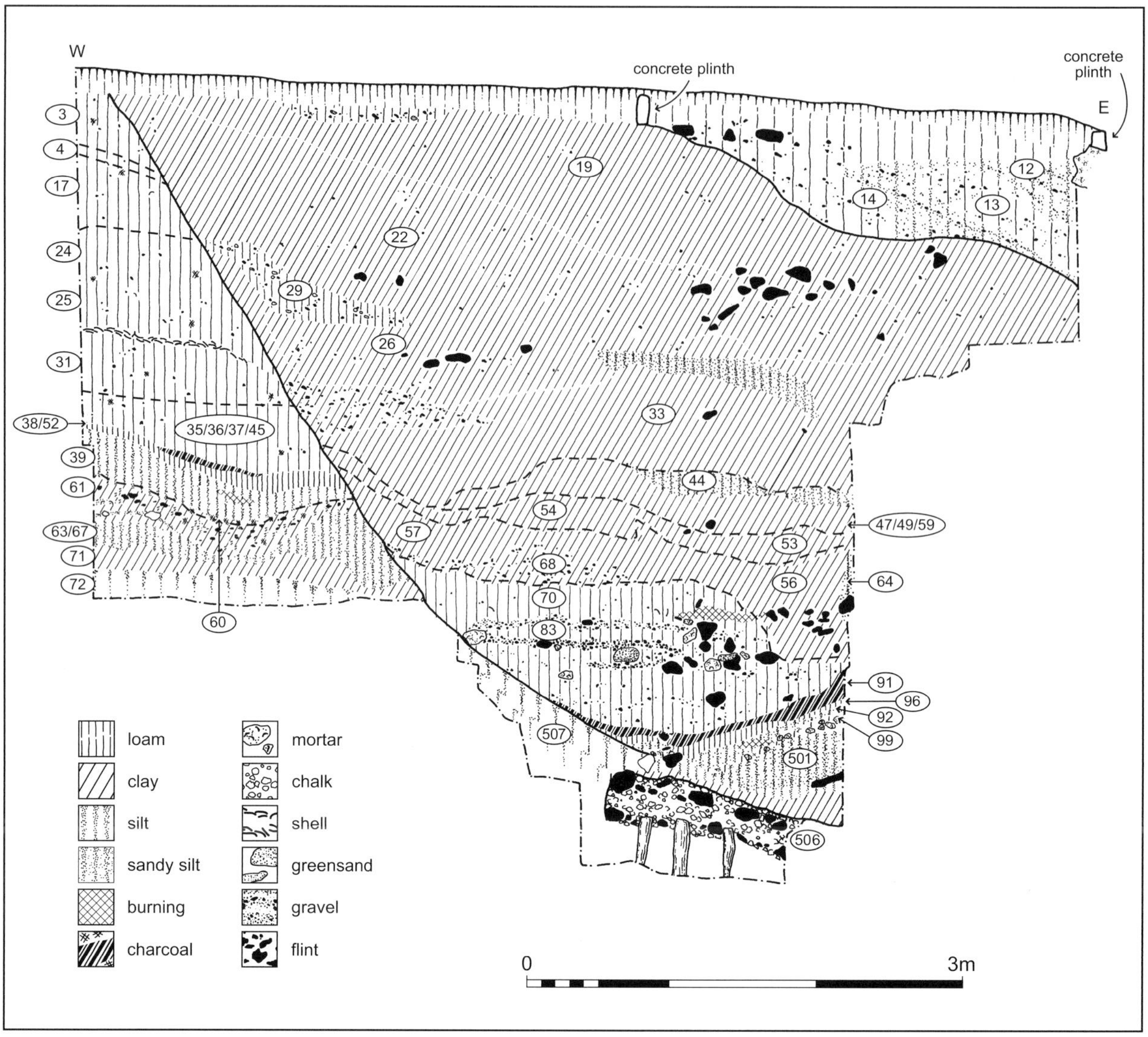

Figure 2.1 South-facing section in Trench 2, including footings of Roman fort wall (506), 'dark earth' sequence, and slumping following the collapse of the Roman fort wall (see Figure 1.3 for location)

Phase 2: Fort construction (Trench 2)

The foundation trench for the Roman fort wall was located in the eastern end of Trench 2 (Fig. 2.1, Pl. 2.1). Because of the constraints of shoring, its eastern edge could not be recorded, while the western side was disturbed through slumping following the collapse of the wall (Phase 13). The footings comprised a grid of oak stakes, between 0.60 m and 0.82 m long driven into the underlying natural (507), which were used to anchor a series of alternating layers of chalk rubble and flint nodules (506), a method of construction that was also noted in earlier excavations (Salzmann and Ray 1906/7, 15–22). Six of the timbers were dated by dendrochronology with the latest ring dating from AD 270, and a suggested felling date for the timbers as a whole of AD 280–300 (see Tyers below, Chapter 4). All further traces of the 3 m thick wall in Trench 2 were removed when it subsequently collapsed. Because of the constraints imposed by the shoring, the base of the fallen Roman wall could not be investigated, though deposits of flint, greensand, ironstone, and mortar rubble at the extreme eastern end of Trench 3 appear to relate to the wall's foundations that were wrenched up when it fell (46, 64, 505).

Upcast from the foundation trench sealed the pre-fort surface to the west. It comprised dumps of mottled yellow/grey silty sand (63/67) containing an intermittent lens of lighter brown gravely sandy clay containing occasional flecks of charcoal (layer 81). Overlying this was a layer of mortar and flint rubble (61), representing the construction horizon for the fort wall, which produced only a few undiagnostic sherds of Roman pottery. A possible post-hole (F65) was located within this construction sequence, that plausibly could relate to scaffold used in the construction of the fort wall.

Phase 3: Sequence inside fort wall (Trenches 1, 2 and 7)

The fort construction horizon (61) was succeeded by a deep sequence of deposits that survived intact at the western end of Trench 2 (Fig. 2.1). A thin lens of light brown clay with abundant charcoal (layer 60) associated with coins of Carausius (287–93) and of Allectus (293–6), but with pottery dating to the late 4th century (*c.* 370+), was sealed by a thick layer of pale mottled yellow/grey silty sand (layer 39), which was in turn sealed by a thin lens of light brown silty clay containing frequent flecks of charcoal (layer 38/52).

Above this, starting at a depth of *c.* 2.4–2.6 m below the present ground surface, lay a deep deposit of fairly homogeneous mid- to dark brown silty loams (layers 17, 24–25, 31, 35–37, 45), with abundant charcoal and occasional lenses of gravel and dumps of oyster shell (e.g., layer 31). The lower 0.2–0.6 m (layers 35–37 and 45) produced pottery dating to the 4th century. From a depth of 2.2 m below the present ground surface, layers 31, 25 and 24 produced a handful of 7th to 11th century sherds from an otherwise overwhelmingly Roman assemblage; layer 17 at the top of this 'dark earth' sequence, produced 12th/14th century material. The upper part of the sequence in Trench 2, at a depth of *c.* 0.6 m (layers 3 and 5), showed greater variability, being generally lighter, with occasional lumps of yellow and red/brown clay, and a distinct mottled orange/brown silty clay (layer 4) dipping from north-west to south-east at and angle of *c.* 20°. Soil micromorphology shows these layers to have been contaminated by cess (see Macphail, Chapter 4 below). Only residual Roman pottery was recovered from layers 3–5. This sequence was truncated during the 1930s when the Ministry of Works undertook a programme of landscaping, giving rise to the present ground surface.

The upper part of the 'dark earth' sequence was also recorded in Trenches 1 and 7. In Trench 1 (Fig. 2.5), the 'dark earth' sequence (layers 235, 242–244, 246, 248, 250–252) was excavated to a depth of 1.8 m (corresponding to layers 17, 24 and 25 in Trench 2, and 718 in Trench 7). At 1.75 m below the present surface, a hearth (245/247/249) associated with a trampled gravel surface was uncovered (layer 243/250). This surface was associated with a particularly high concentration of animal bone, some of which was articulated, and pottery dating to the 12th to 14th centuries, and stratigraphically appears to correspond with a distinct layer of oyster shells at the interface of layers 25 and 31 in Trench 2. The upper part of the 'dark earth' sequence in Trench 1 was truncated by the foundation trench for the Keep's western wall (F253).

Plate 2.1 Wooden piles driven into the natural that formed part of the foundations of the Roman fort wall, revealed at the bottom of Trench 2. See Figure 2.1 for section drawing

Very little of the 'dark earth' sequence (711) at the northern end of Trench 7 survived the earlier excavations by Sands, but at the southern end of Trench 7 (Fig. 2.6), the dark brown silty loam (layer 718) associated with 9th to 13th century pottery was excavated to a depth of 1.4 m (corresponding to layers 17 and 24 in Trench 1). This merged into a mid-greenish brown silty clay loam (layer 734) at a depth of 0.8 m, which at a depth of 0.7 m was sealed by a fairly homogeneous yellow clay, with large pale grey and orange mottles (layer 717). This whole sequence was truncated by slumping (as was the case in Trench 2), the foundation trench for the Keep's northern wall (F749), and an early 20th century excavation (F710).

A large block of the sequence of 'dark earth' and underlying deposits was also excavated in Trench 2 where it had slumped eastwards following the collapse of the Roman fort wall (Fig. 2.1), and no pottery later than the 12th to 13th century was recovered from the top of the 'dark earth' in this displaced block of stratigraphy. This was sealed beneath over 3 m of clay, within which a four-fold division of the deposits can be identified (Fig. 2.1). Firstly, lenses varying between yellow/orange clay (69), yellow/green clay with lenses of gravel (51, 56, 68), grey silty clay (57), very mixed yellow/grey/brown loamy clay (73, 74, 76, 85), with a thin lens of material which slipped off the side of the intact 'dark earth' sequence (58). This was overlain by a series of lenses of dark orange clay with black mottling (48, 50, 53, 54, 62) which may represent slumped parts of the 'dark earth' sequence. Thirdly, there was a complex sequence of tips and dumps including mottled yellow/orange/grey clay (49, 59), orange/dark grey-brown clay (43), and mottled yellow/grey silty sand (possibly redeposited natural: 44, 55). Finally, the upper *c.* 2.5 m part of the

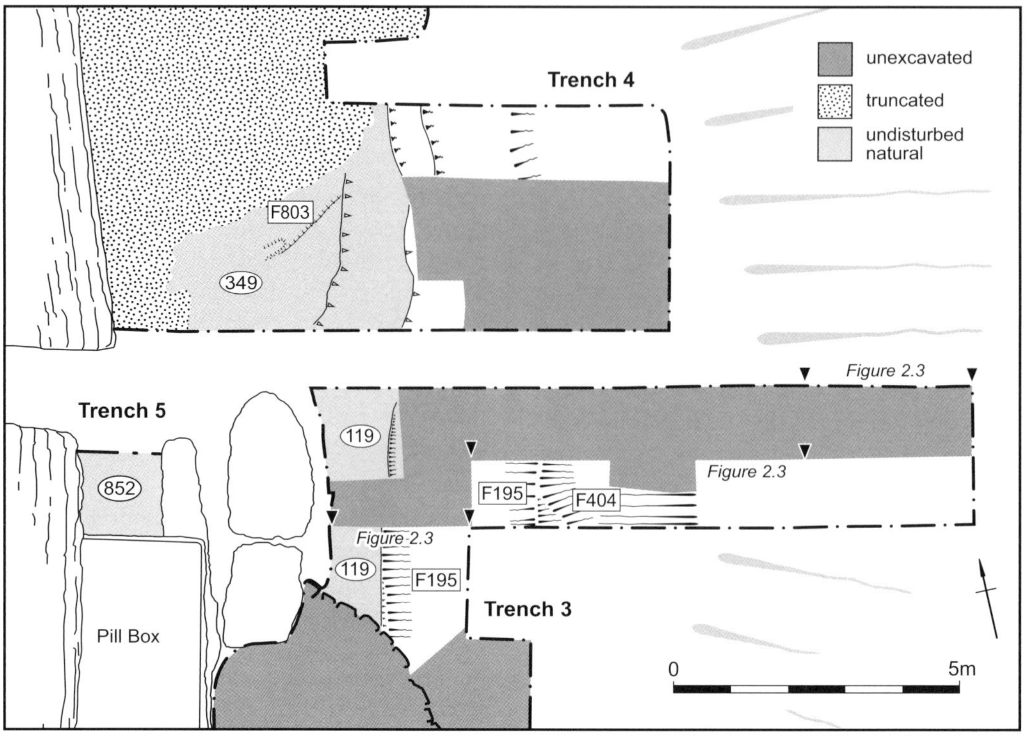

Figure 2.2 Phase 5: slumping of the hillside outside castle to east of Keep (Trenches 3 and 4)

sequence comprised far more homogeneous layers of mottled yellow/orange/light brown silty clay (6–8, 10, 19, 22–23, 26–30, 32–34, 40–42, 47). This upper part of the surviving sequence was particularly uniform, but with occasional layers of light brown silty sand (18), light to mid-brown loam with frequent lumps of chalk, yellow clay and charcoal (21), light grey brown loam with flecks of charcoal, mortar and dressed blocks of greensand (23), and mid-grey/brown silty loam with occasional lumps of chalk and gravel (29). This upper part of this mottled yellow/orange/light brown silty clay was also located in Trench 7 (Fig. 2.6, layers 716, 720 and 733). The majority of the latest pottery from this sequence dates to between the 11th and 13th century, but there is some 12th–14th century pottery from (18) and some 16th–17th century sherds from (32).

There are a number of potential interpretations of this *c.* 3.4 m of yellow/brown clay. One possibility is that it may have been dumped into the hole created after the collapse of the Roman fort wall in order to level the site. This does not appear likely because the general trend of the lenses within the sequence is roughly horizontal rather than spilling down from the west.

A more likely explanation is that the yellow/brown clay represents the upward continuation of the sequence of deposits above the dark earth which slumped downslope when the Roman fort wall collapsed (the yellow clay that Sands (1908) excavated inside the Keep and which was subsequently removed by the Ministry of Works). This clay must have been dumped inside the Keep sometime after its construction as the plinth around the outside of the Keep wall suggests that the medieval ground surface was very similar to that of today, and the interior walls of the keep are made of roughly dressed blocks clearly built as a free-standing wall and not trench-built into earlier material. However, if the yellow/brown clay had been dumped inside the base of the Keep, it might have been expected that traces of a floor surface would have been preserved, though no such evidence was found either in the stratified sequence in Trenches 1, 2 and 7, or the block of slumped stratigraphy in the eastern part of Trench 2.

Phase 4: Pre-slumping deposits in lower trenches

The earliest surviving deposits outside the Roman fort wall were excavated in Trench 5, the north-west corner of Trench 3 and south-west corner of Trench 4 (Fig. 2.2). The upper part of the natural grey silt was recorded in all three locations and showed signs of leaching (Trench 3: 408/415; Trench 4: 376; Trench 5: 852; Figs 2.3, 2.7 and 2.9). In Trenches 3 and 4 it was overlain by layers of reddish orange/brown silty clay (Trench 3: 169; Trench 4: 349), which produced a possibly 5th to 9th century sherd. In Trench 3 this was in turn overlain by mid-greyish brown silty clay (165/167) containing occasional flecks of charcoal and two 11th to 13th century sherds, sealed by a dense layer of reddish brown sandy gravel (119). Part of this sequence of deposits subsequently slumped eastwards (see below, Phase 5; Fig. 2.3), and these displaced deposits (196; 197; 405) produced five further 11th to 13th century sherds.

A heavily truncated cut feature, 0.2 m deep, was located to the south of the North East Tower (F803), cutting into layer 349 and the undisturbed natural (Fig. 2.2). It was filled with a light to mid-brown very silty loam with a large amount of chalky rubble and occasional flecks of charcoal (398), overlain by a mottled light yellow/grey very silty clay with occasional pieces of chalk and flint (393) and a mid-grey/yellow/orange silty clay (387). F803 appears to have been truncated by slumping to the east and the North East Tower, and its fill contained six 11th to 13th century sherds.

Phase 5: Slumping of hillside outside the Castle, and subsequent levelling of the area

The area immediately to the east of the Keep and Roman fort wall was affected by slumping in the form of a series of rotational slips which created two north-south oriented linear depressions in Trenches 3 and 4 (Fig. 2.2: F195 and F404). The westernmost depression (F195) was partly filled by slumped material with the same sequence of layers as in the undisturbed stratigraphy to the west: an intercalated mid-brown/pale grey silty clay (403, presumably derived from some mixing of the natural and slumped material), a reddish brown silty clay (197, equivalent to 169), overlain by mid-greyish brown silty clay (181, equivalent to 165/167), capped by reddish brown sandy gravel (196, equivalent to 119). The lower part of the eastern slump was filled with a very mixed reddish brown silty clay (405) which would appear to be the weathered upper part of the natural sequence equivalent to 403. In Trench 4, the reddish brown silty clay (167) was once again fractured by slumping (layer 367).

This series of depressions and steep scarps created through slumping was subsequently levelled through the dumping of a thick layer of mottled yellow clay which sealed the whole area excavated outside the castle (Fig. 2.4). At the southern end of Trench 3 a reddish orange silty clay (199) was overlain by a mid-grey/brown silty clay (401) (Fig. 2.13). To the south-east of the East Tower a test pit indicated at least 1.3 m of dumped clay, with a mottled reddish brown clay with occasional flecks of charcoal (183), overlain by a very mottled yellow/brown/grey silty clay (171), which merged with a mid-grey/brown silty clay loam with frequent flecks of charcoal, and lenses of gravel (161, very similar to 401) and finally a pale orange/grey silty clay (124). Once again, lenses of gravel and lighter/darker clays indicate dumping from the west.

In the northern part of Trench 3, and the whole of Trench 4, between the East and North East Towers, the dumped sequence comprised a series of very mottled yellow/orange/grey silty clays (Trench 3: layers 118/172/173; Trench 4: 344/364/399/800/801), which at the lowest (eastern) end of Trench 4 were at least 1.5 m thick (Figs 2.3, 2.10, and 2.16). Occasional lenses of gravel, chalk rubble and slightly paler/darker clays highlight a series of tip lines, once again indicate that the clay was dumped from the west. A small area of yellow clay in Trench 5 (layer 853) may also relate to this same episode of dumping (Fig. 2.4).

Similar heterogeneous dumped clays were found in the northern part of Trench 6, and though not stratigraphically linked, they appear to form part of the same dumping episode. The clay itself was not excavated, though it was seen in the sides of later features, including the 1.4 m section provided by pit F633 where it was seen to comprise a heterogeneous dumped deposit of mottled, predominantly yellow/orange silty clay (Figs 2.4 and 2.15: layers 625, 627) very similar to the dumped material in Trenches 3 and 4.

Where excavated in Trench 4 these various dumped clays produced small amounts of 11th to 13th century pottery (layer 401 yielded one sherd which can only be dated to somewhere between the 11th to 14th centuries).

Phase 6: Keep construction and associated features

West and north walls of the Keep

The foundation trenches for the west and north walls of the Keep were sectioned in Trenches 1 and 7, where they were cut into the top of the 'dark earth' sequence. In Trench 1 (Fig. 2.5), a cut at least 1.9 m wide and 0.8 m deep was excavated for the Keep footings (F253), though below this the Keep wall was trench-built into the 'dark earth' sequence. The foundation trench was backfilled with a series of grey/yellow/orange silty, sometimes sandy, clays (217–234, 236–241), from which two 11th to 13th century sherds were recovered. The upper part of the foundation trench was removed in the 1930s during the Ministry of Works landscaping of the site, and a narrow undated trench dug along the inside of the Keep wall may also date to that period (F206/F211).

In Trench 7 a shallow cut at least *c.* 1 m wide and 0.6 m deep was excavated for the foundation trench on the inside of the Keep (Fig. 2.6: F749; its upper part was also truncated during the 1930s

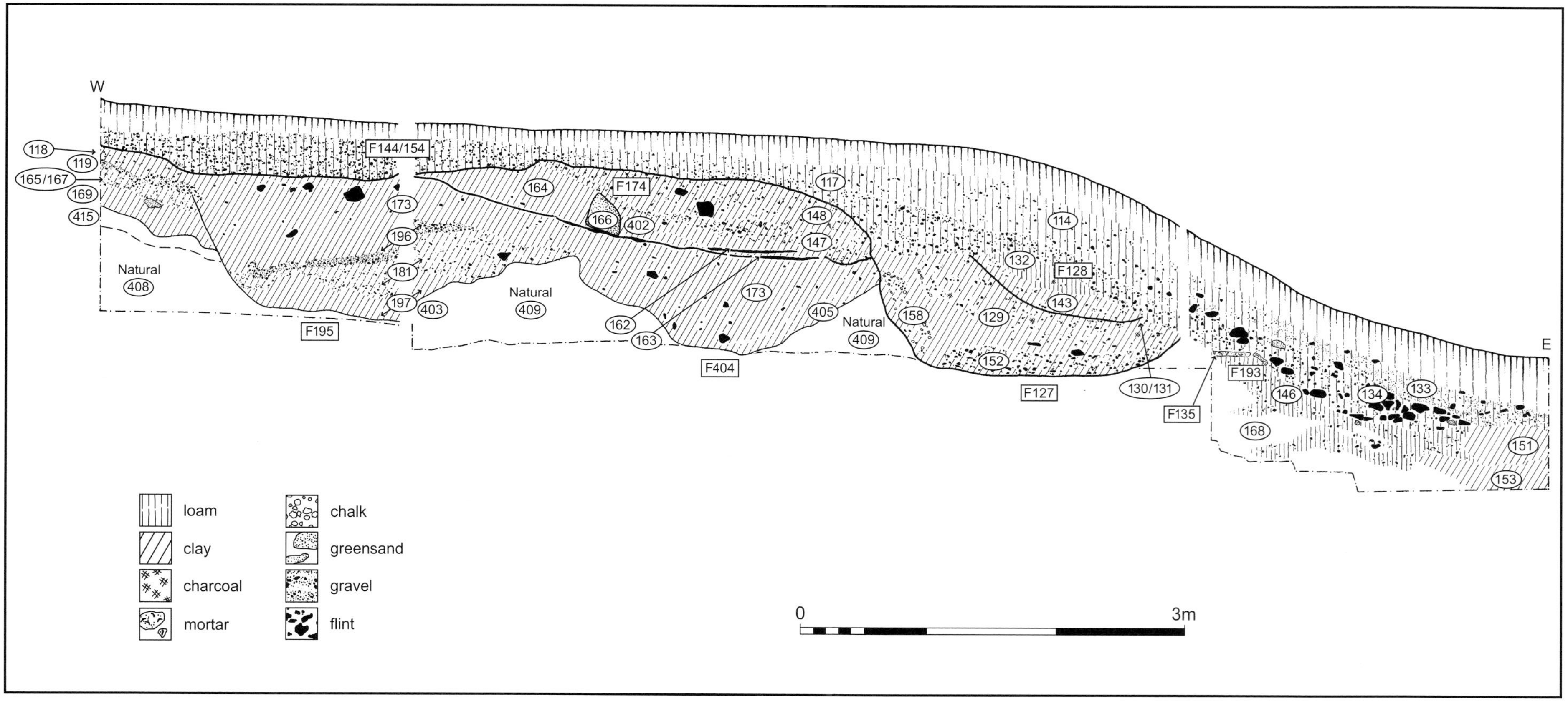

Figure 2.3 South-facing section in Trench 3, including slumping of the natural (Phase 5: F195 and F404), Phase 8 working platform (F166/F174, shown in plan on Figure 2.8), and pit F127 and oven/hearth F128 of Phase 10 (see Figure 2.2 for location)

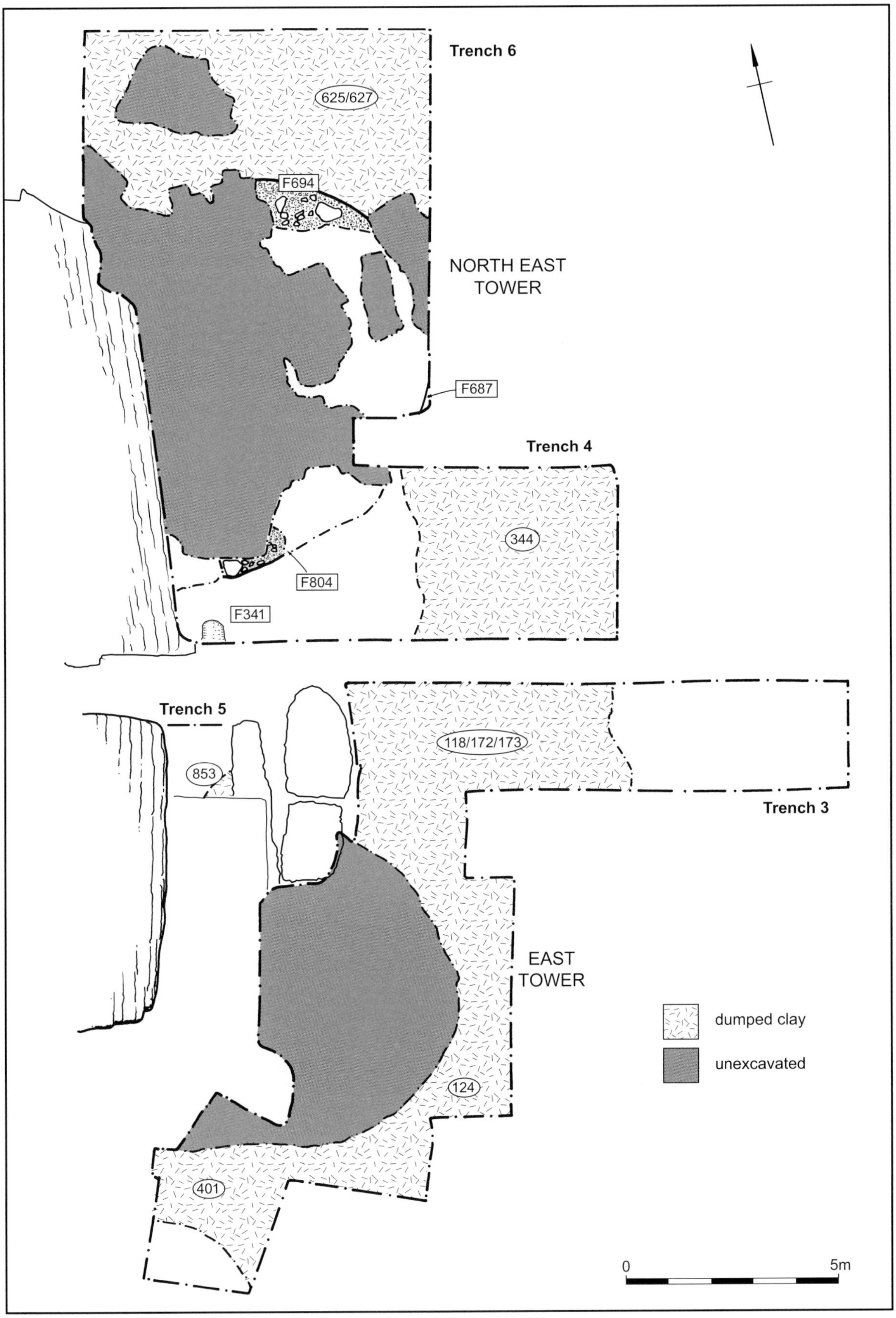

Figure 2.4 Phase 5: dumped clay outside Castle to east of Keep, and surviving fragments of the earliest phase of the Keep's North East Tower (F687, F694 and F804)

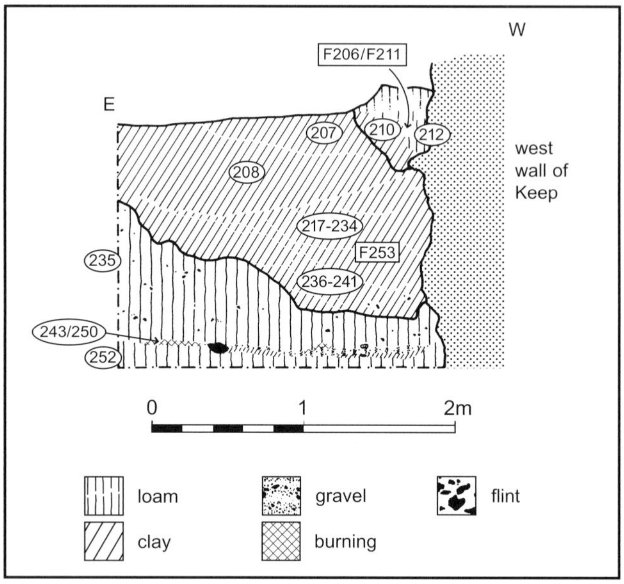

Figure 2.5 North-facing section in Trench 1, including upper part of 'dark earth' sequence (contexts 235, 243/250 and 252) and construction trench (F253) for the west wall of the Keep (see Figure 1.3 for location)

Plate 2.2 General view of Trenches 4 and 6, looking north across the collapsed Roman fort wall, below which fragments of the Keep's North East Tower were preserved (centre foreground): see Plate 2.3 for detail of these footings

Plate 2.3 Surviving fragments of the first phase of the Keep's North East Tower (Phase 6: F804) sealed beneath the more substantial fragments of the second phase (Phase 8: F806). See Figure 2.7 for a section drawing and Figures 2.4 and 2.8 for plans of these two phases

landscaping). It was filled with a distinctive very mottled light grey/green very silty clay, with abundant small rounded lumps of very pale grey clay especially towards the bottom (719), which only yielded a few sherds of residual Roman pottery. A pair of early medieval or later tweezers (SF 142) was also recovered (Fig. 3.10, 20; see Richards below, Chapter 3). From 0.8 m below the present ground surface the Keep was trench built into the 'dark earth' sequence. On the north side of the Keep wall there was a very steep sided cut (F712) filled with a mottled yellow/brown silty clay (713). From 1.0 m below the present ground surface, the Keep wall was trench built.

A possible North East Tower

At its south-east corner the Keep butts against the earlier fort wall where there is a Roman bastion (Fig. 1.3, Pl. 1.5). This would have provided support for the Keep, which was a substantial stone structure, and for this reason, as well as simple symmetry, an equivalent tower is to be expected outside the fort wall at the Keep's North East corner. Two phases of tower were recorded at this point (Pls 2.2–2.3), and though no independent dating evidence was recovered from either phase, apart from the *terminus post quem* of the 11th/13th century provided by the dumped deposits into which the tower's foundation trench was cut (Phase 5 above), it is logical that the earliest was contemporary with the initial construction of the Keep.

The fragmentary remains of a first phase of tower were located in Trenches 4 and 6 (Fig. 2.4). Despite heavy robbing in antiquity three areas of *in situ* masonry survived, on the southern (F804: Fig. 2.7), eastern (F687) and northern (F694) edges of the Tower. The largest fragments (F804 and F694) comprised blocks of semi-cemented pale brown slightly-silty sandy gravels, surrounding large blocks of undressed greensand, resting upon a reddish brown sandy clay with abundant gravel (384), set in a vertical-sided and flat-bottomed foundation trench. The smaller fragment of the tower footings, F687, simply comprised a thin lens of pale brown sandy gravel adhering to the side of the eastern most edge of the foundation trench. All other traces of the earliest phase of the tower were robbed out subsequently.

Associated features south of the North East Tower

Part of what may have been a pit (F341) was excavated in the south-west corner of Trench 4 (Figs 2.4, 2.7 and 2.10). Its southern edge was not located, though it certainly did not extend as far south as Trench 5. The profile of F341 was affected by

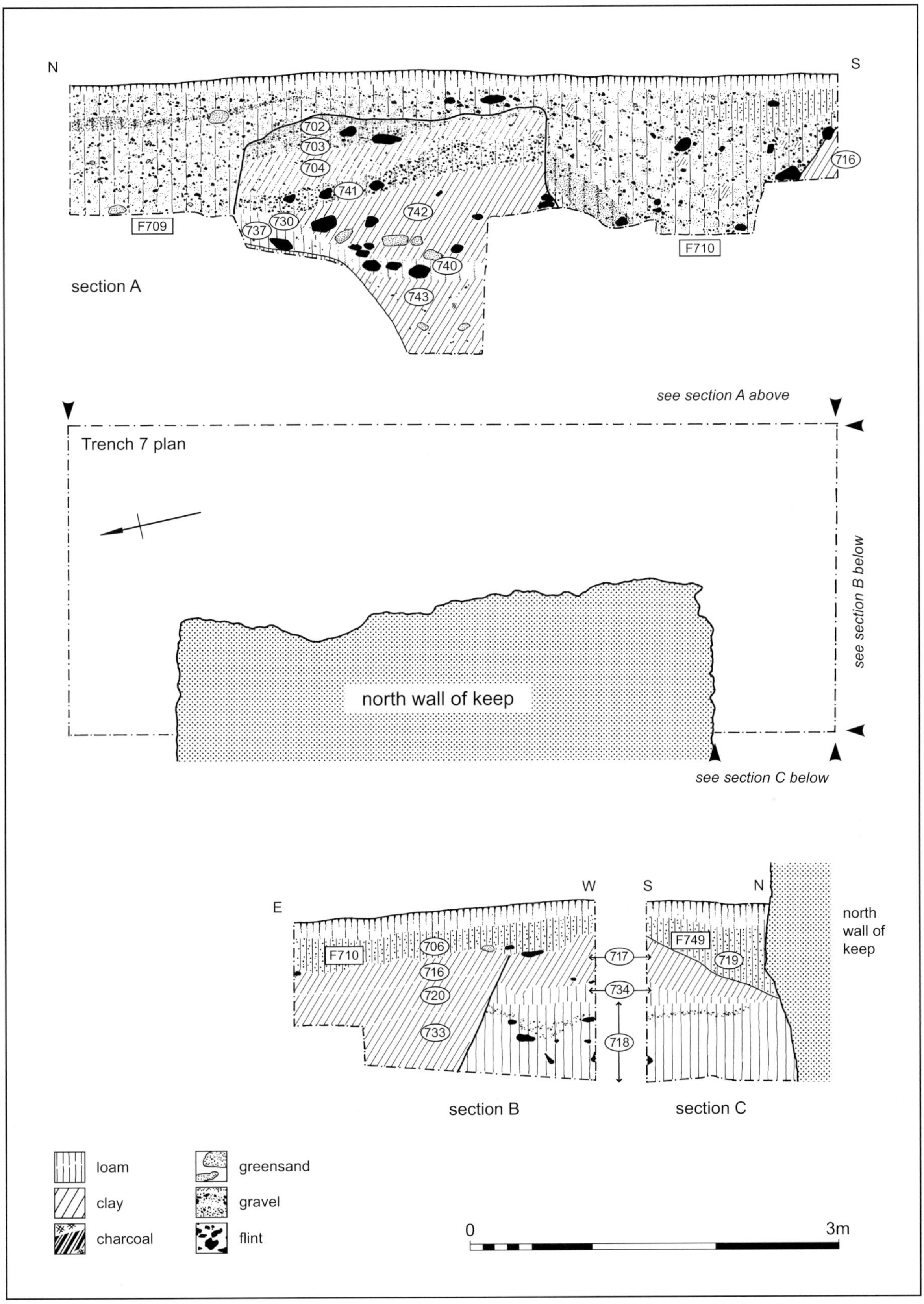

Figure 2.6 Plan and sections of Trench 7, including the foundation trench for the Keep's northern wall (F749) which cuts into the 'dark earth' sequence (contexts 717, 718 and 734), the dumped clay (716, 720 and 733), the backfilling of the robber trench for the Keep's north wall (contexts 702–4, 730, 737 and 740–3), and early 20th century excavations (F709 and F710) (see Figure 1.3 for location)

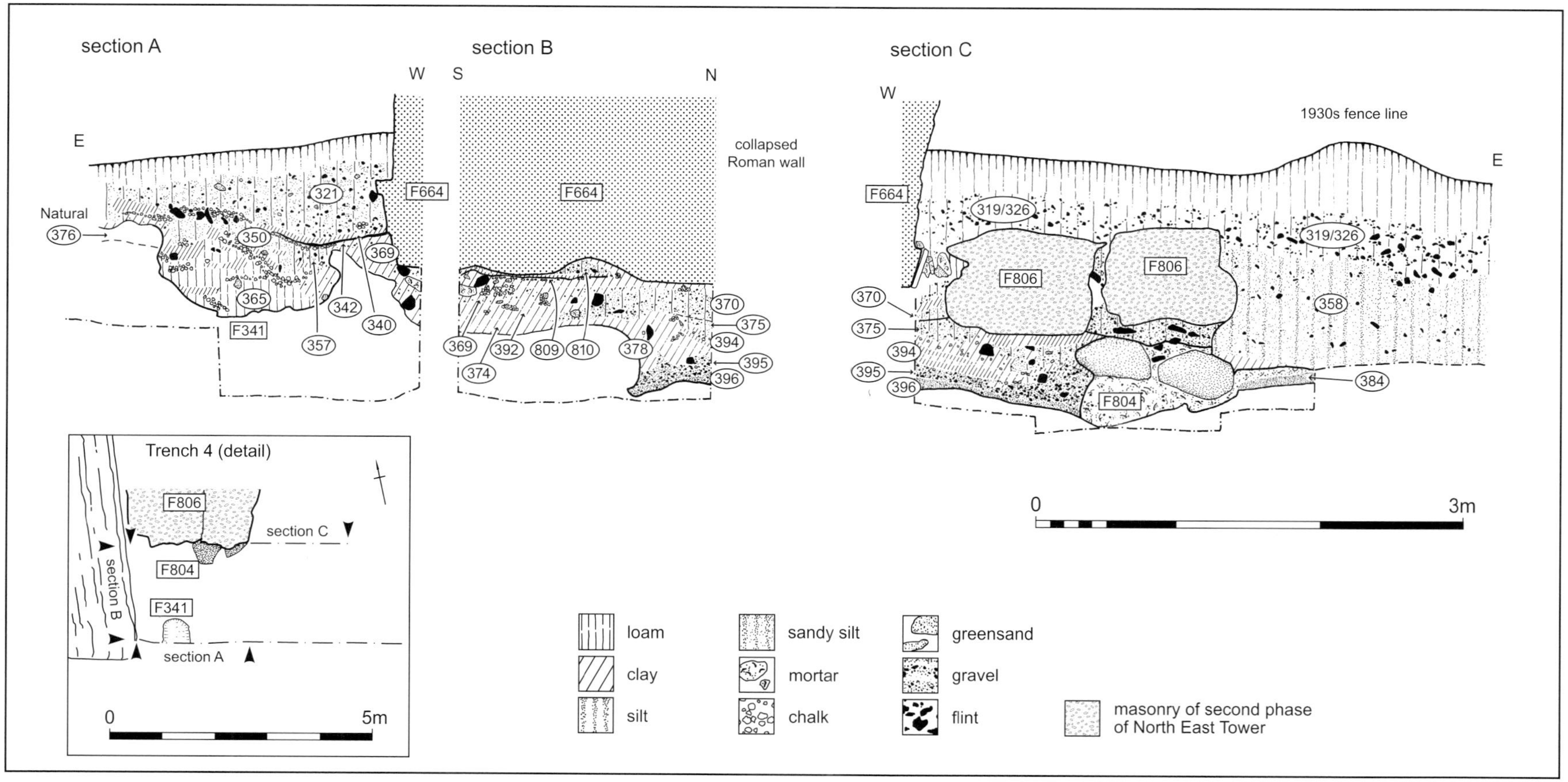

Figure 2.7 Sections in south-west corner of Trench 4, including pit F341, sequence of deposits under the collapsed Roman fort wall (F664), and footings of phases 1 (F804) and 2 (F806) of the Keep's North East Tower

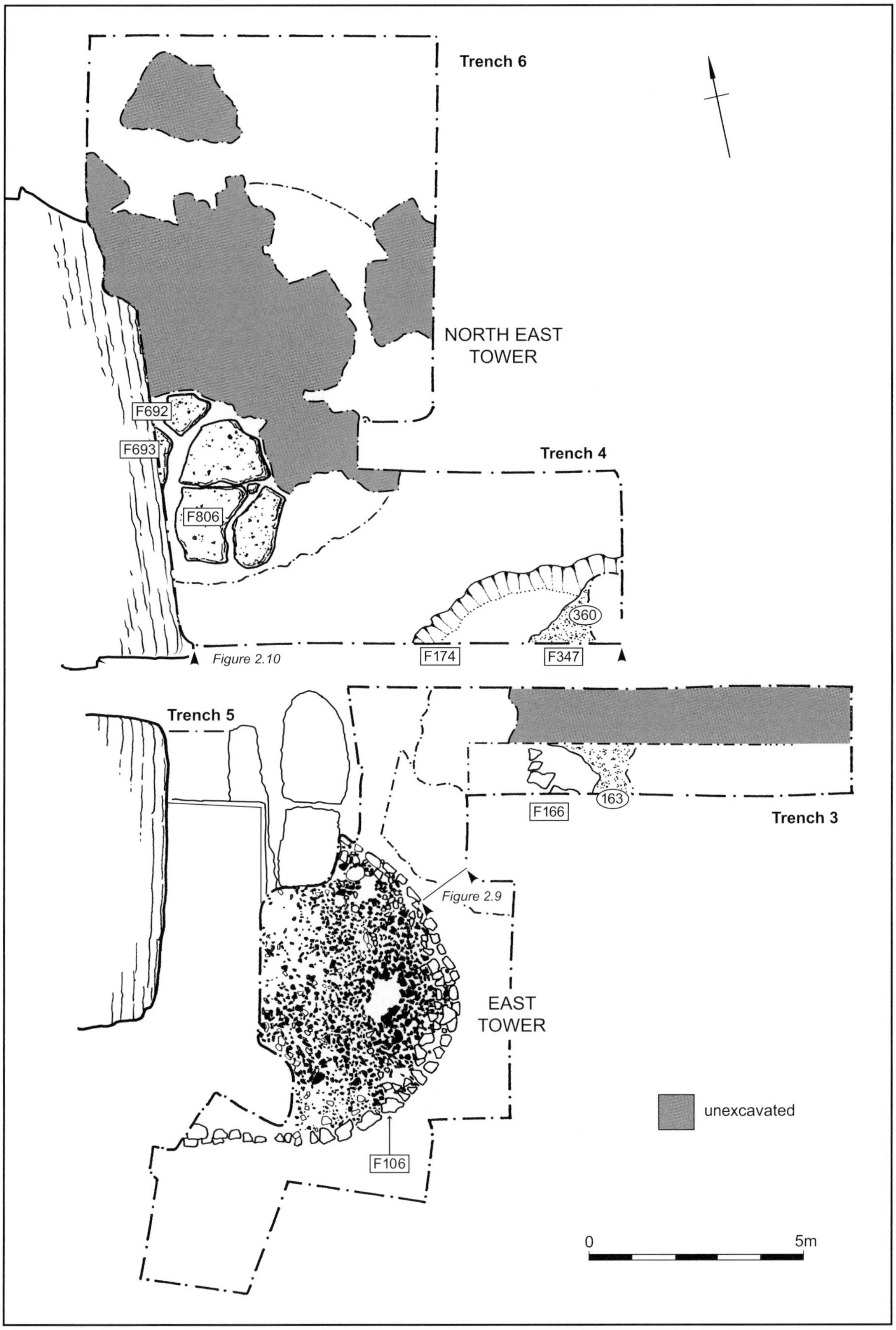

Figure 2.8 Phase 8: surviving fragments from the reconstruction of the Keep's North East Tower (F692, F693 and F806), addition of an East Tower. The working platform (F166/F174/F347) probably relates to this phase (and is shown in section on Figure 2.3)

Plate 2.4 The East Tower of the Keep (Phase 8), looking north-east from on top of the garderobe block inserted in Phase 9. See Figure 2.11 for a plan of this area. The medieval flight of steps were cut down through dumped deposits to provide access to the garderobe block's foundation trench

compression resulting from the collapse of the Roman curtain wall (664), but appears to have been U-shaped with a width of *c.* 1.2 m and depth of *c.* 0.7 m, cut into the natural. It was backfilled with tips and dumps of yellow/orange clay, grey/brown silty clay, chalk rubble, and mid- to dark brown loamy soil (365). This was sealed by a lens of mid-grey/brown sandy gravel (350) and a mid-grey/brown silty clay with lenses of chalk, gravel and charcoal (357). A small assemblage of 11th to 13th century pottery was recovered.

Pit F341 was sealed by a heavily truncated chalk and clay spread (layer 312/318–340/342–809) (Figs 2.7 and 2.10). This surface comprised a layer, *c.* 0.05 m thick, of densely packed chalk rubble (*c.* 5–30 mm in size) (layers 318, 342 and 809), sealed by a thin layer of pale yellow clay (312, 340). In places, a thin lens of charcoal separated the two. A small amount of 11th to 13th century pottery was recovered. The fragmentary survival of 312/318–340/342–809 makes its stratigraphic position difficult to determine. It overlay 349 (the upper, disturbed, part of the natural) to the south of the North East Tower, and sealed the slumped material 367 just to the east, and the dumped yellow clay (344 etc). It also slumped into the top of pit F341, and extended under the collapsed Roman wall F664 (as 809) where it was overlain by a mid-brown silty sand with frequent mixed gravel (810). This section under the collapsed Roman wall also showed that the chalk surface did not extend across the foundation/robber trench of the North East Tower, though it physically overlay layers 369/370 which relate to the first phase of robbing. The stratigraphy here was, however, very disturbed by the compression caused by the collapse of the wall and layers 369/370 may have been displaced southwards beyond their original confines.

It would seem, therefore, that this spread of chalk and clay post-dated the slumping in Phase 5, and the subsequent levelling of the site through the dumping of clay and digging of pit F341, all of which are associated with 11th to 13th century pottery. It also spread across the bottom of a shallow hollow F391, filled by 334 (Fig. 2.10), which contained 13th to 15th century pottery.

Phase 7: Robbing of Phase 1 of the Keep's North East Tower

The remains of the first phase of the Keep's North East tower were subsequently largely dug out, and the robber trench backfilled. Subsequent robbing had largely removed the fill of this first robber trench, and it was only beneath the masonry of the second phase of the North East Tower (F806) that the full sequence survived, comprising a series of dumped deposits with mid- to dark brown sandy gravel and a small amount of chalk and flint rubble (395, 396; Fig. 2.7), followed by intercalated tips of pale yellow silty clay and dark brown sandy gravel with chalk rubble (378/394/805/808), a dark grey/brown silty clay (382) and finally a light orange brown sandy gravel sealed by a horizontal lens of yellow clay (375). All of these lenses were butted up against the surviving fragment of the earliest phase of the Keep's North East Tower (F804), and extended under the masonry of the later tower (F806) and collapsed Roman curtain wall (F664). Four 11th to 13th century sherds were recovered. A small pocket of homogeneous brown silty sand beside the eastern edge of the tower's foundation trench (layer 383) may also relate to the backfilling after the first phase of robbing; eight sherds of 11th to 13th century pottery were recovered.

Phase 8: Remodelling of eastern side of Keep

Second phase of the Keep's North East Tower

The surviving footings of the earliest tower at the north-east corner of the Keep (F804) and material dumped into the robber trench to the west, were sealed by a thin layer of very pale brown mortar (807) which in turn was overlain by a loose sandy gravel containing numerous undressed flint nodules (Fig. 2.7). This was sealed by several large blocks of cemented masonry (F806/F692/F693), comprising a series of carefully laid courses of flint nodules set in a white gravelly mortar (Fig. 2.8). These would appear to be the footings of a second tower structure whose surviving fragments were later heavily robbed and then shattered by the collapse of the Roman curtain wall (F664). No dating evidence was found.

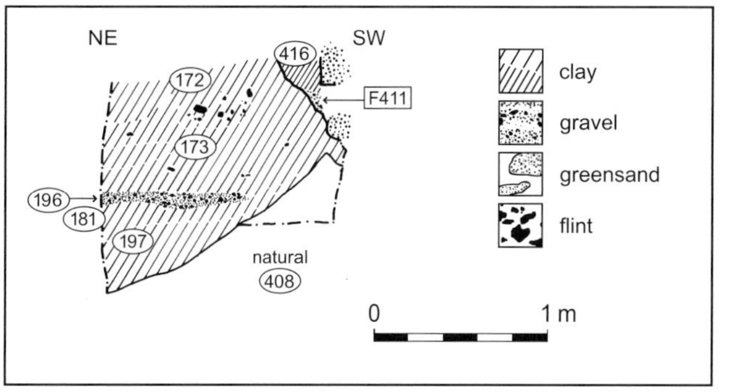

Figure 2.9 North-west facing section through the construction trench (F411) for the Keep's East Tower (see Figure 2.8 for location)

The Keep's East Tower

The footings of another tower were excavated in Trench 3 (Fig. 2.8; Pl. 2.4). In plan, it comprised a nearly D-shaped area marked by a series of well-dressed greensand blocks (F106), with a core of loose sandy gravel with abundant flint nodules (108; very similar to 806 under the North East Tower), the density of which appeared to decrease towards the centre of the tower. The top two surviving courses of greensand facing-stone had very well dressed outer facing surfaces, with fine diagonal tooling, the construction trench (F411) for which was backfilled with a mottled yellow/orange silty clay (Fig. 2.9: 198; 416). Below the lowest course of well dressed masonry, the tower footings were trench-built into the dumped clay sequence of Phase 5, and undisturbed natural grey silt. The lower courses of greensand were undressed and set in the same loose light brown sandy gravel (108) as the overlying flint rubble.

To the south of the East Tower, a layer of light grey/brown silty clay, containing abundant chalk rubble and greensand chips may represent debris from the construction of the tower (Fig. 2.13: 400). It was sealed by a dump of reddish brown silty clay (190), and both were cut by the foundation trench for the later garderobe drain (F407).

The only direct dating evidence for the construction of the East Tower was provided by four sherds of 11th to 13th century pottery from the backfill of the construction trench (198), though a *terminus post quem* of the 11th/13th century is given by the small amount of pottery from the dumped clay sequence into which the Tower was trench-built.

Several strands of evidence suggest that this structure was not contemporary with the earliest phase of the Keep's North East Tower. The profiles of the two construction trenches were very different: the East Tower's was concave, the North East Tower's vertical. Though both used courses of undressed greensand blocks, in the earliest phase of the North East Tower these were set in a semi-cemented sandy gravel (804), while in the East Tower this was very loose (108) and very similar to 806. The plans of the two towers are also different, the North East Tower being broader by around 1 m.

The working platform

The area between the North East and East Towers was occupied by a platform terraced into the slope below the fort wall (F174/F347). This may have been contemporary with the construction of the towers, or a phase of later repair (Figs 2.3, 2.8 and 2.10).

In Trench 3 there was a north-south aligned row of large, partly dressed greensand blocks (F166) towards the bottom of the western slope below the platform (Figs 2.3, 2.8). These may have been to retain a dump of pale yellow silty clay (164), and prevent it spilling onto a series of roughly laid mortar surfaces to the east. In Trench 4, a layer of flint rubble (361) may have served the same function, in retaining the sides of the clay (Fig. 2.10). Though the stone alignment F166 was confined to Trench 3, the mortar surfaces extended into Trench 4. The lower horizon comprised a friable white/very pale brown mortar with frequent small lumps of chalk, forming a relatively hard smooth surface (163/360). This was sealed by a lens of mottled pale yellow/grey silty clay with occasional gravel (390/402), which appears to have spilled down over the floor surface from the west. This was covered by a second, rather softer, surface of friable white/very pale brown mortar with frequent small lumps of chalk but with occasional flint nodules (162/359). These floor surfaces were truncated to the east by substantial pits (F127 and F327), into which parts of the mortar

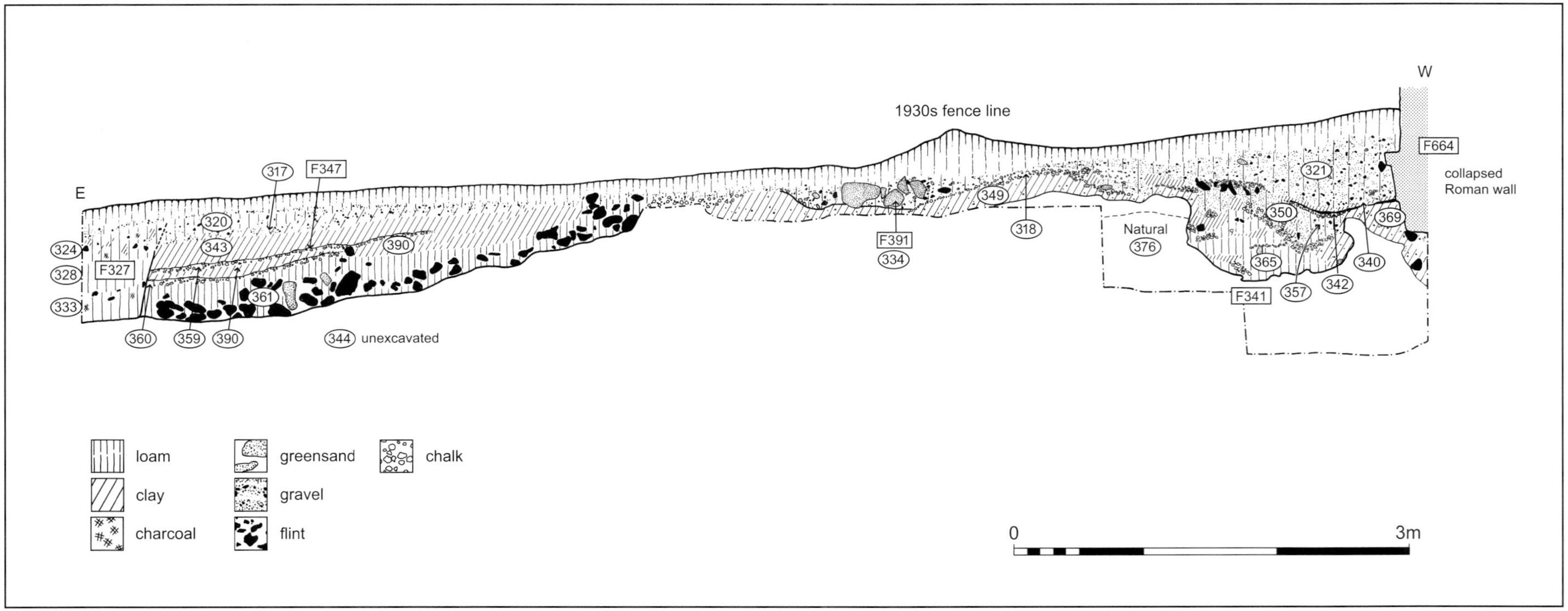

Figure 2.10 North-facing section in Trench 4, including pits F341 and F327, and Phase 8 working platform F347 (the latter is shown in plan on Figure 2.8)

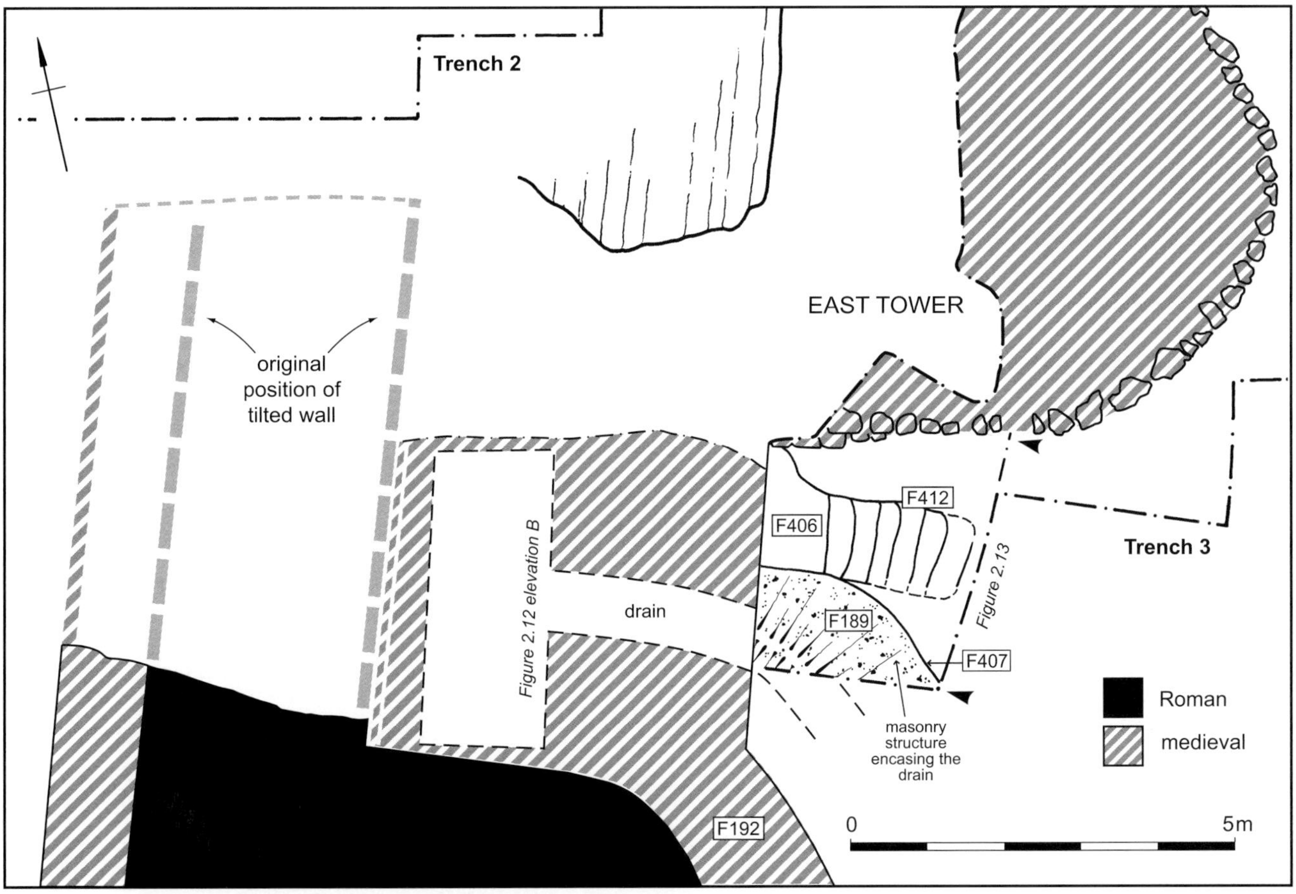

Figure 2.11 Plan of garderobe chamber inserted between the Keep's East and South East Towers in Phase 9 (see Figure 1.3 for location). Note that the fragment of tilted Roman fort wall, with a medieval inner facing, has been restored to its original position (see Figure 2.12 for its actual current position)

surfaces had slumped. No dating evidence was recovered apart from three 11th to 13th century sherds from the clay 164.

This working platform was subsequently backfilled with dumps of pale brown silty clay with abundant lumps of mortar (147), pale yellow/brown silty clay with occasional lumps of mortar and gravel (148), and pinkish orange slightly sandy silty clay (343) which produced three sherds of 11th to 13th century. The dumping of this material would effectively have levelled the area immediately outside the two towers.

Phase 9: Insertion of garderobe tower and drain

The construction of the new East Tower just 3 m to the north of the Roman bastion would have created a recessed area roughly 5 m square which was later filled-in through the construction of a garderobe chamber which now lies beneath one of the Second World War pill boxes (Figs 2.11–2.12). Before the construction of this pill box, which obscured much of the medieval masonry, the southern wall of the garderobe chamber was described by Clarke (1884, 367) as a wall 9 feet (2.74 m) thick and 10 feet (3.1 m) high, which extended some 20 feet (6.1 m) to the north of the Roman bastion that formed the Keep's South East tower. This probably equates with the stretch of wall recorded by Sands (1908, 27), and was constructed at the same time as the base of the Roman bastion and part of the curtain wall to the south was strengthened through the provision of battering around its base (Figs 1.3 and 2.11: F192).

Foundation trenches (F406/F407) for the garderobe and associated drain (F189) were dug into the dumped clay sequence of Phase 5, and underlying natural grey silt (Fig. 2.11). Access for these trenches was provided by a flight of steps also cut into the clay/silt (F412) (Fig. 2.11, Pl. 2.4). The six steps were 1.1 m wide, 0.3 m broad, and 0.08–0.15 m high. On each of the flat surfaces a thin lens (*c.* 1–2 mm thick) of greensand chippings sealed by *c.* 1–2 mm of very mixed orange/brown clay, representing trampled material derived from the construction of the garderobe/battering (which comprised greensand

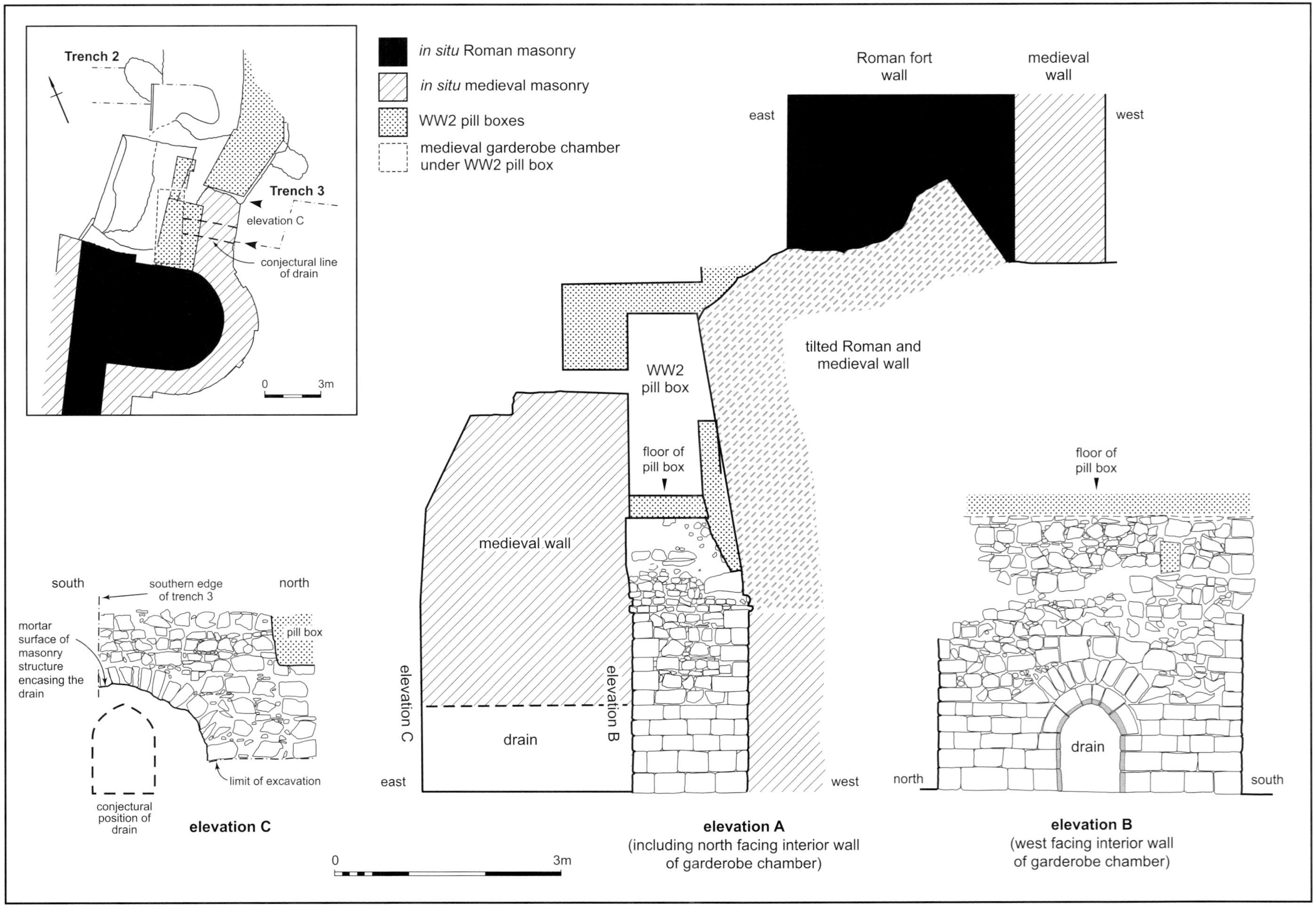

Figure 2.12 East-west section through the garderobe block, and elevation drawings from within the garderobe chamber (elevations A and B) and its outer, east face (elevation C)

blocks). The steps, and foundation trench 406, were backfilled with tips and dumps of yellow/orange clay, chalk and greensand rubble, reddish-brown sandy gravel, mottled orange-grey sandy clay, and pale brown sand with an abundance of flint, greensand and ironstone rubble (176, 188, 413, 414), which yielded six 11th to 13th century sherds.

Internally, the garderobe chamber itself measured 3.98 m by 1.50 m. The lower 1.2 m comprised five courses of extremely well-dressed greensand blocks, the lower course being 0.26–0.28 m high, the second course 0.24–0.26 m, and the remaining three 0.18–0.20 m. Above this undressed greensand rubble and occasional beach cobbles were used apart from the corners which employed well-dressed greensand blocks 0.18 m to 0.22 m in thickness. The wall to the east was 2.8 m thick, through which passed the drain. This was also built of well-dressed greensand blocks, having a flat bottom, vertical sides, 0.75 m apart, and an arched roof rising to a height of 1.14 m.

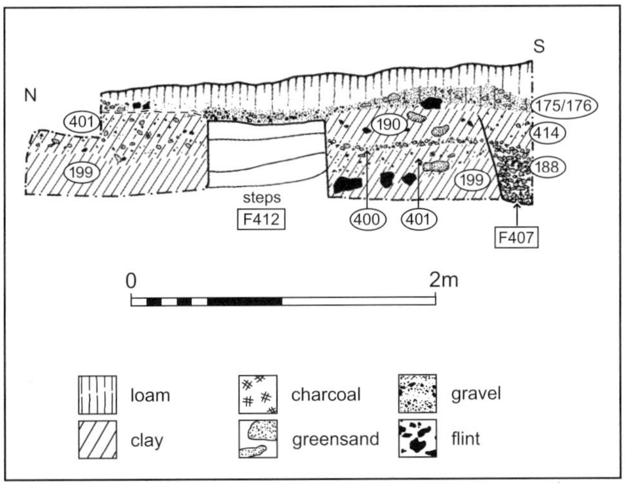

Figure 2.13 West-facing section in south-west corner of Trench 3, showing the construction trench for the garderobe drain (F407) and access steps (F412) shown in plan on Figure 2.11

Phase 10: Features cut into top of yellow clay

A series of features were cut into the top of the dumped clay sequence (Fig. 2.14). Several (F110/F120/F138, F128, F144/154, F327) were also stratigraphically later than the backfilling of the working platform 174/347, though in other cases (F341; F633, F670) all that can be said is that they stratigraphically post-date the dumping of clay in Phase 5, and pre-date the collapse of the Roman curtain wall (Phase 12). In most cases, however, pottery suggests a 13th to 15th century date.

Pit F180

After the foundation trench for the garderobe chamber was backfilled, a sub-rectangular pit was dug, 0.8 m long, 0.5 m wide and 0.5 m deep (Fig. 2.14). The pit showed considerable signs of burning, and was filled with tips and lenses of sand, gravel, stone rubble and charcoal (layers 177; 178; 179; 182). A few sherds of 13th to 15th century pottery were recovered, suggesting that this may relate to one of the documented periods of repair to the Keep at this time (as might F138 and F127: see below).

Pits or hollows F138/F112/F120/F110

A series of shallow pit or hollows was partly excavated to the east of the East Tower (Fig. 2.14). Though their function is unclear, they all appear to have been deliberately backfilled, though not with midden material, and may relate to the clearing up of debris from repairs to the eastern side of the Keep. Feature F138 was 0.4 m deep, and only the lowest 0.1 m of fill survived its truncation by F120 and F110. The pit was lined with 15 mm of orange clay, containing a small amount of very fine gravel (141). This was sealed by 30–50 mm of crushed mortar (140), perhaps indicating that this feature was associated with an episode of repairs to the castle fabric. The feature was then backfilled with a very dark brown silty clay loam (very much like topsoil: 139). There was no dating evidence.

Only a very small part of F112 survived its truncation by F120. It was filled with a mid-brown silty clay loam, and contained a large amount of stone rubble (notably flint and greensand (113). One 11th to 13th century sherd was produced, though F112 cut F154 which contained 13th to 15th century material.

Both F112 and F138 (and indeed F154) were cut by F120, a shallow pit or hollow 0.6 m deep. The lower fill comprised a mid-brown silty sand, containing a little mixed gravel (142). This was overlain by a light to mid-brown slightly sandy loam, also with a little gravel but also frequent undressed fragments of greensand and flint (121, 122). The upper fill, very little of which survived recent disturbance, comprised a lens of dumped yellow clay tipping into the western side of the pit (126). A small assemblage of 13th to 15th century material was recovered.

The last of the series of intercutting features in this area was F110. This shallow pit or hollow, 0.3 m deep, was filled with a fairly uniform dark brown silty loam with occasional gravel and flint nodules (layer 111).

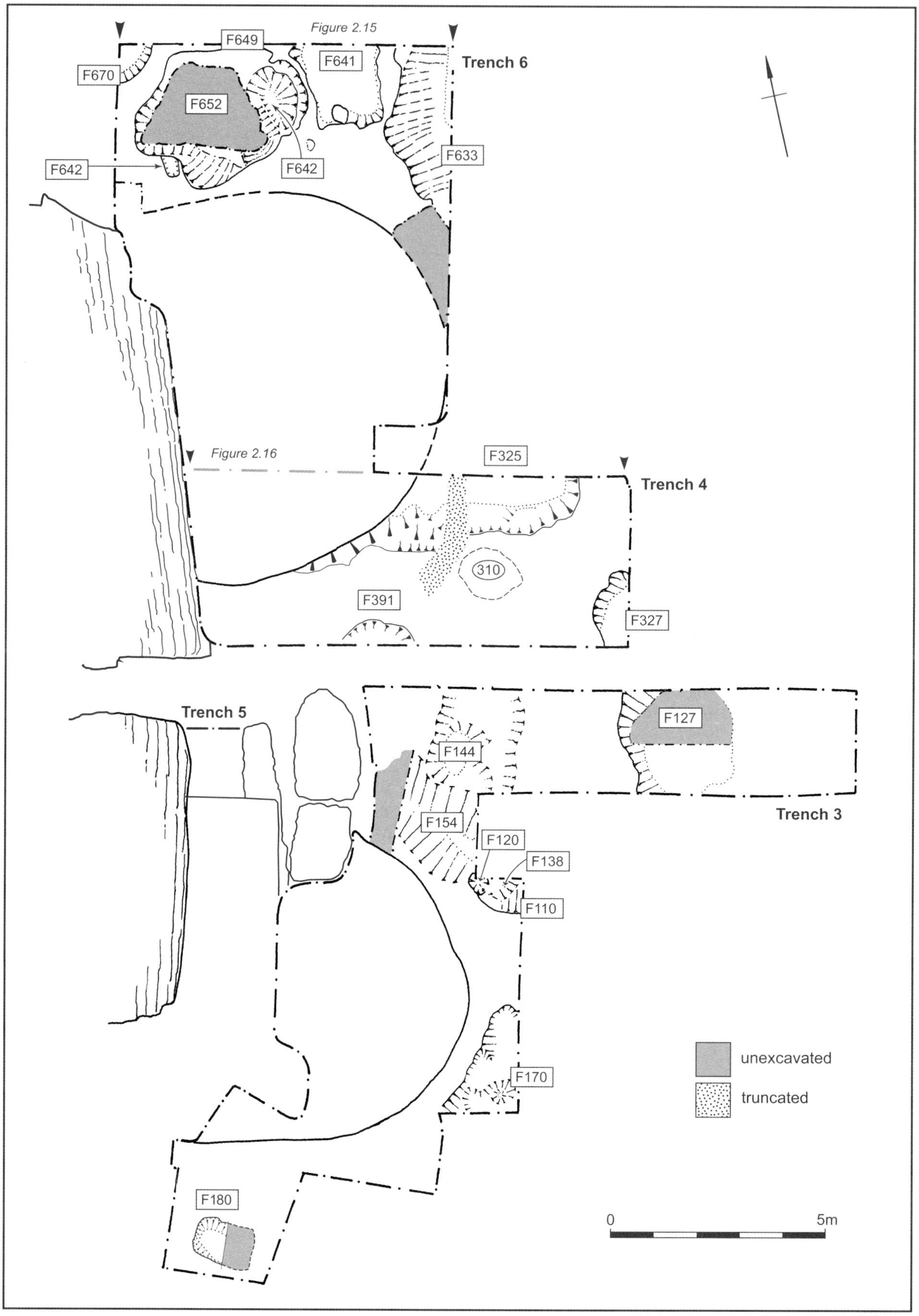

Figure 2.14 Phase 10: features cut into the dumped yellow clay that post-date the construction of the Keep's extra-mural towers

Hollows F144/F154

Two substantial hollows were located between the East and North East Towers, that post-date the backfilling of the working hollow (174/347) (Figs 2.3 and 2.14, below). One of the hollows (F154) was cut by pit F120. The northern hollow, F144, measured *c.* 3.4 m by 2.0 m, and was up to 0.2 m deep. Feature F154 was at least 2.4 m long and 2.0 m wide and lay between F144 and the East Tower. Both were filled with a series of tips and dumps of material: F144 had a sequence of mid- to dark brown silty clay loam with abundant flint rubble and occasional flecks of charcoal (150, 346), overlain by a mottled mid-brown silty clay with frequent gravel and midden debris such as lenses of mussel and oyster shells (145). This was sealed by a layer of mid- to dark brown silty clay loam, with lenses of gravel and occasional rounded flint cobbles (136). The latest pottery was 13th to 15th century. The upper part of the hollow was filled with a very mottled orange/grey/brown slightly clayey silt, with a little gravel and occasional flint nodules (117) which extended beyond the confines of F144 downslope, being cut be another pit F127. Layer 117 in Trench 3 was equivalent to layers 313/317/320/337 in Trench 4 which were cut by pit F327.

Hollow F154 contained a similar sequence. The lowest fill comprised a dark brown silty clay loam with frequent undressed fragments of greensand and flint rubble, along with dumps of whelk shell (137). This was sealed by a series of layers of mid- to dark brown silty clay loam with lenses of gravel and occasional flint cobbles, associated with 13th to 15th century pottery (115, 116, 136). The final fill was a yellow clay (107).

Pit F127 and hearth F128

To the east of F144, a large pit, F127, was cut into the backfilled working platform F174 (Figs 2.3, 2.14). It was oval in plan and filled the full width (2.5 m) of the extension to Trench 3. It may originally have measured *c.* 4 by 3 m, just missing the south-east corner of Trench 4. Its lower fill comprised 0.2 m of very dark grey/brown silty clay, with a large amount of charcoal/organic matter and shells suggestive of domestic refuse (152). The rest of the pit was backfilled with a mid-brown silty clay containing only flecks of charcoal and small fragments of shell (129). A large assemblage of 13th to 15th century pottery was recovered from both 152 and 129. On its western side the fill (129) was intercalated with a series of lenses of mortary material and clay (155, 156, 157, 158) that appear to have slumped from the sides (i.e. 173, 163, 402, 162, 147 and 148).

By the time pit F127 was virtually backfilled (with 129), an oval-shaped hearth or oven (F128) was cut into its surface measuring *c.* 1.8 m by 1.6 m. A thin lens of charcoal (130) no more than 10 mm thick was sealed by a layer of hard burnt clay (131). The hearth/oven was backfilled with a dump of mixed light yellow/brown silty clay (143) and mid-brown silty loam with abundant whelk shell and frequent flecks of charcoal, presumably representing another dump of midden material (132). There were also lenses/tips of fragmentary burnt clay, and chalky mortar/lime. No direct dating evidence was produced, though the soil overlying both features (114) contained 12th to 15th century material.

To the east of the pit/hearth complex (F127/F128) traces of a surface comprising a very hard, very pale brown gravely mortar survived later slumping and truncation (Fig. 2.3: F135). It rested upon a light to mid-brown silty clay containing frequent lenses of chalk rubble (185, 194), which filled a linear hollow *c.* 0.7 m wide and *c.* 0.2 m deep (F193). This may have been a deliberately cut feature as a footing for F135, or a natural linear hollow created through slumping. No dating evidence was recovered.

Both the linear feature F193 and overlying deposits (F135, 183, 194) were cut by a large feature, only a small part of which could be excavated in the north-eastern corner of the trench extension (F417). It was filled with flint rubble (134). No dating evidence was recovered.

Pit F327

Another large pit was cut into the backfilled working platform in the south east corner of Trench 4 (Figs 2.10, 2.14: F327), the contents of which was quite different to F127. The lower fill comprised a mixed yellow and brown clay/silty clay with the appearance of having been dumped (333), containing tips and lenses of mortar, and slabs of a very gravelly mortar similar to F135. In the northern part of F327 this was sealed beneath a mottled, mid-brown silty clay containing lenses of reddish sand, charcoal and burnt clay (329), perhaps the debris from a hearth/oven structure like F128. In the southern part of the pit, layer 333 was sealed by a further dump of mid-brown silty loam, including much domestic refuse (328). The remaining part of the pit was filled with dumped yellow/brown clay, midden material, and lenses of a mid-brown loam similar to topsoil (324). The pit contained 13th to 15th century pottery. An area of flint cobbling (layer 310, Fig. 2.10), associated with 12th to 14th century pottery, in a very shallow hollow to the west of F327 may represent all that remains of

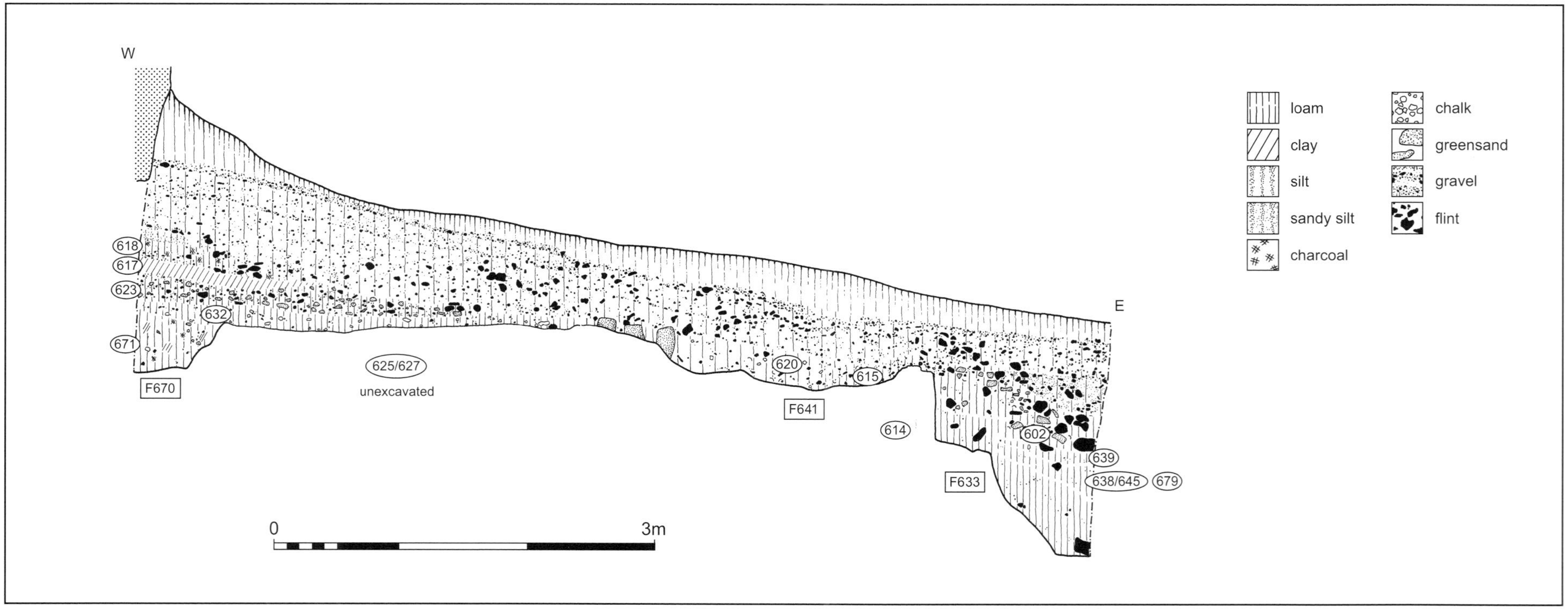

Figure 2.15 South-facing section at northern edge of Trench 6, including pits F633 and F670, and hollow F641 of Phase 10 (see Figure 2.14 for location)

a more extensive roughly made surface; similar cobbling was found between the North East Tower and pit F633.

Pit F325

To the north of F327, part of another shallow pit or hollow (F325) was excavated, which extended beyond the northern edge of Trench 4 (Figs 2.14, 2.16). The lowest fill excavated comprised a mid- to dark brown silty clay loam with frequent gravel and flint rubble (339/348). Some residual 11th to 13th century pottery was recovered.

Hollow F391

Part of a shallow hollow, F391, was uncovered to the south of North East Tower (Figs 2.10 and 2.14). It post-dated chalk spread 318, and may have been created through the subsidence of slumped/dumped deposits. It was filled with a mid-brown silty loam, with frequent mixed gravel and numerous medium to large blocks of undressed greensand (334). Three 13th to 15th century sherds were recovered.

Pit F633

Part of a substantial pit, F633, 1.4 m deep, was recorded in the north-east corner of Trench 6 (Figs 2.14–2.15). The lowest fill, tipping down the western edge of the feature comprised a very mottled, dumped deposit of yellow/orange clay, with lenses of grey clay, mortar, gravel and mid- to dark loamy soil (679). This was sealed by a thick layer of equally mottled yellow/brown silty clay containing lenses of dark brown loam, rich in organic material, burnt clay, mortar and charcoal (638/645), suggesting the periodic dumping and burying of kitchen and other waste. Nothing later than the 11th to 13th century was recovered from the small pottery assemblage. This was sealed by a mid- to dark brown sandy loam with abundant mixed gravel (639), which was once again associated with 11th to 13th century pottery. Above this lay a thick layer of mid- to dark brown silty loam (602), again rich in organic material, but with lenses of oyster shells, burnt clay, charcoal and stone rubble (predominantly flint but with greensand, ironstone and chalk). A substantial pottery assemblage dating to the 13th to 14th century was recovered.

The surface of the dumped clay 625/627 adjacent to F633 was covered in a relatively dense layer of flint gravel and cobbles (614, Fig. 2.15). Though this did not appear to form part of a carefully laid surface, it lay directly below the modern topsoil and so may have been disturbed.

Hollow F641

To the north of pit F633 a shallow hollow (F641), just 0.2 m deep, also extended beyond the northern edge of Trench 6 (Figs 2.14–2.15). On the eastern side this was filled with a mid-brown silty loam (615), which was overlain to the west by a dark brown silty loam, with lenses of gravel, mortar, burnt clay, and abundant midden debris (620). There was also a large amount of flint rubble and a number of larger greensand blocks, including two with mortar still adhering, and 13th to 15th century pottery. An iron strap mount dated to the 15th century or later (SF 124, Fig. 3.10, 30; see Richards below, Chapter 3).

Pit F628

To the west of F641, lay a small oval pit (F628), 0.4 m wide and at least 0.6 m long; it was truncated by another pit F642 (Fig. 2.14). Its fill comprised a mid-brown silty loam, packed with greensand blocks and a number of flints and lumps of yellow clay (629). It contained a small amount of 13th to 15th century pottery.

Pit F649

Another substantial pit (F649) lay to the north of F628, and west of pit F641, which could only be partly excavated due to a substantial fragment of overlying masonry (652) and the associated rubble (648, 674, 685) (Fig. 2.14). The lowest fill that could be excavated was a mid-grey-brown silty clay, containing a large amount of midden debris, including an articulated sheep mandible (691), and a dark brown silty loam with frequent flecks of charcoal and lenses of gravel (668) partly sealed by a dump of mottled yellow/orange silty clay (686). This was sealed by a lens of charcoal (684), which in turn lay beneath a layer of reddish brown silty clay loam with an abundance of charcoal, burnt clay and flecks of mortar and 13th to 15th century pottery (631, 644, 669, 677, 678). To the west of F649, this layer extended over the dumped clay into which the pit was cut. Within the pit F649 this layer of burnt debris was overlain by a mid-brown sandy silt (630) and a series of tips and lenses of dark brown silty loams, containing distinct bands of fine gravel (624). Once again, pottery dated to the 13th to 15th century.

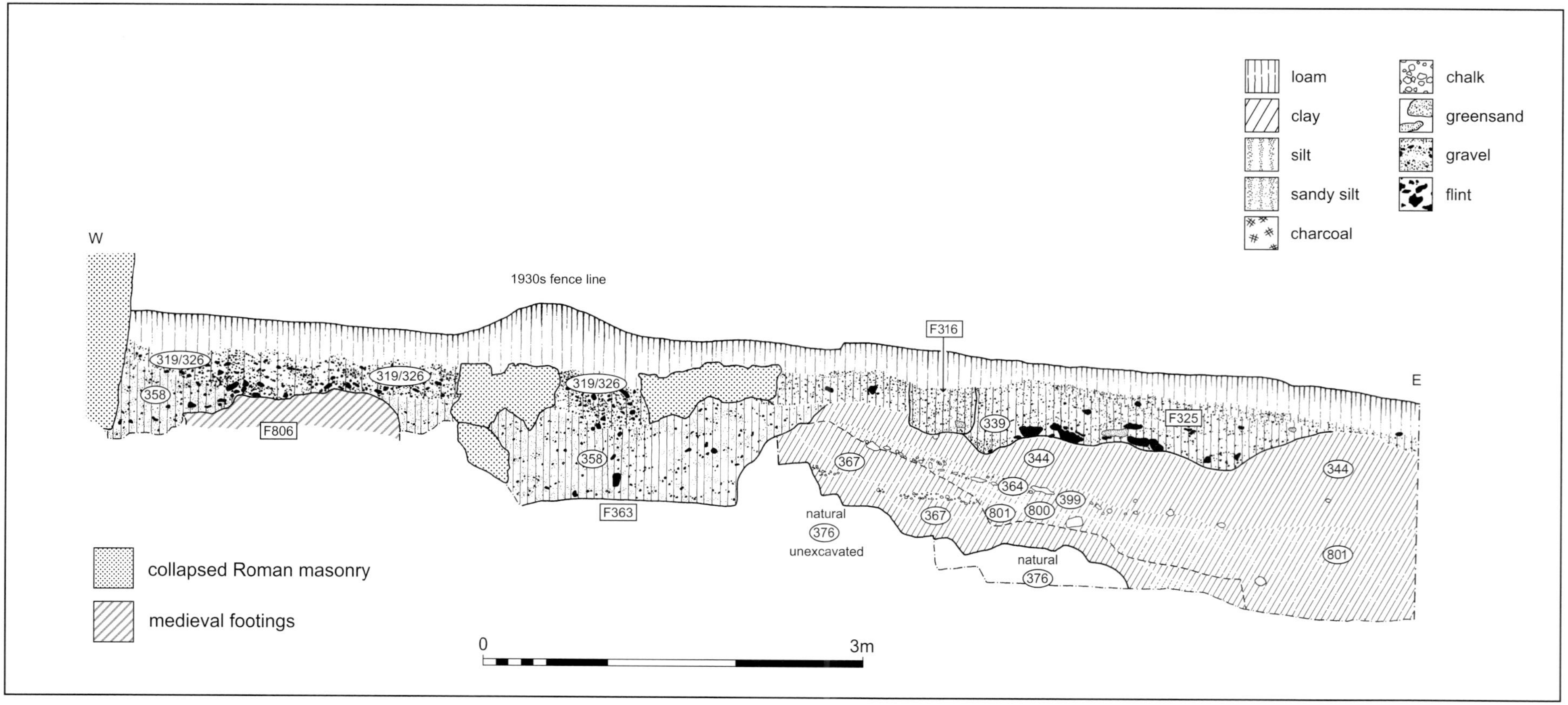

Figure 2.16 South-facing section of Trench 4 (before it was extended to the north during the excavation of Trench 6), including surviving fragments of the second phase of the Keep's North East Tower (F806, Phase 8), and its robber trench F363 (Phase 14) (see Figure 2.14 for location)

Pit or hollow F670

Part of another potentially large pit or hollow lay to the north-west of F649 (Figs 2.14–2.15: F670). It was filled with a mid-brown very silty clay, with frequent lumps of yellow clay, along with abundant gravel and flint rubble (671). The small assemblage of pottery dated to the 11th to 13th century, though it was sealed beneath the burnt layer 644 dating to the 13th–15th century.

Phase 11: Burial of Keep under Mound

At some time following the backfilling of the Keep wall construction trench, a layer of yellow clay was laid over the full extent of Trench 1 (Fig. 2.5, 207/208). This probably represents the base of a substantial mound of yellow clay that illustrations such as Grimm's aquatint (Pl. 1.3) show covering the Keep, and which Sands observed in his excavations of 1908 (Sands 1908, 26–7). The small area excavated in 1993–5 only produced a handful of residual Roman sherds. The mound was removed by the Ministry of Works during the 1930s, and it may have been then that a linear cut was dug alongside the Keep wall (Fig. 2.5, F206/211).

Dumps of yellow clay were a significant component of the fill of Trench 2 (contexts 1–4). These either represented deliberate dumps of material designed to fill the void created by the collapse of the Roman fort wall, or they resulted from the slippage into the gap created by the fall of the wall of clay already dumped within the Keep. The majority of the associated pottery is residual Roman and medieval, but a few sherds of 16th–17th century pottery were recovered from layer 32.

Phase 12: Demolition and partial robbing of Keep Wall and Towers

North Wall of Keep

Trench 7 revealed the fill of the robber trench for the missing part of the Keep's north wall (Fig. 2.6). It was filled with a range of mainly sandy gravels (702–704, 714–715, 730, 736–43). The edges of the robber trench were destroyed by Sand's excavation (F709 and F710). The majority of the pottery was medieval and residual, but layer 737 contained one 16th century sherd.

North East Tower

The Keep's North East Tower was demolished to just below present ground level and the footings largely robbed before the collapse of the Roman curtain wall. The fill of this first phase robber trench was quite distinct from a subsequent phase of robbing (Phase 14). A series of tips and dumps of material butted up against the surviving fragment of the Phase 8 rebuilt tower (F806), and extended to the south and west under the block of Roman wall F664 (Fig. 2.7). These comprised intercalated lenses of yellow/orange silty clay (374), pale grey slightly silty clay (392), a light brown/grey silty clay with occasional mixed gravel (369), a dark brown sandy clay (368), and a mid- to dark grey/brown sandy gravel (370, 377). A similar range of deposits was found between F806 and F692/693 (Fig. 2.8), where a light brown slightly silty sandy gravel (646) was overlain by mid- to dark grey brown silty loam (621). On the northern side of the Tower, another area of more consolidated robber trench fill survived above the intact footings F694 (Fig. 2.4), comprising a mid-brown silty sand, with frequent fine gravel (673, 675). All these deposits associated with the first phase of robbing of the second North East Tower were distinguishable from the later deposits by being firmer and having a greater heterogeneity. Pottery indicates an 18th century date.

Pit F345

A shallow pit, F345, was also cut into the chalk spread 318, and was backfilled with a loose mid-brown silty sandy gravel (338; Fig. 2.17). Though this only yielded four 11th to 13th century sherds the character of the fill was very similar to that of the robber trenches of the North East Tower.

East Tower

At some stage, but prior to the collapse of the Roman fort wall, the East Tower was also demolished, though only to ground level. There is no independent evidence for the date of this robbing.

Phase 13: Collapse of Roman Wall and subsequent deposits

In the north-west corner of Trench 6, a deep stratified sequence of deposits (Figs 2.14–2.15) was excavated which overlay pits F649 and F670, and the block of fallen Roman curtain wall F652 and associated rubble (648, 674, 685) (Pls 2.5–2.6). The lowest in the

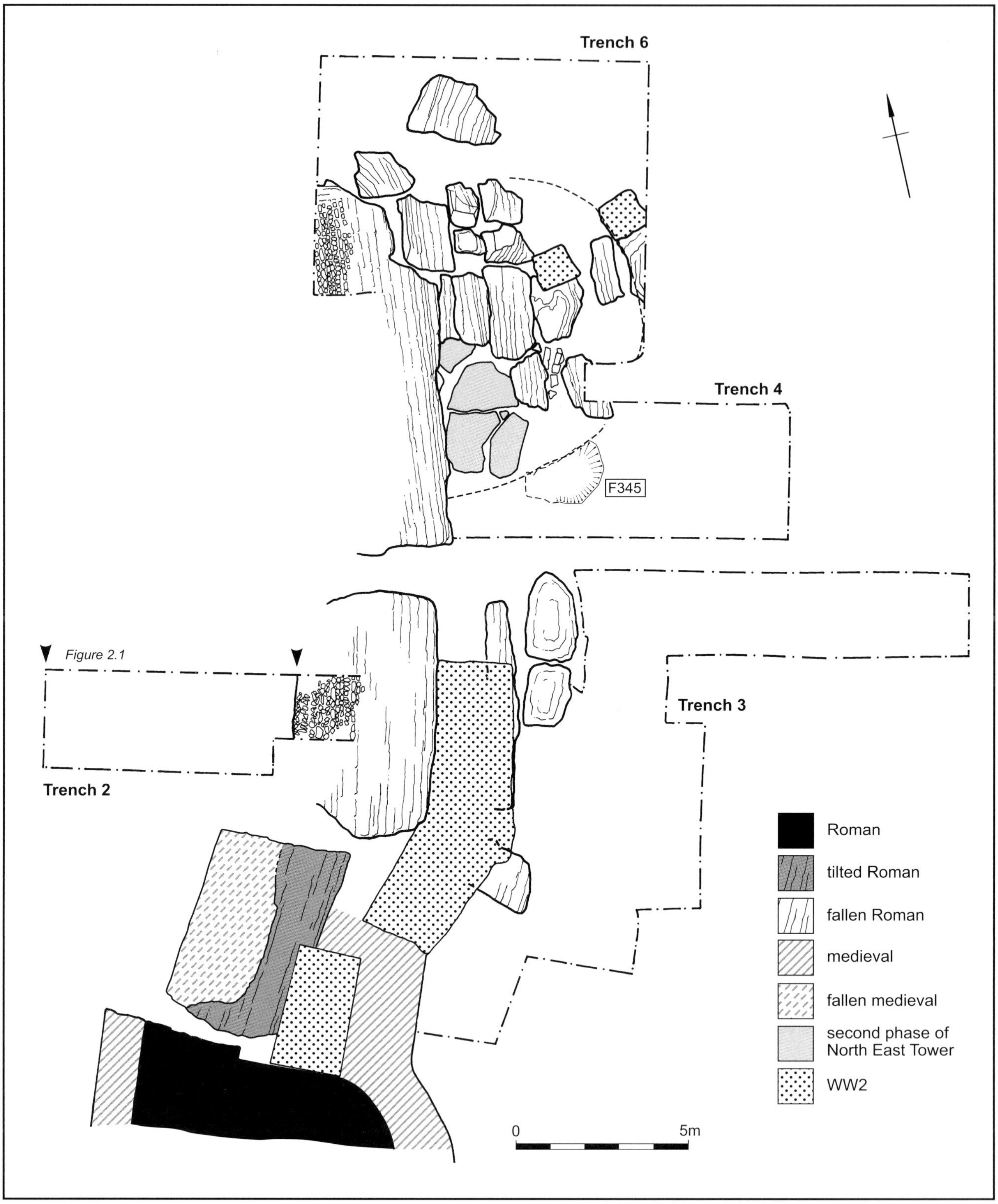

Figure 2.17 Plan of collapsed and tilted fragments of Roman fort wall

sequence of layers was a mid-brown clay loam, with some gravel (643), which overlay the burnt horizon spreading out from F649 (644). Layer 643 was sealed by a mid-brown very silty clay loam containing a large amount of mortar rubble, frequent flint nodules and occasional flecks of charcoal (632). Above this lay a light to mid-brown silty loam with frequent mixed gravel and greensand chips (623). In turn this was sealed by a very mottled yellow/orange/brown silty clay, with frequent lumps of chalk (617). Finally in this sequence lay a dark brown silty clay loam, with abundant flecks of charcoal and burnt clay, and some gravel (618). This sequence was associated with a large amount of 13th to 15th century pottery.

There were few areas where the strata above the fallen Roman wall were not disturbed by the Ministry of Works landscaping of the site. A mid- to dark brown silty loam (640) overlay the backfill of the first robber trench of the second phase, North East Tower (673), and F680; it contained 18th to 19th century pottery. It was sealed by a mottled yellow very silty clay containing flecks of charcoal (637), possibly equating with 617 to the north. Finally, there was a spread of mottled mid-brown silty loam with a large amount of gravel and small lumps of mortar (616).

Phase 14: Further robbing of North East Tower's footings

Although the footings of the North East Tower had been largely dug out during the 18th century, there was a further phase of robbing during the 18th/19th century (Phase 12) (Figs 2.7, 2.16). To the east this robbing went to the very edge of the original foundation trench, though to the north parts of the tower's first phase footings and second phase robber trench were left. The trench was backfilled with a very mixed loose, light-to-mid-brown silty sandy gravel (319/326; 358; 608; 635; 636; 682; 683). To the north, parts of the first phase of tower foundation also survive (F694), along with the backfill of the second robber trench which led to the removal of the North East Tower's second phase (673).

Phase 15: Recent activity

A large part of the sequence in Trench 7 was truncated by two recent excavations (Fig. 2.6, F709, F710). Along with F609 in Trench 6 (Fig 2.18) these are probably the work of Harold Sands (1908, 26–7).

In 1925 the castle was given to the nation, and until the outbreak of War, the then Office of Works carried out a programme of clearance which included completely removing the mound of clay that sealed

Plate 2.5 The collapsed Roman fort wall looking south-west from the north-east corner of Trench 6. See Figure 2.17 for a plan of these wall fragments. The Second World War pill box inserted into the collapsed wall fragments to the west of Trench 3 can be seen top left

Plate 2.6 The collapsed Roman fort wall looking south from the northern edge of Trench 6. The Second World War pill box inserted into the collapsed wall fragments to the west of Trench 3 can be seen top right

the Keep, and then levelling the ground giving rise to the present ground surface (e.g., Trench 2: layers 9, 11–16, Fig. 2.1). The projected line of the Roman fort wall was marked by two concrete plinths (Fig. 2.18). A narrow undated trench dug along the inside of the Keep wall may also date to this period (F206/F211), the fills of which comprised dark brown loamy soils (203, 204, 212) with lenses of crumbly mortar (215) and orange/grey clay (210). A shallow trench F104 excavated around the footings of the East Tower may also date to the 1930s, and a curving gully-like feature located in Trenches 4 and 6 may represent an unsuccessful attempt to locate the North East Tower in a similar way (F316/F322/F634, Fig. 2.18). A rectangular trench dug across the southern part of the North East Tower may also represent an early archaeological investigation (F314).

In May 1940 the castle was refortified and subsequently used as an observation and command

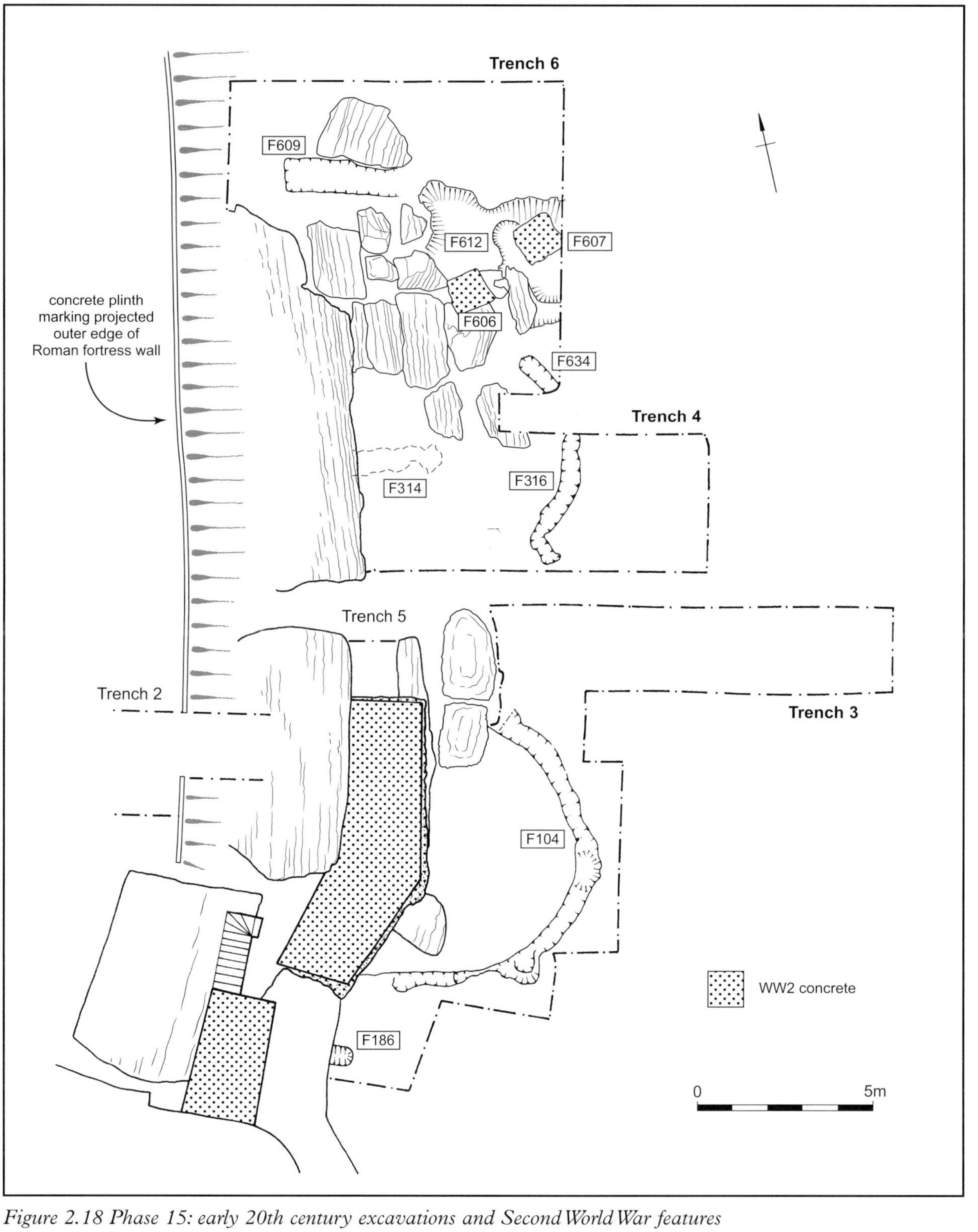

Figure 2.18 Phase 15: early 20th century excavations and Second World War features

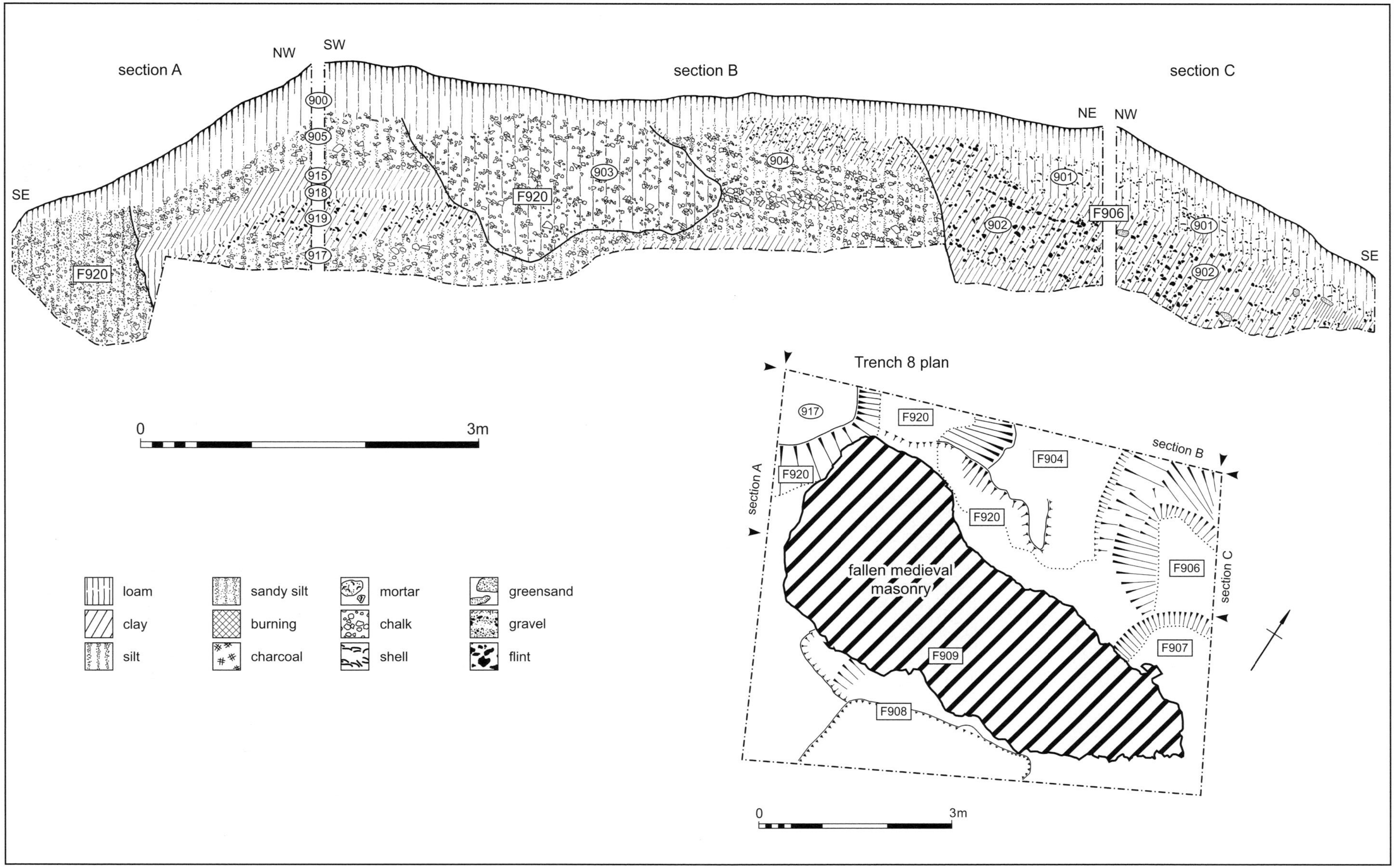

Figure 2.19 Plan, and east-, south- and west-facing sections of Trench 8 (see Figure 1.3 for location)

Plate 2.7 Trench 8: fallen medieval wall south of the postern, from the south

Plate 2.8 Trench 8: fallen medieval wall south of the postern from the west

post by British, American and Canadian troops. Numerous pill boxes were concealed amongst the ruins, two of which were sited within the tumbled mass of masonry on the eastern side of the Keep (Fig. 2.18) and have since been retained as part of the monument. A series of anti-tank blocks (including F606; F607) were also laid in an irregular shaped trench which caused further disturbance to the already highly truncated remains of the North East Tower (F612, layers 605, 611 and 613, see Figs 2.17–18).

Trench 8: Fallen wall south of the medieval postern

Excavations under the direction of Stuart Rigold in 1964 'explored the forework of this [postern] gate and revealed a large piece of fallen baffle-wall, already partly buried when the 13th century refortification began' (Wilson and Hurst 1965, 192). Sands had also earlier explored this mass of fallen masonry (1908, 29).

With no surviving records of the earlier excavations, it was decided in 1995 to reinvestigate and record this fallen piece of masonry in order to determine an appropriate conservation strategy. With only a small area visible above ground in 1995, it was only an assumption that this masonry was the same as that investigated in 1964.

The masonry re-revealed in Trench 8 measured some 7 m by 3 m with a thickness of 2 m (Figs 1.3, 2.19). It lay on the surface of the ground which slopes steeply towards the south-east. The upper surface of the masonry was in good condition: it consisted of single and double courses of roughly dressed greensand alternating with several course of flint (Pls 2.7–2.8). The small portion of the underside which was revealed in the course of emptying the bottom of the 1964 trench showed course of carefully dressed greensand ashlar. While the surviving upper surface probably represented the inside face of the original construction, the underside was presumably intended to be the external face of the wall.

The re-excavation identified four phases of activity which cannot be closely correlated with the phases of the main Keep excavations:

Context group I

The stratigraphy beneath the collapsed wall fragment F909. From bottom to top: 914 (natural), 913 (disturbed top of natural?), 912 (thin layer of pale grey silt), 911 (? buried soil horizon), 910 (layer of yellow-brown silty clay). No pottery was recovered from these layers.

Context group II

Build up of material over the collapsed wall (from the area excavated it is difficult to say whether this is *in situ* dumping or the slumping of material as the wall collapsed, Fig. 2.1). From bottom to top: 917 (greensand chips and loamy soil); 919 (layer of brown clay); 918 (layer of brown loamy soil); 915 (layer of yellow clay); 904, 903 and 905 (layers of greensand chips and loamy soil) (Fig. 2.19). While there is 19th and 20th-century material from 903 and 904, layers 915 and 917 contained (probably residual) 11th to 13th century pottery.

Context group III

Steep-sided cut feature (F906) was found in the north-east corner of Trench 8 (Fig. 2.19). The lower fill comprised a mid- to light brown silty clay (902), the upper fill a mid-brown silty loam (901). The character of the fills suggests that this cut is older than Rigold's excavations. The fills contained both 13th to 15th century pottery and post-medieval sherds of 16th century or later date.

Context group IV

Recent excavations, probably by Rigold in 1964 (Wilson and Hurst 1965, 192; Fig. 2.19): F907 (filled with 900), F908 (filled with 900), F920 (filled with 904). The latest pottery was of 19th and 20th century date.

The re-exposure of this fallen wall fragment confirmed its medieval character and its probable association with the postern gate as an external baffle. The foundations of a wall which projected east from the south side of the postern might well represent the original position of this fallen fragment. It remains unclear when this section of wall fell.

Chapter 3
Finds

Pottery

by Jane Timby with contributions by Alan Vince† and D. F. Williams

The excavations produced a substantial collection of pottery, amounting to some 11,769 sherds, weighing 133.6 kg, dating from the late Roman period through to the 20th century. Of particular interest is a collection of pottery of late Roman to late Saxon date from a deposit of dark earth pre-dating the construction of the Keep (Phase 3). There have been no detailed reports on pottery from any previous archaeological work at Pevensey since that published by Salzmann (1909). This earlier assemblage along with other pre-Second World War excavated material has been studied in depth by Malcolm Lyne and a report prepared (Lyne 2009). Two essentially medieval sites within the adjacent village of Pevensey have also been investigated in more recent years by Dulley (1967) and Barber (1999).

Following some commentary on the condition and character of the pottery and the methodology used, this report is divided into two main sections: first, a chronological discussion of the pottery in terms of the defined stratigraphic sequence and second, a discussion of the Roman and medieval assemblage in a wider local and regional context. A description of the fabrics and associated forms can be found in Appendix 2. The Saxon sherds and medieval imports have been discussed separately by Alan Vince. Representative groups from selected key phases have been illustrated along with other pieces of intrinsic interest.

Condition of the material

Looking at the assemblage as a whole it comprises 41.5% Roman material, 1.5% Saxon, 28.5% medieval and 28.5% post-medieval/modern (by weight). Because of the nature of the site there is an immense amount of redeposition of material throughout all the sequences and a small amount of possible contamination of horizons where later material has penetrated earlier groups. Table 3.1 lists the quantities of sherds for each stratigraphic phase. Overall, pottery was recovered from 293 individual contexts. The largest collection of Roman pottery came from the dark earth deposits (Phase 3) accounting for some 20% of the total assemblage.

The condition of the material is variable. Comparison with vessels illustrated by Lyne (2009) from earlier excavations in the castle and by Dulley (1967) from the village suggests that much of this pottery was in a much better state of preservation. Many of the key diagnostic sherds from the present excavations unfortunately came from redeposited contexts.

Methodology

The pottery fabrics were sorted according to the composition, size and frequency of the macroscopically visible inclusions in the clay body. Representative type sherds were extracted as sorting proceeded for comparison and later identification. The bulk of the Roman coarsewares can be divided into grog-tempered wares and grey sandy wares. Although further refinement of these categories may be possible, for the purposes of this report the fabric divisions have been kept very basic and several groups, particularly with the grey wares, subsequently amalgamated. It is considered that the character of the assemblage in terms of its stratigraphic context and the paucity of knowledge concerning local Sussex industries in both the Roman and medieval periods mitigates against over-refinement of groups at this stage which descriptively sound very similar and contribute little to our overview of the site. Potentially the material could contribute to a detailed in-depth study such as that carried out by Lyne (1994) on the grog-tempered wares, to try and define individual production centres but such work falls outside the remit of this excavation report. There are also a number of small unidentified one-off, yet visually quite distinctive sherds which may potentially be imports (Roman and medieval) but not within any currently known repertoire. Again, without diagnostic material such sherds cannot be confidently identified and await further work on material from the Continent.

The assemblage was fully quantified by sherd count, weight and estimated vessel equivalents (eve) (rim only) and the data computerised using an Excel spreadsheet (available in the archive). Fabrics are referred to in text by their codes after the first mention, details of which can be found in Appendix 2 or by referring to Table 3.2 (Roman/Saxon) and Table 3.7 (medieval/post-medieval).

Table 3.1 Quantity of pottery by stratigraphic phase

Phase	*Wt (g)*	*No*	*Eve*	*Aver*
1	75	10	12	7.5
2	53	6	0	8.8
3	27758	2396	3153	11.5
4	395	56	33	7
5A	171	28	19	6
5Aii	363	45	30	8
5B1	357	29	40	12.3
5B2	421	61	65	7
5C	170	21	3	8
6A	917	80	88	11.5
6B	4	1	0	4
6C	137	12	0	11.4
6D	16	3	0	5.7
7	23	4	5	5.8
8C	14	3	0	4.7
8D	20	3	5	6.7
9	49	8	3	6.1
10	4	2	0	2
10A	22	3	6	7.3
10B	1203	176	128	6.8
10C	112	15	49	7.5
10D	1326	223	230	6.1
10E	21	1	0	21
10G	381	52	21	7.3
10H	332	58	48	5.7
10I	3279	518	195	6.3
10J	718	109	29	6.6
10K	85	7	0	12
10L	2819	339	182	8.6
10M	34	10	10	3.4
10Q	78	9	16	8.7
11A	71	7	6	10.1
11B	54	7	15	7.7
11C	1699	210	108	8
12A	742	104	63	7.4
12B	1774	239	90	7.6
12Ci	100	8	19	12.5
12Cii	10990	910	1108	12
12Ciii	38	7	3	5.4
12Ciiia	3052	237	287	12.9
12Ciiib	1630	140	287	11.6
12Ciiic	588	46	48	12.8
12Ciiid	10509	945	958	11.1
12D	223	38	11	5.9
12E	104	15	1	6.9
13A	4993	369	199	13.5
13B	43	7	0	6.1
13C	1294	187	68	7.5
14A	4691	380	565	12.3
14B	8478	854	687	9.9
14C	2421	267	258	9
14Ciii	30	3	0	10
15	34100	2010	4780	17
17	228	25	160	9.1
18	806	100	42	8
19	1652	185	178	8.9
US	1904	181	240	
Total	**133571**	**11769**	**14551**	

Ceramic sequence

Phases 1–2: Saxon shore fort

The surface of the natural subsoil in Trench 2 (71) produced single sherds of Roman grog-tempered ware and a Dorset Black Burnished ware (DOR BB1) straight-sided dish. Above this, Phases 1 and 2 produced very little pottery with some ten sherds from the former and six from the latter. The presence of a very abraded sherd of Oxfordshire colour-coated (OXF RS) mortarium from (71) in the pre-fort layers (Phase 1) alongside East Sussex handmade grog-tempered ware and sandy grey wares suggests a date in the later 3rd century. Phase 2 belonging to the period of the fort construction yielded typologically undiagnostic body sherds of grey sandy ware. The dendrochronological date and associated coins from this phase indicate a *terminus post quem* of AD 293 for this group (see Chapter 2).

Phase 3: Sequence inside fort wall

(Figs 3.1–3.3, 1–60)

The deep sequence of deposits in Trench 2 produced a substantial quantity of pottery. Lesser amounts of contemporary material came from Trenches 1 and 7. Table 3.3 summarizes the range of fabrics present from the phase as a whole.

The lowest horizon in Trench 2, layer 60, produced a small assemblage of 58 sherds. Within this was a late Roman shell-tempered (ROB SH) hook-rimmed jar, an OXF RS flagon, an Alice Holt storage jar sherd (ALH RE), various grey sandy ware jars and flanged bowls and a small scrap of residual samian. Succeeding layers 39, 38 and 52 all contained good groups of 4th century pottery with a number of ALH RE-type black and grey sandy wares, New Forest colour-coated wares (NFO CC), Overwey jars (OVW WH), DOR BB1 and Oxfordshire white-slipped mortaria (OXF WSM). Perhaps significantly none of these horizons contained any Pevensey colour-coated ware.

The potentially contemporary horizon in Trench 1 with a hearth (245/247/249) and gravel surface (250) is less clear-cut chronologically as there are sherds of Pingsdorf ware and medieval fabric LOCMED1 present in (250) and a further medieval cooking pot from (245) suggestive of a date from the 11th century. Similar material came from the successive horizon (246), including another Pingsdorf sherd possibly from the same vessel as (250). A vitrified sherd from a crucible came from (246). The equivalent horizon in Trench 7 was aceramic.

In Trench 2 the series of spits making up the next horizon, (17, 24–5, 31, 35–7 and 45) produced the bulk of the pottery from the phase. The group can perhaps be split chronologically with the earlier horizons (45 and 37) being notably different in fabric

Table 3.2 Roman and Saxon fabrics

	Fabric	Common Name	Wt (g)	No	Eve
IMPORTS	SAMCG/EG	Central /East Gaulish samian	273	51	41
	ARG RS	Argonne ware	15	2	0
	NAF RS	African red-slip	57	3	19
	MAY CO	Mayen-ware	52	2	4
	RO IM1	French/German import	37	1	11
	RO IM2	?North French import	3	1	0
	NOG WH4	North Gaulish mortaria	10	1	0
	BAT AM1	Dressel 20 amphora	83	2	0
	AMP	?Eastern Mediterranean	32	1	0
	?AMP	?amphora	17	1	9
REGIONAL	ALH RE	Alice Holt grey/black ware	3187	128	361
	OVW WH	Overwey whiteware/Portchester D ware	1752	166	325
	NFO CC	New Forest colour-coated ware	700	106	96
	NFO CCM	New Forest colour-coated mortaria	356	12	40
	NFO WHCC	New Forest whiteware, colour-coated	129	15	10
	NFO WH	New Forest whiteware	15	1	0
	NFO WHM	New Forest whiteware mortaria	68	1	21
	NFO PA	New Forest parchment ware	3	1	0
	LNV CC	Nene Valley colour-coat	6	1	0
	OXF RS	Oxon colour-coated ware	2366	332	399
	OXF RSM	Oxon colour-coated mortaria	352	41	35
	OXF WSM	Oxon white-slip mortaria	499	20	32
	OXF WHM	Oxon whiteware mortaria	744	27	52
	OXF PA	Oxon parchment ware	7	2	7
	MAH WHM	Mancetter-Hartshill mortaria	60	1	10
	ROB SH	Midlands shelly ware	70	4	23
	DOR BB1	Dorset black-burnished ware	953	81	176
LOCAL	PEV CC	Pevensey colour-coated ware	1514	180	248
	PEV WSM	Pevensey white-slip mortaria	91	6	8
	PEV CCM	Pevensey colour-coated mortaria	95	9	5
	GROG1	grog-tempered ware	17171	1319	1393
	GROG2	grog-tempered ware	113	21	18
	GROG3	grog-tempered ware	939	63	92
	GROG	miscellaneous grog-tempered	825	71	18
	GRQTZ	grog and sand tempered	12	2	2
	GROG4	Thundersbarrow-type storage jar	2851	93	15
	GREY1	local grey ware	4921	619	297
	GREY2	local grey ware	8084	983	1085
	GREY3	local grey ware	2740	153	549
	GREY4	black sandy ware	1109	93	141
	GREY5	black sandy ware	65	6	7
	GREY6	grey sandy ware	1491	64	89
	GREY7	grey sandy ware	92	7	35
	GREY8	grey sandy ware	1141	131	279
	GREY9	grey sandy ware	207	8	20
UNKNOWN	MISCOXID	miscellaneous oxidised sandy wares	128	14	14
	MISCGREY	miscellaneous reduced wares	1366	207	229
	WH	miscellaneous whiteware	16	4	0
	WS	miscellaneous white-slipped wares	69	7	0
	LOC CC	miscellaneous colour-coated ware	150	19	0
	MORT	mortaria, source unknown	2	92	0
	R00	unclassified Roman wares	100	39	5
SAXON	SX1-3	sandstone-tempered wares	170	17	4
	SX4-7	local late Saxon flint/sand temp	1640	133	101
	SX8	shell-tempered ware	22	3	0
	ECHAF	chaff-tempered ware	4	1	0
	CHARN	granite-tempered ware	8	1	0
SAXON IMPORT	NF RPT	red painted ?Normandy	100	9	30
	PING	Rhenish ?Pingsdorf ware	104	18	0
	IMP WH	?imported whiteware	5	1	0
Total			59186	5396	6355

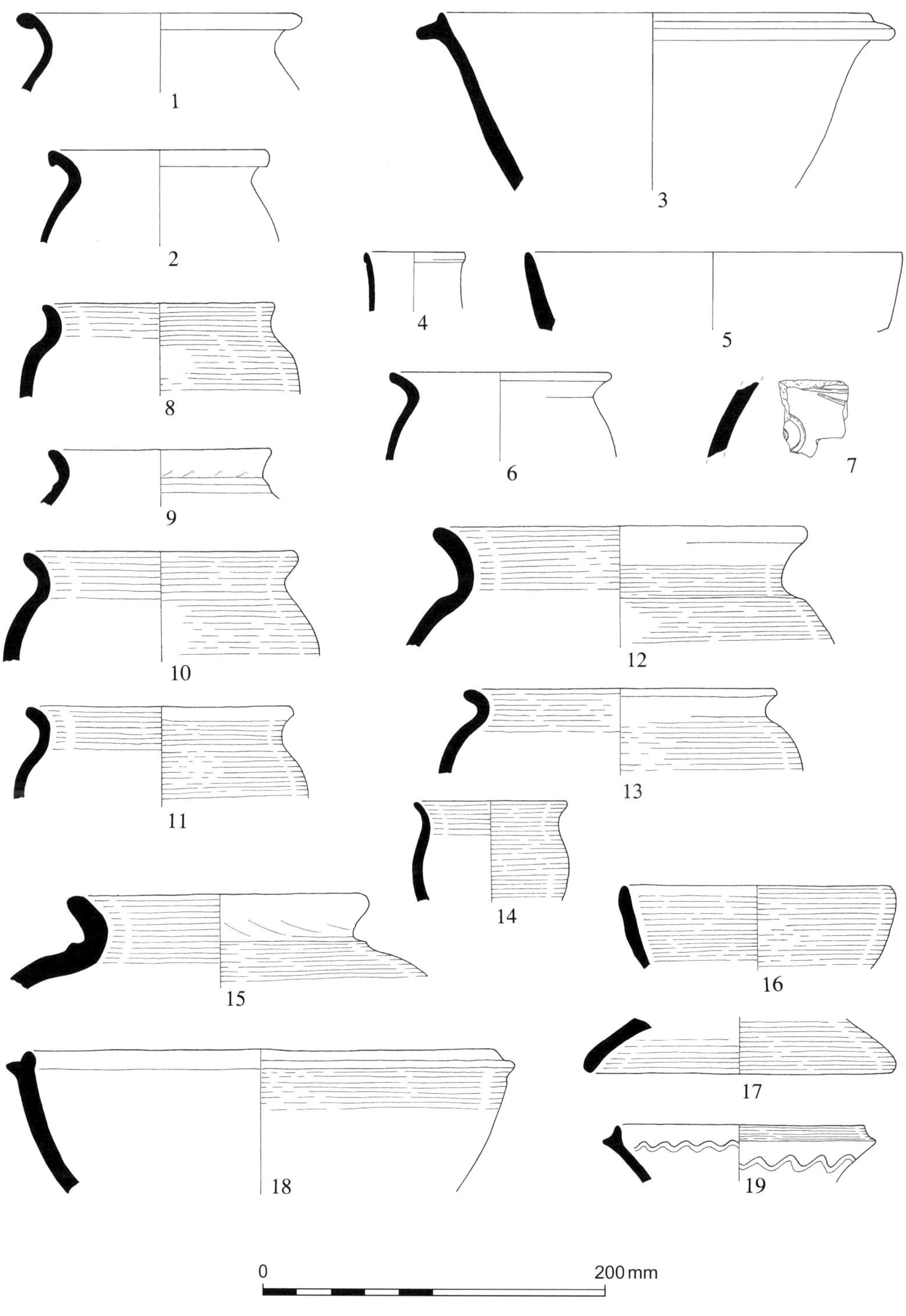

Figure 3.1 Pottery from the 'dark earth' sequence (Phase 3)

composition to the rest of the group, and the section (Fig. 2.1) does indeed appear to show a levelling off or truncation at this point which may have some chronological significance. Contexts 45 and 37 contain exclusively 4th century Roman wares, GROG, ALH RE, DOR BB1, NFO CC, OXF RS, GREY and a small quantity of OVW WH. Pevensey colour-coated wares (PEV CC) are conspicuous by their absence. When Pevensey ware was first recognised by Fulford (1973) the evidence suggested floruit of production towards the middle of the 4th century although five sherds from Portchester may derive from contexts of pre-340 date. Lyne (2009, 99) suggests that it appears around 350 at Pevensey. The presence of a New Forest mortarium of Fulford (1975a) type 104 from (45) along with the Overwey ware suggests that material was accumulating in these deposits up to at least AD 350/60. These particular

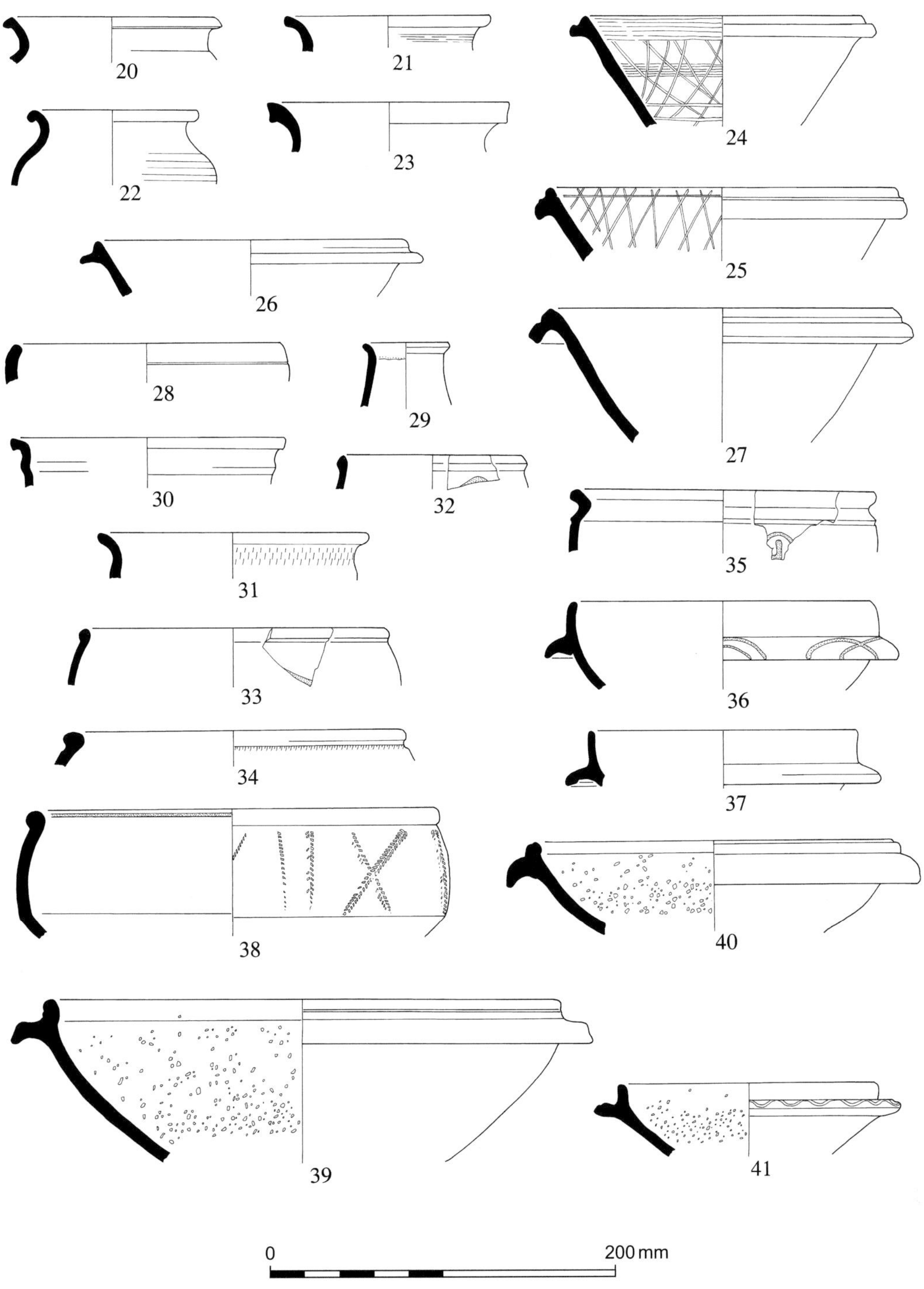

Figure 3.2 Pottery from the 'dark earth' sequence (Phase 3)

groups therefore point to Pevensey ware as perhaps being a little later in date. It appears in substantial quantities in the successive horizons along with a number of other new types including a sherd of imported African red-slipped ware (NAF RS) (Fig. 3.3, 48) and local colour-coated ware. In addition to the Roman wares there are seven Saxon sherds (SX1, SX2, SX4–7) including a late Saxon, everted-rim cooking-pot (SX4–7), three sherds of red-painted ware (NF RPT), and 62 sherds of fabric LOCMED1 including a sherd with an applied thumbed strip (Fig. 3.3, 57). The latest recognisable Roman ware present is the sherd of African red-slip from (31) from a dish (Hayes (1972) type H75), typologically dated to the early-mid-5th century. The Saxon sherds mainly from (24 and 25) include sherds of probable early, and of middle-late Saxon date. The latest wares in the standard fabric LOCMED1, from (17) and (24), appear to date to the high medieval period (11th–13th centuries).

Table 3.3 Summary of pottery from Phase 3 (dark earth)

	Fabric	Common name	Wt (g)	No	Eve
IMPORTS	SAMCG/EG	Central /East Gaulish samian	63	15	15
	ARG SA	Argonne ware	3	1	0
	NAF RS	African red-slip	41	2	13
	AMP	amphora	32	1	0
REGIONAL	ALH RE	Alice Holt grey/black ware	1411	66	210
	OVW WH	Overwey whiteware	899	85	151
	OXF	Oxfordshire wares	1408	153	158
	NFO	New Forest wares	791	80	96
	ROB SH	Midlands shelly ware	77	3	23
	DOR BB1	Dorset black-burnished ware	549	47	87
LOCAL	PEV	Pevensey ware	1012	113	176
	GROG	grog-tempered wares	9953	670	648
	GREY1	grey sandy ware	2497	322	160
	GREY2	grey sandy ware	4195	484	594
	GREY3	grey sandy ware	1207	42	277
	GREY4	grey sandy ware	489	39	98
	GREY6	grey sandy ware	104	3	29
	GREY7	grey sandy ware	35	5	0
	GREY8	grey sandy ware	550	46	171
	GREY9	grey sandy ware	159	4	20
UNKNOWN	OXID	miscellaneous oxidised sandy wares	104	8	6
	GREY	miscellaneous reduced wares	333	57	98
	WS	miscellaneous white-slipped wares	59	4	0
	LOC CC	miscellaneous colour-coated ware	88	10	0
	R00	unclassified Roman wares	43	5	22
SAXON	SX1-3	sandstone-tempered wares	49	7	2
	SX4-7	local late Saxon flint/sand temp	721	53	40
	ECHAF	chaff-tempered ware	4	1	0
	CHARN	granite-tempered ware	8	1	0
LATE SAXON	NFR PT	red painted ?Normandy	50	5	15
	PING	Pingsdorf ware	17	3	0
MEDIEVAL	LOCMED1	local flint/quartz gravel tempered	786	59	44
	ENG2	Medieval regional import	21	2	0
UNDATED	CRUC	crucible	4	1	0
Total			27758	2396	3153

The uppermost dark earth layers in Trench 2 (3, 5) yielded a further 31 Roman sherds. In Trench 7 (718, 721–9) and Trench 1 (235) alongside the Roman wares were 4 Saxon sherds (ECHAF, CHARN, SX2), 47 sherds of late Saxon SX4–7, including 1 pedestal lamp, 2 sherds of NF RPT, 13 sherds of LOCMED1 and 2 sherds of English glazed wares (ENG2). In Trench 1 the uppermost layer (235) also contained a sherd of late Saxon ware (SX4–7), and five medieval sherds (LOCMED1) one with an applied thumbed strip.

In summary the ceramic content of the dark earth deposits point to a long period of accumulation from sometime in the mid-4th century through to at least the 11th century. A possible hiatus in the stratigraphy in Trench 2 between horizons 45/37 and those above is highlighted by the pottery. The majority of early, mid- and late Saxon sherds from the site came from the upper part of the dark earth with no clear-cut sequence apparent. The presence of a marked quantity of medieval wares present raises the question as to whether the contexts from (31) upwards represent a series of dumped soil layers brought in from elsewhere in the late Saxon and early medieval periods (*cf.* Macphail, Chapter 4).

Phase 4: Pre-slumping deposits in lower trenches (Fig. 3.3, 61)

Phase 4 only produced a small group of 56 sherds of rather mixed date with examples of Roman, late Saxon, medieval and post-medieval wares present, the latter from (165) suggesting some contamination. The sealing horizon (119) was aceramic.

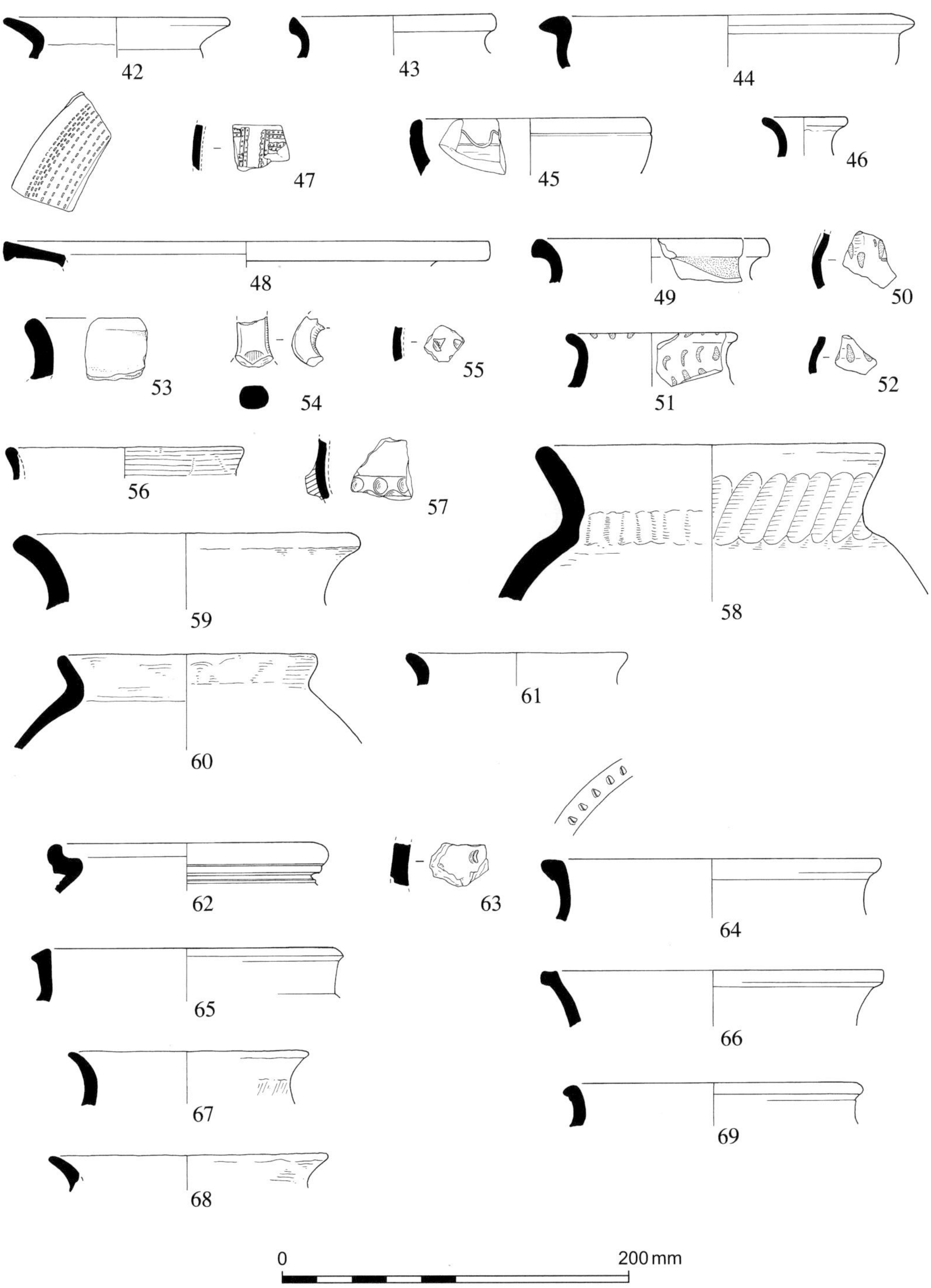

Figure 3.3 Pottery from the 'dark earth' sequence (Phase 3), and Phases 4 and 5

Phase 5: Slumping (Fig. 3.3, 62–9)
The material slumped downslope (Phase 5) produced a total of 73 sherds, of which 65 are Roman, 3 mid–late Saxon and 5 medieval cooking pot (fabric LOCMED1). Of particular note is a sherd of NAF RS, Hayes (1972) type 91 = Bonifay (2004) type 49–50 (see Appendix 2) from (181) dated to the mid-5th–early/mid-6th century and the unidentified imports RO IM1 and RO IM2 from (197). One of the Saxon sherds from (367) is decorated with finger-nail rustication.

The medieval wares are mainly coarse flint-tempered cooking pots, LOCMED1, with three sherds of the slightly finer LOCMED2, a single glazed sherd of Rye-Ringmer (RRING) type and a single South-west French import (SAIM) which is first documented in the early–mid-13th century continuing until the 14th century. A sherd of post-medieval English stoneware from (161) suggests some contamination. A sub-group of Phase 5 with just a small group of 21 body sherds of Roman and

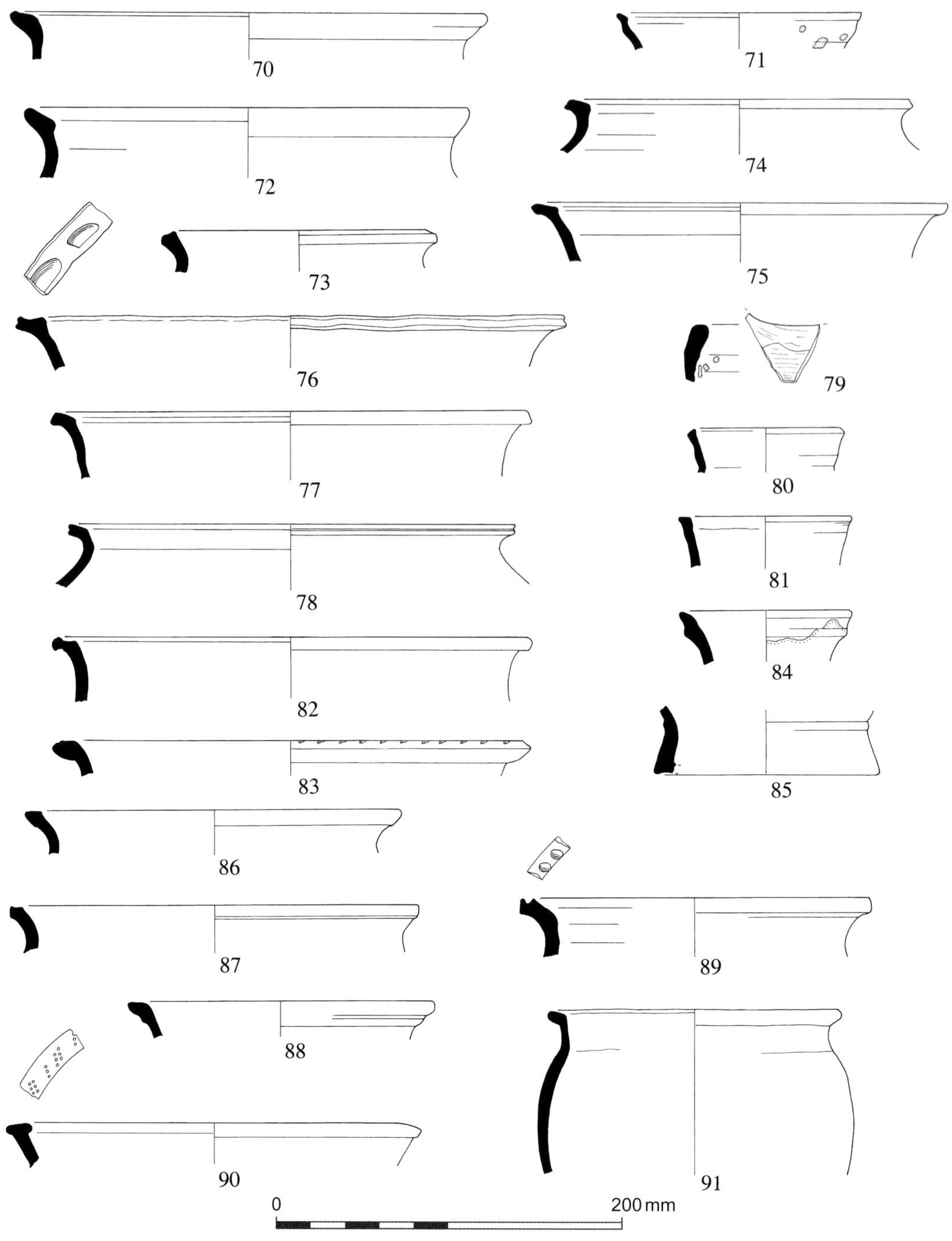

Figure 3.4 Pottery from Phase 10

medieval date has examples of LOCMED1 and two sherds of RRING-type, one with an applied thumb strip suggesting a date in the 12th–13th century.

Phase 6: Keep construction

Phase 6 relating to the keep construction only produced 96 sherds most of which came from the foundation trenches. The majority of the sherds, 73 pieces are of Roman date. Of the remaining seven sherds, six fall within the SX4–7 Saxo-Norman range with one body sherd of LOCMED1 cooking pot (11th–early 13th century). Further unfeatured sherds of LOCMED1 come from Phase 6 so dating from the pottery remains elusive.

Phases 7–9: Robbing of Phase 1 of the Keep's North East Tower

Phases 7, 8 and 9, relating to the possible robbing of the North East Tower, remodelling of the east side of the Keep and the insertion of the garderobe tower and drain, respectively, yielded very little pottery. Phase 7 produced two sherds of a possible Flemish jug (AARD), Phase 8 sherds of LOCMED1 and Phase 9 an intrusive sherd of porcelain.

Table 3.4 Summary of pottery from Phase 10 features

Fabric	*10A wt*	*10A no*	*10B wt*	*10B no*	*10C wt*	*10C no*	*10D wt*	*10D no*	*10G wt*	*10G no*	*10H wt*	*10H no*	*10I wt*	*10I no*	*10J wt*	*10J no*	*10K wt*	*10K no*	*10L wt*	*10L no*	*10M wt*	*10M no*	*10Q wt*	*10Q no*
ROUE																	6	1	8	4				
NFM													219	31					14	3				
NFMS													5	1										
SAIM							5	2					9	3	1	1			4	2				
MISC							5	1					3	1	3	1			11	2				
ENG1			8	1			51	4	10	2	13	2	151	5	15	4			38	2				
ENG2							10	2											56	9				
LOCMED1	3	1	932	153	64	11	915	175	262	35	252	42	1899	317	411	73	13	2	1867	217	34	10	14	1
LOCMED2			24	4	24	1	190	19	72	9	18	4	72	15	180	11	46	1	217	27			41	2
LOCMED3	2	1	55	4			96	13	6	1	17	6	53	10	23	3	10	1	11	3				
MEDFLG			3	1							10	2												
MEDCH															10	1								
WSX			60	5			5	1	6	1														
RRING			23	3	8	1	9	2	25	4			16	1	6	2	10	2	65	9				
WINCH															6	1								
MEDREW					5	1																		
MED00			4	2									68	29	3	2			25	7				
ROMAN	17	1	94	5			30	3					669	89	30	4			417	47			20	5
SAXON							10	1					7	1					86	7				
PMED					11	1					22	2	108	15	30	6							3	1
Total	**22**	**3**	**1203**	**178**	**112**	**15**	**1326**	**223**	**381**	**52**	**332**	**58**	**3279**	**518**	**718**	**109**	**85**	**7**	**2819**	**339**	**34**	**10**	**78**	**9**

wt = g

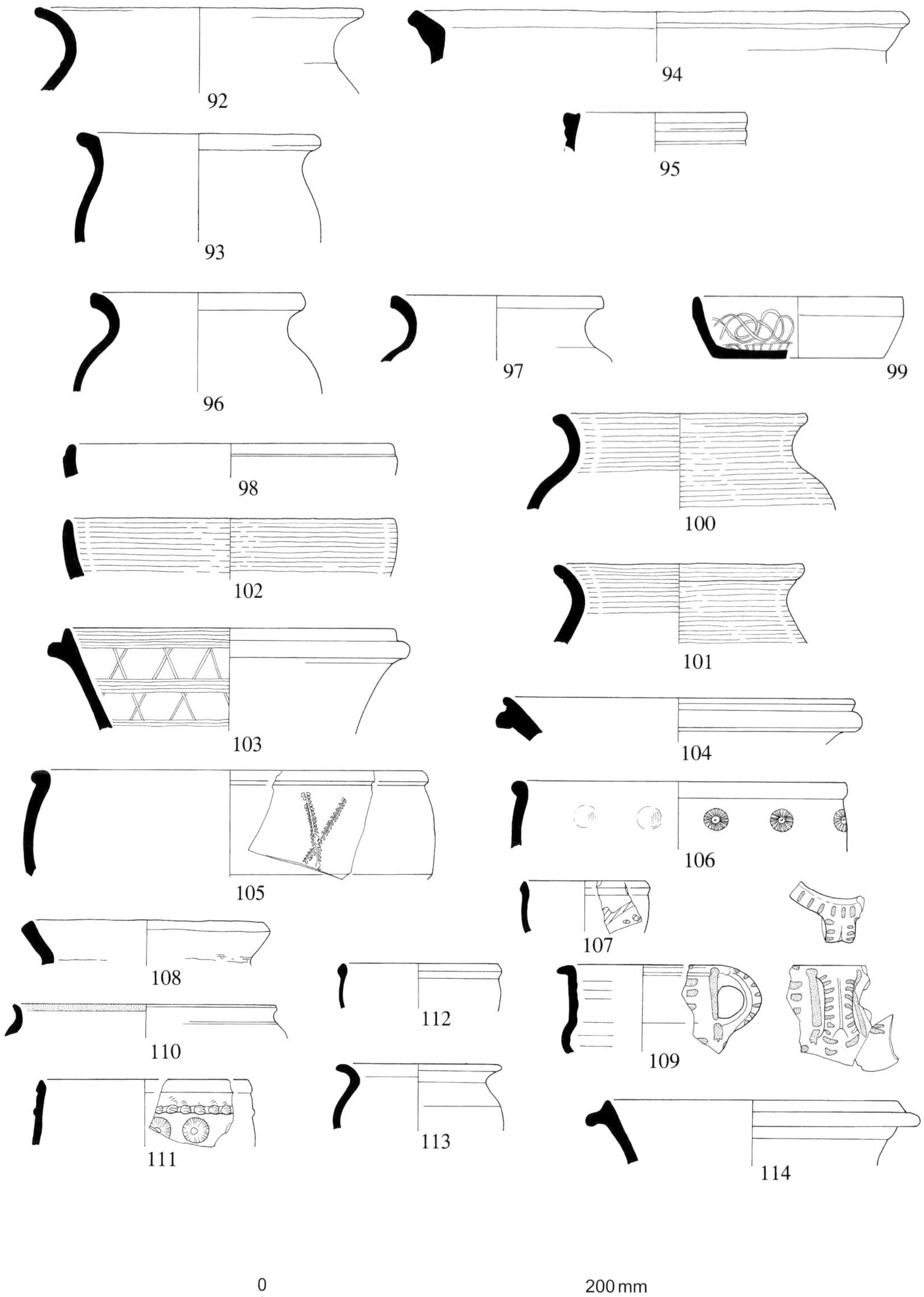

Figure 3.5 Pottery from Phases 10, 12 and 13

Phase 10: Features cut into top of yellow clay (Figs 3.4–3.5, 70–93)

Phase 10 relates to a series of discrete features cut into the top of the natural/dumped yellow clay predating the collapse of the Roman curtain wall. The medieval pottery from these is much more diverse than hitherto with a range of imported wares and several sherds of glazed jug, mainly Sussex types (Table 3.4). Despite the fact that the material came from cut features, most of it appears quite well-broken up with average sherd size between 6 and 8.4 g. The material in F633 is a complete contrast with an average size of 21 g, suggesting that this material may potentially be of a more primary nature. Overall the groups would support a date range in the 13th–14th century.

The largest assemblages were recovered from hollow F144/F154, pit/hearth complex F127/F128, pit F633, hollow F641, and pit F649. Most of the groups contain redeposited sherds of Roman date with a sparse scatter of Saxon pieces. Several fragments of chimney pot were noted, particularly in features F144/F154, F327 and F633. Imported wares were present in F127/F128, F633, F641 and F649. Intrusive post-medieval wares were noted in (307) pit F325, (603) pit F633, which includes a sherd from a Cologne/Frechen mug, (615), hollow F641, and (393), hollow F803 with a Surrey-Hampshire border-ware pipkin sherd (15th–17th century).

Phase 11: Burial of Keep under Mound

Phase 11 produced mostly residual Roman and medieval sherds but layer 32 contained a few sherds of 16th to 17th century pottery.

Phase 12: Demolition and partial robbing of Keep Wall and Towers (Fig. 3.5, 94–5)

Most of the pottery from Phase 11 came from robber trench F673 (Phase 11). The group appears to have been disturbed as several fragments of post-medieval red earthenware are present in layers (673) and (675). Of particular note is the presence of two sherds of Pingsdorf ware (PING). The latest medieval material present appears to be of 13th–4th century currency.

Phase 13: Collapse of Roman Wall and subsequent deposits (Fig. 3.5, 96–114)

The collapse of the Roman wall in Phase 13 and the subsequent deposits resulted in the recovery of a substantial quantity of some 2690 sherds of pottery. Deposits in Trench 6 produced 104 sherds. The lowest horizon (643) was aceramic with most of the sherds coming from the succeeding layers (632), (623), (617–8). These were mainly of medieval date with several imports (NFMS, MISC, ROUE, SAIM), a larger number of local cooking wares and some local Sussex glazed jug suggestive of a date in the 13th–14th centuries.

The pottery from layers associated with the tumbled Roman wall and with a high risk of intrusive material (616, 637, 640) was much more diverse chronologically with several Roman and Saxon sherds mixed in with later material. Imports include sherds of PING, AARD, NFM, ROUL and MISC. Of particular note were several post-medieval/modern sherds including 19th–20th century stonewares and earthenwares, in particular from contexts (637) and (640).

Much of the Phase 13 pottery came from Trench 2 (46, 64 and 525). Of the deposits thought to relate to the Roman wall's foundations, a small group of eight sherds came from (46) of which seven are Roman in date and one a local medieval cooking ware (fabric LOCMED1). A much larger group, some 911 sherds, came from the slumped sequence of dark earth. This group of material essentially mirrors that described in Phase 3 with mainly late Roman, early-late Saxon and some later sherds. Of note amongst the Roman wares is a red-painted flange from a Mancetter-Hartshill mortarium, a single sherd of Dressel 20 amphora and several Pevensey ware vessels including white-slipped mortaria. A grey-ware dish from (83) has an incised cross on the base. The Saxon material includes sherds of SX1 and SX2 and some 40 sherds of late Saxon SX4–7 and NF RPT. Medieval intrusive sherds of cooking ware, English glazed jug and at least four imported sherds (NORG, NFRE).

The slumped yellow clay in Trench 2 produced 1367 sherds with a similar chronological range to the slumped dark earth. The lowest horizons were dominated by late Roman wares including a rare example of an OXF PA shouldered bowl (Young 1977, P32) and a 'blown' waster sherd of PEV CC ware. Further late Saxon sherds were present along with an imported small whiteware sherd with part of a raised strip, probably a Saxon import (IMP WH). Medieval wares were confined to 16 sherds of local fabric LOCMED1. This group was overlain by material thought to have derived from the dark earth sequence. This contained mainly Roman sherds with 19 pieces of local fabric LOCMED1 but no obvious Saxon sherds. The upper sequence is again a mixture of Roman, Saxon and medieval pottery. Amongst the medieval sherds is an imported jug (NFM) from (10) and sherds of local fabrics LOCMED1–2 from layers (6, 8, 10, 19, 26–8, 30, 32–3, 40–1, 47), fabric MEDCH from context 23 and fabric MEDFLG from context 28 showing a certain amount of contamination in the medieval period.

The small group of pottery from the construction trench for the Keep wall contained exclusively later Roman sherds. The linear feature alongside the keep wall (F 206/211) also produced mainly Roman sherds with two small fragments of medieval fabric M1.

Phase 14: Further robbing of North East Tower's footings (Fig. 3.6, 120–2)

The group of 602 sherds from further robbing of the North East Tower's footings comprises 10% Roman, 0.5% Saxon, 49.5% medieval and 39% post-medieval material. Of note amongst the redeposited material is a sherd of 6th-century NAF RS ware (Hayes 1975, type 99C = Bonifay 2004, type 55 Variante C; see Appendix 2) from (608). The medieval material contains a several imported sherds (ROUL, ROUE, SAIM, NFM, NFMS and MISC). It is noticeable that the material from F363/F672 is in a better state of preservation with larger sherds compared with those from F180/F186 and robbing of Keep walls (Trench 7, 702, 703, 704, 714, 715, 730, 736–43).

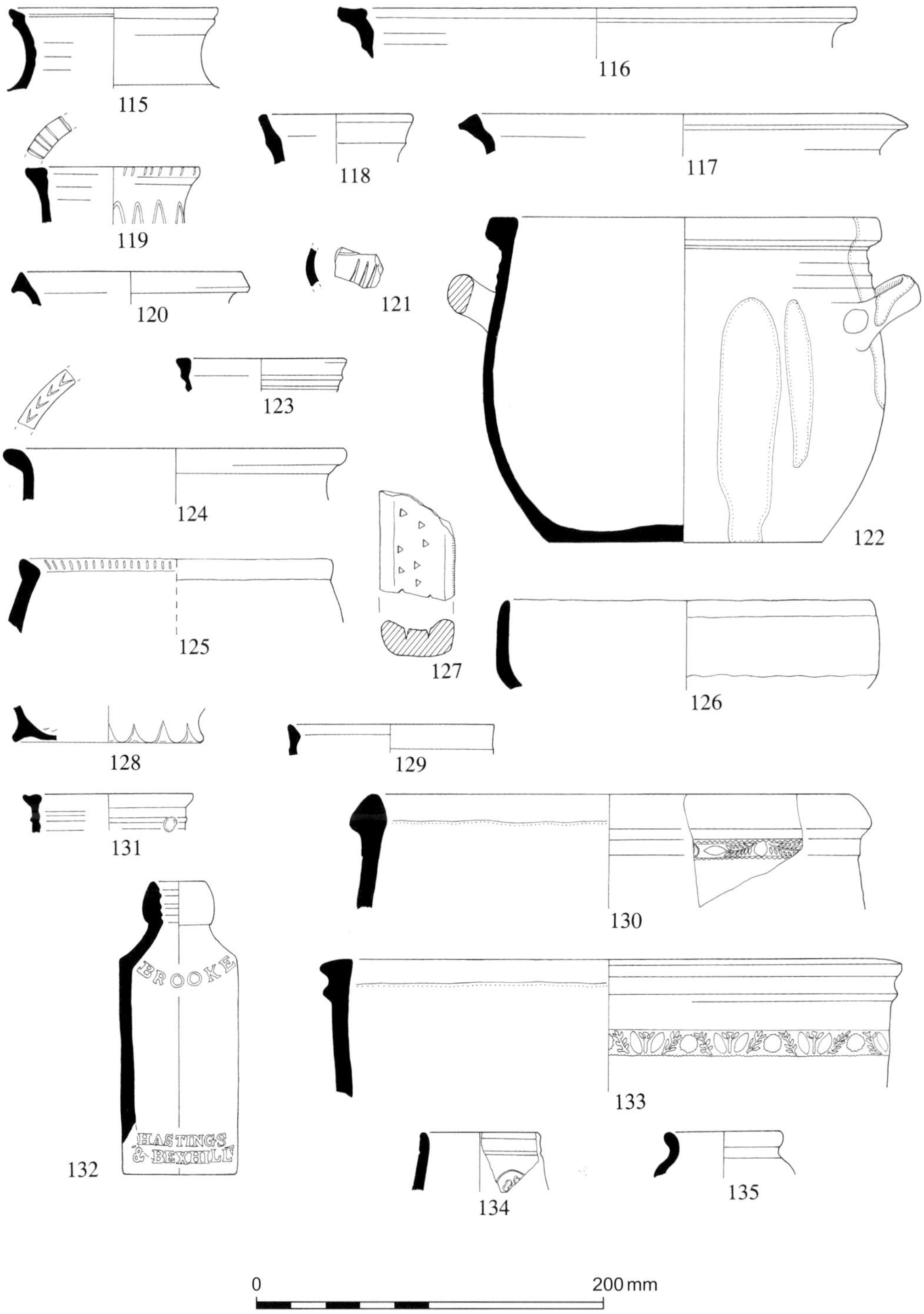

Figure 3.6 Pottery from Trench 8, and Phases 14–15

Phase 15: Recent activity (Fig. 3.6, 123–35)
A large quantity of material was recovered from layers resulting from recent activity and, not surprisingly, this also contains material of mixed date range but with an obviously greater bias towards the medieval and post-medieval periods. Of particular note is the only rim sherd in the assemblage of an imported Mayen ware jar possibly of late Roman date although it could be later (from 9). Other less common sherds include a ROUL medieval jug with an applied flower (from 102). A large number of stoneware bottles were recovered with various trademarks including Brookes of Hastings and Bexhill; Brookes of Eastbourne; W. Reid of Eastbourne; H.T. Floyd, Fairlight Road, Hastings; Hailsham Mineral Water Works; ...rne, Eastwood; Stour... and Boulton/Lambeth (London).

Trench 8 (Fig. 3.6, 115–19)
The stratigraphy beneath the collapsed wall (context group I) did not yield any ceramic material but 25

sherds were recovered from material over the collapsed wall (context group II). This was a mixture of medieval, local cooking wares (12th–14th century) mixed with post-medieval/modern stoneware bottles and china. Feature F906 (context group III) contained a modest group of 100 sherds dating to the later 12th–14th centuries with a single, intrusive, later-earthenware sherd. The group includes seven imported sherds (ROUL, SAIM, AARD, MISC) and three sherds of English glazed ware. The latest material defined stratigraphically is from recent excavations (context group IV) and as might be expected comprised a mixture of Roman, medieval and post-medieval/modern wares in a fairly broken condition.

Table 3.5 Comparison of Roman wares from Pevensey 1993–95 excavations with earlier excavated groups

Type/source	*no*	*1993-5* *no %*	*wt(g)*	*wt %*	*old excavations* *wt %*
IMPORTS					
fineware	56	1	345	*	1
coarseware	4	*	92	*	*
mortaria	1	*	10	*	nr
amphora	4	*	132	*	nr
REGIONAL					
Alice Holt	128	2.5	3187	5.5	11.5
Overwey	166	3	1752	3	3
New Forest	135	2.5	1264	2	3
Nene Valley	1	*	6	*	*
Oxfordshire	423	8	3973	7	7
Mancetter-Hartshill	1	*	60	*	nr
late shelly ware	4	*	70	*	*
Dorset BB1	81	1.5	953	1.5	8
LOCAL					
Pevensey colour-coat	195	4	1700	3	4
grog-tempered	1569	30	21911	38	33
grey sandy wares	2064	40	19850	35	27.5
misc	347	6.5	1810	3	1
Total	**5179**	**100**	**57115**	**100**	**100**

* = less than 1%

Discussion of the Roman pottery

There are relatively few individual Roman assemblages in the immediate area to provide useful comparative data other than with material already recovered from Pevensey itself. The general ceramic trends for the period have been well documented by Pollard (1988) for the Kent area and the grog-tempered production studied by Lyne (1994). In terms of other Saxon shore forts along the south coast the only site with a sizeable published assemblage is that from Portchester to the west (Fulford 1975b), with a smaller group from Lympne to the east (Young 1980). The only other published site spanning the later Roman to Saxon period is that at Bishopstone, near Newhaven (Bell 1977).

A comparison (Table 3.5) of the Roman 1993–95 assemblage with those studied by Lyne (2009) from earlier excavations shows a broadly similar incidence of British fabrics. Close correspondences can be seen in most of the defined classes of ware (figures cited from Lyne's work are based on an amalgamation of the individual groups studied from different chronological horizons; these figures do not reflect the entire assemblage but form a sample of the better groups which were considered worth quantifying). Minor differences occur in the rarer imported classes, which appear to show a greater diversity in the previously excavated material although the overall percentage of imports is similar at around 1%. Of particular note amongst the recent material is the first documented presence of North African red-slipped ware at Pevensey of which at least three vessels are present.

Most of the Roman pottery from the recent work came from the dark earth (Phases 3 and 13). The nature of this horizon does not, unfortunately, allow chronological refinement on ceramic, or stratigraphic grounds, in contrast to the sequences investigated by earlier excavators (Lyne 2009). Previous work has suggested, for example, that the grog-tempered wares (Lyne group A) were insignificant at Pevensey until around AD 350, after which they became the second most important source of supply and after AD 370 the most important until the early 5th century. Grog-tempered wares account for 30% by count (38% by weight) of the present Roman assemblage compared with 33% from the older excavations. Most of the forms are jars which account for 83% of the estimated vessel equivalents (eve). Other types are limited to straight-sided dishes (10.5%), flanged bowls (5.5%), a single flask and a lid.

The revival in the later Romano-British period of grog-tempered pottery is widespread across Kent, Sussex and Hampshire. It was observed at Lympne that 75% of the pottery comprised grog and grey local sandy ware (Young 1980) and it similarly formed one of the main groups documented at Portchester, accounting for *c.* 30% of the 4th century assemblage (Fulford 1975b).

In the earlier assemblages from Pevensey reduced sandy wheel-turned wares, of probable local origin, form the bulk of the domestic pottery in the late 3rd and early 4th century but disappear after AD 350. Alice Holt products played a minor role until *c.* 350 after which they showed a significant increase until the end of the 4th century. Overwey wares appear in the second half of the 4th century to disappear by the early 5th. Dorset Black Burnished ware accounts for approximately 25% of the pottery in the late 3rd century and early-mid-4th century, but thereafter was

Table 3.6 Incidence of Roman forms by EVE

Forms	*Eve*	*%*
jar	3452	60
bowl/dish	1865	32
flask	113	2
jug/flagon	48	*
beaker	95	1.5
cup	6	*
lid	8	*
mortarium	200	3
Total	**5787**	**100**

very insignificant (Lyne 2009, 97). This latter ware does not appear to be so well represented amongst the present group which perhaps shows a greater emphasis on the later wares. Lyne (*idem.*) notes a greater proportion of DOR BB1 bowls/dishes than cooking pots unlike other coarseware suppliers and this is sustained by the present evidence where jars account for 41.5% (eve) compared with 58.5% bowls/dishes.

Several, different, colour-coated industries were supplying south-east England in the later Romano-British period but Oxfordshire colour-coated ware is the most common fineware at both Pevensey and Lympne. Lyne (2009, 99) has demonstrated that OXF RS products increase in importance eclipsing New Forest products in the mid-4th century and remain constant despite the appearance of Pevensey colour-coated ware (PEV CC) after AD 370. At Portchester, perhaps not surprisingly, New Forest products are more prolific, but even these were overwhelmed by OXF RS in the second half of the 4th century (Fulford 1975b). Oxfordshire finewares also dominated the Kent market in the 4th century, with Nene Valley wares forming the second major group and NFO CC just restricted to civitas capitals and Saxon shore forts (Pollard 1988, 141). Nene Valley wares clearly did not travel far to the south/south-east as they are poorly represented at Pevensey, just as they are at Portchester (Fulford 1975b).

A new colour-coated industry, thought to be based in the locality of Pevensey emerged in the later 4th century (Fulford 1973). Pevensey has produced the largest group of these wares including a waster sherd, perhaps from a second, from the recent excavations. The forms closely imitate the Oxfordshire products both in form and decorative finish. It was not marketed far and has only been documented at two sites in Kent, Wye and Lympne (Pollard 1988), with a few sherds from Portchester.

Whilst quite diverse, the range of imports from Pevensey is not all exclusive to the site; it is perhaps quite likely that the existence of the shore forts generated quite a lot of coastal trade. Argonne ware and Mayen ware occur at Pevensey, Portchester and other sites across Kent, with examples of the latter at Lympne. African red-slipped ware has been noted at Garden Hill, Sussex, and Dover (Bird 1977), Chalk (Pollard 1988, 142) and Canterbury in Kent (Bird 1982).

All three shore fort sites have produced small quantities of samian. Morris (1975) has suggested that at Portchester it is unlikely to represent 2nd/3rd-century occupation but probably arrived with the first occupants of the site. Samian was so prolific it would perhaps be unusual if it were absent from a Roman site and it is certainly a common feature of many later Roman assemblages along with Dressel 20 amphora sherds, intimating an extended period of circulation after the end of production for both these products.

A comparison of Pevensey with the later phases of the multi-period site at Bishopstone shows that the occupants of this site were using a similar range of British wares in the 4th century. Grog-tempered wares accounted for *c.* 50% (by weight) accompanied by Overwey wares (8.4%) Alice Holt/New Forest sandy wares (undifferentiated) (10.4%), DOR BB1 (0.8%), New Forest wares (2.5%), Oxfordshire wares (17.2%), and Pevensey ware (10%) (Green 1977, 175). The proportion of finewares to coarsewares is surprisingly high at 31% at Bishopstone compared with just 13% at Pevensey. Young (1980) commented on the low proportion of finewares at Lympne which only accounted for *c.* 10% and at Portchester the figure averages around 15–20% in the 4th century (Fulford 1975b). Without further comparative data it is difficult to determine whether Bishopstone is atypical for some reason or whether the proportions are typical of other civilian sites in the region. It should be noted that the sample size was quite small at just below 1000 g and thus the figures may not be representative.

The range of forms present overall at Pevensey is quite small (Table 3.6), being overwhelmingly dominated by coarseware jars accounting for 60% (eve). The low level of apparent ceramic drinking vessels – beakers only represent 1.5% – was presumably compensated for by glass or other vessels not visible in the archaeological record, unless some of the smaller colour-coated bowls served this purpose. Liquid-serving vessels such as flagons or jugs, and mortaria are also poorly represented and less common items, such as the candlesticks and colanders found at Portchester, are absent. Although no directly comparable figures are available, the impression from the illustrated catalogue at Portchester suggests that beakers, flagons/flasks, lids and mortaria, if not more plentiful in a relative sense, were certainly more diverse.

Anglo-Saxon pottery

by Alan Vince†

(For fabric descriptions see Appendix 2)

A total of 153 sherds (1844 g) of Anglo-Saxon pottery was recovered; there are clearly two distinct groups. The earlier group consists of sandstone-tempered and granite-tempered wares, while the later group consists of gravel-tempered wares. The chaff-tempered sherd could belong to either group, whilst the shell-tempered sherd might belong to the second group, or be of post-Conquest, medieval date.

The early Anglo-Saxon pottery contains decorated and burnished vessels and there is little evidence for the use of the vessels. It is likely, therefore, that they were not primarily used for cooking, which would certainly have led to at least one sherd being sooted. In the absence of a thin section of fabric SX1 it is not possible to say whether or not all the sherds of sandstone-tempered ware are from the same source. Furthermore, it is not possible to say for certain that the chaff-tempered ware is non local. Chaff is a component in the sandstone-tempered fabric and it was not possible to examine the clay matrix without a thin section. The granite-tempered sherd, however, cannot have been locally produced and the well made, burnished nature of the vessel rules out an origin in the south west of England at this period. It is likely, therefore, that the vessel is either from the English Midlands or from Scandinavia.

The dating of the gravel-tempered pottery (SX4–7) is less certain. None of the sherds had any characteristics of early Anglo-Saxon pottery and the form and manufacture of all the featured sherds suggests a mid- or late Saxon date for the majority of the vessels. Similar vessels are known from late mid-Saxon contexts at Southampton and from the earliest deposits in medieval Southampton, thought to date to the 10th or early 11th century (Timby 1988; Brown 1994). There is, however, no obvious difference in fabric between these wares and the medieval coarsewares from the Pevensey site and featureless body sherds might therefore be either of mid- to late Saxon date or later medieval intrusions.

The shell-tempered sherd, SX8, comes from a feature cutting through the Phase 5 clay and could be of post-Conquest, medieval date.

A consideration of the stratigraphic context of these sherds shows that there is no clear progression from deposits containing sandstone-tempered sherds to those containing gravel-tempered ones. Indeed, if anything, the stratigraphic sequence is reversed (the ratio of gravel- to sandstone-tempered sherds is higher in Phase 3 deposits than in later deposits). All of the sherds are small and there is every possibility that all of them, including those in Phase 3, have undergone several cycles of redeposition. The high degree of reworking of these deposits is also indicated by the quantity of Roman pottery found in what are clearly post-Roman deposits.

A model which would fit the ceramic evidence would be that the Phase 3 dark earth was deposited during the late Romano-British period and that its surface remained the ground surface from the 5th century until the construction of the Keep in Phase 6 and that all finds from later deposits are reworked from the Phase 3 dark earth. Whether post-Roman occupation was continuous or consisted of two or more distinct episodes is unknowable from the ceramic evidence. Firstly, neither assemblage is large enough to give a clear view of its character and, secondly, there are in fact few good chronological indicators within the ceramics of this period in southern England except where large quantities of imports are present, as at Southampton.

Medieval pottery

by Jane Timby

(For fabric descriptions see Appendix 2).

Medieval pottery accounted for 28.5% (wt) of the total ceramic assemblage, in total some 4140 sherds. Table 3.7 summarises the main types present by quantity. The imported wares are discussed in more detail by Alan Vince below.

The group was dominated by the local, flint-and-quartz, gravel-tempered ware (LOCMED1), largely used for cooking pots, which account for 74.5% (wt) of the medieval assemblage. Other, potentially local fabrics account for a further 16%, regional imports for 6.5% and continental imports for 2.5% (wt).

The problems of redeposition and contamination of deposits has been highlighted already and with perhaps the exception of some of the Phase 10 features, few of the medieval contexts produced sufficiently large groups of pottery to allow a rigorous stratigraphic analysis of the medieval ceramic sequence. None of the contexts in Phases 4–8 produced more than 10 medieval sherds. In Phase 12 the only significant group came from context 673 and this had post-medieval contamination. The largest groups appear to be from the post-medieval/modern horizons, thus mixed with later material. The sherds are also generally very fragmented.

Streeten (1985) has highlighted the existence of several kilns in the Sussex area dating to the medieval and post-medieval periods although many of these remain unpublished in detail. Place-name evidence suggests that there are many more sites awaiting discovery. Knowledge of the medieval pottery industries in this part of East Sussex is still in quite a formative stage and recent work is proving that some of the previously defined types may not be quite as

Table 3.7 Medieval and post-medieval fabrics

Medieval	*Code*	*Common name/Description*	*Wt(g)*	*No*	*Eve*
IMPORTS	NFRY	North French early glazed ware	40	1	0
	NFRE	?North French unglazed ware	21	6	1
	ROUE	Rouen ware	16	7	0
	ROUL	Rouen ware	34	13	19
	NFM	green-glazed ?Rouen ware	296	45	11
	NFMS	North French green glazed micaceous silty	23	6	0
	NORG	Normandy gritty ware	28	2	0
	SAIM	South-west French mottled glazed ware	68	20	0
	SAIG	Saintonge glazed	5	1	0
	SAIP	Saintonge polychrome-decorated	1	1	0
	AARD	Flemish decorated ware	21	6	1
	MISC	other possible imports	206	29	11
REGIONAL	ENG1	English sandy, source unknown	624	48	29
	ENG2	English sandy, glazed	188	24	0
	TUDGR	Tudor Green	1	1	0
LOCAL	MEDLOC1	local flint, quartz gravel-tempered	24710	3207	1937
	MEDLOC2	local flint, quartz gravel-tempered	2819	302	139
	MEDLOC3	local flint, quartz gravel-tempered	922	149	19
	MEDFL	flint-tempered, low iron clay	28	3	0
	MEDFLG	local flint and glauconitic	67	6	6
	MEDCH	chalk-tempered	53	4	7
	WSX	West Sussex type	252	30	47
	RRING	Rye-Ringmer jugs	907	120	30
	WINCH	Winchelsea	25	2	0
	BOHEM	Bohemian kiln type, Hastings	15	1	10
	MEDREW	late Medieval red earthernware	133	18	0
UNKNOWN	MED00	miscellaneous other	217	37	21
POST-MED	PMESTW	Post-medieval English stoneware	22688	701	4850
	PMISTW	Post-medieval imported stoneware	170	5	0
	PMPSTW	Post-medieval proto-stoneware ?local	105	10	0
	OLIVE	Spanish olive jar	69	3	0
	PMGRE	glazed and unglazed red earthenwares	13478	773	503
	PMTG	tin-glazed earthenware	473	181	0
	PMCH	miscellaneous 'china'	4068	536	437
	PMPORC	porcelain	22	8	6
	BORDY	Surrey-Hampshire border ware	1312	43	7
	PM00	miscellaneous other	280	24	5
Total			**74385**	**6373**	**8096**

clear-cut as originally thought (Barber pers. comm.). The similarities in fabrics across quite wide areas have only proved distinguishable through textural analysis at present (Streeten 1980; 1985). Streeten (1985, 122) has also commented that the identification of marketed products in Sussex on the basis of their fabrics alone is hazardous. Attempting to provenance the local Pevensey material in more detail was, therefore, not considered worthwhile at this juncture and a generalising approach has been adopted.

The flint-tempered tradition (MEDLOC1–3) is related to local Saxon/Saxo-Norman traditions (*cf.* fabrics SX4–7 above). It is regarded as a local product and a Reginald le Potere is named as a tenant of the manor in 1292 (Dulley 1967, 220), suggesting that the kilns continued until at least the late 13th century. Similar wares occur across southern Sussex in the late Saxon-early medieval period, for example at Battle Abbey, where it is clear the tradition continued in East Sussex up to *c.* 1350 (Streeten 1985, 122). The pottery recovered from excavations in the village (Dulley 1967) dating from the 12th century was similarly dominated by a local, flint-gritted ware.

During the 13th century the local wares appear to be augmented by increasing quantities of regional and continental imported sandy wares. From the mid-13th century glazed jugs from the Rye kilns would have begun to feature. The range of imports documented at Pevensey Castle (see Vince below) also features in assemblages from the village, so were clearly not exclusively for the use of the castle occupants, assuming that the material being studied derives from this source. Similarly the material excavated from the Old Farmhouse, Pevensey (Lyne 1999) includes a variety of imported wares alongside the local coarsewares. If the wares excavated from the village reflect usage by the village inhabitants it would seem that the pottery is the result of Pevensey's general status as a port involved in coastal and cross-channel trade, rather than reflecting the status of the Castle. Battle Abbey, only situated some 15 km away, received surprisingly few imported wares in the same period (Streeten 1985, 122).

Pottery production at Pevensey probably ceased in the late 14th-early 15th century. The Rye/Ringmer potters were still supplying the market throughout the 15th century and, in the later 15th century, various fine earthenwares began to appear in the ceramic record at other sites in the Sussex region (Streeten 1985, 114), possibly from the nearby Boreham Street kilns (Barton 1979). Other local production centres operating in the 15th–17th centuries include Graffham, Brede, Lower Parrock, Hartfield and High Lankhurst, Westfield (Streeten 1985, 103–4). A small amount of fine, whiteware from Surrey, including the single sherd of Tudor Green, are likely to have arrived in the 15th–16th centuries.

Imported medieval pottery

by Alan Vince†

One hundred and fifty-six sherds of possible medieval imports were selected for detailed study. They comprise 108 separate vessels. The sherds were recorded by context, so that there are 112 individual records. Twelve distinct wares were identified, accounting for all but 29 sherds. Details of the fabrics can be found in Appendix 2.

Chronology

It seems likely that most of the medieval imports arrived in the layers in which they were found as a result of complex, site-formation processes rather than being dated by their contexts. Since many of the imports found themselves have known date ranges, it is possible to say something about the periods of activity represented by plotting these dates (Table 3.8). This shows that very little of the pottery found need date to before the late 12th century, even if the types themselves were being produced before that. It is clear, though that there is material spanning the 13th and early 14th centuries with roughly equal quantities likely to date to the early 13th and later 13th centuries and a much smaller quantity dating to the early 14th century (*cf.* Lyne 2009, 137).

Table 3.8 Summary of medieval imports

Code	*Sherds*	*Vessels*	*Wt (g)*	*Earliest*	*Latest*
MISC	29	24	206	ND	ND
NFRY	1	1	40	900	1150
PING	18	9	104	1050	1250
NFM	45	16	295.5	1150	1350
NFRE	6	5	21	1150	1350
NFMS	6	6	22.5	1150	1250
NORG	2	2	28	1150	1250
ROUE	7	7	16	1150	1250
AARD	6	6	21	1250	1450
SAIM	20	19	67.5	1250	1450
SAIN?	1	1	0.5	1250	1450
ROUL	13	10	33.5	1250	1350
SAIG	1	1	5	1300	1350
SAIP	1	1	1	1300	1350
Total	**156**	**108**	**861.5**		

Catalogue

Figs 3.1–3.3: Dark earth (Phase 3)

1. Wheelmade, shell-tempered jar blackened on the exterior and interior rim surface. Fabric ROB SH. (60)
2. Hook-rimmed jar in a hard, slightly pimply, grey, sandy ware. Fabric GREY2. (60)
3. Large, flanged bowl in a hard-fired, slightly metallic, grey ware. Fabric GREY3. (52)
4. Colour-coated beaker with a dark-brown interior, black, slightly glossy exterior on a white fabric. Fabric LOC CC. (52)
5. Straight-sided dish with a black-burnished interior. Fabric ALH RE. (52)
6. Wheelmade, sharply-everted-rim jar, slightly sooted on the exterior rim and body. Grey-brown in colour with a blue-grey interior. Fabric GREY2. (52)
7. Bodysherd from a closed form. Fine, sandy fabric with dark-grey surfaces and a red-brown-grey, sandwich-effect core. Burnished. Decorated with an incised, free-style decorative scheme. Fabric GREY2. (38)
8. Simple rim, handmade jar with a burnished finish. Fabric GROG1. (31)
9. Handmade jar with a slight cordon below the everted rim. Luting marks are visible where the rim has been added and shaped. Fabric GROG1. (31)
10 Handmade, everted-rim jar with a burnished finish. Fabric GROG1. (31)
11. Handmade, everted, simple-rim jar, grey in colour with a lighter core. Burnished finish. GROG3. (31)
12. Large, handmade, everted-rim jar with a burnished finish. Dark grey in colour. Fabric GROG1. (31)
13. Handmade, everted-rim jar, burnished on the interior rim face and external body. Fabric GROG1. (31)
14. Handmade beaker with a fine, burnished finish. Fabric GROG. (31)
15. Handmade, storage jar with a slight shoulder cordon. Orange-brown surface with a dark grey core. Partly-burnished finish. Fabric GROG4. (31)

16. Handmade, straight-sided bowl with burnished surfaces. Brown with a grey core. Fabric GROG1. (31)
17. Handmade lid (or shallow dish), burnished on both the interior and exterior surfaces. Brown in colour. Fabric GROG1. (31)
18. Large, handmade, flanged-hemispherical bowl, with a zone of burnishing on the upper exterior surface. Patchy brown-black in colour. Fabric GROG1. (31)
19. Handmade, flanged bowl, decorated with a single, incised-wavy line on the interior and exterior. The zone above the flange is burnished. Fabric GROG1. (31)
20. Everted-rim jar in a hard, grey sandy-ware. Fabric GREY. (31)
21. Everted-rim jar, mottled orange-grey in colour. Fabric OXID. Decorated with a band of burnishing on the inner-rim face and exterior neck. (31)
22. Everted-rim jar with slight rilling on the body. Blackened rim and slight sooting on body. Fabric OVW WH. (31)
23. Everted-rim jar. Fabric OVW WH. (31)
24. Flanged, grey sandy-ware bowl decorated with burnished lines on the interior and burnish on the upper exterior rim-zone. Fabric GREY3. (25)
25. Flanged bowl decorated with burnished lines on the interior. Grey sandy ware. Fabric GREY9. (31)
26. Flanged bowl with a black-burnished, slipped rim and interior surface. Very hard, grey fabric. Fabric GREY3. (37)
27. Dropped-flanged bowl in a light grey, sandy-ware with an orange-red, inner core, Fabric GREY9. (31)
28. Curved-wall bowl. Fabric OVW WH. (31)
29. Colour-coated beaker. Fabric LOC CC. (31)
30. Red-colour-coated bowl. Fabric PEV CC. (25)
31. Red-colour-coated bowl with rouletted decoration. Fabric PEV CC. (31)
32. Red-colour-coated bowl with a slightly-shaped rim. Decorated with white paint. Fabric PEV CC. (31)
33. Beaded rim, red-colour-coated bowl with white-painted decoration. Fabric PEV CC. (31)
34. Beaded rim, red-colour-coated bowl with rouletted decoration. Fabric PEV CC. (31)
35. Red-colour-coated bowl with white-painted decoration. Fabric PEV CC. (31)
36. Red-colour-coated flanged, hemispherical bowl with white-painted, intersecting pairs of arcs on the flange. Fabric PEV CC. (31)
37. Red-colour-coated, flanged, hemispherical bowl. Fabric PEV CC. (25)
38. Large, beaded-rim, carinated bowl in red-colour-coated ware. Decorated with impressed-notched bars, forming crosses separated by vertically-set impressions. The inner-rim edge has a single, white-painted line. Fabric PEV CC. (31)
39. Large, white-slipped mortarium with rounded-quartz, trituration grits. Fabric PEV WSM. (31)
40. White-slipped orange-ware bowl with flint-and-quartz, trituration grit. Fabric PEV WSM. (31)
41. New Forest whiteware mortarium, decorated with a single, wavy line on the flange. Fabric NFO WHM. (31)

Fig. 3.3, 42–60 Dark earth (Phase 3); 61–9 (Phases 4, 5)

42. Everted-rim jar with a black-burnished, slipped, exterior surface and inner-rim face. Fabric GREY8. (31)
43. Jar in a hard, slightly metallic, grey fabric, slightly sooted in the exterior. Fabric GREY3. (31)
44. Bowl in a hard, grey, fine sandy-ware, fabric GREY1. (31), (36)
45. Small dish in a hard, slightly micaceous, fine, sandy fabric with a black-surface slip. Fabric GREY3. Decorated with a single, wavy line and horizontal line on the interior. (31)
46. Flask in a dark grey, sandy ware with a black-surface slip. Fabric GREY7. (37)
47. Bodysherd in a fine, orange, finely micaceous ware with a dark-brown colour-coat. Impressed-stamp decoration. Fabric LOC CC. (36)
48. Dish, Hayes (1972), type 75 with a rouletted flange. Fabric NAF RS. (31)
49. Thickened-rim, wheelmade, everted-rim jar. Decorated with an irregular band of red paint on the exterior below the rim. Fabric NF RPT. (25)
50. Bodysherd from a closed, indented form. Decorated with red-painted, tear-drop motifs. Fabric NF RPT. (31)
51. Jar/pitcher with red-painted decoration. Fabric NF RPT. (31)
52. Small body sherd decorated with red-painted motifs. Fabric NF RPT. (31)
53. Handmade, everted-rim jar. Brown exterior with a grey interior. Fabric SX4–7. (235)
54. Small, loop handle. Fabric SX4–7. (726)
55. Small, split body sherd, dark grey-black in colour. Decorated with stabbed impressions. Fabric SX2. (24)
56. Handmade, simple, everted-rim jar. Highly-burnished-black, exterior surface. Fabric SX2. (25)
57. Bodysherd from a cooking pot/storage jar decorated with an applied-thumbed strip. Red-brown exterior with a grey core. Fabric LOCMED1. (235)
58. Large everted rim, handmade jar with finger-moulding depressions at the neck. Black in colour. Fabric SX4–7. (722)
59. Handmade, everted-rim jar, orange-brown surfaces with a grey core. Fabric SX4–7. (31)
60. Sharply-everted-rim, handmade jar with a smoothed surface. Dark-grey-black exterior with a grey core/interior surface. Fabric SX4–7. (31)

Phase 4

61. Handmade, everted-rim jar, dark grey in colour. Fabric GROG1. (165)

Phase 5

62. Lid-seated jar in a sandy orange-ware with a darker core and slightly blackened exterior surface. Fabric ROIM2. Probably an import. (197)
63. Bodysherd from a handmade jar with finger-nail-impressed decoration. Fabric SX7. (367)
64. Handmade, wheel-finished vessel. Impressed, triangular notches on the upper-rim surface. Fabric LOCMED1. (405)
65. Wheelmade cooking-pot, light brown in colour with a grey core. Fabric LOCMED2. (161)
66. Handmade, wheel-finished cooking-pot. Black in colour with a coarsely gritted, paste. Fabric LOCMED1. (161)
67. Simple, everted-rim, handmade jar, Fabric LOCMED1. (364)
68. Simple, everted-rim, handmade jar. Black in colour with a sooted exterior. Fabric SX7. (364).
69. Wheelmade cooking-pot. Fabric LOCMED1. (364)

Fig. 3.4: Phase 10

70. Wide-diameter, wheelmade cooking-pot. Black-to-red-brown in colour. Fabric LOCMED1. (137)
71. Jug, fabric LOCMED2 variant with a higher frequency of calcareous inclusions. Glaze splatters on the exterior
72. Wide-diameter cooking-pot, wheelmade. A grey-to-black exterior with a red-brown interior and grey core in quite a coarse paste. Fabric LOCMED1. (145)
73. Wheelmade cooking-pot, light-brown-to-grey in colour. Fabric LOCMED2. (125)
74. Wheelmade cooking pot, red-brown in colour with a grey core. Fabric LOCMED2. (152)
75. Wheelmade, thin-walled cooking-pot, black in colour. Fabric LOCMED1. (152)
76. Wide-diameter, handmade, wheel-finished ?dish with a finger-depressed rim. Grey in colour with a dark brown interior. Fabric LOCMED1. (152)
77. Wheelmade ?dish. Black to red-brown in colour. Fabric LOCMED1. (152)
78. Wide-diameter jar, wheelmade. Grey-brown in colour with a red-brown core. Fabric LOCMED1. (152)
79. ?Bowl with a vertical handle. Blackened exterior with a brown, interior surface with glazed splatters. The exterior surface shows knife-trimming marks. Fabric LOCMED1. (152)
80. Wheelmade jug, light brown in colour, unglazed. Fabric LOCMED3. (152)
81. Wheelmade jug, light-red-brown in colour with a grey core. Unglazed. Fabric LOCMED2. (152)
82. Large cooking-pot with a shaped rim. Red-brown-to-grey in colour. Fabric LOCMED2. (125)
83. Thickened-rim cooking-pot with notching on the upper surface. Wheel-turned. Fabric LOCMED1/ (602)
84. Wheelmade jug, glazed colour below the rim. Fabric LOCMED2. (602)
85. Corded base of a jug. Whiteware with a mottled-green glaze. Fabric NFM. (602)

86–8. Wheelmade cooking-pots. Fabric LOCMED1. (602)

89. Handmade, wheel-finished cooking-pot with deeply impressed, oval depressions into the rim surface. Fabric LOCMED1. (601)
90. Hammer-head cooking-pot decorated with comb-impressed dots on the rim surface. Glaze splatters on upper-rim surface. Fabric LOCMED1. (620)
91. Handmade, black cooking-pot, sooted on the exterior. Fabric LOCMED1. (668)

Fig. 3.5 Phases 10 and 12

92. Wheelmade, everted-rim jar, sooted on the inner-rim face. Fabric SX4–7. (691)
93. Handmade, wheel-finished cooking-pot with sooted, interior and exterior surfaces. Fabric SX4–7. (668)
94. Handmade cooking-pot, fabric LOCMED1. (338), Phase 12
95. Jug with a squared rim. Traces of accidental brown paint. Fabric NFM. (338), Phase 12. (ID45)

Collapse of Roman wall (Phase 13)

96. Everted-rim jar. Fabric OVWWH. Blackened-exterior rim. (87)
97. Wheelmade, everted jar. Fabric OVW WH. Sooted exterior rim. (87)
98. Bowl. Fabric OVW WH. (87)
99. Small dish in a grey sandy-ware. The interior is decorated with radiating, burnished lines on the base and squiggles on the wall. The underside of the base also has a squiggled, burnished-line design. Fabric GREY3. (86)
100. Handmade, everted-rim jar, with burnished surfaces. Red-brown-to-black coloration. Fabric GROG1. (90)
101. Handmade everted rim jar with a well-burnished exterior and interior rim face. Black in colour. Fabric GROG1. (87)
102. Simple-rim, handmade bowl, burnished on the interior and exterior surfaces. Light grey interior, darker grey exterior. Fabric GROG1. (87)
103. Flanged-rim bowl decorated with a burnished design on the interior. Fabric GREY3. (89)
104. Flanged-rim bowl with a burnished exterior, but plain interior. Fabric GREY6. (89)
105. Bowl with impressed-stamp decoration. Fabric PEV CC. (90)
106. Beaded-rim bowl decorated with impressed-rosette decoration. Fabric OXF RS. (87)
107. Small, colour-coated bowl with white-painted decoration. Fabric PEV CC. (90)
108. Handmade, everted-rim jar. Grey-black-to-brown in colour. Fabric SX5. (83)
109. Handled cup in a cream fabric decorated with a dark-orange-painted design. Fabric NF RPT. (87)
110. Globular bowl with short, everted rim. Decorated with a band of orange-red paint on the inner rim face. Fabric OXF PA. (51)

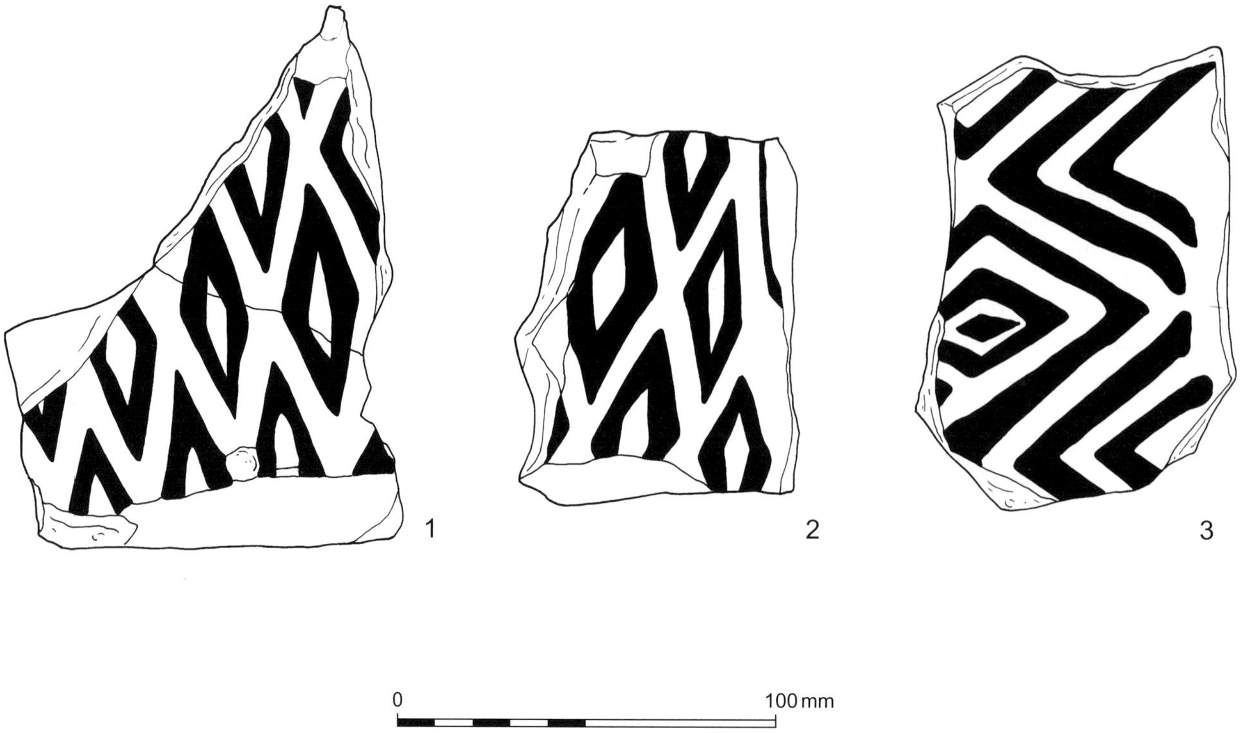

Figure 3.7 Roman stamped box flue tile

111. Bowl decorated with a horizontal-stamped cordon and stamped rosettes. Fabric PEV CC. (50)
112. Small bowl with folded-over rim. Fabric PEV CC. (50)
113. Everted-rim, small jar burnished on the rim and upper shoulder. Fabric GREY7. (50)
114. Flanged bowl with black surfaces and a grey core. Fabric GREY7. (50)

Fig. 3.6: pottery from Trench 8 and Phases 13–15

115. Wheelmade jug/pitcher, plain, dark-orange in colour. Fabric LOCMED2. (902), Trench 8
116–7. Wheelmade and wheel-finished cooking-pots. Fabric LOCMED1. (900), Trench 8
118. Wheelmade jug, plain, mid-orange in colour. Fabric LOCMED2. (900), Trench 8
119. Handmade/wheel finished jug. Plain, dark-orange with incised decoration on the rim and upper neck. Fabric LOCMED1. (900), Trench 8
120. Wheelmade, light-brown jug/pitcher with a cream fabric. Fabric MISC. (683), Phase 14
121. Small, redeposited, handmade body sherd from a carinated vessel with grooved decoration. Fabric SX1. (742), Phase 14
122. Substantial part of a double-handled chamber-pot. Red earthenware, glazed internally orange-brown with darker-brown, glazed dribble on the exterior. Fabric PMGRE (608), SF 135, Phase 14
123. Jug with a mottled, yellow-brown external glaze. Fabric ROUL (323), Phase 15
124. Wheelmade cooking pot with impressed decoration on the upper-rim surface. Fabric LOCMED1. (605), Phase 15
125. Handmade cooking-pot with impressed decoration on the inner-rim face. Black with a red-brown interior. Fabric LOCMED1. (114), Phase 15
126. Handmade dish, mid-red-brown with a grey core. Blackened in the external base area. Fabric LOCMED2. (175), Phase 15
127. Strap handle from a jug/pitcher with triangular-stabbed decoration. Unglazed, light brown with a grey core. Fabric LOCMED3. (114), Phase 15
128. Pinched base from a jug. Fabric MISC. ID78. (114), topsoil
129. Jug rim sherd with a dark-green glaze over a white slip. Fabric AARD. ID26. (103), Phase 15
130. Large, red-earthenware bowl with band of impressed-relief decoration. Internally glazed. Fabric PMGRE. (302), Phase 15
131. Glazed jug with an iron wash on the rim. Decorated with an applied, white clay-pellet on red. Fabric ROUL. ID28. (600), topsoil
132. Complete, English stoneware-bottle with the name Brooke and Hastings & Bexhill impressed. Fabric PMESTW. (600), topsoil
133. Red-earthenware bowl, internally glazed with band of relief decoration. Fabric PMGRE.(300), topsoil
134. English, stoneware jar with the edge of a stamped motif. Fabric PMESTW. (600), Phase 15
135. English, stoneware jar. Fabric PMESTW. (600), Phase 15

Ceramic building material

by Jane Timby

A substantial quantity of ceramic building material (brick, tile and chimney pot) was retained. In total, approximately 2,560 fragments were recovered from Phases 1–15, with further substantial quantities of very fragmented material from the unstratified/topsoil contexts. The material was scanned to assess its composition, note the main types present and extract any unusual fragments. Apart from Roman tile fragments recovered from the collapsed wall (362), most of the ceramic building material was in a very fragmented state with no complete measurable items with the exception of post-medieval bricks from the upper levels.

Roman

The first occurrences of Roman building material come from Phases 1 and 2 with two fragments, one an *imbrex*, recovered from the former (contexts 71–2) and 11 pieces of flat tile/*tegulae* from the latter (61). Context (66) F65, possibly associated with the fort construction (Phase 2), contained two fragments, a *tegula* and a relief-patterned box flue. Two other examples of box flue, probably decorated with the same die, came from (722) (Phase 3) (Fig. 3.7, 1) and (613) (Phase 14B) (Fig. 3.7, 2) which match with Betts *et al.* (1994) die 21 (fabric 1). Several other examples of this type have been noted both from Sussex and the London area in contexts dating from the early Flavian to early 2nd century. Examples from Sussex, in particular, include Wiggonholt, Westhampnett, Angmering, South Malling, Southwick, Chichester and Bullock Down, Eastbourne. The distribution suggests a kiln source in south-west Sussex in the Chichester-Arundel area (*ibid.* 19). Pevensey at present falls at the eastern-most limit of the distribution. The dark earth (Phase 3) produced another roller-stamped tile from (3) (Fig. 3.7, 3). The fragment probably matches with Betts *et al.* (1994) die 83, for which there is no useful dating and only a poor type example. Further examples are recorded from the bath-house at Wiggonholt (*ibid.* 133).

In general the dark earth (Phase 3) contained a much larger collection of ceramic building material, some 470 Roman fragments including both roofing tile (*tegulae* and *imbrices*) and combed box-flue. Very little Roman tile was associated with Phases 4–9, the only fragment of particular note being a flat *mammata* tile from Phase 4. More material was recovered from the features cut into the top of the yellow clay (Phase 10), many of the pieces too fragmentary to identify further, but pieces of roofing tile and box flue are present.

The collapsed Roman wall (362) produced several large fragments of flat tile with mortar attached to the upper and lower surfaces. One fragment has a length of 365 mm and a thickness of 40 mm (width unknown). Two pieces have incomplete paw prints, probably from a cat. Contexts associated with the collapsed Roman wall (Phase 13) similarly produced numerous Roman tile fragments with further examples of combed, box-flue tile alongside the roofing tile and flat tile intermixed with later post-Roman material.

Catalogue of illustrated pieces (Fig. 3.7)

1. Roller-stamped tile, Betts *et al.* (1994), die 21. (722), Phase 3
2. Roller-stamped tile, Betts *et al.* (1994), die 21. (613), Phase 15
3. Roller-stamped tile, Betts *et al.* (1994), die 83? (3), Phase 3

Medieval

The earliest occurrence of medieval building material is six fragments of possible chimney pot in Phase 3, (31) (Fig. 3.8) and a small quantity of medieval brick/tile in (17). Further fragments of chimney pot were found throughout the sequence but unfortunately all too abraded to allow any form of reconstruction. Chimney pots are a common feature of medieval Sussex and several complete examples have been published by Dunning (1961) with further discussion by Barton (1979). Some better preserved examples, dated to the late 13th-early 14th century, have been previously recorded from Pevensey by Dunning (1967, fig. 66) who noted two fabrics: a coarser one containing much flint-and-quartz-sand grit and a finer, sandy type. Approximately 60–70 fragments were recovered from the recent excavations, all of which appear to equate with the coarse version. The presence of pieces from the dark earth suggests that they could potentially be quite early. Most of the fragments came from Phases 10–15.

With the exception of the fragments from the dark earth and one tile from Phase 10, recognisable medieval ceramic building material does not manifest itself until Phase 14 and from features associated with recent activity (Phase 15).

Catalogue of illustrated pieces (Fig. 3.8)

1. Fragment of chimney pot in a coarse flint-tempered fabric. (677), Phase 10
2. Fragment of chimney pot. Smoothed surfaces with internal blackening. (200), unphased

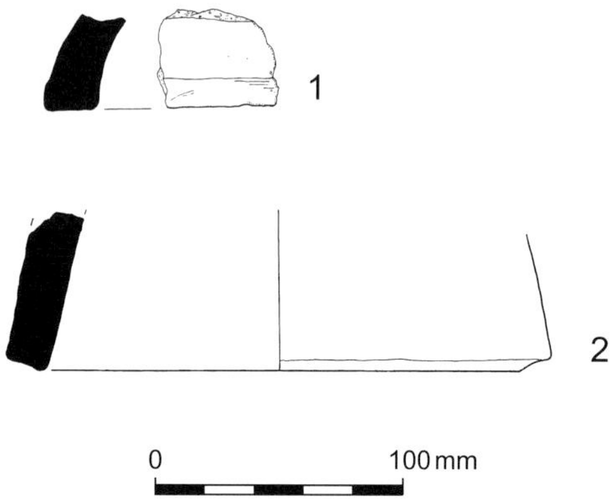

Figure 3.8 Medieval chimney pot

Coins

by Richard Reece

Since only a small number of coins were found in the present excavations (Tables 3.9–3.10) few firm suggestions can be made on their interpretation. But when they are amalgamated with the excellent lists prepared by Malcolm Lyne (2009, 63–77) from earlier work a clearer picture emerges.

On their own, the present coins suggest that there was little occupation of the site before the later 3rd century. The 4th century coins fall into two main groups around AD 326 and 345 and the absence of coins struck between 330 and 345, normally the most common coins on any site, makes the distribution very unusual. The two concentrations, as well as the low representation of coins of 330–345, are mirrored in the finds from Portchester (Reece 1975).

Table 3.9 Roman coin list

1	Carausius,	Pax, mm/ML, RIC 101
1	Allectus,	Pax, mm S/A/ML, RIC 28
1	Maximian I,	no complex mm, rev illeg
2	Radiates	rev illeg (2)
1	?Barbarous Radiate	pierced, rev illeg
1	Follis	very corroded, reverse uncertain
4	Constantine I	RIC7London as 10,16, 289; HK 92
2	Crispus	RIC7London230,291
1	Constantine II	RICTLondon 237
2	Constans	HK 148, 638
3	Theodora	HK as 113 (3)
1	Constantius II	CK as 25
5	House of Constantine	HK as 87, as 137, as 963: CK ?as 25 reverse illegible (1)
1	Valens	CK as 528
1	Gratian	CK364
2	House of Valentinian	CK as 296, as 514
1	House of Theodosius	CK as 162
2	Counters	Barnard France 74, Germany 82
3	Uncertain	illegible (1), corroded (2)
1	Victoria	6d 1890
36 Total		

When all the coins are put together, the method put forward in 1995 (Reece 1995) is applied, and the assemblages of other shore forts are added the diagram in Figure 3.9 results. The values for Richborough (Rich corr) (Table 3.11) have been produced by bringing the uniquely high values for the period 388–402 back to an average value and re-calculating the percentages.

The general interpretation of the diagram is that the British mean for a whole range of sites is represented by the zero line in Figure 3.9. When values go downwards in relation to that line it means that that particular site is accumulating coins at a lower rate than the average British site. When values rise that site is accumulating faster than average. In general the five shore forts represented accumulate coins more slowly than average up to about AD 150. Reculver then begins to "take off" while the other forts remain somewhat inert. Reculver grows gently up to 260 and then develops quickly up to 294 when it levels out and becomes average. After 330 it falls back and remains below average in its loss of coins until the end.

In 260 the other four forts change their patterns of accumulation, but in very different ways. Lympne levels out, Richborough rises slightly, and Portchester and Pevensey continue to drop. Lympne rises to a peak in 348 and then drops away. Portchester and Pevensey begin to rise after 294 to 317, but then diverge. Portchester grows to a peak in 348 and then declines while Pevensey levels out in 317, drops again after 330 to a rather remarkable low, then keeps rising from 348 to 388.

With these diverse coin profiles I find it almost impossible to consider a unified command of any such thing as the Saxon Shore, but, if such a command did exist I would suggest that its life was briefly between about 290 and 320, after which its forts went their separate ways.

The story of Pevensey told solely from the coins as judged against a British average is of establishment shortly before 300, a first phase, or a false start from 300 to 330, a pause from 330 to 348 and then strong growth almost up to the end. Comparison with the archaeological findings should be instructive.

Metalwork

by David Richards†

This is a comparatively small metalwork assemblage, reflecting the limited areas examined during the three seasons of work (*cf.* Mayes and Butler 1983; Keen and Hanks 1993).

In spite of the number of Roman coins recovered (see Reece, above), there is a disappointing quantity of recognisable artefacts from this period. Two

Table 3.10 Roman coin list

Context	*SF no.*	*Authority*	*Date*	*Reference*
1	2	Counter Germany 82	?16thC	Barnard 82
1	1	House of Constantine ?	310-330	rev illeg
22	11	Gratian	375-78	CK364
25	18	Constantine I	335-37	HK92
25	22	Theodora	337-40	HKas113
30	27	? Crispus	324-26	RIC7London as 291
30	33	Constantine II	320-24	RIC7London 237
30	26	Crispus	320-24	RIC7London 230
30	31	House of Constantine	335-41	HK as 87
30	28	Constans	345-48	HK638
30	36	Uncertain	Late 4C	illegible
31	43	Constans	345-8	HK148
33	42	House of Valentinian	364-78	CKas514
36	61	Follis, very corroded	294-310	uncertain
36	98	Theodora	337-40	HKas113
36	56	Constantius II	350-60	CK as 25
37	62	Radiate, very corroded	260-90	rev illeg
43	71	Very corroded	3-4C	illeg
59	84	House of Constantine	343-48	HK as 963
60	82	Carausius, Pax, mm /ML	286-93	RIC 101
60	82	Allectus, Pax, mm S/A/ML	293-96	RIC 28
76	87	Maximian I, no complex mm	286-94	rev illeg
83	90	?Barbarous Radiate, pierced	260-90	rev illeg
83	101	House of Theodosius	388-402	CK as162
89	109	House of Valentinian	364-78	CK as 296
103	4	Victoria 6d	1890	
121	367	? Constantine I	310-17	RIC7London as 10
131	700	Valens	364-78	CK as 528
141	637	Radiate, worn	260-75	uncertain
157	725	Constantine I	320-24	RIC7London 289
219	49	House of Constantine	345-48	HKas137
234	69	Constantine I	310-17	RIC7London16
247	74	Corroded fragments	3-4C	Illeg
600	132	Counter France 74	?15thC	Barnard 74
rabbit burrow		Theodora	337-40	HKas113
US	116	House of Constantine	350-60	CK ? as 25

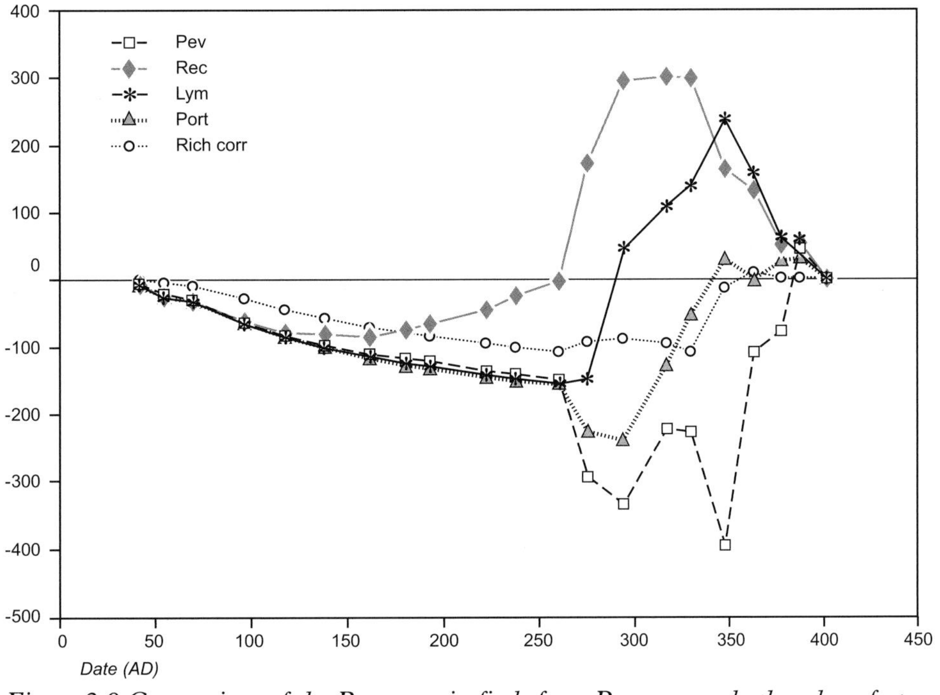

Figure 3.9 Comparison of the Roman coin finds from Pevensey and other shore forts (for the methodology used to create this graph see Reece 1995)

Table 3.11 Comparison of Roman coins from Pevensey and other shore forts

Date	*Pev*	*Rec*	*Lym*	*Port*	*Rich corr*
41	0	0	0	0	184
54	1	0	0	1	404
69	0	1	0	0	142
96	0	2	0	0	386
117	0	2	0	0	93
138	0	8	0	0	76
161	2	9	1	0	112
180	1	13	0	0	37
193	0	9	0	0	14
222	0	21	0	0	53
238	0	18	0	0	13
260	0	18	0	2	39
275	0	205	29	43	4759
294	31	164	63	69	4099
317	43	16	15	75	351
330	13	25	14	67	855
348	25	71	66	188	10127
364	124	34	1	31	3237
378	46	17	2	78	2849
388	42	3	0	5	115
402	4	3	0	14	1705
Total	**332**	**639**	**191**	**573**	**29650**

Date	*Pev*	*Rec*	*Lym*	*Port*	*Rich corr*
41	-8.423405797	-8.423405797	-8.423405797	-8.423405797	-2.217672239
54	-23.05664332	-26.06869151	-26.06869151	-24.32349081	-6.237325575
69	-31.06507189	-32.51217486	-34.07712008	-32.33191938	-9.456546727
96	-64.51464332	-62.83185583	-67.52669151	-65.78149081	-29.88756841
117	-83.69842903	-78.88575109	-86.71047723	-84.96527653	-45.93476053
138	-99.23164332	-81.89940356	-102.2436915	-100.4984908	-58.90473704
161	-110.6686898	-85.27603938	-114.4692323	-117.9596337	-72.58847686
180	-118.598213	-75.87332286	-125.4108037	-128.9012051	-82.28215622
193	-122.6855702	-65.87617296	-129.4981608	-132.9885622	-85.89733798
222	-135.6157845	-45.94253748	-142.4283751	-145.9187765	-97.04003119
238	-141.7158559	-23.87359482	-148.5284466	-152.018848	-102.7016541
260	-148.9405702	-2.929295021	-155.7531608	-155.7531608	-108.6110226
275	-294.5046416	172.3204051	-149.4847715	-226.2736023	-93.66919187
294	-336.0787191	294.0238509	45.41058897	-240.8023255	-90.37055757
317	-224.0977182	301.5259031	106.407549	-127.4493446	-96.0695177
330	-226.618306	298.9723194	138.028764	-52.1981121	-108.910307
348	-397.0226954	164.3778364	237.872908	30.19402493	-13.06446784
364	-110.1502194	130.9644741	156.4870101	-2.326253428	9.487725247
388	45.40616437	52.75952146	57.45435714	33.02154737	-0.049858709
402	0	0	0	0	0

bracelet fragments (6 and 10; Fig. 3.10) are the only certainly Roman copper alloy artefacts, and even one of these came from a context which produced a late or post-medieval lace-tag (5). Some of the badly encrusted pieces, probably nail stems, from the 1993–5 excavations might be Roman, but even X-ray photography would not help with identification.

Thus, most of the identifiable artefacts among the 38 copper alloy objects and 24 iron artefacts in the catalogue are medieval or later. Typical are the copper alloy lace-tags and the strap-ends. The two tweezers (20 and 28; Fig. 3.10) although not unlike their Roman predecessors, have very close parallels from nearby Hamwic (Hinton 1995). The unworn Tournai jeton (61) and the remarkable gold wedding ring (62; Fig. 3.11) are both 15th century.

The discrete group of small pins with twisted wire heads (51; Fig. 3.10) are probably from the late 17th or, more likely, the 18th century (Caple 1983). However, the larger solitary pin could be earlier (Egan and Pritchard 1991, 301).

Due to the continuity of typological form in iron implements, most of these items are even less amenable to dating on typological grounds than those in copper alloy. As discussed above some items, including the hold-fasts or rivet-and-rove plates (29; 16, 47a) do occur in Roman contexts (Manning 1985, 132 and figs R74–81) but, at Pevensey, the absence of other contemporary metal objects – except coins – makes it safer to assign them also to the medieval period. While the copper alloy objects are mainly from dress or domestic use, the ironwork includes some structural material and weaponry (arrowheads) as well as brooches and dress fittings.

In all, 62 metal objects were recovered from 38 contexts, but only seven of the latter yielded more than one find, suggesting a degree of residuality rather than concentration of usage. Two contexts (22 and 30/31) in Trench 1 produced five and ten metal objects respectively.

Some 450 nails were recovered during the excavation, 177 alone from context 35 in Trench 6. The latter range in date from a medieval 'fiddle-key' horseshoe nail to 19th century factory-made cut nails.

Catalogue (Figs 3.10–3.11)

All dimensions are given in millimetres. Small finds numbers are enclosed in [ ] whilst context numbers are placed within ( ). L. = length; dia. = diameter; th. = thickness; w. = width.

Phase 3

1. Copper alloy. ?Bar. 60 L. (25) [23] Not Illustrated
2. Copper alloy. ?Coin. Heavily corroded roughly circular fragment. 8 dia. (31) [38] Not Illustrated
3. Copper alloy. ?Strap end fragment, slightly tapering. 22 L. (31) [39] Not Illustrated
4. Copper alloy. Strap. Thin and curved, possibly from a belt fitting. 38 L. (31) [41] Not Illustrated
5. Copper alloy. Lace-tag. Slightly tapering, both ends damaged. 31 L. (31) [44] Not Illustrated
6. Copper alloy. Bracelet, fragment, made from a thin flat strip decorated with single, widely spaced grooves around the exterior edge. Similar to an example from Brancaster (Cool 1985, 205 no. 21), among other sites. Roman, 4th century. 60 dia. (31) [47]
7. Copper alloy. Flat curved fragment. 15 L. (31) [46] Not Illustrated
8. Copper alloy. ?Strap end or buckle plate fragment. 30 L. (31) [50] Not Illustrated
9. Copper alloy. ?Coin. Thick heavily corroded disc, but plain on both faces. 28 dia., 4 th. (37) [63] Not Illustrated
10. Copper alloy. Cable-twist bracelet fragment. Again, similar to a Roman example from Brancaster, for which Cool (1985, 205) suggests a tentative, 4th century date. 28 L. (250) [76]
11. Copper alloy. Irregular, crescent-shaped object. 38 L. (252) [77] Not Illustrated
12. Copper alloy. Three fragments of thin strip, none greater than 10 L. (36) [99)] Not Illustrated
13. Copper alloy. Fragment (dross). <1 g. (725) [158] Not Illustrated
14. Iron. ?Arrowhead. A sharply pointed spike, almost certainly not a nail stem. It is broken off at the blunt end leaving no trace of socket or tang. Possibly Type 7 (Ward-Perkins 1964). 96 L. (25) [60] Not Illustrated
15. Iron. Nail or stud. Unchecked corrosion has caused severe delamination. A large dome-headed stud or nail with broken, untapered, surviving stem. 120 L., 60 head dia. (242) [78)] Not Illustrated
16. Iron. Rivet-and-rove plate. A short, square-sectioned stem is clenched over a rove whose shape is concealed by corrosion products and not well shown in the X-ray. The use of these objects in castle architecture is unclear but they have been recovered in several excavations. 60 L. (250) [75] Not Illustrated
17. Iron. ?Needle case. Heavily corroded, the X-ray shows a symmetrically tapering object hollow to the tip. The form is similar to the cases used to carry needles or other sharp implements when not in use, but these are commonly made of copper alloy. 69 L. (31) [55] Not Illustrated
18. Iron. Knife blade. A sharply tapering and pointed blade with a broad back curving down slightly to the point. The cutting edge has been worn by sharpening. No trace of the tang survives but there is a spot of copper alloy near the broad end which may be the remains of a rivet. 95 L. (723) [147]

Phase 5

19. Copper alloy. Toggle fastening. Cruciform head with large undercut hole and damaged butt-end. 44 L. (183) [95]

Phase 6

20. Copper alloy. Tweezers. Badly corroded, formed from a plain strip. Early medieval or later in date with parallels from Hamwic (Hinton 1995, 44). 40 L. (719) [142]
21. Copper alloy. Lace tag. 37 L. (337) [94] Not Illustrated
22. Iron. ?Horseshoe. Completely shrouded in dirt and corrosion products. X-ray photographs suggest a flat curved object which might be a large horseshoe but there is no sign of nails or nail holes. (117) [6] Not Illustrated
23. Iron. Arrowhead. Heavily corroded. The X-ray reveals a socketed missile with a long tapering point, perhaps a type of 'bodkin' for armour piercing (Ward-Perkins 1964, fig. 17, no. 8). 110 L. (116) [3] Not Illustrated
24. Copper alloy. Bar mount. Thin and tapering with a single perforation. 28 L. (152) [52] Not Illustrated
25. Copper alloy. Needle case. Hollow cylinder, probably originally filled with felt or greasy wool to protect needles when not in use. 57 L. (152) [79] Not Illustrated
26. Copper alloy. Rectangular, cross-section strip with one small, central perforation. Each end of the strip terminates in a loop. The larger loop is butt-jointed and

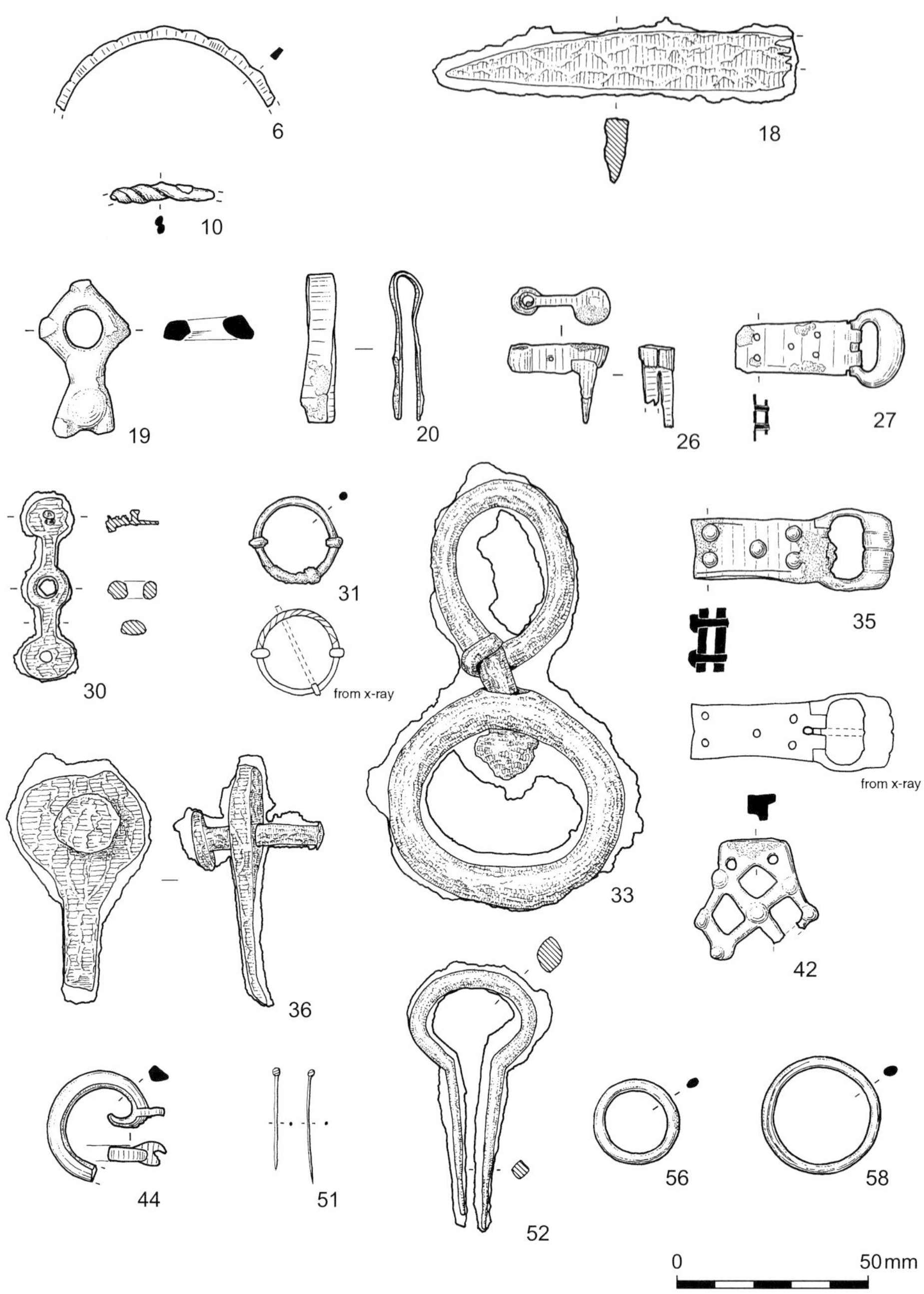

Figure 3.10 Roman and medieval metalwork

encloses the heads of two small rectangular spikes (one broken) 25 L. (152) [80]

27. Copper alloy. Strap-end, buckle and plate. Part of tongue surviving, plate has five perforations. 45 L. (324) [73]
28. Copper alloy. Pair of tweezers, formed from a plain strap. 35 L. (324) [91] Not Illustrated
29. Iron. Hold-fast. The top of a T-shaped hold-fast or clamp. The foreshortened shaft has a sub-rectangular cross-section. 75 L. (324) [93] Not Illustrated
30. Iron. Bar mount. A strap-mount with two, equal-diameter terminals and a central lobe. One rivet survives in this mount, which was plated with white metal. The form is perhaps developed from the mounts illustrated in Egan and Pritchard (1991) so that a date later than the 15th century can be postulated. However, the context is associated with the construction of the Keep and pottery of 11th to 13th century date. 50 L. (620) [124]
31. Iron. Annular buckle or brooch. A neat, white-metal-plated ring made from twisted iron strip. Two beaded 'stops' on opposing sides of the ring and a fragment of the butt end of the pin or tongue. 24 dia. (615) [137]
32. Iron. Joiners-dog fragment. Heavily encrusted and corroded. A flat, tapering strip; the sharp point is clinched. This is one arm of a typical cramp or 'dog'. The surface appearance suggests this object may have been in contact with fire. 60 L. (677) [149] Not Illustrated

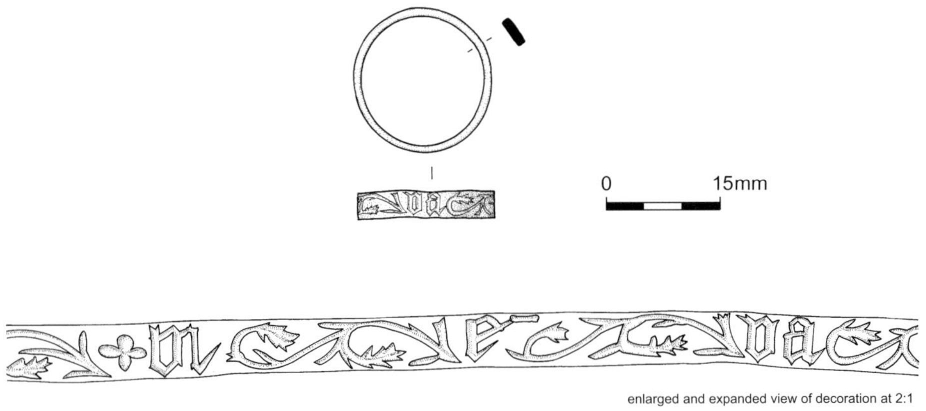

Figure 3.11 15th century gold wedding ring (62)

33. Iron. Swivel hook. A ring, *c.* 50 dia., is widened and pierced to hold a long mushroom-headed rivet. The latter is then bent into another ring locked against itself to make the whole object into a figure of eight. Swivel rings are typically from hoisting apparatus, civilian or maritime. Date uncertain ?16th–19th centuries. 115 L. [677] (150)

Phase 12

34. Iron. Split pin. The comparatively uncorroded state of this object suggests this is a relatively modern object. 621. [338] (97) Phase 11C Not Illustrated
35. Copper alloy. Strap-end buckle. Oval, with an ornate, bulbous outer edge. The thick rectangular plates of the strap-end show traces of gilding. X-rays also show at least three rivets. The tongue (missing) was of iron. Late 13th century (Egan and Pritchard 1991, 44 and 46). 52 L. (675) [143]
36. Iron. Unknown object. Spoon-shaped with the circular end pierced with a flat-headed rivet in place. The 'handle' is a rectilinear extension broken off at the end. The X-ray does not assist identification. The rivet may have held something like scale plates or a knob to the disc. It is not impossible that this is the hilt of a dagger. 64 L. disc 36 dia. (673) [148]

Phase 13

37. Iron. Knife tang or buckle tongue. Tapering to a blunt point, the other (broken) end is flatter and rectangular in cross section. The X-ray merely confirms the shape. 37 L. (632) [123] Not Illustrated
38. Copper alloy. Rod or bar with one rounded end. Probably made from a heavily-leaded alloy. 34 L. (640) [155] Not Illustrated
39. Copper alloy. Pin or needle, sharply bent. Flat, rectangular cross-section at point, tapering out to square at the ?eye end. 981. (22) [8] Not Illustrated
40. Copper alloy. Bar, roughly cast. 36 L., 10 w., 5 th. (22) [9] Not Illustrated
41. Copper alloy. Lace-tag, fragment. 27 L. (22) [14] Not Illustrated
42. Copper alloy. Mount or strap end with two perforations for attachment, with open lattice decoration. 33 L. (30) [34]
43. Copper alloy. Four pieces of corroded alloy. (40) [72] Not Illustrated
44. Copper alloy. Part of a broken buckle? 30 dia. (54) [85]
45. Copper alloy. Disc, possibly a token. Possible inscription on one face. 24 dia. (76) [87] Not Illustrated
46. Copper alloy. Disc. A thin ovoid fragment of a once circular disc? There is a neat, punched hole and a possible legend around the more regular curve. 20 dia. (83) [90] Not Illustrated

47a. Iron. Rivet-and-rove. An X-ray shows both parts in more detail, although the plan shape of the rove is not shown. (381) Not Illustrated

47b. Iron. Three stem fragments similar to the above, but do not seem to conjoin. One fragment is clearly pointed and might be the end of an arrowhead. (22) [16] Not Illustrated

48. Iron. ?Nail stem. Too corroded to determine its section. There is a small spike, probably of corrosion product sticking out of one end, otherwise the rod is untapered. 46 L. (22) [15] Not Illustrated
49. Iron. Rivet stem. A damaged and fragmentary stem, the head is missing but a piece of ?rove is attached at the other end. 50 L. (30) [161] Not Illustrated
50. Iron. ?Arrowhead. The absence of any evidence for socket or tang makes identification of this heavy missile difficult but possibly it is the head of another type 8 (Ward-Perkins 1964, fig. 18). 72 L. (30) [161] Not Illustrated

Phase 14

51. Copper alloy. Seven dress pins. All have heads made from twisted wire, stamped to a globular shape. All show traces of a silvery coating. These pins are late post-medieval or even 17th century (Caple 1983). The complete examples are 26–33 L. (608) [133]
52. Iron. Object. An ovoid head terminates in two, parallel, tapering arms of square section. The general form is

like a split shank staple but this appears to be a more specialised implement. 70 L. (608) [134]

53. Copper alloy. Thin, corroded alloy strip. Possibly a binding strip. 32 L. (178) [92] Not Illustrated
54. Iron. Ferrule. Slightly tapering with open socket, broken off at the narrower end. Probably from an implement rather than a weapon. 48 L. (178) [35] Not Illustrated
55. Iron. Object. A tapering, square-sectioned bar, flattened and broken off at the wider end where it seems to bifurcate at the break, or perhaps hold a rivet. Obviously an implement, use unknown. 80 L. (737) (?) Not Illustrated

Phase 15

56. Copper alloy. Ring, oval cross-section, slightly flattened on the faces. This, together with traces of iron at one spot probably derived from an iron-tongue, indicate that this is not a finger ring. Probably part of a dress buckle or plain brooch. 22 dia. (610) [139]
57. Iron. Strip. A slightly curved, flat piece, possibly decorative or a piece of binding. 60 L. (105) [115] Not Illustrated
58. Copper alloy. Ring, cast from a dark grey alloy. Slightly ribbed cross section, little evidence of wear. 30 dia. (15) [03]
59. Copper alloy. Length of wire. Loosely coiled into four turns and twisted in places. ?For making pins. 40 dia., 0.5 th. (103) [7] Not Illustrated

Topsoil

60. Copper alloy. Pin, with oval, wire-wound head. Possibly 16th century. [100] (70) Not Illustrated
61. Copper alloy. Jeton. A remarkably unworn stock jeton of the 'Crown' series, from the design on the obverse. These counting tokens emanated from Tournai in Belgium about 1450. There is a close parallel in Mitchener (1988). (600) [132] Not Illustrated
62. Gold ring. An engraved gold ring lettered +VI E- VA. The letters are separated by patterns in trailing vine-like decoration. Mr John Cherry of the British Museum has examined the ring and suggested a 15th century date. He also suggested that the engraving may have held coloured enamel, making this a high quality object. However, examination of the engraved cuts under a high power microscope in the Engineering Department, University of Reading, failed to detect any undercutting or traces of enamel. The ring is very light and pale in colour, possibly with a lighter metal to produce a low-carat gold. 22 dia. 1.72 g (701) [138]
63. Iron. Key. A late or post-medieval key with kidney-shaped handle and single cruciform ward. The terminal spike is missing. (600) Not Illustrated

Slag and minerals

by David Richards†

A total of 15.35 kg of slag was recovered from the excavations. Of this total, more than 12 kg, or 78%, was recovered in 1995, largely from Trench 6. Six large pieces, totalling 8 kgs came from the topmost layers of this trench (and are therefore unstratified) but smaller amounts of similar slag was recovered from other contexts, particularly those associated with a large pit (F649), in Phase 10 of 13th to 14th century date.

The small amounts (2.35 kg.) of slag from the first two seasons of excavations were spread between Trenches 1–4 and are, with one exception, undistinguished and mainly small (<200 g) pieces of a greyish-black, crystalline slag of medium density. Charcoal or ferrous inclusions were occasionally noted and some have exterior surfaces with earth and stones adhering. Tentatively, this material was identified as hearth-bottom slag from smithing work, rather than smelting slag.

The exception, from context 23, Phase 13, in Trench 2, is an irregular piece weighing 300 g, highly vesiculate with a black or purple vitrified exterior, the hollow centre containing a mass of tabular crystals. Professor J. R. L. Allen FRS (University of Reading) has kindly examined this specimen, suggesting it is either an early blast-furnace slag, or a piece of highly vitrified lining material. The first evidence for blast-furnace smelting in the Weald is AD 1594–1620 (Crossley 1975) and as other evidence now suggests that context 23 is not later than the 14th century (Chapter 2), the latter explanation is probably the correct one.

In 1994 three small pieces of reddish-purple ore, weighing 180 g, were recovered, two from contexts 246 and 250 (Phase 3) in Trench 3 and one from context 338 (Phase 12) in Trench 4. The writer is grateful to the late Professor P. Allen FRS (University of Reading) who has commented on the ore samples, which are in his opinion of local origin, almost certainly weathered sideritic ore from the Wealden Clay (Lake *et al.* 1987 31–35, 91). The silts of the Cuckmere river, only a few miles north-west of Pevensey, contain much ore from the same source.

In spite of the lack of other definite evidence, such as tap-slag, in the assemblage at this stage, the presence of this ore was suggestive of a smelting operation nearby. This is reinforced by the large amounts of dense, vesiculate black/grey slags recovered from Trench 6 in 1995. Some of these large lumps show evidence of 'raddling', that is being raked, from the bottom of a large furnace while still plastic. These have been described as woostite/fayalite slag typical of material from relatively high-temperature furnaces, i.e. above 1200°C (Professor J. R. L. Allen pers. comm.). In 1995 other pieces of ore, tap-slag and vitrified lining were recovered from Trench 7, adding to the earlier evidence for smelting.

Trench 6 was a comparatively small area (10 x 9 m) at the north-east corner of the Keep, where the larger quantity of distinctive slag (above) was recovered from the upper layers. Whether a larger area would have produced more slag is a matter for speculation. In the lower layers, very similar slag is associated with a number of features (pits) which seem to be of earlier date (Phase 10, F649). Where the material originated is also unclear, since no structural evidence for a furnace within, or adjacent to the castle has been found.

Stone

by Ruth Shaffrey

The stone types found during the excavations partly reflect the types of stone which are found in the fort walls. One of the most common materials was a pale cream to slightly peach-coloured sandstone which may be from the Ashdown Beds of the Hastings Beds and are Lower Cretaceous in age. These rocks do exist around Brighton and Worthing but are poorly exposed and, if exploited, unlikely to have come from this area. They also outcrop more locally around the Pevensey area and are therefore most likely to be from a local source. Other, locally available materials include the chunks of chalk and the many dressed blocks and smaller fragments of Upper Greensand which are likely to be from Eastbourne (White 1926, 84). There were also many mainly sub-angular fragments of Sussex 'Marble' also known as Small Paludina Limestone. There were frequent fragments of ironstones similar to those used in the walls which are probably from the Tunbridge Wells Sandstone.

Roman glass

by Denise Allen

Four certain and six possible fragments of Roman glass were recovered. All fragments have an outer layer of whitish-iridescent weathering. A small quantity of Roman vessel glass is also reported by Lyne (2009, 89–90).

1. (167) Fragment of blue-green glass, its curvature suggesting that it came from the lower part of the neck of a large bottle. Diam of neck *c.* 40 mm. PH 24 mm. Such vessels were extremely common during the first two centuries AD, and because of the large numbers in circulation, residual fragments are often found in later contexts.
2. SF 106 (89) Flat fragment of blue-green glass. PH 22 mm. Both surfaces appear relatively smooth and unpitted, and this is therefore more likely to be a body fragment from a prismatic bottle than a piece of window glass. 1st to 2nd century AD.
3. (58) Tiny fragment of blue-green glass with one rounded edge. PH 10 mm. There appears to be a slight curvature along the length of the rounded edge, and it is therefore more likely to be a vessel rim than the edge of a piece of window glass. As there is no discernible evidence of rotary-polishing over the surfaces, it is probably the fire-rounded rim of a blown vessel. It could belong to a wide variety of forms and cannot be closely dated within the Romano-British period.
4. (47) Rim fragment of a bowl of pale yellow-green glass. Rim outflared and cracked-off flat; sides taper downward, with upper part of an oval indent extant, pushed in whilst the glass was still warm and pliable. Diameter of rim *c.* 120 mm. PH 23 mm. This is a well-recognised late Roman form, known as an indented truncated-conical bowl. It was in use during the 4th century, and appears to have been most common during the second half of that period. Two examples were found at Lullingstone Roman Villa, Kent, and many further finds are listed with reference to these (Cool and Price 1987, 118–119, 137, nos 375–376, fig. 30). Seventeen fragments from a minimum of six vessels were found in excavations at Colchester (Cool and Price 1995, 104–5, nos 720–731, fig. 6.8).

The six fragments of possible Roman glass are listed below. These are all featureless and therefore more difficult to identify with certainty, but having the appearance and colour of typical late Roman glass:

1. (83). Three fragments of pale yellow-green glass
2. (53). Fragment of pale yellow-green glass
3. (70). Fragment of pale olive green glass, surfaces streaky
4. (87). Fragment of pale olive green glass, surfaces streaky
5. (90). Flat fragment of pale olive green glass – piece of double-glossy, cylinder-blown window glass?
6. (89). Fragment of greenish-colourless glass

Medieval window glass

by Edward Carpenter

Six small fragments of medieval window glass were found. The condition of the glass varies but all are opaque due to corrosion which took place while the glass was buried. None of the fragments show any signs of surface pitting on their exterior surface. All dimensions are maximum.

GLW 1 Two fragments join to form this piece. One edge is grozed. The decoration is of two-stripe strapwork running parallel with the grozed edge. The thicker band is 2 mm wide the other less than 1 mm wide. They are separated by a gap of 1 mm. The thinner line is nearest the grozed edge. Length 36 mm; width 19 mm; thickness 2.5 mm.

GLW 2 This fragment has one grozed edge. There is no surface decoration. Length 26 mm; width 16 mm; thickness 2.5 mm.

GLW 3 This fragment is the best preserved of the group. At the centre there are two vertical parallel lines. Either side are diagonal lines each tapering to a point, those on the left pointing to the bottom right and those on the right pointing to the bottom left. Length 29 mm: width 19 mm; thickness 2 mm.

GLW 4 This fragment is badly decomposed and is laminating. There is no trace of any surface decoration. Length 15 mm; width 12 mm; thickness 1 mm.

GLW 5 This small fragment has a two-stripe strapwork design painted parallel to the grozed edge, and is of the same scale to the design on GLW 1. The thinner line is nearest the grozed edge. Length 18 mm; width 17 mm; thickness 2 mm.

GLW 6 Two fragments join to form this rectangular piece. Some of the design is obscured. A painted line follows the edge of the glass, set within this outline is a motif of single-veined petals or leaves, the veins emerging from the lower painted line. One edge is possibly grozed. Length 33 mm; width 20 mm; thickness 3 mm.

Chapter 4
Environmental evidence

Animal bones

by Adrienne Powell and Dale Serjeantson

A substantial assemblage of animal bone was recovered from the excavations, amounting to an estimated total of some 20,000 hand retrieved fragments (Serjeantson nd.). However, many of the bone-bearing contexts spanned wide date ranges and some medieval contexts included a substantial quantity of re-worked Roman material, so have minimal potential for providing information on diet and husbandry. In addition, bone was retrieved from a column sample taken through the build up of the dark earth deposit but the quantity of bone from the column was small and is not considered in this report. Here, only contexts closely dated by pottery have been included in the analysis: this comprises three groups: 1) 4th century AD, 2) 11th–13th century AD and 3) 13th–15th century AD.

Methodology

Most of the assemblage was retrieved by hand, but samples from three contexts from the Phase 10 pits on the eastern side of the Keep produced bone and marine shell from the >10 mm sieve residue. Only one of these sampled contexts fell within the closely dated material.

Bone has been identified to species where possible, and sheep and goat bones have been distinguished using the criteria of Boessneck (1969) and Payne (1985). The sheep-sized and cattle-sized categories include vertebrae which could not be identified to species and ribs, proximal ends only. Bone in these categories has not been included in the percentage of identifiable bone in Table 4.1, although the quantities do include fragments which were only identifiable as bird or fish.

The assemblage was recorded using the 'bone zone' system described by Serjeantson (1996). This produced a basic fragment count, or number of identifiable specimens (NISP). Since differential fragmentation and survival may affect the relative proportions of species and anatomical elements present in an assemblage, the minimum number of elements (MNE) was calculated in addition to the NISP. This was based on the sum of the most frequent zone for each element and was calculated for the main domestic animals only. Minimum numbers of individuals (MNI) were derived from the most common element in the MNE counts for these species, taking side into account.

The incidence of burning and butchery was noted and quantified, with the latter categorised as either chop marks, knife cuts or saw marks and the location on the bone fragment recorded. The incidence of carnivore and rodent gnawing was also recorded. The surface preservation of the fragments indicates the degree of post-depositional destruction; it may mask evidence for butchery and carnivore gnawing and usually also reduces the proportion of the bones which can be aged. Here, the surface condition was recorded for each identifiable fragment on a scale of 1 to 4, where condition 1 is excellent and condition 4 is poor.

Ageing has been based on tooth wear and epiphyseal fusion, although the latter is generally less reliable. Timing of epiphyseal closure is based on Sisson and Grossman (Getty 1975). Tooth wear in the main food mammals was recorded following Grant

Table 4.1 Summary of animal bones, hand-retrieved only

	4th C	*11th–13th C*	*13th–15th C*	*Total*
Horse	2	3	3	8
Cattle	165	291	133	589
Sheep/goat	57	303	202	562
Sheep	3	63	60	126
Goat	0	0	2	2
Pig	142	341	179	662
Dog	2	2	3	7
Cat	0	7	10	17
Red deer	16	3	0	19
Red/Fallow deer	0	0	2	2
Fallow deer	0	2	0	2
Roe deer	1	5	1	7
Wild boar	4	1	2	7
Fox	0	1	0	1
Hare	2	6	3	11
Rabbit *	0	0	1	1
Rat sp.	1	1	1	3
Bird	25	121	122	268
Fish	0	55	51	106
Sheep-size mammal	52	251	183	486
Cattle-size mammal	94	190	61	345
Unidentified	646	1825	1123	3594
Total	**1212**	**3471**	**2142**	**6825**
% Identified	*34.7*	*34.7*	*36.2*	*35.1*

* intrusive

Table 4.2 Taphonomic characteristics of identified bones

Date	*Area*	*Gnawed*	*Rodent*	*Butchered*	*Burnt*	*Total*
4th C		23.5	0.2	19.4	1.2	566
11th–13th C	Pre-Keep	10.6	0.4	11.1	1.3	822
	Outside Keep	21.6	0.4	10.9	1.3	825
13th–15th C	Outside Keep	22.9	0.0	14.8	1.1	1020
Total		**19.5**	**0.2**	**13.7**	**1.2**	**3233**

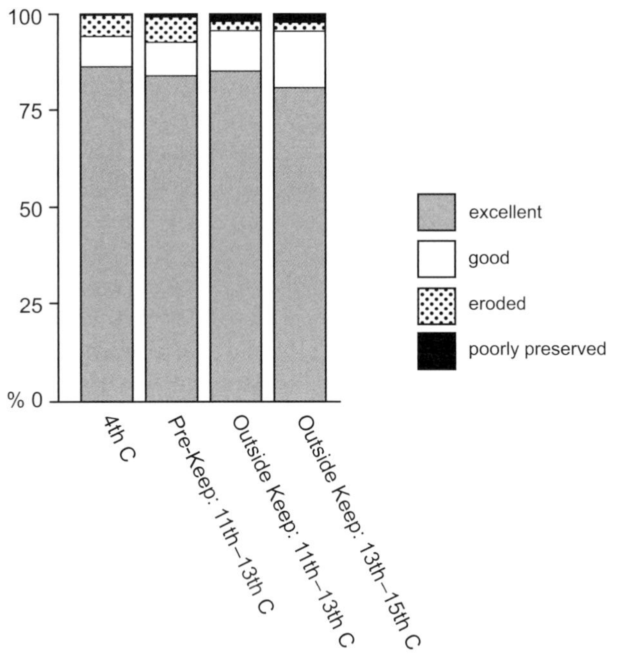

Figure 4.1 Preservation of bone surface. Surface preservation of bones was recorded as (1) excellent, (2) good, (3) eroded, and (4) poorly preserved

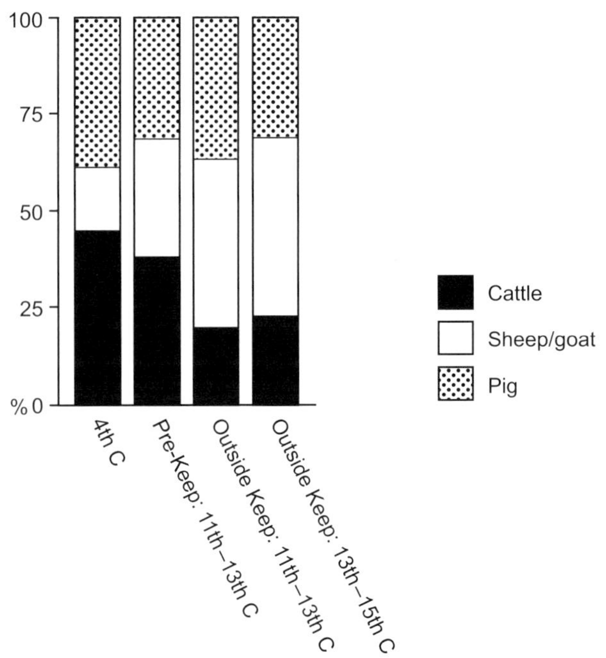

Figure 4.2 Spatial and temporal variation in the distribution of the main domestic animals (cattle, sheep/goat and pig)

(1975) with attribution to age stages based on O'Connor (1988). Measurements on the crown heights of cheek teeth (Levine 1982) were also used to age horses. The material was sexed where possible: cattle, sheep and goats on their pelves (Getty 1975, Grigson 1982); pigs on the morphology of the upper and lower canine teeth (Schmid 1972); equids on canines and pelves (Getty 1975).

Measurements taken are based on von den Driesch (1976) and Payne and Bull (1988). Withers heights for the main domestic species were calculated using the factors quoted in Driesch and Boessneck (1974).

The assemblage

The species composition for the hand-retrieved material is shown in Table 4.1; there is a total of 6825 fragments with most (>80%) coming from the two medieval groups. The level of identification is 35% overall and is consistent between the groups. Most of the identifiable bone in all three groups is from the main domestic mammals, cattle, sheep/goats and pigs, but this proportion decreases through time from 87% in the 4th century to 83% in the 11th–13th century and 74% in the 13th–15th century. Other domestic mammals, horse, dog, cat, are not well represented in the assemblage and the bones of these species are outnumbered by those of hunted wild mammals. The bird and fish bone assemblages are relatively small, but their proportional contribution increases through time, particularly in the 13th–15th century group:

	4th	*11–13th*	*13–15th*
Mammal (%)	94	85	78
Bird (%)	6	10	16
Fish (%)	0	5	7

The bones from the sieved sample from context 152 (13th–15th century) add little to the hand-retrieved material: two sheep/goat bones, one domestic-fowl-size, posterior phalanx and one cervical vertebra from a sheep-sized mammal.

The taphonomic characteristics of the hand-retrieved material, excluding unidentified fragments, are summarised in Table 4.2. Burnt bone is almost completely absent in all phases as is rodent-gnawed bone. Carnivore-gnawed bone, in contrast, occurs at high levels in both the Romano-British and 13th–15th century groups and is still common, although less frequent, in the 11th–13th century material. Similarly, the Romano-British and later medieval phases contain moderately high levels of butchered bones while these are less frequent in the earlier medieval group.

It is possible that this difference in observed frequency of gnawing and butchery marks owes something to variation in preservation. To investigate this, the medieval material was divided into three groups: pre-Keep (11th–13th century), outside Keep (11th–13th century) and outside Keep (13th–15th century) and the condition of bone surface in each group quantified. Figure 4.1 shows this graphically and it may be seen that the pre-Keep material contains slightly more bone with poorer surface preservation than the other medieval groups: 8% compared with 4% eroded and poorly preserved (conditions 3 and 4). When the degree of gnawing and butchery is calculated for the two 11th–13th century groups separately, it appears that, slight though the difference in surface preservation is between the two groups, it has biased the survival of this evidence. Carnivore gnaw-marks occur on 11% of fragments from the pre-Keep group but are twice as frequent (22%) in the better preserved material from the outside Keep, almost identical to the Romano-British and 13th–15th century groups. Butchery marks have a similar frequency in both groups, but in the pre-Keep group chop marks (which are less vulnerable to post-depositional destructive processes than the shallower and finer knife marks) comprise 76% of the butchery evidence while in the outside Keep group they make up 66%. Furthermore, as Figure 4.2 shows, the pre-Keep group also contains a higher percentage of cattle bones than either of the other two medieval groups.

The main domestic mammals

Species representation

The relative abundance of the main domestic mammals is compared in Figure 4.3 using NISP, MNE and MNI calculations for each of the three phases. The calculations using the different methods give broadly similar results, except for the 11th–13th century when MNI suggests a significantly higher proportion of sheep than the other two counts. In the Romano-British group cattle bones are predominant and pig bones are almost as numerous but sheep and goat bones are poorly represented; all methods of quantification show this same pattern. The high representation of cattle is typical of a Romano-British assemblage (King 1978) but the high proportion of pig bones is unusual by this period and in this region (Grant 1989): at both Chichester (Levitan 1989) and Portchester (Grant 1975) pig follows both cattle and sheep in frequency.

In marked contrast, both medieval groups show sheep to have been the predominant animal. The NISP and MNE figures suggest a slightly greater frequency of cattle bones in the earlier medieval

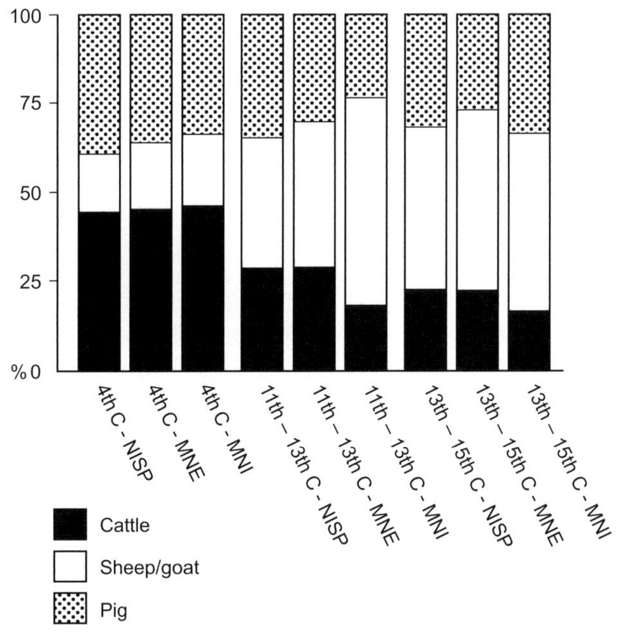

Figure 4.3 Relative proportions over time of the main domesticated mammals (cattle, sheep/goat and pig), calculated from the number of identified specimens (NISP), minimum number of elements (MNE), and minimum number of individuals (MNI)

Table 4.3 Minimum number of elements (MNE) and overall minimum number of individuals (MNI) of the main domestic mammals, 4th century

Element	*Cattle*	*Sheep*	*Pig*	*Total*
Horn core	0	0	-	0
Skull	2	0	4	6
Mandible	7	6	6	19
Atlas	2	0	2	4
Axis	0	1	1	2
Scapula	5	4	8	17
Humerus	5	4	9	18
Radius	6	3	4	13
Ulna	0	0	4	4
Pelvis	6	5	3	14
Sacrum	0	0	0	0
Femur	12	3	6	21
Tibia	5	3	7	15
Patella	0	0	0	0
Astragalus	5	0	4	9
Calcaneus	0	2	1	3
Tarsals	5	0	0	5
Carpals	2	0	0	2
Metacarpal	1	4	5	10
Metatarsal	3	3	2	8
Phalanx I	7	0	2	9
Phalanx II	12	0	1	13
Phalanx III	4	0	0	4
MNE total	**89**	**38**	**69**	**196**
% main domestics	*45.4*	*19.4*	*35.2*	
MNI	**7**	**3**	**5**	**15**
% MNI	*46.7*	*20.0*	*33.3*	

Table 4.4 Minimum number of elements (MNE) and overall minimum number of individuals (MNI) of the main domestic mammals, 11th–13th century

Element	*Cattle*	*Sheep*	*Pig*	*Total*
Horn core	4	3	-	7
Skull	3	1	6	10
Mandible	11	18	20	49
Atlas	2	6	2	10
Axis	2	2	1	5
Scapula	9	11	11	31
Humerus	9	20	16	45
Radius	7	38	9	54
Ulna	10	9	15	34
Pelvis	11	15	8	34
Sacrum	0	0	0	0
Femur	7	8	11	26
Tibia	15	35	17	67
Patella	1	0	1	2
Astragalus	4	5	3	12
Calcaneus	12	7	8	27
Tarsals	3	0	4	7
Carpals	4	0	0	4
Metacarpal	7	11	11	29
Metatarsal	5	18	14	37
Phalanx I	16	16	6	38
Phalanx II	12	1	1	14
Phalanx III	9	1	1	11
MNE total	**163**	**225**	**165**	**553**
% main domestics	*29.5*	*40.7*	*29.8*	
MNI	**9**	**28**	**11**	**48**
% MNI	*18.8*	*58.3*	*22.9*	

Table 4.5 Minimum number of elements (MNE) and overall minimum number of individuals (MNI) of the main domestic mammals, 13th–15th century

Element	*Cattle*	*Sheep*	*Pig*	*Total*
Horn core	1	1	-	2
Skull	1	2	4	7
Mandible	4	5	7	16
Atlas	2	3	1	6
Axis	0	3	0	3
Scapula	3	20	11	34
Humerus	2	20	11	33
Radius	4	28	9	41
Ulna	3	8	6	17
Pelvis	2	17	12	31
Sacrum	1	0	0	1
Femur	3	10	5	18
Tibia	4	16	5	25
Patella	0	0	0	0
Astragalus	2	5	3	10
Calcaneus	6	9	6	21
Tarsals	4	1	0	5
Carpals	3	0	0	3
Metacarpal	7	10	9	26
Metatarsal	6	11	2	19
Phalanx I	6	11	3	20
Phalanx II	10	2	1	13
Phalanx III	8	0	0	8
MNE total	**82**	**182**	**95**	**359**
% main domestics	*22.8*	*50.7*	*26.5*	
MNI	**5**	**15**	**10**	**30**
% MNI	*16.7*	*50.0*	*33.3*	

group but this is not supported by the MNI figures and can be linked with the high frequency of cattle in the 11th–13th century pre-Keep material. The MNI figures also indicate a greater contribution by pig in the later medieval phase.

Carcass representation and utilisation

The MNE representation of cattle, sheep and pig bones is given in Tables 4.3–4.5 for the 4th century, 11th–13th century and 13th–15th century groups respectively. The pattern of body parts present is broadly similar in each phase in that elements from all areas of the skeleton, cranial, trunk, limb and extremity regions, tend to occur in all the main species. The rarity of the small bones from the extremities, particularly in sheep and pig, may be attributed to the hand-retrieved nature of the assemblage.

Figure 4.4 compares the percentage-body-part representation for cattle in the three phases: the values are derived from the actual MNE for each part as a percentage of the expected MNE, based on the MNI, if whole carcasses were originally deposited on site. The 4th century graph shows a very low representation of metapodials suggesting either that some cattle were butchered elsewhere or that skins were removed with the feet attached and further processed elsewhere. The predominance of distal femur and the lack of such robust elements as distal humerus and distal tibia are unusual features of this assemblage, and may be linked to the butchery of cattle long bones, discussed below. In contrast, the graph of the 11–13th century cattle reflects a more typical pattern where survival bias acting on an assemblage containing all butchery stages results in a tendency for high frequency of robust and/or early-fusing bones. Once again, the metapodials are relatively under-represented, although, in the 13th–15th century graph this is reversed and the metapodials show the best survival rates. The contrast with distal tibia suggests that although all stages of carcass processing appear to be represented, this latest group contains a relatively high proportion of bones removed from the carcass early in the butchery process.

Figure 4.5 compares the body-part representation for sheep/goat between the three phases. The pattern for the 4th century group suggests, like the 11th–13th century cattle assemblage, an assemblage with complete sheep-carcasses acted on by preservational

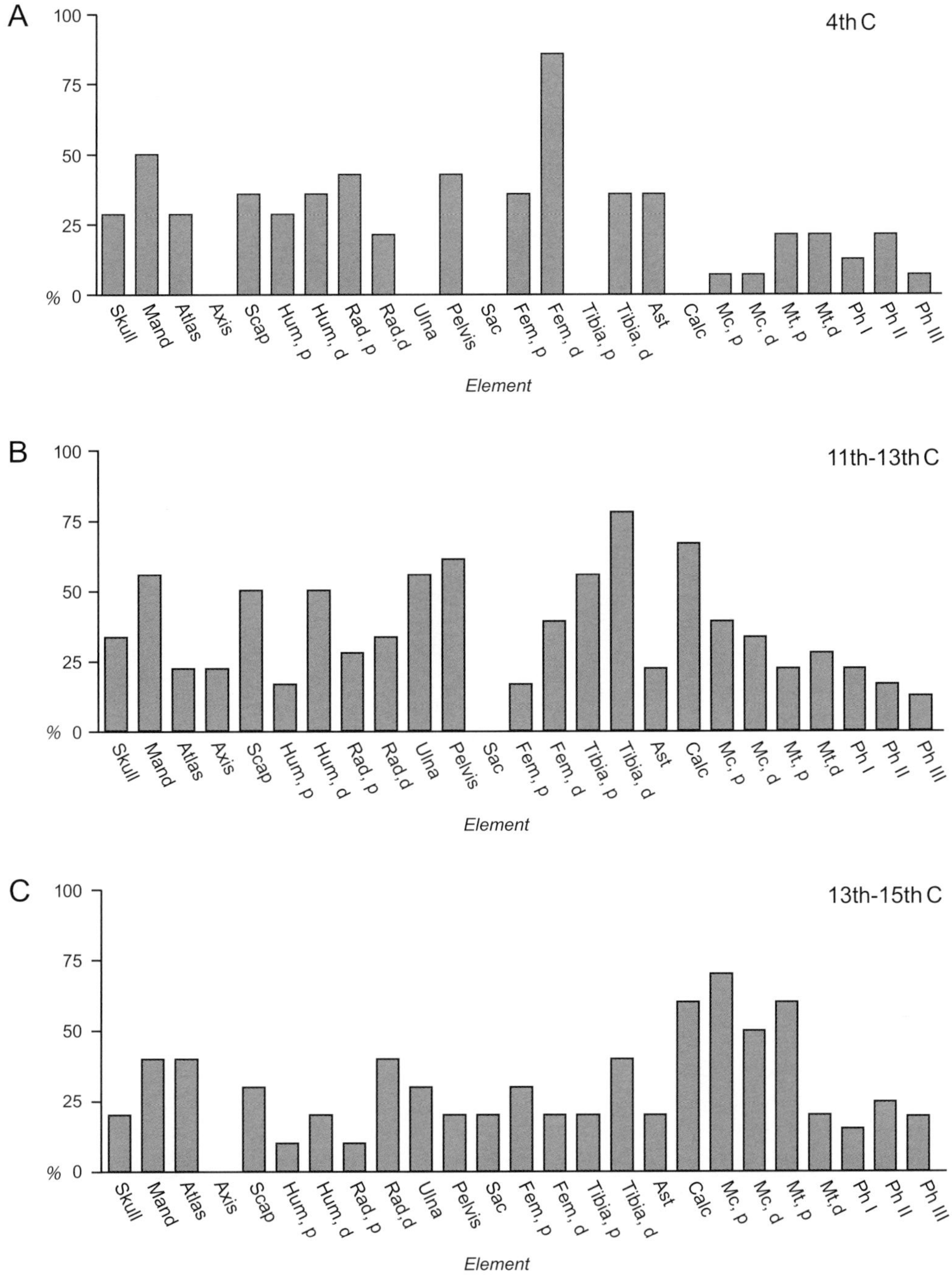

Figure 4.4 Body part representation (%): cattle

biases. The 11th–13th century group shows a lower contribution by primary-butchery waste elements, major limb bones are predominant. The 13th–15th century group similarly contains relatively little primary butchery waste, suggesting that (as may also have been the case in the 11th–13th century) some meat was imported as dressed carcasses or sides. The meaty axial bones are present in higher numbers, but the imbalance in frequency between bones from the front and back limbs suggests the selection of forequarter joints.

Figure 4.6 examines the body part representation in the pig assemblage. The 4th and 11th–13th century groups show similar patterns: the high occurrence of cranial parts and high meat-yielding elements suggesting that complete carcasses were present. The low representation of extremity bones is probably due to survival and retrieval biases. The 13th–15th century material shows a much lower representation of cranial bones than the earlier two groups and bears a distinct resemblance to the contemporary sheep assemblage, suggesting that here too there was some

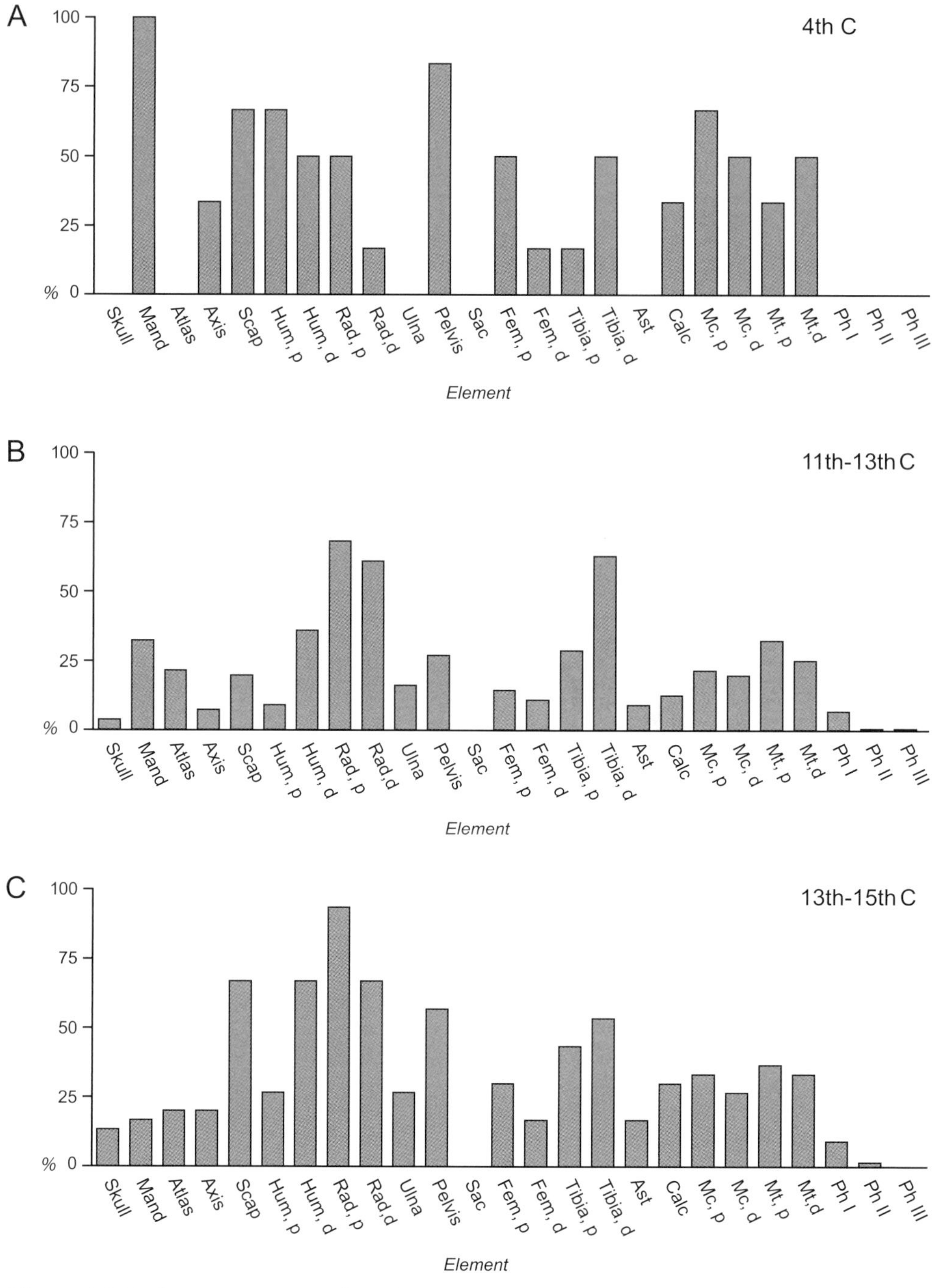

Figure 4.5 Body part representation (%): sheep/goat

importing to the site of joints of pork or bacon, and in particular of forequarter joints.

The distribution of butchery marks by species and phase is shown in Table 4.6. Most of the butchery evidence consists of chop marks although there is a decrease in their frequency between the Romano-British and medieval groups. The high frequency of chop marks in the assemblage as a whole is largely due to their preponderance in the cattle material which shows a greater incidence of butchered bone than either sheep or pig in the Romano-British and earlier medieval group although, surprisingly, not in the later medieval group. The latter may correlate with the body part evidence for the 13th–15th century group, which suggested that, unlike the cattle, a greater proportion of mutton and pork or bacon was imported to the site as joints in this phase.

Cattle

The Romano-British, cattle-butchery pattern mainly shows evidence of carcass division or later processing stages: only one bone, a phalanx I with a knife mark, indicates skinning. The scarcity of skinning evidence is consistent with the interpretation of body-part

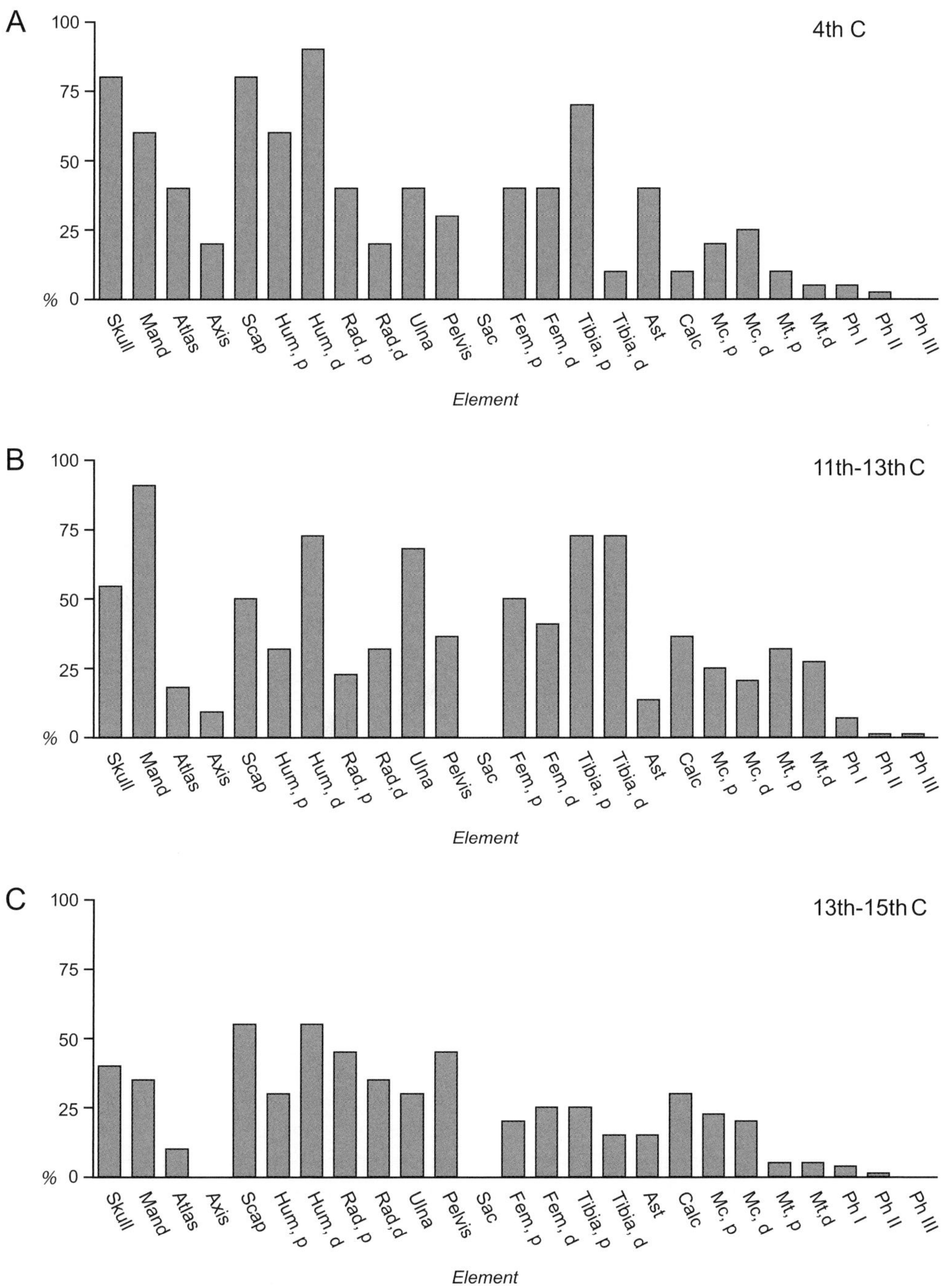

Figure 4.6 Body part representation (%): pig

frequency for this phase. The evidence of disarticulation and jointing, for example, distal humeri with chops around articulation, a femur chopped through the head, a mandible with chops at the hinge etc., suggests butchery was concentrated at major joints. Some butchered bones, such as femora, are only small fragments (not more than 25% complete), a pattern characteristic of the intensive carcass-processing practised in Britain and elsewhere at some urban and fortified sites in the Empire. Many of the butchered cattle-sized vertebrae are split longitudinally, laterally or medially to the sagittal; others show transverse chop marks. Where direction can be determined they are always chopped from the ventral surface, suggesting beef carcasses were split open from the belly, probably while lying on the ground.

The cattle-butchery pattern in the earlier medieval group again shows little evidence of skinning: a single phalanx I with transverse knife-marks. Carcass division is still concentrated around the major joints, particularly the elbow and hip, although the tibia, radius and metacarpal also show evidence of midshaft butchery. One axis, chopped at the cranial end,

Table 4.6 Distribution (%) of butchery marks by species

	Chopped	*Cut*	*Both*	*Sawn*	*Total (n)*	*% butchered of total*
4th century						
Horse	0	100	0	0	1	50
Cattle	92.7	2.4	4.9	0.0	41	24.8
Sheep	55.6	44.4	0.0	0.0	9	15
Pig	85.7	9.5	4.8	0.0	21	14.8
Red deer	33.3	33.3	0.0	33.3	3	18.8
Wild boar	100	0	0	0	1	25.0
Bird	0	100	0	0	3	12.0
Cattle-sized	100	0	0	0	24	25.5
Sheep-sized	71.4	28.6	0.0	0.0	7	13.5
Sub-total	**83.6**	**12.7**	**2.7**	**0.9**	**110**	
11th–13th century						
Cattle	83.3	13.9	0	2.8	36	12.4
Sheep	59.3	40.7	0	0	27	7.4
Pig	54.8	45.2	0	0	31	9.1
Red deer	50.0	50.0	0	0	2	66.7
Roe deer	100.0	0.0	0	0	1	20.0
Hare	100.0	0.0	0	0	1	16.7
Bird	16.7	83.3	0	0	12	9.9
Cattle-sized	90.6	9.4	0	0	32	16.8
Sheep-sized	81.6	18.4	0	0	38	15.1
Sub-total	**68.3**	**31.0**	**0.0**	**0.7**	**142**	
13th–15th century						
Cattle	93.3	6.7	0.0	0.0	15	11.3
Sheep	51.3	48.7	0.0	0.0	39	14.8
Pig	56.0	44.0	0.0	0.0	25	14.0
Bird	27.3	72.7	0.0	0.0	11	9.0
Cattle-sized	90.0	10.0	0.0	0.0	20	32.8
Sheep-sized	80.5	17.1	2.4	0.0	41	22.4
Sub-total	**67.5**	**31.8**	**0.7**	**0.0**	**151**	

indicates the removal of the head from the rest of the body. Butchery on the vertebrae seems to follow the same pattern as in the 4th century. Evidence for other carcass-processing activities comprises two horn cores, one sawn, the other chopped, indicating removal of the horn for working.

Since there are fewer butchered cattle bones in the 13th–15th century group than in the earlier two groups the pattern presented is much sketchier. There is no skinning evidence but an occipital bone bears a chop mark indicative of removal of the head and a horn core has been chopped through towards the tip to remove the horn sheath. Other marks evidence the division of the carcass, mainly at the major joints but there is one tibia which has been chopped through midshaft. The cattle-size vertebrae indicate a change in butchery at this time: evidence for midline splitting of the carcass occurs for the first time, out of eight vertebrae showing longitudinal splitting, five are split along the sagittal plane rather than laterally or medially to it. This pattern generally correlates with butchery of a suspended carcass and its appearance at this site is relatively late: at Flaxengate, for example, it appears in the 10th century (O'Connor 1982) and becomes increasingly common from the mid-11th century.

Sheep

There are too few butchered sheep bones from the 4th century material for a clear pattern to emerge. However, there is evidence of removal of the head in a transversely chopped axis and of further disarticulation in a pelvis with chop marks around the acetabulum.

The evidence from the 11th–13th-century sheep material is greater. There is possible evidence for the method of slaughter in an axis with transverse cut marks on the ventral surface. Subsequent preliminary stages of carcass processing are only represented by transverse knife cuts indicative of skinning on four metapodials. Long bone ends display cuts from disarticulation at the joints and a pelvis with a vertical chop on the medial surface of the ilium probably indicates subdivision of the trunk into smaller units. Two radii display knife marks consistent with filleting. Cranial fragments show several types of butchery.

Three skulls were split open paramedially: this could have occurred when a carcass was split into sides but the presence of a split atlas and an unsplit axis suggests that heads were removed from the body at an early stage of butchery with the atlas attached then split at a later stage to extract the brain. Two cases of chop marks by mandibular hinges suggest removal of the jaw, possibly to facilitate removal of the tongue. There is one example of horn removal in a male horn core which has been chopped through.

The 13th–15th century sheep bones include a higher number of bones from the post-cranial skeleton than the earlier material. The method of slaughter is suggested by an atlas and an axis with transverse ventral cuts as in the 11th–13th century specimen. Skinning techniques removed either the whole foot with the skin, indicated by a metacarpal with cuts around the proximal articulation, or took just the toes, indicated by a phalanx I with cut marks. Consistent with the paucity of primary butchery waste, the only instance of butchery on cranial material was a horn core chopped down the posterior which may indicate chopping open of the skull. Carcass disjointing seems to have used more 'high impact' techniques than in the 11th–13th century, suggested by chopping through the distal articulations of humerus and radius, a femur chopped below the head and a scapula chopped through transversely near the glenoid articulation. Other evidence of carcass subdivision is in a few ilia with vertical chop marks on the medial surface. Knife marks on several scapulae and a scrape along a radius shaft indicate filleting. One proximal metacarpal split lengthways probably indicates marrow extraction.

Pig

Skinning evidence is absent in the pig material from the 4th century deposits, which is perhaps unsurprising given the low frequency of extremity bones in this phase. Four mandibles which were split lengthways through the mandibular symphysis could be evidence of splitting the carcass into sides or, as in the sheep, of splitting the skull at a later stage of butchery to extract the brain. The butchery marks and fragmentation patterns of the atlas and axis present do not decide the issue. Disarticulation is evidenced by chop marks at major limb joints such as the elbow and shoulder. A humerus, chopped and broken open midshaft, indicates marrow extraction.

In the 11th–13th-century pig material skinning evidence is present in the form of vertical knife cuts on the buccal surface of the mandible and possibly in the transverse cut marks around the shaft of a humerus and an ulna. As in the earlier group, four mandibles, chopped lengthways through the symphysis, suggest the splitting of the carcass into sides. However, in this group there is an unsplit axis which is chopped anteriorly, suggesting that, as with the contemporary sheep, splitting of heads probably occurred after their removal from the body in order to extract the brain. Again, dismemberment is evidenced at the major limb joints, for example a femur chopped through below the head is mirrored by chopping into the acetabula of two pelves, and subdivision of the trunk into smaller units is shown by the vertical cut on the medial surface of an ilium. Filleting marks are present too, on the shafts of the major long bones.

In the 13th–15th century material transverse cuts on two pig astragali possibly represent removal of the foot perhaps with the skin. Chop marks into the caudal surface of an atlas may reflect removal of the head while two mandibles chopped through the symphysis indicate the subsequent splitting-open of the skull. Filleting cuts are present on a humerus midshaft and stripping of meat from the skull is probably represented by chop marks parallel to the tooth row on a mandible and a maxilla and cuts on the temporal process of a zygomatic bone.

Vertebra fragments of sheep or pig from the 4th century indicate that the carcasses of the smaller stock were split paramedially, as practised with the cattle. In contrast, in the 11th–13th century two fifths of the vertebrae were split in the sagittal plane while the remainder were split paramedially. This differs from the pattern in cattle but may just indicate chopping for stews or soups. Transversely chopped vertebrae indicate this or dividing the carcass into smaller joints. Chopping is still, as in cattle, from the ventral surface. Ribs display chop marks at or through the articulation with the spine. In the 13th–15th century material sagittally split vertebrae are less common, only two occur while nine are split paramedially. The vertebrae are also chopped through transversely and in the horizontal plane. A sheep lumbar-vertebra with ventral paramedial chop marks on both transverse processes is probably evidence of removal of ribs from the spine as are several ribs chopped through the head. One, pig lumbar-vertebra has been chopped through paramedially from the dorsal surface, removing the left transverse process. This departure from the usual pattern of chopping through from the ventral surface, splitting the animal from its belly, may be related to the probable change, observed in the cattle vertebrae, to suspending carcasses for butchery.

Ageing and sexing

Cattle

The epiphyseal fusion data for cattle are shown in Table 4.7. In the 4th century there is no evidence for the deaths of very young calves, and subsequently, although there is a small number of bones from animals killed in the second year, it appears that the major kill-off was between two and three years, with over 40% of bones in this age group being unfused.

Table 4.7 Age at death of cattle from bone fusion

4th century

Age at Fusion	*Element*	*Fused*	*Unfused*	*Total*		*% UF*
7-10 months	Scapula	5	0	5		
"	Pelvis	6	0	6	< 1 yr	0
12-15 months	Radius, p	7	0	7		
15-18 months	Phalanx II	11	0	11		
15-20 months	Humerus, d *	6	1	7		
20-24 months	Phalanx I	6	0	6	< 2 yr	3.2
24-30 months	Tibia, d	3	1	4		
"	Metapodial, d	1	2	3	< 3 yr	42.9
36-42 months	Femur, p	2	2	4		
42 months	Femur, d	3	2	5		
42-48 months	Humerus, p	2	0	2		
"	Radius, d	0	3	3		
"	Tibia, p	2	1	3	< 4 yr	47.1
Total		**54**	**12**	**66**		

11th–13th century

Age at Fusion	*Element*	*Fused*	*Unfused*	*Total*		*% UF*
7-10 months	Scapula	9	0	9		
"	Pelvis	13	0	13	< 1 yr	0
12-15 months	Radius, p	5	0	5		
15-18 months	Phalanx II	12	0	12		
15-20 months	Humerus, d	3	0	3		
20-24 months	Phalanx I	15	1	16	< 2 yr	2.8
24-30 months	Tibia, d	10	3	13		
"	Metapodial, d	7	1	8		
36 months	Calcaneus	4	4	8	< 3 yr	27.6
36-42 months	Femur, p	2	0	2		
42 months	Femur, d	5	1	6		
42-48 months	Radius, d	3	2	5		
"	Ulna, p	0	3	3		
"	Tibia, p	2	3	5	< 4 yr	42.9
Total		**90**	**18**	**108**		

13th–15th century

Age at Fusion	*Element*	*Fused*	*Unfused*	*Total*		*% UF*
7-10 months	Scapula	3	0	3		
"	Pelvis	2	0	2	< 1 yr	0
12-15 months	Radius, p	1	0	1		
15-18 months	Phalanx II	9	1	10		
15-20 months	Humerus, d	1	0	1		
20-24 months	Phalanx I	6	0	6	< 2 yr	5.6
24-30 months	Tibia, d	2	1	3		
"	Metapodial, d	5	2	7		
36 months	Calcaneus	3	0	3	< 3 yr	23.1
36-42 months	Femur, p	1	0	1		
42-48 months	Radius, d	3	1	4		
"	Tibia, p	1	1	2	< 4 yr	28.6
Total		**37**	**6**	**43**		

* includes 1 neonate

Table 4.8 Tooth wear stages of cattle, sheep/goats and pig, following O'Connor (1988). N: neonatal; J: juvenile; I: immature; S: subadult; A: adult; E: elderly

		N	*J*	*I*	*S*	*A*	*E*	*Total*
Cattle	4th C	1	0	0	0	3	2	6
	11th–13th C	0	0	0	2	5	0	7
	13th–15th C	0	0	0	0	3	1	5
	Total	**1**	**0**	**0**	**2**	**11**	**3**	**18**
Sheep	4th C	0	0	0	3	3	0	6
	11th–13th C	0	0	0	0	13	3	18
	13th–15th C	0	0	0	0	5	0	5
	Total	**0**	**0**	**0**	**3**	**21**	**3**	**29**
Pig	4th C	0	0	1	0	2	0	5
	11th–13th C	0	0	3	11	6	0	21
	13th–15th C	0	0	2	2	4	0	8
	Total	**0**	**0**	**6**	**12**	**12**	**0**	**34**

Table 4.9 Main domestic animals: summary of sexed material

Species	*Date*	*Male*	*Female*	*Element*
Cattle	4th C	0	2	pelvis
	11th–13th C	0	2	pelvis
	13th–15th C	0	1	pelvis
Sheep	4th C	1	0	pelvis
	11th–13th C	1	2	pelvis
	"	1	0	atlas
	"	1	0	horn core
	13th–15th C	5	7	pelvis
Pig	4th C	1	1	mandible
		1	0	mandibular canine
	11th–13th C	3	7	mandible
		6	2	mandibular canine
		0	4	maxilla
		0	1	maxillary canine
	13th–15th C	3	2	mandible
		3	0	mandibular canine
		1	0	maxilla

This suggests prime beef animals were being supplied to the Roman fort. However, over half the bones in the group fusing between three and four are fused, suggesting a high proportion of skeletally-mature cattle were also supplied. The dental data confirm the fusion evidence, and one mandible of a neonatal calf is the only evidence of young animals at the fort. The age at death of the cattle – with predominantly older animals – resembles that at contemporary Portchester.

The 11th–13th pattern is similar in the proportions surviving their first two years and surviving beyond four years, but in this period the supply of younger beasts was spread over the third and fourth years. In the 13th–15th century material there is still little evidence for animals killed at less than two years of age and none in their first year. The main juvenile kill-off was again in the third year but a much higher proportion of bones than in the earlier groups came from animals which survived beyond skeletal maturity. There are too few mandibles for the tooth-wear data to provide a detailed picture, although those which are available (Table 4.8) are consistent in each phase with the pattern suggested by the epiphyseal fusion.

As Table 4.9 shows, the few cattle pelves which could be sexed are all from females.

Sheep

The epiphyseal fusion data for sheep is shown in Table 4.10. The few ageable bones from the 4th century suggest that no animals were killed in their first year of life and that some animals had survived into adulthood. The mandibles suggest a higher proportion of juveniles than do the bones, but are also few in number.

The 11th–13th century fusion data show a small proportion of deaths in the first year of life, including a radius from a neonate. There is a larger kill-off in the second year and another by the end of 42 months, however, a large proportion of animals still survived beyond this point: 47% of bones fusing between two and three and a half years are fused. This evidence is supported by the dental data which show an older profile than in the 4th century. The 13th–15th pattern is very similar to the earlier medieval group. Although it shows a slightly higher proportion of bones from animals surviving two years and slightly more dying by three and a half years, there is still the high number of bones from animals surviving into adulthood: 45% of the latest-fusing bones.

There is more sexable sheep material than cattle but this is mainly from the 13th–15th century group which displays an unusually large proportion of males. This almost certainly relates to the importance of the medieval wool industry which made it worthwhile to keep castrated males into adulthood, hence the large proportion of bones from adult animals.

Pig

The fusion data for the 4th century pigs, while scarce (Table 4.11), indicate a small kill-off of animals in their first year, then a substantial kill-off in the second year and then a small but still substantial kill-off between two and three and a half years, with 25% of bones in this last group coming from animals which survived into adulthood. The age profile is quite different for the 11th–13th century pigs: there is only a slightly higher kill-off in the first year but most (84%) of the bones fusing between one and two years of age are unfused and there is no evidence for pigs

Table 4.10 Age at death of sheep and goats from bone fusion. UF = unfused (%)

4th century

Age at Fusion	*Element*	*Fused*	*Unfused*	*Total*		*% UF*
3-4 months	Humerus, d			0		
"	Radius, p			0		
5 months	Scapula	1		1		
"	Pelvis	5		5		
5-7 months	Phalanx II			0		
7-10 months	Phalanx I			0	< 1 yr	0
15-20 months	Tibia, d	2		2		
20-24 months	Metapodial, d		1	1	< 2 yr	33.3
36 months	Calcaneus	1	1	2	< 3 yr	50.0
36-42 months	Femur, p	1	2	3		
42 months	Humerus, p			0		
"	Radius, d			0		
"	Ulna, p			0		
	Femur, d			0		
"	Tibia, p			0	< 4 yr	66.7
Total		**10**	**4**	**14**		

11th–13th century

Age at Fusion	*Element*	*Fused*	*Unfused*	*Total*		*% UF*
3-4 months	Humerus, d	12	0	12		
"	Radius, p *	10	1	11		
5 months	Scapula	4	1	5		
"	Pelvis	11	2	13		
7-10 months	Phalanx I	15	0	15	< 1 yr	7.1
15-20 months	Tibia, d	14	4	18		
20-24 months	Metapodial, d	9	3	12	< 2 yr	23.3
36 months	Calcaneus	2	3	5	< 3 yr	60.0
36-42 months	Femur, p	2	1	3		
42 months	Humerus, p	1	0	1		
"	Radius, d *	4	3	7		
"	Ulna, p	1	3	4		
	Femur, d	1	1	2		
"	Tibia, p	5	1	6	< 4 yr	39.1
					< 3.5	42.9
Total		**91**	**23**	**114**		

13th–15th century

Age at Fusion	*Element*	*Fused*	*Unfused*	*Total*		*% UF*
3-4 months	Humerus, d	11	3	14		
"	Radius, p	14	2	16		
5 months	Scapula	15	0	15		
"	Pelvis	14	0	14		
5-7 months	Phalanx II	2	0	2		
7-10 months	Phalanx I	10	0	10	< 1 yr	7.0
15-20 months	Tibia, d	7	0	7		
20-24 months	Metapodial, d	5	2	7	< 2 yr	14.3
36 months	Calcaneus	5	2	7	< 3 yr	28.6
36-42 months	Femur, p	2	4	6		
42 months	Humerus, p	0	2	2		
"	Radius, d	5	4	9		
"	Ulna, p *	1	1	2		
	Femur, d	0	1	1		
"	Tibia, p	0	2	2	< 4 yr	63.6
Total		**91**	**23**	**114**		

Table 4.11 Age at death of pigs from bone fusion. UF = unfused (%)

4th century

Age at Fusion	*Element*	*Fused*	*Unfused*	*Total*		*%UF*
12 months	Scapula	7	0	7		
"	Humerus, d	5	0	5		
"	Radius, p	2	1	3		
"	Pelvis	1	0	1		
"	Phalanx II	1	0	1	< 1 yr	5.9
24 months	Metapodial, d	4	5	9		
"	Phalanx I	1	1	2	< 2 yr	54.5
36-42 months	Femur, p	0	2	2		
42 months	Radius, d	0	1	1		
"	Femur, d	1	0	1	< 4 yr	75.0
Total		**22**	**10**	**32**		

11th–13th century

Age at Fusion	*Element*	*Fused*	*Unfused*	*Total*		*% UF*
12 months	Scapula	4	1	5		
"	Humerus, d	9	2	11		
"	Radius, p	2		2		
"	Pelvis	4	0	4		
"	Phalanx II	1		1	< 1 yr	13.0
24 months	Tibia, d	1	6	7		
"	Metapodial, d	4	27	31		
"	Phalanx I	2	4	6	< 2 yr	84.1
24-30 months	Calcaneus		7	7	< 3 yr	100.0
36-42 months	Ulna, p		8	8		
"	Femur, p		6	6		
42 months	Humerus, p		1	1		
"	Radius, d		3	3		
"	Femur, d		5	5	< 4 yr	100.0
Total		**27**	**70**	**97**		

13th–15th century

Age at Fusion	*Element*	*Fused*	*Unfused*	*Total*		*% UF*
12 months	Scapula	4	0	4		
"	Humerus, d	2	1	3		
"	Radius, p	3	2	5		
"	Pelvis	5	4	9		
"	Phalanx II	1	0	1	< 1 yr	32
24 months	Tibia, d	0	3	3		
"	Metapodial, d	0	9	9		
"	Phalanx I	1	2	3	< 2 yr	93
24-30 months	Calcaneus	0	4	4	< 3 yr	100
36-42 months	Ulna, p	1	2	3		
"	Femur, p	0	2	2		
42 months	Radius, d	0	3	3		
"	Femur, d	0	2	2		
"	Tibia, p	0	1	1	< 4 yr	91
Total		**17**	**35**	**52**		

Table 4.12 Measurements of horse and cattle, after Levine (1982) and Driesch (1976)

Horse							
M1/M2		*Length*	*Crown height*	*Breadth*			
	4th C	24.2	28.2	25.2			
Cattle							
Horn core		*Min diam*	*Max diam*	*Length*			
	11th–13th C	45.6	63.7	176			
	"	46.5					
Scapula		*GLP*	*BG*	*LG*	*SLC*		
	4th C	63	40.6	43.4			
	"	56.5	40.6				
	"	57.4					
	11th–13th C	55.2	38.6	46.6	39.9		
	"	55.6	37.4	46.8	40.7		
	"	62.6	44.7	55.7			
	"	67.5	45.3	53			
	"		43	51			
Humerus		*BT*	*HT*				
	4th C	65.10	40.70				
Radius		*BFp*					
	4th C	65.6					
	"	72.7					
	11th–13th C	65.6					
	"	59.7					
Tibia		*Dd*	*Bd*				
	4th C	42.6	55.6				
	11th–13th C	44.0	57.1				
	"	51.3	66.2				
	13th–15th C	36.2	49.8				
Metacarpal		*GL*	*Dp*	*Bp*	*SD*	*Dd*	*Bd*
	11th–13th C	177.8	32.2	46.9	27.6	27.4	55.8
	"	177.2			28.1	28.9	50.9
	"		31.6	51.7			
	13th–15th C	179	33.6	55.5	31.6	32.1	56.8
	"	176.2	29.8	48.2	23.8	26.9	49.6
	"		30.3	48.8			
	"					27.8	49.5
Metatarsal		*Bp*					
	13th–15th C	40.2					
Calcaneus		*GL*					
	11th–13th C	147.9					
	"	110.8					
	"	118.2					
	13th–15th C	110.7					
	"	114.5					

Table 4.13 Measurements of sheep / goat, after Driesch (1976)

Scapula	*GLP*	*BG*	*LG*	*SLC*
4th C	30.1	18.8	24.2	19.1
11th–13th C	30.2	18.0	24.4	19.0
"	33.3		25.9	19.8
"		19.1		18.3
"		17.5	17.3	
"				19.6
13th–15th C	29.9	19.2	23.7	17.7
"	35.4	24.1	28.1	21.5
"	31.2	19.0		19.2
"	31.6	18.8	24.9	
"	29.3		22.8	
"		17.6		15.8
"				19.3
"				18.0

Humerus	*Bd*	*BT*	*HT*	
11th–13th C	28.8	26.5	18.0	
"	32.0	29.4	17.5	
"	30.2	27.7	17.9	
"	32.1	27.4	17.5	penning elbow
"			18.9	
13th–15th C	28.6	27.1	17.7	
"	31.5	26.9	18.6	
"	28.6	25.1	17.3	
"	28.3	25.6	16.6	
"	31.4	27.5	18.2	
"		27.9	17.9	
"		26.2		

Radius	*BFp*	*Bd*	*BFd*
11th–13th C	26.9		
"	24.9		
"	25.1		
"	27.7		
"	27		
"		27	21.9
"			22.3
13th–15th C	27.3		
"	27.1		
"	28.1		
"	25.9		
"	27.4		
"	25.6		
"	26.4		
"	28.2		
"		27.4	23.4
"		28.2	23.5
"		26.5	22.9
"		26.4	24.3
"		25	22.2

Tibia	**Withers**	*Dd*	*Bd*
4th C		19.4	24.4
"		20.6	25.5
11th–13th C		19.0	23.6
"		18.2	24.8
"		20.7	25.4
"		18.8	24.0
"		18.3	24.7
"		19.3	24.2
"		19.9	25.5
"		20.1	23.7
"		20.9	25.4
"		19.9	25.9
"		20.9	26.2
"			22.5
13th–15th C		20.5	24.6
"		18.9	
"		19.0	23.8
"		17.9	21.4
"		17.4	22.7

Metacarpal		*GL*	*Dp*	*Bp*	*SD*	*Dd*	*Bd*
4th C				25.1			
11th–13th C			14.9	21.3			
"			14.4	19.6			
"			14.1	20.2			
"			15.9	22.0			
"					15.1	25.9	
"					14.7	22.8	
13th–15th C	**581**	118.9	14.9	21.7	12.5	15.7	
"			16.1	22.1			
"			16.1	22.0			
"			16.7	22.9			
"			15.1	20.8			

Metatarsal		*GL*	*Dp*	*Bp*	*SD*	*Dd*	*Bd*
11th–13th C	**581**	128	17.6	18.5	10.7	14.6	21.9
"	**587**	129.2	18.5	19.4	10.4	15.5	23.3
"			17.4	18.5			
"			18.8	19.8			
"			19.7	19.8			
"			18.9	18.9			
"			19.8	20.1			
"			20.2	19.5			
"						14.5	22.1
13th–15th C			19.0	18.4			
"			19.5	19.1			
"			18.3	18.2			
"			18.9	19.2			
"			19.6	20.0			
"						16.8	24.8
"						15.4	23.9
"						15.2	23.2

Calcaneus		*GL*
13th–15th C	**580**	50.9
"	**570**	50.0

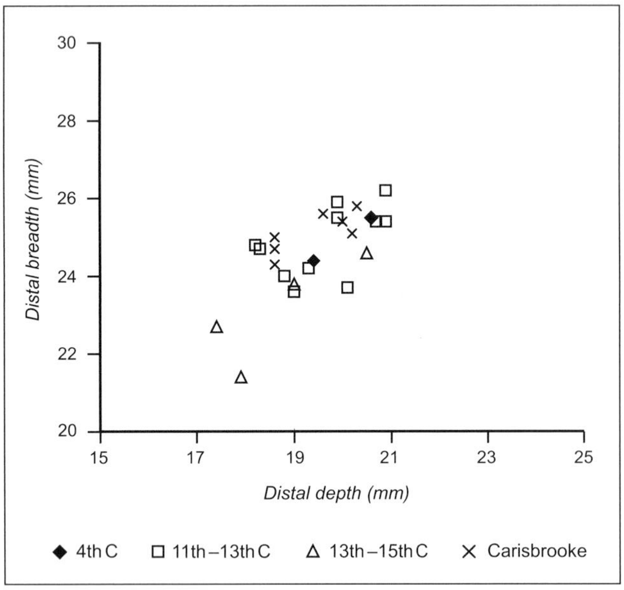

Figure 4.7 Sheep/goat tibia: distal depth (Dd) x distal breadth (BD) (mm)

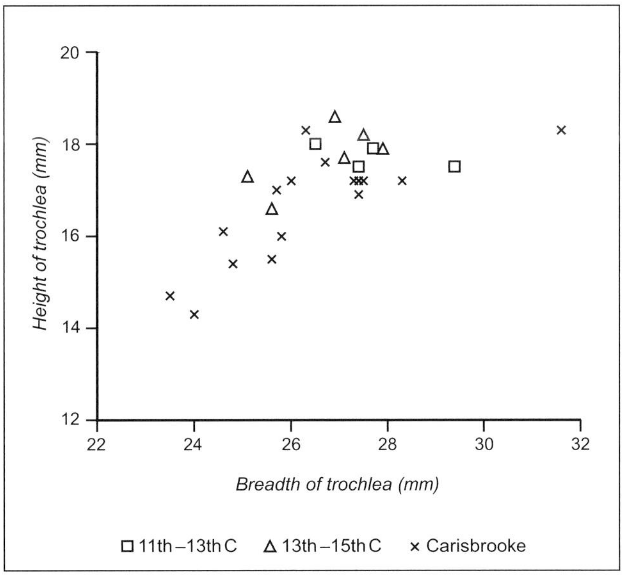

Figure 4.8 Sheep/goat humerus: breadth of distal trochlea (BT) x height of trochlea (HT) (mm)

older than three years. The 13th–15th century pigs show a similar pattern, although there is an even higher representation of animals killed in their first two years and one bone from an animal older than three years. The evidence for animals from a restricted age-range, containing no very young juveniles (tooth wear stages N and I) and no skeletally adult animals suggests that pigs were not kept at Pevensey Castle itself in either of the medieval phases.

The pig assemblage supplied the largest number of elements which could be sexed, a corollary of the fact that sex determination in this species was made on the durable teeth and mandibles. The 11th–13th century material suggests a preponderance of females. Few of the sexable mandible could be aged, but of five specimens where this was possible, males are represented by an immature and an adult while the females are represented by three sub-adult mandibles. The relatively young age of the females, sub-adult rather than adult, suggests a relatively intensive culling-regime.

Analysis of size

Cattle bones produced relatively few measurements (Table 4.12), insufficient for detailed analysis. However, the pattern, noted by Grant (1977) in the Portchester Castle assemblage, of size decrease between the Romano-British and medieval cattle, is not confirmed here. Four metacarpals yielded withers height estimates of 1.085 m and 1.089 m for the 11th–13th century group and 1.079 m and 1.096 m for the later group. Although the size of the distal tibia is comparable with that from contemporary assemblages such as Carisbrooke (Smith 1994) and Portchester, other bones, for example radius and scapula, appear to have been from relatively smaller animals.

The sheep bones yielded a larger suite of measurements (Table 4.13). The scattergram of sheep tibia in Figure 4.7 suggests firstly, that no change in size occurred between the Romano-British and medieval phases; secondly, that Carisbrooke sheep and 11th–13th century sheep from Pevensey were comparable and, furthermore, hints at a size decrease between this earlier medieval group and the later 13th–15th century group. This possible distinction in size between the earlier and later medieval groups can also be seen in the graph of sheep, distal-humerus measurements (Figure 4.8). However, for this element the larger sample from Carisbrooke overlaps both ranges from Pevensey suggesting that the smaller size of the sample from Pevensey may be showing a spurious pattern.

The measurements on the distal humerus of pig (Table 4.14 and Fig. 4.9) suggest a wider size range in the medieval group compared with the Romano-British group, but again this may be an artefact of the sample size.

Pathology

Few examples of pathological material were observed and, apart from the dog bones from the Romano-British phase described below, almost all are medieval. Specimens exhibiting abnormal developmental traits include a cattle mandible (11th–13th century) with a retained dP4 and both the M1 and M2 lacking the bovine pillar and a sheep mandible (13th–15th century) lacking the P2. This

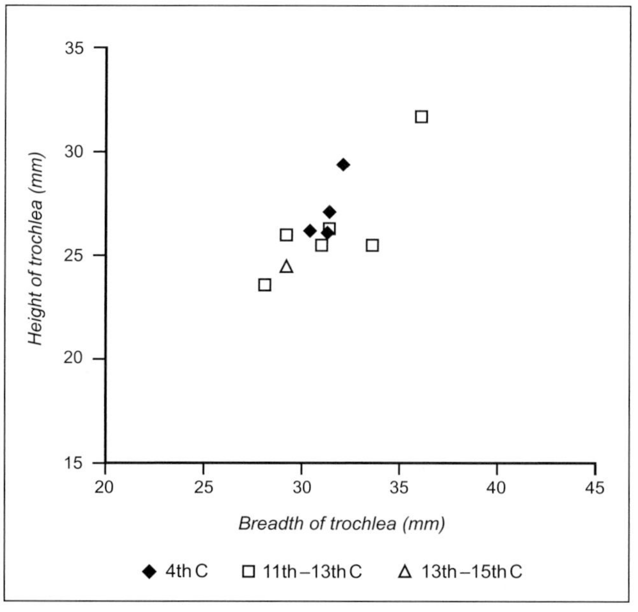

Figure 4.9 Pig humerus: breadth of distal trochlea (BT) x height of trochlea (HT) (mm)

sheep mandible is one of ten in the assemblage which display the congenital presence of an accessory buccal foramen below the P2 or P3. The trait is present in material from all phases, but is greater in frequency in the two medieval groups, occurring in one out of six 4th century mandibles but in seven out of 18 from the 11th–13th century and two out of five from the 13th–15th century. One of the few elements which might suggest poor husbandry is a pig maxilla showing rotation of the P4. This could indicate overcrowding in the jaw as the result of malnutrition in the animal as a juvenile.

Other domestic mammals

Domestic mammals other than cattle, sheep and pigs are poorly represented in all phases which, in particular the rarity of dog remains, is consistent with the source deposits being composed almost entirely of food waste.

Horse bones occur as small fragments with only few capable of measurement (Table 4.12). Of the few present in each period, only three provide any ageing information. An upper first or second molar from the 4th century came from an individual older than 14 years; a proximal fragment of radius from the 11th–13th century group is fused; and, from the 13th–15th century group, a very worn male canine from an animal probably between 8–13 years old. Although this is a very small sample, the maturity of the animals is what one would expect given the nature of the site. Only one bone exhibits evidence of butchery: a proximal humerus shaft fragment from the 4th century which shows a knife cut; the bone also exhibits gnaw marks. The cuts could represent filleting of the meat. Horse flesh was avoided by the Romans themselves, but continued to be eaten among some of the groups within the Empire and by the Saxons and other peoples on the fringes of the Empire employed to defend the borders of the later Empire.

Table 4.14 Measurements: pig (top) and wild boar (below), after Payne and Bull (1988) and Driesch (1976). Possible wild animals are also indicated

M_3		*Breadth*				
	13th–15th C	15.0				
Scapula		*GLP*	*BG*	*LG*	*SLC*	
	4th C	36.7	28.2	31.7	24.8	
	"	40.5	28.3	34.2		
	"	32.5	23.2	30.0		
	"				25.0	
	11th–13th C	37.2	26.8	31.9		wild?
	"	31.0	20.4	25.8		
Humerus		*Bd*	*BT*	*HT*	*HTC*	
	4th C	42.7		28.6		
	"	38.7	32.1	29.4	19.0	
	"	37.1	31.3	26.1	17.0	
	"	38.5	31.4	27.1	18.7	
	"	35.7	30.4	26.2	18.0	
	11th–13th C	43.8	36.1	31.7	20.2	
	"	38.0	31.4	26.3	19.3	
	"	36.6	31.0	25.5	17.6	
	"	34.0	29.2	26.0	17.8	
	"	34.1	28.1	23.6	15.6	
	"	40.3	33.6	25.5	19.2	
	"	41.6				
	"				16.5	
	13th–15th C	36.3	29.2	24.5	18.2	
Radius		*Bp*				
	4th C	28.1				
	11th–13th C	25.7				
	13th–15th C	24.6				
	"	28.6				
Tibia		*Dd*	*Bd*			
	11th–13th C	23.8	29.2			
Metacarpal		*GL*	*SD*	*Bd*		
	4th C	77.1	16.7	18.6		wild?
	11th–13th C	67.5		15.8		
Metatarsal		*GL*	*LeP*	*SD*	*Bd*	
	11th–13th C	77.4	76.2	12.4	15.4	
Wild boar						
Radius		*GL*	*Bp*	*Bd*	*BFd*	
	4th C	179.8	32.6	38.4	32.4	wild
Metacarpal		*GL*				
	13th–15th C	57.8	(Mc 5)			wild

All of the ageable dog remains, an ulna and lumbar vertebra from the 4th century and a mandible from the 11th–13th century, are from adult animals. Both the Romano-British specimens exhibit pathology: the vertebra shows lesions typical of spondylosis with both cranial and caudal articulation affected; the ulna, from a large animal, shows remodelling and extra bone growth around the proximal articulation (possibly from a sprain or dislocation which was allowed to heal), although the articular surface is itself little affected. The two 11th–13th century specimens (context 137) are mandibular fragments, body and ramus, which may belong to the same individual. The jaw is robust and has well-spaced teeth. The 13th–15th century specimens are both isolated teeth.

Cat, although absent from the Romano-British deposits, is the most common of the non-food domestic mammals. It is represented mostly by isolated limb bones in both medieval groups but other body parts present include a mandible (13th–15th century), a scapula (11th–13th century) and two, probably paired, pelves (11th–13th century). One of the four, ageable bones from the 11th–13th century are juvenile, as are four of the nine, ageable bones from the 13th–15th century; these bones are all from older juveniles rather than young kittens. None of these bones exhibit any sign of skinning or other butchery, unlike at some contemporary sites such as Launceston Castle (Albarella and Davis 1994), Faccombe Netherton (Sadler 1990) and Castle Mall (Albarella *et al.* 1997), where the evidence suggests cats were exploited for their skins.

Wild mammals

The bones of game animals occur in every period (Table 4.1). They are most frequent in the 4th century deposits, where they comprise 6% of the total for the mammals which were eaten. The percentages for the 11th–13th century and 13–15th century groups are 2% and 1%, respectively. The cervids are the most common and of these red deer (*Cervus elaphus*) is the predominant species due to the frequency of its bones in the Romano-British group. These are still relatively few but at least two individuals are represented, one a juvenile, and the elements present (radius, ulna, pelvis, lumbar vertebra, femur, tibia and metapodials), suggests that whole carcasses were brought to the site. Two other elements exhibited butchery evidence: the lumbar vertebra had cut marks on the ventral surface of the right transverse process and the pelvis had been chopped close to the acetabulum. The remains include three fragments of antler: one tine and two shed antler burrs, one of which retained enough of the beam to show that the brow tine had been sawn off.

In contrast to the 4th century, in the 11th–13th century red deer is less frequent than roe deer (*Capreolus capreolus*) and is represented by distal limb bones only: calcaneus, metatarsus and first phalanx, whereas the roe deer bones in the same phase include a scapula and radius in addition to three metapodial fragments. Although a small sample, this suggests that red and roe deer carcasses may have been treated differently by 11th–13th century hunters. The roe scapula exhibits a chop mark at the articulation. Both species are represented by a minimum of one individual. Fallow deer (*Dama dama*) is only definitely represented by two tibiae, both right, from the 11th–13th century group.

Wild boar (*Sus scrofa*) was distinguished from domestic pig by its greater size (Table 4.14). The species is rarely identified on historic period sites in southern England. It is represented here by a group of bones from the same 4th century context (52), which includes an articulating radius and ulna and an atlas from the same context which exhibits chop marks on both the dorsal and ventral surfaces, evidence of the dismemberment of the carcass. As well as a very large lateral metacarpal and axis, other fragments of pig from the medieval period were large enough to raise the possibility that wild boar as well as domestic pigs were present. Wild boar thrive, not only in woodlands but also in marshes such as would have been present in the Pevensey Levels before they were drained. These wild boar may well have been hunted from the Roman fort.

Hare (*Lepus europaeus*) is also present in all phases but is most common in the 11th–13th century group where its bones outnumber those of other game mammals. One bone from this group, a pelvis, shows evidence of butchery in the form of a slice across the blade of the ilium. The hare, unlike wild boar, favours dryer, more open country.

The remaining wild mammals in the assemblage are minimally represented. Fox (*Vulpes vulpes*) is represented by a single, isolated radius from the 11th–13th century group. The single rabbit (*Oryctolagus cuniculus*) bone from the 13th–15th century may be intrusive. Rat (*Rattus* sp.) is present as a single specimen in each phase. The presence of vermin within the Castle, may have been the impetus for keeping cats.

Birds

Method

The bird bones were identified by Adrienne Powell using the reference collection at the University of Southampton. Those bones of domestic fowl which can be distinguished from pheasant and guinea fowl (MacDonald 1992) were recorded as domestic fowl

Table 4.15 Identified bird bones (NISP)

	4th C	*11th–13th C*	*13th–15th C*	*Total*
Domestic fowl	5	11	16	32
cf. Domestic fowl	14	38	28	80
Goose, domestic	0	14	9	23
Goose, domestic/greylag	0	14	15	29
Mallard cf. domestic *Anas platyrhynchos*	0	9	6	15
Peafowl *Pavo cristatus*	0	0	1	1
Rock/Stock dove *Columba livia/oenas*	0	0	2	2
Subtotal domestic + domestic?	19	86	77	
Per cent domestic + domestic?	*86.4*	*92.5*	*89.5*	
Small goose	0	1	0	1
Teal *Anas crecca*	1	1	1	3
Crane *Grus grus*	0	3	2	5
Oystercatcher *Haematopus ostralegus*	0	0	1	1
Woodcock *S colopax rusticola*	1	0	0	1
Golden Plover *Pluvialis apricaria*	0	0	1	1
cf. Curlew ? *Numenius arquata*	1	1	0	2
Gull ? Lesser black-backed *Larus cf fuscus*	0	1	1	2
Buzzard *Buteo buteo*	0	0	1	1
Razorbill *Alca torda*	0	0	2	2
Subtotal wild	3	7	9	
Per cent wild	*13.6*	*7.5*	*10.5*	
Domestic fowl size	0	7	6	13
Goose size	0	1	1	2
Unidentified	3	20	29	52
Total	**25**	**121**	**122**	**268**

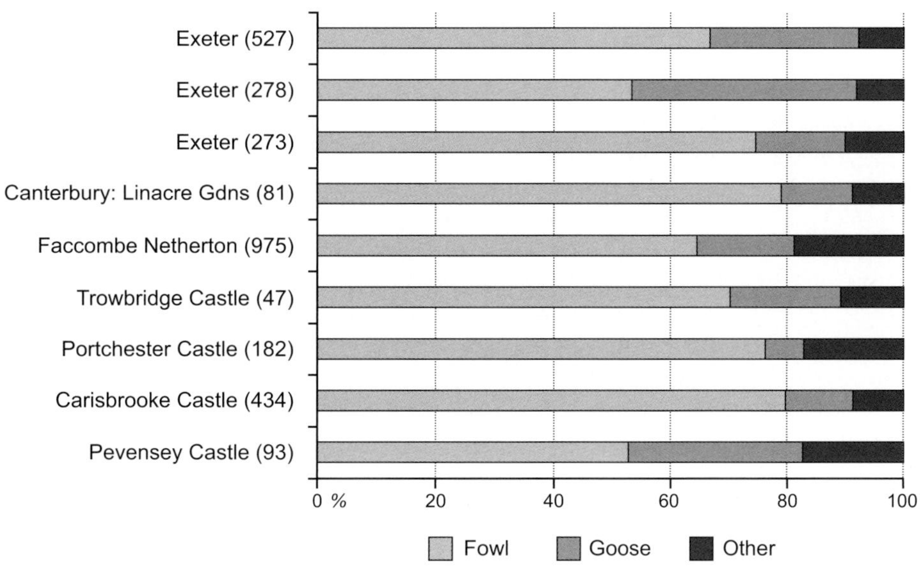

Figure 4.10 Relative abundance of domestic fowl, goose and other birds at Pevensey and other 11th to 12th century sites

Table 4.16 Bird bone measurements

Domestic Fowl

Coracoid	*GL*	*Lm*	*Bb*	*Bf*
11th–13th C	52.9	50.4	13.5	11.9
"	56.4	53.6	14.9	12.5
"	57.5	54.7		12.7

Scapula	*Dic*
4th C	12.7
11th–13th C	12
"	12.3

Humerus	*GL*	*Bp*	*SC*	*Bd*
4th C				15.9
"				15.8
11th–13th C	75.4	19.4	7.4	15.3
"	62.9	16.7	6.4	13.3
13th–15th C	63.4	17.5	6.1	13.3
"				15.5
"				13.4

Radius	*GL*	*Bd*
4th C		7.3
13th–15th C	57.7	6
"		5.4

Ulna	*GL*	*Bp*	*Dip*	*SC*	*Did*
4th C					10.1
"					10.0
11th–13th C	70.8	9	14.1	5.1	10.5
"					7.8
13th–15th C	7.8	11.8			

Carpometacarpus	*GL*	*L*	*Bp*	*Did*
4th C	38.9	36.2	11.5	6.7
"			12.8	
11th–13th C	33.7	31.4	10	7.4
"	37.5	34.8	10.8	6.8
"			10.7	
13th–15th C	31.4	29.4	9.8	6.1

Femur	*GL*	*Lm*	*Bp*	*Dp*	*SC*	*Bd*	*Dd*
11th–13th C	69.2	64.9	14	9.8	7.2	13.9	12.1
"	64.8	60.4	12.3	8.7	5.5	12.1	10.9
"	73.5	69.3	13.8	9.7	5.9	13.6	11.6
"		59.2	12.7	8.9	6.1	12.4	10.4
"			13.8	9.5			
13th–15th C			15.2	11.5			
"			14.2	9.5			
"						13.9	11.8

Tibiotarsus	*GL*	*La*	*Dip*	*SC*	*Dd*
11th–13th C	98.2	101.8	12.3	5.4	10.9
"	86.9	90.4	11.2	5.1	9.8
"					9.7
"					10.9
13th–15th C					11.1

Tarsometatarsus	*GL*	*Bp*	*SC*	*Bd*
4th C	64.2	11.5	5	10.9
"		13.2		

Anser

Scapula	*Dic*
11th–13th C	20.9

Humerus	*GL*	*Bp*	*SC*	*Bd*
13th–15th C	161.8	33.9	11.3	23.1

Radius	*Bd*
11th–13th C	10.4

Carpometacarpus	*GL*	*Bp*	*Did*
11th–13th C	97.4	22.6	12.6
13th–15th C			11.9

Femur	*GL*	*Bp*	*Dp*	*SC*	*Bd*
11th–13th C		20.5			
13th–15th C	79.0	19.9	17.3	9.1	21.2

Tibiotarsus	*La*	*Dd*	
11th–13th C	124.6	15.2	*albifrons / leucopsis?*
"		15.9	

Anas

Humerus	*Bp*
13th–15th C	13.7

Ulna	*GL*	*Bd*	*Dip*	*SC*	*Did*
11th–13th C	48.0	5.9	7.3	3.3	6.6

Tibiotarsus	*Bd*	*Dd*	
4th C		6.3	*Anas crecca?*
11th–13th C	8.9	9.7	

and others as probable identifications (Table 4.15). The 'zones' present on the main skeletal elements were recorded (Cohen and Serjeantson 1996, 109–112) and the data used to calculate MNE, as with the mammals. The developmental stage of the tibiotarsus and tarsometarsus was recorded, and porosity of other skeletal elements, so that age could be calculated. Domestic fowl were sexed on the presence or absence of a spur or spur scar and medullary bone in the femur. Butchery cuts were noted. Selected measurements were taken from the suite illustrated by Driesch (1976).

Relative numbers

Bird bones comprised 6% of material from the later Romano-British period (4th century AD), 10% from the immediate post-Conquest period (11th–13th centuries AD) and 16% from the later medieval period (13th–15th centuries AD). Though the percentage of bird bones is not especially low, especially from medieval contexts, some aspects of the assemblage suggest that the contexts excavated did not contain dense concentrations of kitchen and table waste in which bones of small as well as large birds can survive well, such as were present at Portchester (Grant 1985, 246) and St Gregory's Priory (Powell *et al.* 2001). At Pevensey there are few bones of birds smaller than teal, geese are relatively frequent, and the assemblage includes few unidentifiable bird-bone fragments of bird bone (Table 4.15). All these are usually a function of relatively poor survival and recovery.

Several contemporary sites in the region have substantial bird bone assemblages. Examples from the late Romano-British period include the fort at Portchester (Eastham 1975) and the towns of Chichester (Cattlemarket site) (Levitan 1989, 260–1) and Silchester (Serjeantson 2000a). From the medieval period, as well as Portchester (Eastham 1985), good samples of bird bones have been recovered from Carisbrooke Castle (Serjeantson 2000b), Trowbridge Castle (Bourdillon 1993), the manor of Faccombe Netherton (Sadler 1990) and the towns of Exeter (Maltby 1979) and Canterbury (Driver 1990). Comparison with these allows this small assemblage to be seen in the context.

Domestic birds

Of the small sample of bird bones from the 4th century AD, most (19, including probable identifications) are from domestic fowl (90%). Compared with contemporary late Roman assemblages, Pevensey has a lower percentage of domestic fowl (Fig. 4.10). Relative numbers are higher than at the late Roman sites further west, Portchester and Chichester. Bones which were complete enough to be measured (Table 4.16) are too

Table 4.17 Medieval domestic fowl: minimum number of elements (MNE) and overall minimum number of individuals (MNI)

Element	*4th C*	*11th–13th C*	*13th–15th C*	*Total*
Coracoid	2	7	1	10
Scapula	1	2	0	3
Humerus	3	5	9	17
Radius	3	1	4	8
Ulna	2	7	3	12
Furcula	0	1	1	2
Sternum	0	1	2	3
Pelvis	1	0	0	1
Sacrum	0	1	0	1
Femur	1	8	5	14
Tibia	0	8	10	18
Carpometacarpus	2	3	2	7
Tarsometatarsus	4	2	6	12
Total	**19**	**46**	**43**	**108**
MNI	*3*	*6*	*6*	*15*

few to show size trends. The only part of the carcass of domestic fowl which is under-represented at Pevensey is the leg (Table 4.17): the femur and tibiotarsus are usually among the bones which survive well, but they are few or absent here. All bones except one are from adult birds (Table 4.18). No tarsometatarsi with spurs were found, but one of the four tarsometatarsi has the spur scar which forms while the scar is developing but has not yet attached to the bones; this suggests a ratio of one cockerel to three hens. The domestic fowl eaten at Pevensey appear to be birds which were kept for both eggs (see Macphail, below, for evidence of egg shells) and meat. In the Empire, and probably in Britain, cockerels were kept for divination and sacrifice, but a higher percentage of adult males with spurs, as in the Silchester forum, might be expected.

In the earlier medieval period just over half the bird bones are from domestic fowl, a smaller percentage than in the earlier period and lower than at many contemporary sites (Fig. 4.10). There are rather fewer tarsometatarsi than the other bones from the carcass (Table 4.17), so the sample is composed of those parts of the carcass which were eaten. Either the feet were removed before the birds were brought to the Castle or were discarded elsewhere. No more than 20% of the bones are from immature birds (Table 4.18), a percentage which is very similar to that on contemporary sites. Medullary bone is present in two of the eight femurs and one of the three tarsometatarsi has a short, thick spur. The fowls consumed therefore include pullets (immature birds), capons (males) and hens, some of the latter killed for the pot while still in lay.

Fowls are fewer than half of all bird bones in the 13th–15th century deposits. Nearly twice as many as

Table 4.18 Medieval domestic fowl: immature bones (%)

	11th–13th C *% immature*	*s*	*13th–15th C* *% immature*	*s*
Coracoid	28.6	1	0.0	7
Humerus	20.0	10	40.0	5
Radius	0.0	5	0.0	1
Ulna	28.6	3	66.7	7
Carpometacarpus	0.0	2	0.0	3
Femur	12.5	6	33.3	8
Tibiotarsus	20.0	11	45.5	10
Tarsometatarsus	33.3	12	50.0	3
Total	**20.5**	**50**	**38.0**	**44**

in the earlier medieval period are immature, which is in keeping with the trend observed elsewhere in the Later Middle Ages (Albarella 1997). As more meat was eaten, a higher proportion of immature birds were fattened for consumption. All parts of the carcass are present. Neither of the two tarsometatarsi of adult fowls is spurred and medullary bone was present in one of the four femurs.

The other domestic birds include goose, peacock and possibly duck and pigeon. A few of the goose bones were clearly domestic from their size and robusticity (Table 4.16), but most could be identified only to wild or domestic grey lag. In the earlier medieval group, half of the goose bones are also compatible with the wild grey lag goose *Anser anser* while the late medieval geese are all compatible in size with domestic goose. None of the bones of mallard exceeded in size those of the wild mallard, so either or both may be present.

Geese were common at the inland town of Silchester, and ducks were numerous at Portchester and present at the Chichester Cattlemarket site but none were found at Pevensey. In the 11th–13th century material, unlike in the 4th century when goose was absent, the relative number of goose bones is higher than has been found on other contemporary sites (Fig. 4.10). While this may suggest that more geese were kept and eaten than at some other sites, it may also result from the fact that bones of goose survived preferentially to the smaller fowl bones. In view of the nature of the assemblage, it is not surprising that bones of pigeon (*Columba livia/oenas*) are few; all are of the size of domestic pigeons. Certainly domestic is the peacock (*Pavo cristatus*). The peacock was favoured for the banquets laid on for royalty and the nobility as they made their progress round the country. There are few finds from medieval England, but one bone was present at Carisbrooke Castle and another at post-Conquest Faccombe Netherton. A peacock bone was also found in later medieval deposits in Canterbury.

Wild birds

Three bones of wild birds were recovered from late Roman deposits: woodcock (*Scolopax rusticola*), teal (*Anas crecca*), and probable curlew (*cf. Numenius arquata*). Though total numbers are few, wild birds represent over 10% of all bird bones, more than in later periods. These species would all have been found close to the Roman fort, in the marshes of the Pevensey Levels, and are found among food remains at other Roman sites. Woodcock in particular is often found on Roman sites (Parker 1988) and is, for instance, the principal wild bird at Silchester. The taste for woodcock seems to have been introduced as part of the Romanisation of Britain.

In the 11th–13th century deposits, all of the seven bones from wild birds are likely to be from food remains, with the possible exception of the gull, a lesser black-backed or herring gull. Since the gulls would have been found within or immediately outside the Castle, this bone may be from a natural casualty. The most unexpected wild bird is the crane (*Grus grus*), which is rare on medieval sites in southern Britain, although the Pevensey Levels are very much the type of habitat in which the crane would have bred. The other wild birds would also have been found on the Levels and the mouth of the River Ashburn. Place-name evidence suggests that cranes were formerly bred in Sussex (Boisseau and Yalden 1998). All – even the crane – were obtained by hawking in the medieval period, as well as by nets and decoys.

The range of species identified in the later medieval contexts is similar to earlier: it includes crane, teal, buzzard, herring or black-backed gull, razorbill and (?)golden plover. The two buzzards, common (*Buteo buteo*) and rough-legged (*B. lagopus*) cannot reliably be separated osteologically. Both adapt to the role of scavengers around human settlements (Mulkeen and O'Connor 1997), so this bone may be an incidental inclusion. The razorbill was represented by two carpometacarpi, one with cut marks, showing that it had been butchered. Razorbills are found in the English Channel and are usually caught during the breeding season from the cliffs on which they nest. They may have been breeding on Beachy Head, but are also sometimes captured accidentally by fisherman. There was also a minor trade in the middle ages, of seabirds preserved in salt in a similar fashion to fish, so these birds may have been imported. The other species could have been captured on the estuary and marshes in the hinterland of the Castle.

The range of wild birds in the 11th–13th centuries is similar to that at Portchester and Carisbrooke Castle. The relative abundance (Fig. 4.10) shows that wild birds are also frequent at Portchester and at the wealthy manor of Faccombe Netherton, while they are fewer in the towns. This no doubt reflects the fact that the occupants and visitors to the Castle expected to obtain birds for consumption both by purchase and hunting. The increase in wild birds in the later middle ages reflects a national trend: birds were captured for sale in towns such as Winchester and London (Drummond and Wilbraham 1991), as well as being hunted for consumption by the nobility.

Fish

The small, fish-bone assemblage was recovered from medieval contexts only. The species identified (Table 4.19) are predominantly larger fish, as is usual when the material has been collected by hand. The unidentified component is also mostly fragments of large fishes. The data consequently are informative mainly about the large fish which were commercially caught and traded, but not about smaller fish which were also caught and eaten at the time.

Cod (*Gadus morhua*) is the only gadid species identified in the earlier phase, while in the later phase haddock (*Melanogrammus aeglefinus*) and ling (*Molva molva*) are also present in small numbers. Conger eel (*Conger conger*) is the next most common overall and in the 13th–15th century group outnumbers the identified gadids. The gadid and conger bones were assigned to size class where possible: large (>1000 mm), medium (<1000 mm >300 mm) and small (<300 mm). The size distribution is shown in Table 4.20.

It is likely that the larger and also the medium-sized fish were preserved and purchased for consumption, possibly from a distance. In the south of England, conger eel, found in the English Channel and traded in quantity from the Channel Islands (Coy 1985), is typically more common than cod, while large ling are rarely found before the later middle ages. Given the proximity to the seashore, any of the fish could have been caught locally, but the size of the gadids suggests that the Castle was mainly supplied by purchase on a large scale rather than by local fishermen.

Other species found are common eel (*Anguilla anguilla*), and flatfish. Bones from smaller species, including whiting and herring, which is known to have been an important part of the medieval diet, are absent, in contrast to fish assemblages from comparable sites such as Battle Abbey (Locker 1985) and Portchester (Coy 1985) and St Gregory's Priory Canterbury (Powell *et al.* 2001) where many fish bones were recovered from contexts in which fish bone was well preserved. This partly reflects the hand-retrieved nature of the assemblage and probably also preservational bias against the fragile bones of fish in the contexts from which bone was recovered.

Table 4.19 Medieval fish bones

	11th–13th C	*13th–15th C*	*Total*
Cod *Gadus morhua*	19	3	22
Haddock *Melanogrammus aeglefinus*		2	2
Ling *Molva molva*		1	1
Gadid	4	4	8
Conger eel *Conger conger*	3	5	8
Common eel *Anguilla anguilla*	1		1
Plaice/flounder Pleuronectid		1	1
Flatfish		1	1
Fish n.f.i.	12	33	45
Total	**39**	**50**	**89**

Table 4.20 Size class of large gadids, ling and conger eel: large >1,000 mm, medium 300–1,000 mm, small <300 mm

	Large	*Medium*	*Small*
Cod	9	3	
Haddock		2	
Ling	2		
Gadid n.f.i.	7		
Conger eel	3	2	1

However, bones of the large gadids and conger are as robust as those of domestic fowl, so the relative paucity of bones of these probably reflects a minimal consumption of fish. At Carisbrooke Castle, for instance, bird bones survived well and were numerous, but fish – of all sizes – are quite rare.

Discussion

Late Romano-British period

The bones all appear to be from food remains, though the presence of worked antler and cattle limb-bone splinters which were heavily chopped as at some other Roman towns and forts may also hint at some industrial activity. There is no good evidence that animals were raised at the fort, though the body parts found do suggest that the pigs and sheep were slaughtered on site. Joints of cattle may have been imported, or hides removed for processing elsewhere. The cattle were mostly prime or adult animals, as at Portchester. Beef was the principal meat here as at urban and other military sites (King 1978). Pig is more frequent than at contemporary sites and the range of ages at which they were killed suggests that the husbandry regime was not especially intensive. Mutton was less often eaten than would be expected on a rural site of the period. The occupants also possibly ate horse flesh. We have no information as to whether any fish were eaten, since the fish most often eaten at this time were smaller species of which the bones are only recovered in very favourable conditions, but they carried out some hunting for wild boar and other species, which must have been present in the marshlands nearby. The food remains are compatible with the interpretation of Pevensey as a garrison which was manned by Romanised Britons, although the possible consumption of horse flesh, the taste for pork and for hunting would also fit with the possibility that the fort was manned by peoples from northern Europe where these tastes were found at the time.

11th–13th century

There are minor differences between the material which predates the Keep and that from outside the Keep, but in the main the bones suggest similar patterns of food supply and consumption. Some features of the assemblage fit with what is found elsewhere at the time. The age to which sheep were kept is greater than it is earlier, and more wethers were kept. Pigs were regularly slaughtered in their second year, females as well as males, to provide bacon as well as pork. The percentage of sheep increases from the Romano-British period. Fowls were kept for eggs more than for meat, as elsewhere in medieval England.

At Pevensey the meat eaten was mainly beef, but rather more pork and bacon and less mutton was consumed than would be expected in a town or village, and in this Pevensey resembles Early Norman Carisbrooke Castle and Portchester. There are hints that the beef and mutton was brought to the site in joints, though pigs were slaughtered on site. The scarcity of fish would again fit with the fact that occupants of a garrison would have been less likely to buy and eat fish in quantity than those in different types of communities such as churchmen and lay households which were more punctilious in their observance of fast days. The wild mammals and birds suggest that the occupants and visitors were permitted to hunt; with crane and wild boar probably locally caught. These and the other wild fowl and mammals confirm that aristocratic visitors spent time at the Castle, but the low percentage of meat from hunted mammals suggests, as it did at Carisbrooke, that for most of the time the occupants of the Castle were eating routine fare.

13th–15th century

In some respects food consumption at Pevensey again follows trends which were occurring nationally. Sheep become more frequent and cattle and also domestic fowls were younger when slaughtered. The increase in the percentage of fish bones may be reflecting a national trend towards higher consumption of the larger preserved fish, rather than herring. This also follows a trend seen elsewhere in towns and other settlements in the south. Butchery methods become more professional, with midline splitting of carcasses. Pig rearing was more intensive, with animals younger (but not presumably smaller) when slaughtered.

In this period as in earlier times, the bones fit well with what might be expected at a site which was garrisoned rather than run as a manor. Judging from the parts of the body found, it is more likely that cattle were slaughtered and consumed at the Castle, rather than imported as joints, although mutton and pork or bacon were also imported as joints, the age at death does not suggest that the stock were raised at the Castle itself. Other aspects of the assemblage confirm the occasional visits of the wealthy owner or the king (when these were not the same person): a peacock was brought to the site, to eat, or to impress, or both, and hunting continued on a small scale. While it partook in national trends in animal husbandry and food consumption, it has also been possible to identify features which can be taken as confirmation that the Castle functioned as a fort and garrison throughout the earlier part of its long history in the defence of the shores of the south of England.

Timber piles

by S. J. Allen

Eight pieces of waterlogged wood were recovered during the 1994 excavations (see Figs 2.1, 4.11, Pl. 2.1). All were pieces of piles used to anchor the chalk rubble foundation of the Roman curtain wall excavated in the upper trench. Each pile was sampled for dendrochronology and stored prior to recording.

The clingfilm had in some cases split or been torn at the tip of some of the piles with the result that some peripheral drying out had taken place. Fortunately the wood was still in a sound and solid condition. More seriously, the sampling of the timbers had removed complete slices of material from each pile which had not been recorded, and that part of the timber which had been sawn away above (1–6, 8) or below (7) the dendrochronological sample had been disposed of, without record. Some cleaning of the wood had taken place either on site or before sampling; the remaining clay was carefully washed off prior to recording.

The recording process followed was that used by the Museum of London with some modification – the timbers had been lifted and little information was available on their position in the ground or relative levels. One face of each timber was drawn in detail at 1:2, choosing that which was best preserved or most informative.

The wood used to make these piles was oak (*Quercus* sp.), of varying growth rates. The pieces used were from trunk wood, rather than branch wood, fairly straight grained and with few knots. No bark

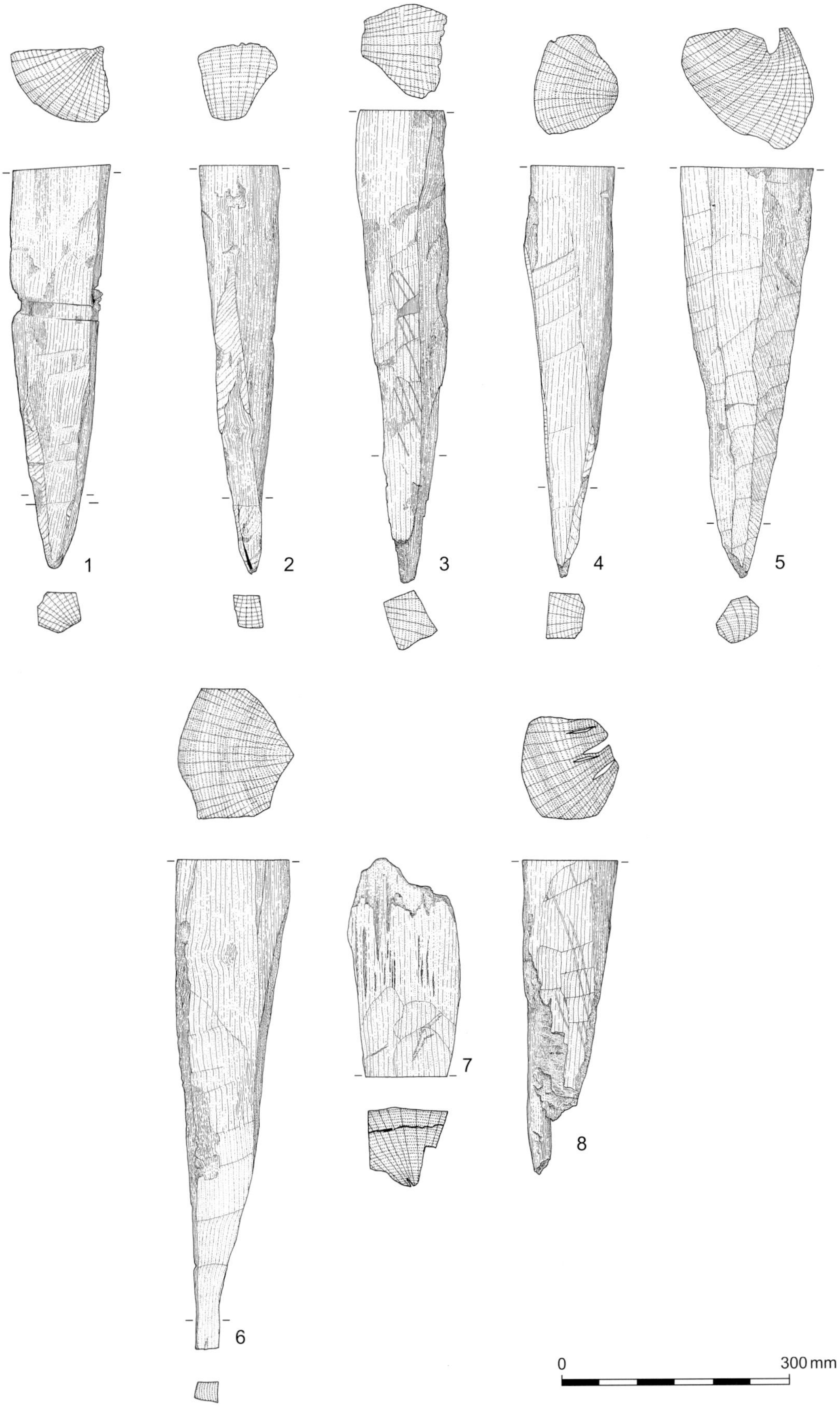

Figure 4.11 Timber piles from the foundations of the Roman fort wall

was present. Sapwood was difficult to identify macroscopically, being stained the same colour as the heartwood, but appeared to be present on a number of the pieces. With these reservations, the estimated minimum diameter of the parent logs range from 0.3–0.5 m, small to medium sized trees.

No evidence was found that would indicate reuse of any of these timbers or of any seasoning. It appears that the piles were made and used very soon after felling. The flat end of the point on 6 may be a relic of the initial conversion, with felled parent tree being cross cut into logs of particular lengths. No marks survive which would determine whether this was done with an axe or saw.

The cross-sections indicate that more than one pile could have been obtained from the same log. The character of the wood surfaces away from the hewn points indicate that the logs were split lengthways along the medullary rays (i.e. radially cleft) rather than sawn. One end of each pile was then hewn to a point. The toolmarks indicate that this was done with the blade working along the grain at a slight angle leaving (where they survived) slightly curving signature marks, suggesting the use of an axe rather than an adze. The blade was slightly curved and more than 88 mm broad. Distinct signature marks were identical, meaning that these two pile points were hewn with the same axe at practically the same time.

No evidence was found to suggest that the piles had been treated in any way prior to burial, to prolong their survival in the ground.

Catalogue

All dimensions are in millimeters. The figure in brackets is the original length of the pile as measure prior to sampling for dendrochronology. 'Upper end' and 'lower end' are used relative to the position of the pile as found.

1. Pile point, hewn to a hexagonal cross-section point. 525 (660) l, 125 w, 105 th. Oak, quartered, severe recent damage, upper end sawn away.
2. Pile point, hewn to a sub-rectangular cross-section point. 535 (800) l, 100 w, 100 th. Oak, radially cleft with possible sapwood, severe recent damage, upper end sawn away.
3. Pile point, hewn to a rectangular cross-section point. 620 (820) l, 140 w, 100 th. Oak, radially cleft with possible sapwood, upper end sawn away.
4. Pile point, hewn to a pentagonal cross-section point. 540(730) l, 130 w, 110 th. Oak radially cleft, tip broken, upper end sawn away.
5. Pile point, hewn to a hexagonal cross-section point. 535(690) l, 180 w, 145 th. Oak, radially cleft with possible sapwood, tip broken, upper end sawn away.
6. Pile point, hewn to a rectangular cross-section point. 645(800) l, 160 w, 142 th. Oak radially cleft with possible sapwood, upper end sawn away.
7. Pile top, hewn to a sub-rectangular cross-section point. 285(600) l, 140 w, 102 th. Oak, radially cleft with possible sapwood, split longitudinally, lower end sawn away.
8. Pile point, hewn to a rectangular cross-section point. 420(640) l, 140 w, 124 th. Oak radially cleft with possible sapwood, severe recent damage, upper end sawn away.

Tree-ring analysis

by Ian Tyers

Dendrochronological analyses was undertaken on a group of waterlogged Roman piles from beneath the east wall of the Roman fort within Pevensey Castle. Eight piles were exposed, with a further six visible in the sections of the trench. The piles, *c.* 0.6–0.8 m in length, were in rows aligned at right angles to the line of the wall and set at intervals of *c.* 0.25 m (see Figs 2.1, 4.11, Pl. 2.1, and Allen above).

Methodology

The eight available samples were placed in a deep-freeze until they were solid. Once frozen the surfaces were cleaned using surforms and scalpels. After the samples had thawed, the ring sequence from each sample was assessed for its suitability for dendrochronological analysis. Unsuitable samples are usually those with either unclear ring sequences, or fewer than 50 rings, or timbers from non-oak trees (at least for the provision of routine dates).

The complete sequences of growth rings in the samples that were selected for dating purposes were measured to an accuracy of 0.01 mm using a micro-computer-based travelling stage. The ring sequences were plotted onto semi-log graph paper to enable visual comparisons to be made between sequences. In addition cross-correlation algorithms (Baillie and Pilcher 1973; Munro 1984) were employed to search for positions where the ring sequences were highly correlated. These positions were checked using the graphs and, where these were satisfactory, new mean sequences were constructed from the synchronised sequences. The *t*-values reported below are derived from the original CROS algorithm (Baillie and Pilcher 1973). A *t*-value of 3.5 or over is usually indicative of a good match, although this is with the proviso that high *t*-values at the same relative or absolute position must be obtained from a range of independent sequences, and that these positions are supported by satisfactory visual matching.

All the measured sequences from this assemblage were compared with each other and those that were found to cross-match were combined to form a site

Table 4.21 *Details of tree-ring samples*

Sample number	*Description*	*Sample type*	*Species*	*No of rings*	*No of sap rings*	*Dimensions (mm)*	*growth rate (mm/year)*	*Result*	*Date of sequences*	*Cross section*
1	Pile	slice	*Quercus*	114	0	135 x 110	1.0	undated		1 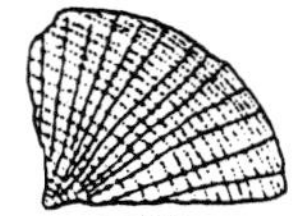
2	Pile	slice	*Quercus*	36	12	110 x 110	1.3	undated		2 
3	Pile	slice	*Quercus*	94	0	145 x 110	1.2	dated	AD 177-270	3 
4	Pile	slice	*Quercus*	110	0	140 x 110	0.9	dated	AD 136-245	4 
5	Pile	slice	*Quercus*	124	0	180 x 150	1.3	dated	AD 131-254	5 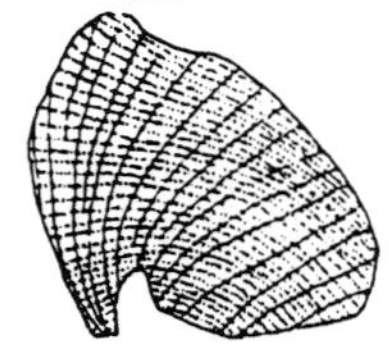
6	Pile	slice	*Quercus*	110	0	170 x 150	1.3	dated	AD 147-260	6 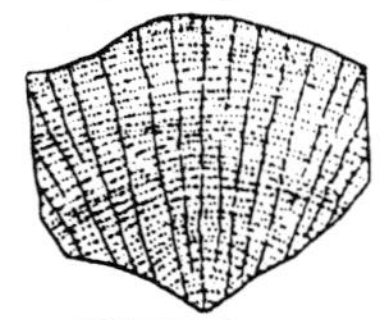
7	Pile	slice	*Quercus*	115	0	110 x 105	1.0	dated	AD 147-261	7 
8	Pile	slice	*Quercus*					rejected		8 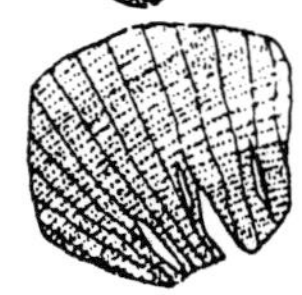

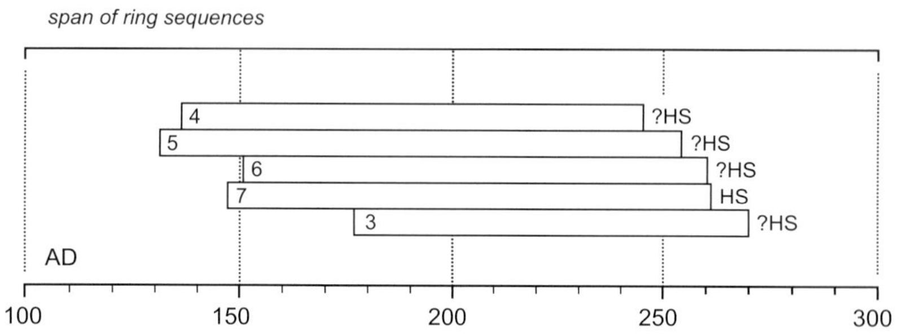

Figure 4.12 Bar diagram showing the relative positions of the dated tree-ring sequences from Pevensey Castle. White bars: heartwood rings; HS: heartwood/sapwood boundary

Table 4.22 Correlation between the dated tree-ring material from Pevensey

Sample	*t*-values samples			
	4	*5*	*6*	*7*
3	5.4	8.4	7.4	6.0
4		11.0	10.2	8.1
5			10.3	9.0
6				6.4

master-curve. This master curve and the remaining unmatched ring sequences were then tested against a range of reference chronologies, using the same matching criteria: high *t*-values, replicated values against a range of chronologies at the same position, and satisfactory visual matching. Where such positions are found these provide calendar dates for the ring-sequence.

These tree-ring dates can initially only date the rings present in the timber. Their interpretation relies upon the nature of the final rings in the sequence. If the sample ends in the heartwood of the original tree, a *terminus post quem* (*tpq*) for the felling of the tree is indicated by the date of the last ring plus the addition of the minimum expected number of sapwood rings that may be missing. This *tpq* may be many decades prior to the real felling date. Where some of the outer sapwood or the heartwood/sapwood boundary survives on the sample, a felling date range can be calculated using the maximum and minimum number of sapwood rings likely to have been present. Alternatively, if bark-edge survives, then a felling date can be directly utilised from the date of the last surviving ring. The sapwood estimates applied throughout this report are a minimum of 10 and maximum of 55 annual rings, where these figures indicate the 95% confidence limits of the range. These figures are applicable to oaks from the British Isles (Hillam *et al.* 1987). The dates obtained by the technique do not by themselves necessarily indicate the date of the structure from which they are derived. It is necessary to incorporate other specialist evidence concerning the re-use of timbers and the repairs of structures before the dendrochronological dates given here can be reliably interpreted as reflecting the construction date of phases within the structure.

Results

All the samples are oak (*Quercus* sp.). Six of these timbers proved to be suitable for the technique. Sample 2 had too few rings, and sample 8, although including enough rings, contained a highly compressed sequence within which individual rings could not be resolved (Table 4.21).

The six measured sequences were compared with each other and five of these were matched together to

Table 4.23 Dating of the master curve from Pevensey Castle, AD 131–270. t-*values with dated reference chronologies. All the reference curves are independent*

Area	*Reference chronology*	*t*-value
London	Baynards Castle, City of London (Morgan 1980)	5.6
	Billingsgate, City of London (Hillam 1990)	6.2
	County Hall Ship, Lambeth (Tyers 1994a)	4.4
	Guys Hospital, Southwark (Tyers unpubd)	5.7
	Guildhall Yard, City of London (Tyers 1994b)	4.0
	New Fresh Wharf, City of London (Hillam and Morgan 1986)	4.5
	St Peters Hill, City of London (Hillam 1992)	4.3
	Tower of London, Tower Hamlets (Hillam 1983)	4.7
Elsewhere	Magor, Wales (Nayling pers comm 1994)	5.8
	Ireland - Teeshan (Baillie pers comm 1982)	3.9
	Holland (Jansma pers comm 1994)	4.2
	S Germany (Becker 1981)	4.9
	NW Germany (Hollstein 1980)	5.0

form a single sequence (Fig. 4.12). All the material exhibited marked bands of slower growth. Hence, although the quality of matches between these samples is very good (Table 4.22), they do not necessarily indicate that they are derived from the same tree. It is likely however that they are derived from a single woodland area. This sequence was found to match to an extensive range of chronologies (Table 4.23) and is dated AD 131–270. The remaining measured sample has failed to produce a visually and statistically acceptable match and is thus undated by the technique. The site master chronology PEVENSEY, dating from AD 131–270 inclusive is listed in Table 4.24.

Interpretation

The absence of sapwood on any of the dated samples prevents the production of a precise felling date for the assemblage. Instead, estimates of the number of sapwood rings likely to have been lost need to be added to the dates of the last surviving rings.

The last ring present on any dated timber is AD 270 on sample 3. The addition of the minimum number of rings likely to have been present on the lost sapwood (10 rings) means that a *tpq* of AD 280 can be calculated for the felling of this timber. In addition, the outer edge of sample 7 (dated to AD 261) is identified as the heartwood/sapwood boundary. This indicates that only sapwood is missing from this sample and thus the minimum and maximum estimated number of missing sapwood rings (10–55) can be added to the end date of this timber. This indicates felling between AD 271 and AD 316. The felling date ranges of samples 3 and 7 can be combined since there is no evidence that the timbers are re-used (see Allen, above) and only one phase of construction is present (see Chapter 2). A date of felling for all the timbers between AD 280 and AD 316 is therefore indicated by samples 3 and 7.

This date range can be further refined because the other three dated samples are all recorded as ending at the possible heartwood/sapwood boundary. This type of record indicates that the last ring present survives around part of the sample circumference, as would be expected for the true boundary, but that it was impossible to eliminate other factors such as post-depositional decay that could have created the same type of outer edge although not at the true boundary. The clustering of the end-dates on these samples between AD 245 and AD 260 may indicate that these are reliable identifications. Applying the number of sapwood rings likely to have been lost (10–55) from these samples suggests a felling dated range of between AD 280 and *c.* AD 300 for all samples.

If the material was used green, which appears to be normal Roman practice (Hanson 1982), this interpretation indicates construction on this part of the fort site between *c.* AD 280–300.

Discussion and conclusions

There is considerable interest in the phasing of the Roman 'Saxon Shore' forts. A full account of the implications of this result is clearly beyond this report (see Fulford and Tyers 1995). However, a number of chronologically related points are made below:

A late 3rd century foundation date for Pevensey Castle would imply:

1. The coin evidence hitherto used to provide a date for the fort is suspect,

Table 4.24 Ring-width data of the site master curve for oaks from Pevensey Castle AD 131–270

Year		*ring-widths (0.01 mm)*										*Number of trees per year*									
AD	131	242	426	408	393	518	274	275	249	389	301	1	1	1	1	1	2	2	2	2	2
		268	310	286	184	252	148	147	143	111	185	2	2	2	2	2	2	3	3	3	3
AD	151	254	262	274	186	246	179	137	123	127	116	4	4	4	4	4	4	4	4	4	4
		179	173	177	165	142	100	153	165	151	109	4	4	4	4	4	4	4	4	4	4
		182	139	132	173	153	174	118	155	113	87	4	4	4	4	4	4	5	5	5	5
		71	67	70	67	76	64	84	110	151	191	5	5	5	5	5	5	5	5	5	5
		140	70	69	71	86	118	121	75	68	66	5	5	5	5	5	5	5	5	5	5
AD	201	84	73	78	61	84	81	72	67	82	92	5	5	5	5	5	5	5	5	5	5
		58	75	67	59	92	62	65	85	92	93	5	5	5	5	5	5	5	5	5	5
		79	80	66	71	51	50	52	42	59	148	5	5	5	5	5	5	5	5	5	5
		116	82	87	104	95	61	48	67	79	82	5	5	5	5	5	5	5	5	5	5
		85	85	85	69	57	63	65	68	118	101	5	5	5	5	5	4	4	4	4	4
AD	251	64	76	99	104	120	106	105	94	104	121	4	4	4	4	3	3	3	3	3	3
		163	193	243	211	169	174	181	224	260	201	2	1	1	1	1	1	1	1	1	1

Sample Column (depth m)	*Prunus* sp. Sloe	*Pomoideae* sp. hawthorn, apple etc.	*Alnus glutinosa* alder	*Corylus avellana* hazel	*Fagus sylvatica* beech	*Quercus* sp. oak	?*Poplus* or *Salix* sp. poplar or willow	*Faxinus excelsior* ash	*Estimate of quantity*
-2.40 to -2.45	+	+	-	+	-	+	-	+	+++
-2.30 to -2.40	+	+	-	+	-	+	-	-	+++
-2.20 to -2.30	+	+	-	+	-	-	+	+	+++
-2.10 to -2.20	+	+	+	+	-	+	-	+	++
-2.00 to -2.10	-	+	-	+	-	+	-	-	+++
-1.90 to -2.00	-	+	-	+	-	+	-	-	+++
-1.80 to -1.90	+	+	+	-	-	+	-	+	+++
-1.70 to -1.80	-	+	+	+	-	+	-	+	+++
-1.60 to -1.70	-	-	-	-	-	-	-	+	+
-1.50 to -1.60	-	-	-	-	-	+	-	-	+
-1.40 to -1.50	-	-	-	-	+	+	-	-	+
-1.30 to -1.40	-	+	+	-	-	+	-	-	++
-1.20 to -1.30	-	-	-	-	+	-	-	-	+
-1.10 to -1.20	-	-	-	+	+	+	-	-	++
-1.00 to -1.10	-	+	-	+	-	+	-	-	++
-0.90 to -1.00	-	-	-	+	+	+	-	-	++
-0.80 to -0.90	-	-	-	+	+	+	-	-	++
-0.70 to -0.80	-	-	-	+	+	+	-	-	+
-0.60 to -0.70	-	-	-	-	+	+	-	-	+
-0.50 to -0.60	-	-	-	+	-	-	-	-	+
-0.40 to -0.50	-	-	-	-	-	+	-	-	+
-0.30 to -0.40	-	-	-	+	-	+	-	-	+
-0.20 to -0.30	-	-	-	+	+	+	-	-	+
-0.10 to -0.20	+	-	-	+	-	+	-	-	++
Pit *Ctx*									
F.127 152	-	-	-	+	+	+	-	-	+++
F.633 602	-	-	-	-	+	+	-	-	+
F.633 638	-	+	-	-	+	-	-	-	+

Table 4.25 Charcoal from the column and selected medieval pits

2. The non-standard layout is not indicative of a late construction,
3. The foundation post-dates the only other dendrochronologically dated defensive installation in southern Britain, the London 'riverside wall' dated to *c.* AD 255–270,
4. That although Pevensey is later than the currently accepted dates for many of the 'Saxon Shore' forts, it is not by as much as hitherto thought,
5. The foundation of the fort may relate to the Carausian period, rather than the later events with which it is often associated.

The dendrochronological analysis of waterlogged timbers from foundations at Pevensey Castle produced a tree-ring chronology dated AD 131–270. The timbers were probably felled in the period AD 280–300. This evidence is the first independent dating evidence, i.e. not derived from pottery typologies or coins, from a 'Saxon Shore' fort for the commencement of construction activities on the site.

Charred plant remains

by Mark Robinson

Excavations around the collapsed eastern wall of Pevensey Castle showed that there was a substantial accumulation of dark earth or midden sediments behind the line of the Roman wall. They began to form after the construction of the Roman wall, which

Table 4.26 Charred plant remains (excluding charcoal) from the medieval pits

	Pit	*F.127*	*F.633*	
	Context	152	602	638
	Sample Volume (litres)	10	10	10
	No. of Items / litre	7.0	1.9	2.1
CEREAL GRAIN				
Triticum dicoccum Schübl. or *spelta* L.	emmer or spelt wheat	-	-	2
Triticum sp. - short free-threshing grain	rivet or bread-type wheat	4	2	-
Triticum sp.	wheat	-	-	6
Hordeum vulgare L. - lateral grain	six-row barley	-	1	-
Hordeum sp. - hulled grain	hulled barley	2	-	-
Hordeum sp.	barley	6	3	2
Avena sp.	oats	5	1	1
cf. *Avena* sp.	oats	6	1	1
cereal indet.		21	-	6
Total cereal grain		**44**	**8**	**18**
CHAFF		-	-	-
OTHER CROPS				
cf. *Vida sativa* L.	fodder vetch	6	-	-
WEED SEEDS				
Chenopodiaceae indet.	fat hen, orache etc	1	1	-
Vida or Lathyrus sp.	vetch or tare	2	-	-
cf. *Vicia or Lathyrus* sp.	vetch or tare	1	3	-
Rumex sp.	dock	4	-	-
Eleocharis S. Palustres sp.	spike rush	1	-	1
Schoenoplectus lacustris (L.) Pal.	bulrush	I	-	-
Gramineae indet.	grass	3	5	2
weed seeds indet.		7	2	-
Total weed seeds		**20**	**11**	**3**

has a *terminus post quem* of AD 280–300 from the oak piles on which it was supported (see Tyers, above). Sedimentation occurred over a long time span, with Roman material in the lower part of the deposit and Saxon material from the upper part. Samples from two medieval pits (Phase 10) outside the Keep, which contained domestic refuse, were examined for charred plant remains. Pit F127 (context 152) is of 13th–15th century date and pit F363 (contexts 602 and 638) is of 11th–14th century date.

Methods and Results

A sequence of 24 samples each of 10 litres was taken at 0.10 m intervals from the top to the bottom of the dark earth. Samples, each of 10 litres, were also taken from three contexts from the medieval pits. The samples were subjected to water flotation onto a 0.5 mm mesh to recover charred plant remains. The non-floating residues were sieved over a 2 mm mesh primarily to retrieve bones and marine mollusc shells.

The dried flots were scanned at x10 magnification under a binocular microscope for charred seeds, chaff and charcoal. Charred seeds are present in 20 of the samples from the column and all three pits, although chaff was not recorded. Charcoal is present in all the flots. The charcoal was broken transversely and examined at up to x400 magnification. Table 4.25 records the charcoal taxa identified in each sample and gives a relative estimate of total quantity. The seed results for the pits are given in Table 4.26.

Charred seeds from the column

The period spanned by the dark earth sequence is one in which major changes occurred in the main arable crops of England. Unfortunately, the concentration of grain in the deposits is very low, averaging less than 0.3 grains per litre and chaff remains, which are particularly important for species identifications, are entirely absent. Most of the grain is unidentifiable. The grain does no more than hint at some of the crop changes that occurred over the period. *Hordeum* sp., some of which could be identified as *H. vulgare* (six-row hulled barley), is present throughout the sequence. The only grain to resemble *Triticum spelta* (spelt wheat) is from -2.10 to -2.20 m, towards the bottom of the sequence, whereas wheat grains from -1.20 to -1.30 m and -0.90 to -1.00 m are of the short-grained, free-threshing type which is so characteristic of later Saxon or medieval assemblages. *Avena* sp. (oats) is absent from the lower part of the sequence. Other charred seeds are few and, apart from *Corylus avellana* (hazel nut), from -1.90 to -2.00 m and -1.80 to -1.90 m, are from possible arable weeds.

Charred crop remains are often very abundant on settlements of both late Roman and late Saxon date. Given the high concentrations of other occupation debris in the dark earth, rather more grain might have been expected. A possible explanation for the lack of chaff and the small quantities of grain recovered could be the specialised nature of Pevensey Castle. Perhaps most of the crop-processing activities, which usually occur on settlement sites and result in remains becoming charred, were occurring elsewhere.

Charcoal from the column

Charcoal is present throughout the sequence, although it tends to be fragmentary rather than in large pieces. The sequence can be divided into three zones on the basis of the taxa present. Between -2.45 and -2.10 m, the Roman part of the sequence, a wide range of taxa is present including *Prunus* sp. (sloe etc), Pomoideae (hawthorn etc), *Alnus glutinosa* (alder), *Corylus avellana* (hazel), *Quercus* sp. (oak) and *Fraxinus excelsior* (ash). From -2.10 to about -1.70 m, the same group is present with less *Prunus* sp. Above about -1.50 m, which would be Saxon or medieval in date, to the top of the deposit, the assemblages are characterised by *C. avellana*, *Fagus sylvatica* (beech) and *Quercus* sp.

There are rather higher concentrations of charcoal towards the bottom of the deposit, but the charcoal could all have been from domestic hearths. The charcoal from the first two zones perhaps represents the collection of fuel from a variety of sources including hedgerow or scrub as well as perhaps woodland. Alder perhaps grew on parts of the Pevensey Levels. The restricted range of taxa and the absence of thorny species from the top zone suggests a woodland source, perhaps a managed coppice with standards, for fuel. The presence of beech charcoal is interesting because, although native, this tree has apparently increased greatly in abundance over the past 1,000 or so years. Its changes in distribution are not well understood. Beech charcoal was also identified from 12th–14th century AD contexts at Pevensey High Street (Robinson 1999).

Charred remains from the pits

The samples from both medieval pits (F127 and F633) contain grains of mixed cereals along with weed seeds. Three of the cereals, free-threshing *Triticum* sp. (rivet or bread-type wheat), hulled *Hordeum vulgare* (hulled six-row barley) and *Avena* sp. (oats), were all major crops in medieval England. *Triticum dicoccum* or *spelta* (emmer or spelt wheat) would be more typical of the Romano-British period and it is possible that these grains from context 638 from pit F633 were residual. Unfortunately, chaff, from which their identity could be confirmed, is absent. The carbonised seeds possibly represent mixed waste from late stages of cleaning of cereal crops with various other plant debris, *Schoenoplectus lacustris* (bulrush), for example, being a tall emergent aquatic plant. Six, large legume seeds, possibly of *Vicia saliva* (fodder vetch), are present from context 152, which also raises the possibility that the remains from pit F127 were burnt animal fodder.

The charcoal belongs to the same taxa that were identified from the medieval part of the midden sequence and likewise probably represents fuel.

Marine molluscs

by E. M. Somerville

During the excavations at Pevensey Castle from 1993 to 1995 a considerable amount of marine shell was retrieved. The shell from all of the Phases 1 to 13 has been examined. Pottery analysis indicates that analysis of molluscan material from three groups of contexts (i) late Roman to 5th century (LR) – from Phase 3 and part of Phase 13; (ii) pre-Keep medieval to 12th to 13th century (earlier medieval = EM) – the remaining Phase 3 contexts; (iii) exterior of Keep, medieval to 15th century (Later medieval = LM) – from Phase 10 contexts; would be most informative, and these groups, particularly EM, contained the bulk of the shell from the site. In addition, a fourth group of contexts comprising Phase 6 (Keep construction) and the remainder of Phase 13 (associated with the collapse of the Roman wall) is included in the analysis, and may well be considered to be in the same date range, on the basis of the associated pottery, as the earlier medieval (EM). A fifth group of shell from those contexts, from a number of phases, where the associated pottery gives a post-medieval date (PM) is included for comparison, although, with some material in this date range not examined, any conclusions about the small assemblage from this group have to be tentative.

The report considers species representation in the five groups of contexts listed above; taphonomic considerations, primarily in relation to the oyster; data on whole shells and intra-site comparisons of oysters, cockles and whelks. Finally, the assemblage is compared briefly with other material from the locality.

Methods

Shell was washed carefully so as to preserve any surface information about epifauna (after the first season the shell was sorted for post-excavation analysis but left unwashed). All shells were identified to species (Fish and Fish 1989). Fragments smaller than approximately 5 mm^2 were discarded. Bivalves were categorised, counted and weighed as complete right/left valves, right/left umbos, unsided umbos and fragments, whereas gastropods were categorised, counted and weighed as complete, apices and fragments. These counts were used for the calculation of the minimum number of individuals (MNI) represented in the five groups of shell. MNI was calculated both for each context within the group (summed MNI – ΣMNI) and for the whole group (group MNI). For bivalves the MNI was taken as the greater of the two numbers for the sided valves and umbos plus half the number of any unsided umbos, while for gastropods the MNI was the total of whole shells and apices. Where a species was only represented by fragments then an MNI of 1 was assigned to that context. If a species was only present in one context of a group, then the MNI for that context is reported, and no group MNI given.

For bivalves, the maximum length (from umbo to opposite margin) and width (orthogonal to length) were measured for whole valves. Whole oyster shells were also scored for a number of other characteristics including shell shape, individual shell weight, age and the extent to which the surface of the shell bore the marks of infestation by one or more of the polychaete worm species *Polydora ciliata*, *P. hoplura* and the burrowing sponge *Cliona celata*. The presence of these species was noted as well as the presence/absence of other encrusting or adhering organisms, including conspecifics. For gastropods, the maximum length (from apex to base) and width (orthogonal to length) were measured, and a note was made of any infesting or encrusting organisms, as well as any indications of interruptions to shell growth.

All the information was entered onto an Excel Spreadsheet, a copy of which has been deposited in the site archive.

An important aspect of the methodology used on this and other studies of marine molluscs from the south-east of England (Somerville unpublished data) is a check on individual repeatability in measuring shell. Before starting to work on the archaeological material those involved completed a recording exercise on a sample of oyster shells collected from the banks of the Arun just behind Shoreham harbour. These are probably the residue of a major oyster industry there in the last century, when Shoreham was the collecting area and transit point to the railway.

From this initial recording exercise two measures can be calculated. The first is an individual measure of repeatability (Harper 1994) which is defined as:

$$\text{Repeatability, } R = (B - W) \,/\, B + (N-1)W$$

Table 4.27 Marine mollusca analysis: repeatability scores

Initials	*Repeatability #*	*F value**	*df**	*p**
LS	0.994	488.1	59,120	<0.0001
PS	0.999	2411.4	32,66	<0.0001
DY	0.991	325.4	32,66	<0.0001
JB	0.999	2488.8	35,72	<0.0001
Group	0.995	696.4	24,75	<0.0001

calculated as given in the formula above; * values from ANOVA table

where *B* is the variance between individuals, *W* the variance within individuals (more often these are called the mean squares in an ANOVA table) and *N* is the number of times a single shell was measured.

Approximately 30 shells were measured three times, at intervals of at least 48 hours. Table 4.27 gives the measures of repeatability obtained for those working on the material from Pevensey Castle. The group score given in the Table 4.27 is calculated in the same way as the individual measure of repeatability, but using one set of measurements from each of the individuals concerned. Strictly speaking, both these measures are of consistency rather than accuracy. However, intuitively, it would seem unlikely that different people would make the same mistakes on the same shells, which would be necessary if the group score did not reflect a tendency for measurements to cluster around the same absolute value – the actual length of the oyster shell.

Results

Species representation in the five groups of contexts

The ΣMNI and group MNI (calculated as described above) and the total weight of shell is given in Tables 4.28–4.31 as a summary of the distribution of shell (scientific names are given in the headings for these tables, but elsewhere in this report the common names are used).

Oysters were found in all five groups of contexts, and were the major part of the shell by weight in all. Whelks were most numerous in the LM group, but were also present in reasonable numbers in EM, in fact mainly in the Phase 6 contexts, which may date from the Keep construction. A few specimens derive from contexts with a pottery *tpq* of AD 350+ (LR group) and 'Roman' (context 365 – EM group).

Cockles, mussels and winkles are present throughout the post-Roman and medieval deposits, but the last two species only become common in the LM group of deposits. Cockles are also well represented there and in the EM group of deposits. An interesting association is that of the netted whelk and the whelk. Both species could be caught in pots,

*Table 4.28 MNIs and weight for oyster (*Ostrea edulis*), cockle (*Cerastoderma edule*) and mussel (*Mytilius edulis*)*

Group	Oyster			Cockle			Mussel		
	Σ MNI	*Group MNI*	*Weight (gms)*	*Σ MNI*	*Group MNI*	*Weight (gms)*	*Σ MNI*	*Group MNI*	*Weight (gms)*
LR	172	158	4224.5	5	5	13.7	17	13	84.8
PKM	313	283	10536.7	237	230	900.3	26	22	72
EM	270	241	8433.2	48	41	128.6	35	30	103.4
EK	2048	1991	48817.2	336	307	1218.6	130	98	428.8
PM	117	105	4390.1	16	13	100.1	7	6	26.3

Table 4.29 MNIs and weight for other bivalves (scallop, Pecten maximus*;* Venerupis *sp. and saddle oyster,* Anomia ephippium*)*

Group	Scallop			*Venuperis* sp			Saddle oyster		
	Σ MNI	*Group MNI*	*Weight (gms)*	*Σ MNI*	*Group MNI*	*Weight (gms)*	*Σ MNI*	*Group MNI*	*Weight (gms)*
LR	1	1	3						
PKM				2	n/a	1.9			
EM				1	1	3.8			
EK	1	n/a	0.7	3	1	10.1	1	1	0.6
PM									

*Table 4.30 MNIs and weight for whelks (*Buccinum undatum*), netted whelks (*Hinia reticulata*) and winkles (*Littorina littorea*)*

Group	Whelk			Netted whelk			Winkles		
	Σ MNI	*Group MNI*	*Weight (gms)*	*Σ MNI*	*Group MNI*	*Weight (gms)*	*Σ MNI*	*Group MNI*	*Weight (gms)*
LR	2	2	13.8				1	n/a	1.9
PKM	8	3	30.6				19	18	52.7
EM	115	114	584.1	11	11	15.9	9	8	26.2
EK	4447	4444	26142.6	157	157	264.8	128	128	430
PM	114	114	1003.5	4	n/a	9.6			

Table 4.31 MNIs and weight for other gastropods (limpet, Patella vulgaris*; sting-winkle,* Ocenabra erinacea*; dog whelk,* Nucella lapillus*;* Dentalium *sp.)*

Group	Limpet			Sting-winkle		Dog whelk		Dentalium	
	Σ MNI	*Group MNI*	*Weight (gms)*	*MNI*	*Weight (gms)*	*MNI*	*Weight (gms)*	*MNI*	*Weight (gms)*
LR	6	5	34.3						
PKM	14	10	63.9						
EM	2	n/a	3.1						
EK	2	2	3.1	1	5.1				
PM						1	5	1	0.1

but given that the netted whelk is generally considered inedible, and the shells were largely intact, the presence of this species may indicate that the whelk catch was sorted on site. Since the characteristic depth-range of the netted whelk is 0–15 m, with a total range down to 40 m, compared to the much wider range of 0–1200 m for the larger edible species (Peacock 1993), the association of the two may indicate that at least some fishing for whelk was close inshore.

No species were found which could not be found today along the English Channel coast, although oysters are no longer found near Pevensey, the local beds having been fished out in the 19th century (Salzmann 1907).

Taphonomic considerations

Although the MNIs reported above are impressive, the amount of whole, that is measurable shell, is considerably smaller. The spreadsheets in the archive give the detail relating to preservation of the different species in the five groups of contexts. This section will examine the data from the oysters to see if there is any general trend in fragmentation across the site. Since such an exercise must use the proportions of shell in different categories of preservation, it is important to restrict this exercise to those contexts with larger amounts of shell. An arbitrary figure of a total of 50 valves plus umbos was used as a minimum for inclusion in this analysis. A total of 19 contexts contained sufficient shell to be considered. These contexts and the percentage by weight of whole valves, sidable umbos (where generally at least half of the shell is present, enabling inspection of the muscle scar) and unsided umbos (where generally less than one third of the shell is present) plus fragments are given in Table 4.32.

Although the difference between a measurable whole valve and a sidable umbo is very important for the analysis of the oysters, in terms of actual amount of shell attrition it is markedly less than the difference between either of these categories and the more fragmentary material. It is also unfortunately possible that the reduction of a whole valve to a sidable umbo can occur during and after excavation, although it is less likely that an initially whole valve would be reduced to an unsided umbo.

It is impossible to tell from the shell alone whether the breakage occurred before final deposition, into rubbish pits in the case of the LM contexts, and it would be interesting to compare the breakage patterns of both bones and artefacts from these contexts. The amount of reduction of the shell seems to fall into two groups – less than an eighth of the weight as fragments and more than a quarter of the weight as fragments. The two very large deposits of shell in the LM group of contexts fall into the former

Table 4.32 Fragmentation of oyster shell

Group	*Context*	*% whole valves*	*% sidable umbos*	*% unsided umbos plus fragments*
LR	52	22.1	73.1	4.8
	45	12.8	77.2	10.0
PKM	24	2.8	62.1	35.1
	25	13.6	48.0	38.4
	31	22.2	66.7	11.1
EM	83	5.8	53.1	41.1
EK	115	7.7	66.1	26.3
	117	25.4	61.9	12.7
	129	50.9	38.3	10.8
	137	8.5	65.6	25.9
	145	38.1	53.2	8.8
	152	62.6	26.9	10.5
	320	6.9	55.4	37.7
	601	12.7	59.1	28.2
	602	4.8	78.4	16.8
	620	15.3	50.3	34.4
	639	16.3	75.3	8.5
	645	20.7	72.1	7.2
	668	38.8	61.1	0.1

Table 4.33 Fragmentation of cockle shell

Group	*Context*	*% whole valves*	*% sidable umbos*	*% unsided umbos plus fragments*
PKM	31	58.8	29.9	11.3
EK	152	82.1	9.2	8.7
EK	602	40.9	31.7	27.7

Table 4.34 Fragmentation of whelk shell

Group	*Context*	*% whole shell*	*% apices*	*% fragments*
EK	115	15.7	79.1	5.2
EK	129	52.5	45.6	1.9
EK	137	13.5	74.7	11.9
EK	152	63.5	32.2	4.3
EK	320	27.9	65	7.1
EK	620	27.6	62.7	9.7

Table 4.35 Comparison of degree of fragmentation for oyster, cockle and whelk

Context	*Rank for* Oyster	*Rank for* Cockle	*Rank for* Whelk
31	3	2	
115	6		3
129	2		1
137	5		6
152	1	1	2
320	8		4
602	4	3	
620	7		5

Table 4.36 Numbers of whole shells of different species for the five groups of context

Group	Oyster	Cockle	Mussel	*Venerupis* sp.	Whelk	Netted whelk	Winkle	Limpet	Dog whelk	*Dentalium* sp.
LR	22L 21R	4L 0R						2		
PKM	23L 22R	120L 114R					13	4		
EM	25L 31R	19L 8R		1L	11	11	6			
EK	170L 374R	227L 236R	9L 7R		1149	144	104			
PM	10L 9R	5L 5R			19	4			1	1

group and it is striking that the most fragmented shell comes from the one sufficiently large deposit of shell in a Phase 13 context (31) where the excavation indicates that this material was not in its original position.

Other shell from these deposits was analysed in a similar way, although relatively few deposits yielded sufficient material, using the criterion of a total of 50 shells. Probably the best way to compare contexts is by rank, where 1 is the context with the least percentage of fragments by weight (Table 4.35).

Although the numbers of comparable contexts for oysters and cockles is too small for statistical testing, inspection shows that the amount of fragmentation is broadly comparable between the different species. For oysters and whelks it is possible to calculate the Kendall rank correlation coefficient, $\tau = +0.4$, but this proves to be non-significant. However, the comparison with whelks suffers from the fact that the analysis of gastropods counts all apices as equivalent, which would be the same as lumping together all the umbos for a bivalve.

The comparison between the fragmentation pattern for oysters and other marine molluscs is therefore inconclusive, but it would still be interesting to look at other evidence for the amount of fragmentation of material within the contexts considered here in order to see what may be deduced about the rapidity with which material was transported to its final point of deposition.

Table 4.37 Shell height data for netted whelks

Group	*Number of shells*	*Mean height (mm)*	*Standard deviation*
EM	11	25.01	2.56
EK	51	24.79	2.80
125	17	23.93	2.27
137	55	24.58	2.23
620	17	23.71	3.68

The arguments so far about taphonomy implicitly assume that there has been no differential deposition of material. The oyster's left valve is cup-shaped and may be used to serve the mollusc at table, although it must be admitted that this would probably not be the case if the oysters were cooked in with other food. Consequently, a bias in the distribution of right and left valves could be taken as indicating differential disposal of waste. For the 19 contexts considered here, the context was considered to be biased if 70% or more of the valves and umbos came from only one side. No context was biased by that criterion, and only one came close (context 45 with 67% left-hand shells).

Data on whole shells

Table 4.36 shows the numbers of whole shell for the five groups described in the introduction. For bivalves both right and left shells are enumerated. It is clear that the spread of numbers is very uneven, and consequently the analyses of variance reported below have to be interpreted cautiously. Single large contexts are reported on separately to the combined data for the rest of their group. There is no further description in the text of those species for which there are literally only a handful of whole shells. Oysters, cockles and whelks are discussed in the next section.

Mussels

Whole mussels are only found in one group. The average length of the left valves was 41 mm and the width 23 mm. This is rather small, but given the very poor survival of mussel shells it is unwise to take this figure as representative of the size of mussels being harvested. Indeed, it was noticeable that some of the umbos clearly came from larger shells.

Winkles

Winkles are only found in any numbers in the LM group of contexts, and only one context (602) yielded a large sample. The overall mean shell height was

Table 4.38 Shell length data for oysters

Group	*No.*	*Mean length left valve (cm)*	*Standard deviation*	*No.*	*Mean length right valve (cm)*	*Standard deviation*
LR	22	7.02	1.19	21	6.44	1.06
PKM	23	7.88	1.23	22	7.08	1.20
EM	25	6.94	1.46	31	6.8	1.29
EK	98	7.4	1.39	140	6.56	1.27
152	54	7.27	1.85	114	6.38	1.15
602	18	7.2	1.31	120	6.3	1.60
PM	10	8.62	1.23	9	7.81	1.19

22.9 mm, and the mean height for context 602 alone was virtually identical at 23.5 mm. The range of shell heights was 12–35.6 mm overall, although the range for context 602 was somewhat narrower at 18.5–29.6 mm. The range of shell heights could indicate that the winkles were taken from all levels of the shore (Warner 1997) although this does require extrapolation from modern data from the Solent, on a gravel and mud substrate.

Netted Whelks
Netted whelks were found in both EM and LM groups. Because three of the contexts in the latter group contained reasonable numbers of netted whelks, the data for these are given separately from the combined data for the other LM contexts. As the Table 4.37 shows, there is little variation in the size of the shells, and the only noticeable difference in distribution is the occasional presence of some juveniles.

The presence of this presumed inedible species is puzzling, as discussed above. In terms of its distribution within the different period groupings determined for the site there is an association with the presence of the common whelk (see above). This association holds good at the context level, in that whelk was present in every context where netted whelks were found, but the reverse is not the case. Since the characteristic depth distributions of the two species differ, this may indicate that fishing for whelks was carried out at a variety of depths.

Intra-site comparisons of oysters, cockles and whelks

The data from the analysis of whole shells are used to address the following questions. Is there any evidence for change over time in the size of the shells? Do the characteristics of the shells indicate whether the source(s) of the molluscs change over time? Can any deductions be made about the management of this resource? Some of these themes will be examined by comparing the Pevensey Castle material with that from other sites.

Oysters
Table 4.38 gives the mean length of both right and left valves for the five groups of contexts, with the two large contexts in LM (152 and 602) treated separately.

Apart from the small PM sample, the shells are fairly consistent in size. Plots of the frequency distributions (in project archive) showed a good approximation to a normal distribution for left valves. Right valves, especially from the LM group, have a small second peak of very small shell – which may have come from the adhering shells. Because of this possible confounding factor, only the data from left valves was used for the analysis of variance. The results show that the small sample of larger PM shells is different from the rest, but there are no differences in size within the late Roman and medieval groups (Table 4.39).

Data were collected on individual shell weights and plots were constructed of length versus weight, as it proved difficult to ascertain the age of the oyster valves by counting the growth lines at the umbo. The expectation was that any shells which are conspicuously heavy for their length could be considered as either those from older animals which had escaped previous harvest or from shells which are growing poorly. Such small shells are called 'dumpy' or 'stunters', and in a management system which used relaying of shells would be rejected (Cole 1956). Although there were some shells which were both large and heavy, the plots for both right and left valves showed a consistent and fairly tight relationship between length and weight, indicating that the oysters were all growing at much the same rate, at least in

Table 4.39 Results of one-way analysis of variance on length of left oyster valves

Groups compared	*F value*	*df*	*P*
EK,152,162	0.238	2,167	NS
LR,PKM,EK	2.378	2,140	NS
PKM,EM,EK	2.772	2,143	NS
ALL	2.89	6,243	<.01

Table 4.40 Shape characteristics of whole oyster shells

Group	Side	No.	Distorted	Ribbed	Side	No.	Distorted
LR	L	22	13	19	R	21	17
PKM	L	23	10	17	R	22	18
EM	L	25	16	21	R	31	26
EK	L	98	63	96	R	140	113
152	L	54	35	44	R	114	79
602	L	18	13	16	R	120	81
PM	L	10	6	9	R	9	5

Table 4.41 Shape characteristics of oyster umbos and presence of adhering shells

Group	Side	No.	Distorted	Adh shell	Side	No.	Distorted	Adh shell
LR	L	127	92	27	R	91	62	4
PKM	L	143	61	13	R	129	60	2
EM	L	26	15	1	R	18	9	

terms of each group. There may be some hints at different growth rates for the different groups, but more data are needed before this analysis can be extended any further. However, Winder (1992) reports some evidence for variation in growth rate in oysters from archaeological sites she has examined.

The shape of oyster shells can give some indication of the conditions under which they have grown (Smith 1987), and may indicate whether they come from a natural or managed bed, as relaying of oysters allows them to grow freely and attain a smooth, undistorted profile. The results are summarized in Table 4.40.

Because of the relatively few whole valves in the earlier contexts, a count was made of the sidable umbos in terms of shape and adhering shell (Table 4.41). What is striking throughout is the amount of distortion of the shell, which is often more noticeable at the umbo as well as the number of adhering shells, particularly on the left valves (see Tables 4.42–4.43 for data on whole shells). All of this is indicative of a naturally growing reef of oysters, with good recruitment of spat (oyster larvae). The presence on a few shells of attached pebble, mussel or cockle shell and inverted barnacles indicates that no provision was being made for the capture of spat on prepared surfaces with relaying.

Some shells in all periods had notches at their base which may have been produced by opening the shell. These were predominately on the right valves. Relatively little evidence for reuse of shell was seen in the form of holes pierced through the shell (*cf.* Holden 1963), and all the instances of this came from LM contexts, particularly in context 602.

Oysters, like other molluscs, often become the substrate for other marine organisms (Tables 4.42–4.43), of which two polychaete worms (*P. ciliata* and *P. hoplura*) and a burrowing sponge (*C. celata*) can be considered as infesting since they penetrate the shell and can cause considerable damage. Other polychaetes may build their tubes on the oyster shell, either sand tubes (probably built by *Sabellaria spinulosa*) or calcareous tubes (where these are intact they are clearly those of *Pomatoceros triqueter*), but these probably do little harm to the oyster. Bryozoa (probably *Electra pilosa*) are found on shells, and appear to be benign. Barnacles, or rather the plates indicating where barnacles were attached, are found infrequently. Adhering shell is the result of oyster spat settling onto established shells. Conjoined shells, that is when both are of a similar size, were relatively rarely found, but any extra damage to one shell would put the pair into the 'adhering' category. Patterns of epifauna can indicate whether the oysters all come from a similar habitat.

Although there appears to be an increase in the number of species of infesting organisms in LM, including contexts 152 and 602, this could be an artefact of the much larger numbers of shells. The presence in 602 alone of the most potentially damaging of the infesting species is interesting, but the overall incidence and amount was quite small. For all the groups examined, it is clear that *P. ciliata* is the main infesting organism, but, even at its most severe this did not seriously damage the shells. *P. ciliata* is also indicative of a shallow-water habitat (Cole 1956; Smith 1987), as are the bryozoans, sandtubes, and barnacles, whereas the calcareous tubes may indicate a slightly deeper habitat (Fish and Fish 1989). More actualistic data are needed on this, as well as further investigation of the co-occurrence of the different organisms. There were no clear trends in the amount of infestation by the three potentially damaging species. Although left shells tend to have more varied epifauna, the infestation rates were not consistently greater for left shells in all groups of shells.

Cockles

In terms of whole shells, the earliest (LR) and latest (PM) deposits yielded insufficient numbers for further analysis. Table 4.44 gives the average length of the left valve for the other groups. Since cockles are equivalve, the data from the somewhat more evenly distributed whole left valves have been used for statistical analysis. Although there is no clear trend in terms of change in size with period, the differences between these four groups of shells are significant ($F = 15.449$, df 3,370, $p<0.0001$). A plot of the distribution of sizes showed that the EM group has a considerable proportion of small (20 mm) valves.

Whelks

The criteria used for a complete shell, which was that both the siphon had to be complete and there had to be at least three full whorls in the spire, led to the rejection of quite a number of larger shells. If the damage to the shell occurred after disposal, then the values reported here may owe as much to taphonomy as to fishing strategy.

Although there is no significant difference between the groups (F=0.0428, df 5,1173, p>0.05), there are obvious differences in the variability in shell height in the different groups, with context 152 in pit F127 having a considerable number of small shells (Table 4.45). There are also considerable differences in the incidence of *P. ciliata* marks on the shells, although it should be noted that this infestation is usually slight. Until more comparative data are available, including actualistic data, it is difficult to interpret these differences. The presence of *P. ciliata* on the shells is consistent with a shallow water origin for the whelks, as discussed above with respect to the presence of netted whelks. Growth interruptions are not severe, which could indicate a relatively benign habitat for the whelks, but again, further actualistic and comparative data are needed.

Table 4.42 Infesting, encrusting and adhering organisms on left oyster valves

Group	*No.*	*pc*	*ph*	*cc*	*st*	*adh shell*	*bryo*	*calc*	*barn*
LR	22	17			1	3	5	5	
PKM	23	15			1	6	4	3	
EM	25	20			1	10	6		
EK	98	54	3		7	23	19	13	2
152	54	24	2		11	29		2	
602	18	7	6	6	3	12	5	5	1
PM	10	6				4			

KEY: pc – *P. ciliata*; ph – *P. hoplura*; cc – *C. celata*; st – sandtube; adh shell – adhering oyster shell of all sizes; bryo – bryozoan; calc – calcareous tubes; barn – barnacle

Table 4.43 Infesting, encrusting and adhering organisms on right oyster valves

Group	*No.*	*pc*	*ph*	*cc*	*st*	*adh shell*	*bryo*	*calc*	*barn*
LR	21	17					1		
PKM	22	7				3		1	
EM	31	21				2			
EK	140	97	5		1	6	15	2	3
152	114	66	5		2	2			1
602	120	48	43	12	2	11	7	7	1
PM	9	3						1	1

KEY: pc – *P. ciliata*; ph – *P. hoplura*; cc – *C. celata*; st – sandtube; adh shell – adhering oyster shell of all sizes; bryo – bryozoan; calc – calcareous tubes; barn – barnacle

Discussion

Although the presence of marine molluscs has often been noted from a number of archaeological sites in Sussex, it is only relatively recently that the characteristics of the assemblages have been reported in any detail. In general, the main species found at Pevensey Castle have also been found in Lewes, at the Friary site (Somerville 1996), the Priory (Somerville 1997) and at St Nicholas Hospital (Somerville unpublished data), at Lydd in Kent (Somerville unpublished data) and in the town of Pevensey (Dulley 1967; Somerville 1999). However, cockles are only found in quantity at Lydd and Pevensey, and the numbers of whelks and winkles found is very variable. Because the dating at these sites is based on pottery assemblages, it is difficult to make direct comparisons in terms of changes in species representation over time. Dulley (1967) reports only finding whelks in quantity at the excavations in post *c.* 1300 contexts in Pevensey town, and it would therefore appear that the Castle population was exploiting this resource slightly earlier, as whelks are present in considerable numbers in LM contexts which have a pottery *tpq* of 11th–13th century, as well as being occasionally present in small numbers in much earlier (LR) contexts. However, it is likely that the LM occupation outside the Keep concentrates around the beginning of the 14th century.

Oysters were found at all the sites listed above, and, albeit with the same caveat about dating, it is instructive to compare the sizes reported. At Lewes Friary, the mode for right valve length was 70 to 89 mm, and, at St Nicholas Hospital, average, right-valve lengths were between 77 and 82 mm for the medieval material. From Pevensey town the earliest group (11th/12th century to 12th–13th century) had an average right valve length of 68 mm, rising to 79 mm in the 13th to 13th–14th century group and dropping back to 69 mm in the 14th to 14th/15th century group. At Lydd the average length of valves (both sides combined) was 61 mm in the 12th–13th century group, 78 mm for the 13th–14th century group and 76 mm for the 14th–15th century group.

These sites did not yield material comparable to the LR or PM phases from Pevensey Castle, so the comparison is with the range of medieval material

Table 4.44 Shell length data for cockles

Group	*Number of valves*	*Average valve length (cm)*	*Standard deviation*
PKM	119	2.47	0.34
EM	27	2.34	0.28
EK	58	2.54	0.31
152	170	2.3	0.23

Table 4.45 Shell height data for whelks

Group	*Number of whole shells*	*Average shell height (mm)*	*Standard deviation*	*% of shells with* P. ciliata	*% of shells showing growth interruptions*
EM	11	47.14	5.573	9.1	9.1
EK	318	49.73	6.335	21.1	11.0
129	58	47	7.78	41.4	5.2
137	85	46.71	5.6	47.1	5.9
152	688	47.60	31.89	62.6	10.9
PM	19	49.64	7.131	21.1	5.3

which gave values for left valves of 69 mm (EM) and 72–74 mm (LM) and for right valves of 68 mm (EM) and 63–66 mm (LM). These values are smaller than those for Lewes and Pevensey town, but are closer to those from Lydd. The Pevensey Castle sizes are, however, quite close to the general average for 'medieval' (11th to 16th century) of 75 mm for left and 64 mm for right valves given by Winder (1992). Modern farmed oysters would be expected to reach these dimensions between three and six years of age (Walne 1974). Thus the Pevensey Castle oysters are somewhat smaller than comparable assemblages from Sussex, which is surprising given the coastal location of the site, and the contrast is probably most marked with the oysters found in the town.

In terms of infesting, adhering and encrusting species, however, the oysters from the town and the Castle are very similar, with *P. ciliata* being the commonest species, although the town shells had more *C. celata* and *P. hoplura*. This general pattern was also found at Lydd, and contrasts with the shells found at Lewes, where the number of epifaunal species was much lower, and *C. celata* was the most common. Both town and Castle shells at Pevensey had a marked representation of adhering shell, and a fair number of distorted shells, which contrasts with all other sites. More detailed comparisons would be needed to establish whether all the Pevensey material comes from a similar locality, but this is certainly a possibility.

Lydd produced vast quantities of cockles, and is the only site of this group to have done so. The sizes are very similar to those for the Pevensey Castle material, although the conspicuously small cockles (length 210 mm) from the 14th–15th century group are unmatched by any group of material from Pevensey. For both these sites, the small average size throughout the medieval period is puzzling, especially since the modern cockle fisheries in the Burry Inlet, South Wales had a bye-law passed in 1959 which forbade the removal of cockles smaller than 230 mm (Hancock and Urquhart 1966). Since the Welsh bye-law was set on the basis of investigations intended to maintain a viable cockle industry, it would appear that the cockles harvested from both Lydd and Pevensey were in danger of being over-exploited.

The whelks from Pevensey Castle have a very low mean height of 47.0 mm–49.64 mm, compared both to the average from Lydd of 62.7 mm for the 12th–13th century group and 59.8 mm for the 14th–15th century group as well as to a modern sample from Shoreham of 62.1 mm–62.4 mm (Nicholson and Evans 1997) and a modern commercial sample from Pevensey bay of 65.42 mm (Bonnell pers. comm.). Indeed, the Pevensey whelks are so small that they would not have been sexually mature (Kideys *et al.* 1993) and the fishery would therefore have been unsustainable. The fact that the average size of whelks at Pevensey remains consistent from the EM to PM groups indicates that this argument is flawed in some way, possibly because of the unanswerable question of the intensity of the fishing pressure. It has already been noted that the criteria used for 'whole' shells may have excluded a number of larger whelks, and therefore the mean value is inaccurate. Clearly there are issues which need further investigation, and it is unfortunate that Dulley's (1967) report did not included data on the size of the whelks.

Overall the Pevensey marine mollusc assemblage is striking for the very large numbers of whole shells in some of the later (LM) contexts. It is also noteworthy that there is very little change in the shells' metrics or other characteristics over the medieval period. The oysters closely resemble those found nearby in the town, although they are smaller, and both assemblages from Pevensey contrast with those from further east at Lewes, which bears witness to the variable morphology of the oyster, as well as indicating that in the medieval period there were a number of different Sussex oyster fisheries. Although the database is less extensive for the two other main species represented at Pevensey, it is possible that the fisheries for cockles at the eastern end of Sussex and western end of Kent were in danger of over-exploiting their stocks, and the same may have been true more locally for the whelk fishery at Pevensey. It is therefore somewhat ironic that there are today still whelks and cockles in the vicinity, but the oysters have disappeared.

Soil micromorphology

by Richard I. Macphail with a contribution by Johan Linderholm

Summary

A total of 18 thin-sections of nine bulk samples from Roman, Saxon and medieval deposits were studied through soil micromorphology, bulk chemistry and microchemistry. Despite the dating difficulties encountered at the site, a number of phases have been identified which may possibly relate to successive occupations at Pevensey Castle. Roman deposits associated with the digging of the fort construction trench and several, subsequent contexts are present that could inform our understanding of the construction and occupation of the fort. Late Roman 'dark earth' formation seems to have begun with a midden spread of soil that may record 'domestic' campfires, and small amounts of constructional and industrial debris. 'Dark earth' continued to develop as a calcareous brown earth soil (typical of many 'dark earth' sites across England and mainland Europe), during the Romano-British and later occupation of the fort, where ash, food and latrine waste were the dominant-included midden components. Evidence of more intensive stocking of herbivores and omnivores may possibly mark a focusing of Norman (pre-Keep) occupation in this south-east corner of the fort. Increased intensity of stocking during the 'Norman' occupation of 'dark earth' is a phenomenon noted at two sites in London. More intensive dumping of latrine waste or garderobe outflow is recorded in the uppermost (pre-Keep) Norman 'dark earth' levels, which again may reflect a concentration of human occupation and the presence of the Norman Castle.

Although long considered to be a later 4th century construction, dendrochronological dating of the wooden piling that supported the Roman fort wall indicates felling around AD 280–300 (see Tyers, above), while coins from associated constructional dumps suggest a *terminus post quem* of AD 293 for the construction of the fort (see Chapter 2). Pottery analysis was undertaken to phase the site, including the Roman and 'dark earth' levels that have been sampled for soil analysis (see Timby, Chapter 3). Soil samples collected in 1994 were assessed, with new samples being taken by Ian Dormor and P. E. J. Wiltshire during the excavation of 1995, which were also assessed (Macphail 1994–1996). The study of 'dark earth' at Pevensey Castle has been carried out against a background of moderately well-dated contexts of Roman through to Saxon/medieval sequences at Deansway, Worcester, No. 1, Poultry and Guildhall Yard East, London and Whitefriars, Canterbury (Macphail 1994; Macphail and Cruise 1995). Equally, 'dark earth' is of continuing European interest (Galinié 2000; Macphail and Cruise 2000; Macphail *et al.* in prep).

Research objectives

The 'dark earth' was investigated at Pevensey Castle because, unlike many other sites, such as those in north-west Southwark, London (Cowan 2003), it appeared to represent a continuous development from the late 3rd century until about 1200, and thus was potentially able to provide soil data that might answer both general questions concerning its formation and specific enquiries into land use from Roman to medieval times at Pevensey.

The general questions are:

- When did the 'dark earth' form and under what kind of land-use and environmental conditions?
- How is it composed and how far does it represent redeposited or re-worked stratigraphy?
- How can the results from the study area improve the excavation, investigation and understanding of 'dark earth' from elsewhere in Europe?

More specific to the history of Pevensey Castle are:

- What is recorded in the deposits associated with the late Roman 'shore fort'?
- What occupational activities can be deduced from the lower, 5th–11th century 'dark earth'?
- What changes in land-use can be identified from the upper, 11th–13th century 'dark earth'?

Samples and methods

Ten, undisturbed Kubiena box samples (thin sections M1–10) were collected in 1994 from Trench 2; (eight samples of 2.5 m thick dark earth; one sample of the piling substrate at 5.0 m) and Trench 3 (one sample of 11th to 13th century buried soil) (Table 4.46). Of all the soil samples collected in 1995, two, overlapping 0.5 m long monolith cores from 'dark earth' in Trench 7 were selected for processing (thin sections M1a–2e; bulk samples 1xA–1xE). In all, 18 thin-sections and nine bulk samples were analysed from 13 archaeological contexts.

Soil micromorphology

Thin-sections of 8 cm and 7.5 cm were impregnated with a crystic resin mixture and manufactured into thin sections at Stirling University and Spectrum Petrographics, Oregon (Murphy 1986). Thin sections were viewed at a number of magnifications from x1, up to x400 under the polarising microscope and employed plane polarised light (PPL), crossed

Table 4.46 Soil micromorphology: microfacies types (soil microfabric types and associated data)

Material	*Sample no. examples*	*Sampling depth (cm), soil micromorphology (SM), bulk data (BD), microprobe (probe), elemental map (EM)*	*Location, phase, interpretation, comments*
			PEV 94 Upper Trench (2), north facing section
Soil Microfabric 8/ Microfacies 8	*M1*	44–52 SM: homogeneous, massive with planar/prismatic microstructure with burrows; 20–25% voids, dominant moderately accommodated planes & chambers; *Coarse Mineral*: C:F, mainly 60:40, as MF2b; *Coarse Organic/Anthropogenic*: many coarse sand to gravel-size flint, decalcifying mortar, chalk, pottery & sandstone/silts/Greensand some partially to strongly burned, occasional burned shell & humic soil, occasional wood charcoal (max. 6 mm), rare, ubiquitous occasional to many coprolitic material – bone & amorphous types (autofluorescent under Blue Light), inc. large (15 mm) 'cess-pit nodules' (patterned but colourless, isotropic except for patches of low order interference colours, autofluorescent); rare frags humified plant frags; rare instance of sand-size vesicular (siliceous?) slag; *Fine Fabric*: heavily speckled & dotted, dark yellowish brown to yellowish (PPL), v. low interference colours (close porphyric, speckled & rarely crystallitic, XPL), greyish brown with many black specks (OIL); abundant amorphous organic matter, rare humified tissue frags & many to abundant fine charred material, occasional to many phytoliths & rare diatoms, with rare ash; *Pedofeatures*: rare instances of secondary sparitic $CaCO_3$; many to abundant yellowish (Fe/P?) impregnative staining, associated with amorphous & autofluorescent coprolitic material, & rare amorphous iron void coating formation; rare thin <500 µm organic excrements, occasional loose v. broad burrow fills & v. abundant broad organo-mineral excrements, with rare biogenic calcite (earthworm granules showing decalcification).	Context 3 (12th–13thC Norman/residual Roman?); Heterogenous soil containing frequent dark brown humic soil frags juxtaposed to common yellow, phosphatic soil containing ashes, charcoal, phytoliths of probable cess origin ('yellow clay'?). Frequent inclusions inc. chalk, frags sandy brown soil (Eb?) & layered silt/sand of prob. constructional material origin; pottery, & Greensand as well as shell & bone. Phosphatic (probable cess) & calcitic void infillings also occur. Midden deposit incl. cess with additional ubiquitous relic? building materials. *(Continued Midden dumping including large amounts toilet/garderobe (cess) waste, indicative of increased occupation intensity?)*
Soil Microfabric 8/ Microfacies 8	*M2*	75–83 SM: homogeneous, massive with planar microstructure with burrows; 15–20% voids, dominant moderately accommodated planes & chambers; *Coarse Mineral*: C:F, mainly 60:40, as MF2b; *Coarse Organic/Anthropogenic*: many coarse sand to gravel-size flint, decalcifying mortar, pottery & sandstone/silts/Greensand some partially to strongly burned, occasional burned shell, rare wood charcoal, rare, ubiquitous occasional to many coprolitic material – bone & amorphous types (autofluorescent under Blue Light), rare instances fish bone; rare frags humified plant fragments & fungal bodies; *Fine Fabric*: heavily speckled & dotted, dark yellowish brown to yellowish (PPL), v. low interference colours (close porphyric, speckled & rarely crystallitic, XPL), greyish brown with many black specks (OIL); abundant amorphous organic matter, rare humified tissue frags & many to abundant fine charred material, occasional to many phytoliths & rare diatoms, with rare ash; *Pedofeatures*: rare impure clay intercalations & coatings; rare instances secondary sparitic $CaCO_3$; abundant yellowish (Fe/P?) impregnative staining, associated with amorphous & autofluorescent coprolitic material, & amorphous iron void coating formation; occasional loose very broad burrow fills & v. abundant broad organo-mineral excrements, with rare biogenic calcite (earthworm granules showing decalcification).	Context 17 (12th–14thC Norman): Biologically mixed homogeneous soil with v. abundant phosphatic pedofeatures, some areas containing ashes, fine charcoal & phytoliths. Inclusions of many coprolitic remains sometimes associated with yellow staining. Secondary iron & calcitic void features. *(Midden dumping inc. large amounts toilet/garderobe (cess) waste, indicative of increased occupation intensity?)*
Soil Microfabric 7/ Microfacies 7	*M3*	106–110 SM: heterogeneous, massive/prismatic with fine blocky & chambered microstructure, with relic laminae; 25–30% voids, dominant planes, chambers & complex packing voids; *Coarse Mineral*: C:F, mainly 60:40, as MF2b, with broad patches/layers of 40:60 (phytoliths-rich)(SM7a); *Coarse Organic/Anthropogenic*: many coarse sand to gravel-size flint, decalcifying flint tempered mortar & sandstone/silts/Greensand – some burned, occasional wood charcoal (<6 mm and as 5 mm size scatters, occasional chalk, ubiquitous occasional coprolitic material – bone & amorphous types (autofluorescent under Blue Light), rare shell & pottery (x1); rare instances ash patches; many amorphous & reddish brown strongly humified (sometimes ferruginised) tissue frags, sometimes partially laminated, & occurring as at least four 0.5–2 mm layers at 108, 108.5, 109, and 110 cm (likely layers of herbivore dung); rare instances root traces (ferruginised sections 0.5–1.5 mm) & eggshell; *Fine Fabric*: heavily speckled & dotted, dark yellowish	Context 17 (12th-14thC Norman): Relatively well-preserved reddish-brown plant remains (highly humified herbivore dung?) and laminated organic matter (stabling crust?) occur as laminae, sometimes in a very open biological fabric that displays thin organic excrements. Preservation has been enhanced by ferruginisation that has also affected *in situ* roots. This is intercalated with a finer phytoliths-dominated ash residue, compared with the 'dark earth' in general.

		brown to brownish (PPL), low interference colours (close porphyric, speckled & occasionally crystallitic, XPL), greyish brown with many black & brown specks (OIL); abundant amorphous organic matter, occasional humified tissue frags & many to abundant fine charred material, occasional phytoliths & rare diatoms, with occasional ash; frequent SM7a – heavily speckled yellowish brown (PPL), v. low interference colours to isotic (open porphyric, speckled & rarely crystallitic, XPL), greyish brown with occasional black specks (OIL); many amorphous organic matter, many fine charred material, many phytoliths & rare diatoms, with rare ash; *Pedofeatures*: rare dusty clay void coatings; rare instances secondary microsparitic $CaCO_3$; many ferruginised humified organic matter (tissue & amorphous 'dung') & roots, with occasional iron impregnation of discontinuous 4 x 11 mm patches & 3 mm wide laminae (poss. Fe/P impregnation); with rare biogenic calcite (slug & earthworm granules showing decalcification); occasional patches <500 µm organic excrements (humified organic matter), abundant broad & v. broad organo-mineral excrements & burrow fills, commonly aggregated.	*(Likely ash midden dumping interspersed with stabling/domestic animal refuse disposal as stock were concentrated?)*
Soil Microfabric 6/ Microfacies 6		110–114 SM: As soil microfabric type 6, with non-crystallitic fine fabric and rare decalcifying earthworm granules and instances of slug plates.	Context 24 (7th–11thC Saxon/Roman): Soil at base of slide is both homogeneous & highly compacted, & earthworm burrows have penetrated this layer. Dominantly decalcified 'dark earth'. *(Continuing 'dark earth' soil formation in midden spreads containing relic Roman material)*
Soil Microfabric 6/ Microfacies 6	*M4*	134–140 SM: homogeneous, massive with channel, blocky & coarse burrow microstructure; 15–20% voids, dominant channels, with planes, chambers & medium vughs; *Coarse Mineral*: C:F, mainly 60:40, as MF2b; *Coarse Organic/Anthropogenic*: many coarse sand to gravel-size flint (max. 30 mm long), decalcifying mortar & sandstone/silts/Greensand some partially to strongly burned, occasional wood charcoal (<7 mm, and a possible l mm thick layer at 156 cm), rare chalk & sand-size humic soil inclusions, ubiquitous occasional coprolitic material – bone & amorphous types (autofluorescent under Blue Light); *Fine Fabric*: heavily speckled & dotted, dark yellowish brown (PPL), low interference colours (close porphyric, speckled & rarely crystallitic, XPL), greyish brown with many black specks (OIL); many amorphous organic matter & many to abundant fine charred material, occasional phytoliths & rare diatoms, with rare ash; *Pedofeatures*: v. abundant bow-shaped passage fills (interlaced like intercalations), with rare biogenic calcite (earthworm granules showing decalcification); occasional iron & manganese impregnative stains & likely iron phosphate nodules; v. abundant broad & very broad organo-mineral excrements & burrow fills.	Context 24 (7th–11thC Saxon/Roman): Long weathered & earthworm worked 'dark earth' of once-ash-rich midden material with relic humus, phytoliths, fine coprolitic material, of likely waste ground origin. Fine nature of material, apart from gravel size stones etc, could indicate dumping of sweepings? One dumping episode at 156 cm marked by scatter of wood charcoal & burned brickearth/massive local silts. Above this band coarser inclusions appear to be more abundant, comprising burned brickearth clay, flint, chalk as well as shell. Possible junction of 2 similar dumped deposits, the lower being more midden-like & the upper containing building debris. *(Continuing 'dark earth' soil formation in midden spreads containing relic Roman material)*
Soil Microfabric 6/ Microfacies 6	*M5*	152–160 SM: homogeneous, massive with channel, blocky & burrow microstructure; 15–25% voids, dominant channels, with planes, chambers & medium vughs; *Coarse Mineral*: C:F, mainly 60:40, as MF2b; *Coarse Organic/Anthropogenic*: many coarse sand to gravel-size flint, decalcifying mortar & sandstone/Greensand, only rare wood charcoal (mainly <1 mm size) rare chalk fine sand-size siliceous vesicular slag; ubiquitous occasional coprolitic material – bone, amorphous, plant tissue (articulated phytoliths – bran?) types (autofluorescent under Blue Light); *Fine Fabric*: heavily speckled & dotted, dark yellowish brown (PPL), moderate interference colours (close porphyric, speckled & occasionally crystallitic, XPL), greyish brown with many black specks (OIL); many amorphous organic matter & many to abundant fine charred material, occasional phytoliths & rare diatoms, with rare ash; *Pedofeatures*: v. abundant bow-shaped passage fills (like intercalations), with rare biogenic calcite (slug & earthworm granules showing decalcification); v. abundant broad & v. broad organo-mineral excrements & burrow fills, commonly aggregated.	Context 24 (7th–11thC Saxon/Roman): long weathered and earthworm worked 'dark earth' of once-ash-rich midden material with relic humus, phytoliths, fine coprolitic material, of likely waste ground origin. Fine nature of material, apart from gravel size stones etc, could indicate dumping of sweepings? *(Continuing 'dark earth' soil formation in midden spreads containing relic Roman material)*

Soil Microfabric 5/ Microfacies 5	*M6*	183–185.5 SM: moderately heterogeneous, massive with channel, blocky & burrow microstructure; 25% voids, dominant channels, with planes, chambers & medium vughs; *Coarse Mineral*: C:F, mainly 60:40, as SMF2a & MF2b; *Coarse Organic/Anthropogenic*: occasional eggshell, including 3–4 layers of *c.* 52 frags, 360 μm wide & <1.5 mm in length; also one frag. 1200 μm wide & 4 mm long; ubiquitous fine bone & coprolitic material (yellow nodules with vivianite centres); chalk, shell, burned soil & siliceous 'plant remains', rare wood charcoal & pot & 1 sand-size heterogeneous brown stained human-like one; *Fine Fabric*: heavily speckled & dotted, dark yellowish brown (PPL), moderate interference colours (close porphyric, speckled & occasionally crystallitic, XPL), greyish brown with many black specks (OIL); many amorphous organic matter & many to abundant fine charred material, rare to occasional phytoliths & rare diatoms, with rare ash; *Pedofeatures*: rare to occasional (in burrow features) (200–400 μm) bow-shaped v. dusty clay to intercalations (foci of fine charred & amorphous organic matter silty clay); abundant biological mixing & passage features; rare weathered slug & earthworm granules.	Context 25 (7th–11thC Saxon/Roman): strongly earthworm worked midden deposits, containing *in situ* dumps of eggshell (2 species of bird?; general fine to coarse coprolitic material, some likely human, & small amounts charcoal & perhaps increasing amounts phytoliths; ashes ubiquitous, as below, but again biogenic calcite showing affects of weathering. *(Continuing 'dark earth' soil formation in midden spreads containing relic Roman material)*
Soil Microfabric 4/ Microfacies 4	*M6*	185.5–191 SM: heterogeneous, massive with channel, blocky & burrow microstructure; 20% voids, dominant channels, with planes, chambers & medium vughs; *Coarse Mineral*: C:F, mainly 60:40, as SMF2a; *Coarse Organic/Anthropogenic*: abundant coarse to fine (<1.5 mm) sandstone, Greensand & brickearth-like frags, some sand 'soil' frags showing relic rooting porosity; many wood charcoal; occasional coprolites including 2 sand-size blackish bone dog-like ones, shell, chalk, burned soil & burned siliceous material; rare v. fine eggshell & mortar; *Fine Fabric*: heavily speckled & dotted, dark to pale yellowish brown (PPL), moderate interference colours (close porphyric, speckled & commonly crystallitic, XPL), greyish brown with many black specks (OIL); many amorphous organic matter & many to abundant fine charred material, rare phytoliths & diatoms, with rare to occasional ash; *Pedofeatures*: rare iron mottling around sandstone & other frags & rarely impregnating the soil matrix; v. dominant fabric mixing (burrowing), with rare biogenic calcite (granules), commonly showing decalcification.	Context 31 (7th–11thC Saxon/Roman): Layer strongly characterised by Hastings Beds, local & burned soil, in generally once ash-rich midden material, which seems to have undergone rooting & minor weathering; seems to contain fewer relic Roman building debris. *(Continuing 'dark earth' soil formation in midden spreads containing relic Roman material)*
Soil Microfabric 3b/Microfacies 3b	*M7*	234–238 SM: massive with channel, blocky & burrow microstructure; 20% voids, dominant channels, with planes, chambers & medium vughs; *Coarse Mineral*: C:F, mainly 60:40, as SMF2a and SMF2b; *Coarse Organic/Anthropogenic*: occasional to many wood charcoal (mainly mm size), inc. some yellow-stained charcoal, occasional gravel & coarse sand-size sandstone, mortar (weathered mortar & plaster), chalk, burned charcoal-rich soil & flint, rare, fine sand-size siliceous vesicular slag (melted sand or phytoliths?) with rare (x3) round or semi-circular siliceous pseudomorphs of monocotyledonous plant (straw thatch?) remains with vesicles/vascular pores (eg, 1400 μm diam.), burned sediment (x1: mixture of fine sand/coarse silt with phytoliths, diatoms & relic organic matter fragments – coastal mud?) & shell; ubiquitous coprolitic bone & coprolites (yellow phosphate – with vivianite – cemented charcoal nodules [x3] – 'nightsoil'?) – especially in burrow fills; *Fine Fabric*: heavily speckled & dotted, dark yellowish brown (PPL), moderate interference colours (close porphyric, speckled & occasionally crystallitic, XPL), greyish brown with many black specks (OIL); many amorphous organic matter (to abundant in burrow fills) & many to abundant fine charred material, rare (but more than in SMF2) phytoliths & diatoms, with rare to occasional ash; *Pedofeatures*: rare thin (100 μm) v. dusty clay coatings (affecting 1 burrow fill); occasional infills of yellow and brownish yellow amorphous iron & phosphate, with commonly associated vivianite formation (cess?); also concentrated around organic matter & charcoal (see above – 'nightsoil'); v. abundant burrow/passage feature mixing of the deposit (both small [200–300 μm] slug plates (calcite) to large (1.6 mm) earthworm granules, some in general matrix showing decalcification.	Context 36/37/45?(Late Roman 4th century): Similar Roman 'dark earth' soil formation as below, but with much less coarse wood charcoal, but with inclusion of siliceous pseudomorphs/melted silica of prob. burned straw (thatch?) origin; contains similar small quantities anthropogenic inclusions, relic of Roman period & phosphate/charcoal nodules & coprolitic bone, but is later affected by small amounts of inwash of cess, & cess material being burrowed into soil; slug granules present & may reflect the amounts of amorphous organic matter present whereas earthworm granules occur in coarse earthworm burrows. *(Initial stages of 'dark earth' formation in relic Late Roman deposits and continuing low intensity Romano-British? midden deposits)*

Soil Microfabric 3a/Microfacies 3a	*M7*	238–242 SM: massive with channel, blocky microstructure; 20–25% voids, dominant channels, with planes, chambers & medium vughs; *Coarse Mineral*: C:F, mainly 60:40, as SMF2a and SMF2b; *Coarse Organic/Anthropogenic*: abundant wood charcoal, including 1–2 mm diam. twig wood, many gravel-size pottery, mortar (weathering mortar & plaster), iron-stone & flint, rare coarse sand-size heavily burned coarse silty daub (grey with rubified edges, & with plant frag. pseudomorphs), fine sand-size siliceous slag, shell & chalk; coprolitic bone & coprolites (yellow phosphate – with vivianite – cemented charcoal nodules – 'nightsoil'?), charcoal-rich soil frags; *Fine Fabric*: heavily speckled & dotted, dark yellowish brown (PPL), moderate interference colours (close porphyric, speckled & occasionally crystallitic, XPL), greyish brown with many black specks (OIL); many amorphous organic matter & many to abundant fine charred material, rare (but more than in SMF2) phytoliths & diatoms, with rare ash; *Pedofeatures*: rare thin (50–100 µm) v. dusty clay coatings; rare (but concentrated around organic matter & charcoal) yellow & brownish yellow amorphous & radial patterned amorphous iron & phosphate, with commonly associated vivianite formation; abundant burrow/passage feature mixing of deposit (single earthworm granule).	Context 39, 38/52 ? – (Late Roman 4th century): Strongly earthworm-worked charcoal & moderately anthropogenic debris-rich 'dark earth' soil layer; as charcoal is largely intact, this contribution to 'dark earth' soil formation was short-lived prior to next layer (camp-fires); presence of burned soil & twig wood charcoal could suggest small domestic fires, while, in addition, strongly burned & melted silty daub & siliceous slag indicate 'industrial' activity too; building debris in the form of plaster & mortar also present alongside latrine waste. Presence of diatoms & phytoliths, with strong homogenisation by earthworms (earthworm granule), reflects broad pedological nature of developing 'dark earth' here. *(Possible spread of charcoal, soil & latrine waste that includes small amounts of constructional, domestic & 'industrial' waste, poss. reflecting last 'Roman' fort activities)*
Soil Microfabric 2a–c/Microfacies 2aKc	*M8*	242–246 SM: massive with coarse layering of: 242–243 (SMF2c): sharp curved and sloping boundary from SMF2b to SMF2c, marked by horizontally laid wood charcoal frags; loose, massive & heterogeneous; 25% voids; channel & chambers; *Coarse Mineral*: C:F, mainly 60:40, as SMF2a; *Coarse Organic/Anthropogenic*: occasional wood charcoal, rare bone & burned bone & coprolitic frags, burned soil – as below; *Fine Fabric*: speckled & dusty brown (PPL), moderate interference colours (close porphyric, speckled, XPL), pale yellowish brown to brown, with occasional black specks (OIL); occasional fine amorphous organic matter with abundant fine charcoal, rare phytoliths & rare ash crystals; *Pedofeatures*: occasional thin (50–100 µm) v. dusty clay coatings; rare (but concentrated around organic matter & charcoal) yellow & brownish yellow amorphous & radial patterned amorphous iron & phosphate, with commonly associated vivianite formation; rare micritic calcite void coatings; many burrow/passage feature mixing of the deposit. 243–245 (SMF2b): massive with channel & chamber microstructure; 20% voids; channel & chambers; *Coarse Mineral*: C:F, 30:70–60:40, as SMF2a; *Coarse Organic/Anthropogenic*: as SMF2b, but fewer; *Fine Fabric*: heavily speckled & dusty darkish brown (PPL), low to moderate interference colours (close porphyric, speckled, XPL), pale yellowish brown to brown, with many black specks (OIL); many to occasional fine amorphous organic matter with abundant fine charcoal, rare phytoliths & rare ash crystals; *Pedofeatures*: occasional thin to thick (50–400 µm) v. dusty clay coatings & void infills – poss. some intercalations; rare (but concentrated around organic matter & charcoal) yellow & brownish yellow amorphous & radial patterned amorphous iron & phosphate, with commonly associated vivianite formation; rare micritic calcite void coatings; abundant burrow/passage feature mixing of the deposit. 245–246 (SMF2a): massive and heterogeneous; 20% voids, vughs & chambers; *Coarse Mineral*: C:F, 70:30, very dominant silt & fine sand-size quartz, with few mica & v. few glauconite; *Coarse Organic/Anthropogenic*: many gravel-size to sand-size flint, ironstone, Hastings Beds (silts & glauconitic sandstone) & pottery, with many coarse (<9 mm) size wood charcoal, occasional burned soil (& grey & also rubified strongly burned daub) & silty rock & burned chalk, rare coprolitic bone, phosphatic & vivianite nodules, burned shell, chalk, shell, patches of wood ash, poss. dung (x1), frags of amorphous organic matter/lignified bark?; *Fine Fabric*: speckled & dusty darkish brown to dark reddish brown (PPL), moderate interference colours (close porphyric, speckled & crystallitic, XPL), pale yellowish brown to brown, with many black specks (OIL); many to occasional fine amorphous organic matter with many fine charcoal,	Context 61 (Late Roman, *c.* AD 370+): 242–243 (SMF2c): Moderately earthworm-worked likely (erosive?) wash/fill of soil and anthropogenic inclusions/occupation debris. *(Subsequent foundation trench cleaning episode)* 243–245 (SMF2b): Earthworm-worked layer composed of poss. ditch-fill silty clay (rich in fine charcoal) and silty and sandy natural; secondary/associated inwash of dusty clay & phosphatic solutions in evidence, alongside coprolitic material; soil becoming rather homogenised before burial by SMF2c. *(Cleaning of foundation trench infilled with charcoal-rich silt & latrine waste)* Context 63/67 (Late Roman, *c.* AD 370+): 245–246 (SMF2a): Basal earthworm-worked deposit of wood charcoal, ash, burned soil & sandstone silty to fine sandy soil (some humic topsoil frags)(& some fine midden bone & coprolite waste), as relic of pre-wall construction occupation involving fires, middening & digging; earthworm burrowing & secondary calcium carbonate formation are evidence of period of weathering, prior to SMF2b formation,

		rare phytoliths & rare to occasional ash crystals; *Pedofeatures*: occasional thin (50–100 µm) v. dusty clay coatings & void infills – poss. some intercalations; occasional (but concentrated around organic matter & charcoal) yellow & brownish yellow amorphous & radial patterned amorphous iron & phosphate, with commonly associated vivianite formation; rare micritic calcite void coatings; abundant burrow/passage feature mixing of the deposit.	which also produced dusty clay coating features. (*Occupation contemporary with foundation trench construction?*)
Soil Microfabric 1b/Microfacies 1b	*M8*	246–250 SM: as SMF1a, but dominantly composed of coarse silt; massive & heterogeneous, with relic laminae; 15% voids, coarse chambers & fine channels; *Coarse Organic/Anthropogenic*: rare flint (x2), pot (x4) & mortar (x2) containing flint & glauconite, & rare wood charcoal (x5); *Fine Fabric*: pale brown to grey, speckled (PPL), low interference colours (close porphyric, speckled b-fabric, XPL), pale grey with common yellow patches (OIL); many thin amorphous organic matter & staining relic of geology & weakly iron stained; *Pedofeatures*: rare clay infills; many iron impregnations of relic bedding, with sharp edged iron hypocoatings to channels; many (eg 1–4 mm wide) burrows at junction with SMF2 above, with occasional burrow fills below.	Context 71 (Truncated Hastings Beds?): Massive, root & likely earthworm-burrowed, truncated natural geological coarse silts; with rare anthropogenic inclusions, but abundant iron impregnation of newly formed porosity & relic bedding; burrowed upper junction with Roman activity layer. (*Truncated geological substrate*)
Soil Microfabric 1a/Microfacies 1a	*M10*	550–558 SM: *Structure*: massive & laminated (1–3 mm); 5% voids, vughs, & complex & simple packing voids; *Coarse Mineral*: C:F (limit at 10 µm), 95:05; very dominant well-sorted (laminae of) v. fine silt-size & subangular coarse silt-size quartz; few mica & v. few opaques; *Fine Fabric*: v. pale brown to grey, speckled (PPL), low interference colours (close porphyric, speckled b-fabric, XPL), pale grey (OIL); apparent absence of organic matter but rare thin iron staining; *Pedofeatures*: rare (single instance) 3 mm wide silt & clay infill, moderately well oriented; rare iron staining.	Context 510 (Geology: piling substrate): Massive and finely laminated Hasting Beds? silts, with instance of clay & silt inwash, likely result of disturbance possibly dating to piling. (*Piling substrate*)
			PEV 94 Lower Trench
Soil Microfabric 8/ Microfacies 8	*M9*	SM: As SMF 8, but crystallitic and ash-rich; occasional sand-size secondary likely phosphate nodules.	Context 17?: Dark earth below 11th–12th C masonry wall; foundation debris of mortar, chalk, Greensand clasts & anthropogenic inclusions (bone & coprolite) buries 'dark earth' that partially retains its calcitic ash-rich nature (origin of 'yellow clay'?)
			PEV 95 Trench 7
Soil Microfabric 6 & 7?/Microfacies 6 & 7?	*M1a*	24.0–31.0 SM: As SMF6 (poor sample), but includes sand-size patches of likely wood ash (grey micritic crystals with typical very thin excremental fabric) & likely iron impregnated ash residues, with moderate interference colours (see microprobe, below) BD: moderately humic (5.5% LOI) and moderately phosphate-rich (2350 ppm P_2O_5), with moderately low MS (93 x $10^{-8}SIkg^{-1}$), & low Pratio (1.4). Probe: impregnated fabric – eg, 3.84% Fe, 5.16% Ca, 0.157% P & 2.982% S (see Table 4.47); Elemental map shows mortar frag. juxtaposed to Fe (Mn and P) cemented soil containing Ca/P bone-coprolites.	Context 717 (no pottery): Strongly homogenised 'dark earth'. The once ash-rich deposit has undergone partial decalcification & iron impregnation. Enhanced P ratio may result from the inclusion of organic dung residues.
Soil Microfabric 8 /Microfacies 8	*M1b*	41.0–45.0 SM: As SMF6 (poor sample), with yellowish brown stained sandy soil, indicative of Fe & P impregnation (from cess?)(see microprobe, below). BD: moderately humic (5.3% LOI) & moderately phosphate-rich (2550 ppm P_2O_5OI), with moderately low MS (96 x $10^{-8}SIkg^{-1}$), and low Pratio (1.0). Probe: (impregnated soil area) – e.g. 12.4% Si, 1.96% Al, 1.79% Fe, 0.486% Ca and 1.17% P (see Table 4.47). Elemental maps show yellow staining is from P/Ca/Fe (Mn) complexes.	Context 734 (no pottery): Strongly homogenised 'dark earth'. The once ash-rich deposit has undergone partial decalcification & inputs of Fe/Ca/P-rich cess (toilet waste) have contaminated patches of the soil particularly with P.

Soil Microfabric 6/ Microfacies 6	*M1c*	46.0–52.0 SM: homogeneous, massive & prismatic with planar microstructure; 20–25% voids, dominant planes, chambers & medium vughs; *Coarse Mineral*: C:F, mainly 60:40, as MF2b; *Coarse Organic/Anthropogenic*: occasional coarse sand to gravel-size flint, decalcifying mortar & sandstone/silts/Greensand some partially to strongly burned, rare wood charcoal, rare chalk, ubiquitous occasional coprolitic material – bone & amorphous types (autofluorescent under Blue Light); many shell; *Fine Fabric*: heavily speckled & dotted, dark yellowish brown (PPL), low interference colours (close porphyric, speckled & rarely crystallitic, XPL), greyish brown with many black specks (OIL); many to abundant amorphous organic matter & many to abundant fine charred material, occasional phytoliths and rare diatoms, with rare ash; *Pedofeatures*: v. abundant bow-shaped passage fills (interlaced like intercalations), with rare biogenic calcite (earthworm granules showing decalcification); v. abundant broad & v. broad organo-mineral excrements & burrow fills; strong aggregation of excremental fabric. BD: moderately humic (5.4% LOI) & moderately phosphate-rich (2580 ppm P_2O_5), with moderately low MS (90 x $10^{-8}SIkg^{-1}$), & low Pratio (0.9).	Context 734 (no pottery): strongly homogenised 'dark earth', with partially homogenised inclusions of humic soil and humified, possible herbivore dung. The once ash-rich deposit has undergone partial decalcification that also affected biogenic calcite (earthworm and slug). Relic amounts of organic matter (LOI), phosphate, low P ratio and magnetic susceptibility data testify to dumping of burned organic and phosphate-rich waste.
Soil Microfabric 6 & 7/Microfacies 6 & 7	*M1d*	54.0–60.0 SM: homogeneous, massive with fragmented prismatic & blocky microstructure; 20–25% voids, dominant planes & simple packing voids; *Coarse Mineral*: C:F, mainly 60:40, as MF2b; *Coarse Organic/Anthropogenic*: many coarse sand to gravel-size flint, decalcifying mortar (including Greensand clasts) & sandstone/silts/Greensand some partially to strongly burned, rare wood charcoal, rare chalk, ubiquitous occasional coprolitic material – bone & amorphous types (autofluorescent under Blue Light); rare shell; rare fine inclusions of humified organic matter; single instance of 4 mm size amorphous/humified organic matter coprolite & stained soil area (omnivore?)(see microprobe); *Fine Fabric*: heavily speckled & dotted, dark yellowish brown (PPL), low interference colours (close porphyric, speckled & rarely crystallitic, XPL), greyish brown with many black specks (OIL); many to abundant amorphous organic matter & many to abundant fine charred material, occasional phytoliths & rare diatoms, with rare ash; *Pedofeatures*: v. abundant bow-shaped passage fills (interlaced like intercalations), with rare biogenic calcite (earthworm granules showing decalcification); v. abundant broad & v. broad organo-mineral excrements & burrow fills; strong aggregation of excremental fabric. BD: moderately humic (5.2% LOI) and moderately phosphate-rich (3010 ppm P_2O_5), with moderately low MS (110 x $10^{-8}SIkg^{-1}$), & low Pratio (1.0). Probe: (amorphous organic coprolite) – eg, 1.89% Fe, 5.24% Ca & 1.82% P (see Table 4.47). Elemental map shows organic coprolite to be impregnated with P/Ca/Fe(Mn) complexes with patches of pure Ca/P.	Context 718 (Roman & Saxon, some 13th C pottery): Strongly homogenised 'dark earth', with rare inclusions of partially homogenised inclusions of humic soil & humified, animal dung, with 1 phosphatised (omnivore) coprolite frag. The once ash-rich deposit has undergone partial decalcification that also affected biogenic calcite (earthworm & slug). Relic amounts of organic matter (LOI), phosphate, low P ratio & magnetic susceptibility data testify to dumping of burned organic & phosphate-rich waste, which may possibly have been worked by pigs.
Soil Microfabric 6/ Microfacies 6	*M1e*	62.0–68.0 mm SM: homogeneous, massive with prismatic & planar microstructure; 15–20% voids, dominant planar voids, with fine channels; *Coarse Mineral*: C:F, mainly 60:40, as MF2b; *Coarse Organic/Anthropogenic*: many coarse sand to gravel-size flint, chalk, decalcifying mortar & sandstone/silts/Greensand with some partially to strongly burned, rare wood charcoal, rare pottery, ubiquitous occasional coprolitic material – bone & amorphous types (autofluorescent under Blue Light); *Fine Fabric*: heavily speckled & dotted, dark yellowish brown (PPL), low interference colours (close porphyric, speckled & rarely crystallitic, XPL), greyish brown with many black specks (OIL); many amorphous organic matter & many to abundant fine charred material, occasional phytoliths & rare diatoms, with rare ash; *Pedofeatures*: v. abundant bow-shaped passage fills (interlaced like intercalations), with rare biogenic calcite (earthworm granules showing decalcification); v. abundant v. broad (10 mm) loose burrow fills; v. abundant broad & v. broad organo-mineral excrements & burrow fills.	Context 718 (Roman & Saxon, some 13th C pottery): strongly homogenised 'dark earth', with partially homogenised inclusions of humic soil & humified, possible herbivore dung. The once ash-rich deposit has undergone partial decalcification that also affected biogenic calcite (earthworm and slug).

Soil Microfabric 6 and 7/Microfacies 6 and 7	*M2a*	43.0–50.0 SM: homogeneous, massive with channel, prismatic & coarse burrow microstructure; 15–20% voids, dominant channels, with planes, chambers & medium vughs; *Coarse Mineral*: C:F, mainly 60:40, as MF2b; *Coarse Organic/Anthropogenic*: many coarse sand to gravel-size flint (some burned), decalcifying mortar & sandstone/silts/Greensand some partially to strongly burned, rare wood charcoal, rare chalk & many sand & gravel-size humic soil inclusions, ubiquitous occasional coprolitic material – bone & amorphous types (autofluorescent under Blue Light); rare shell; *Fine Fabric*: heavily speckled & dotted, dark yellowish brown (PPL), low interference colours (close porphyric, speckled & rarely crystallitic, XPL), greyish brown with many black specks (OIL); many to abundant amorphous organic matter & many to abundant fine charred material, occasional phytoliths & rare diatoms, with rare ash; *Pedofeatures*: v. abundant bow-shaped passage fills (interlaced like intercalations), with rare biogenic calcite (earthworm granules showing decalcification); v. abundant broad & v. broad organo-mineral excrements & burrow fills; strong aggregation of excremental fabric. BD: moderately humic (5.3–5.6% LOI) & moderately phosphate-rich (2790–2950 ppm P_2O_5), with moderately low MS (100-107 x $10^{-8}SIkg^{-1}$), & low Pratio (1.0).	Context 734 (no pottery): strongly homogenised 'dark earth', with partially homogenised inclusions of humic soil and humified, possible herbivore dung. The once ash-rich deposit has undergone partial decalcification that also affected biogenic calcite (earthworm and slug). Relic amounts of organic matter (LOI), phosphate, low P ratio and magnetic susceptibility data testify to dumping of burned organic and phosphate-rich waste.
Soil Microfabric 6/ Microfacies 6	*M2b*	59.0–65.0 SM: homogeneous, massive with coarse burrow microstructure; 20–25% voids, dominant chambers & packing voids, with fine channels; *Coarse Mineral*: C:F, mainly 60:40, as MF2b; *Coarse Organic/ Anthropogenic*: occasional coarse sand to gravel-size flint, chalk, decalcifying mortar & sandstone/silts/ Greensand with some partially to strongly burned, rare wood charcoal, ubiquitous occasional coprolitic material – bone & amorphous types (autofluorescent under Blue Light); *Fine Fabric*: heavily speckled & dotted, dark yellowish brown (PPL), low interference colours (close porphyric, speckled & rarely crystallitic, XPL), greyish brown with many black specks (OIL); many amorphous organic matter and many to abundant fine charred material, occasional phytoliths & rare diatoms, with rare ash; *Pedofeatures*: v. abundant bow-shaped passage fills (interlaced like intercalations), with rare biogenic calcite (earthworm granules showing decalcification); v. abundant v. broad (10 mm) loose burrow fills; v. abundant broad & v. broad organo-mineral excrements and burrow fills.	Context 734 (no pottery): Strongly homogenised 'dark earth'. The once ash-rich deposit has undergone partial decalcification that also affected biogenic calcite (earthworm and slug).
Soil Microfabric 6/ Microfacies 6	*M2c*	66.0–72.0 SM: Aas SMF6 (poor sample) BD: moderately humic (5.4% LOI) & moderately phosphate-rich (2950 ppm P_2O_5), with moderately low MS (101 x $10^{-8}SIkg^{-1}$), & low Pratio (1.0).	Context 718 (Roman & Saxon, some 13th C pottery): Fine fabric, coarse inclusions & chemistry comparable to samples M2a & M2b. These data testify to dumping of burned organic & phosphate-rich waste, & lengthy period of homogenisation.
Soil Microfabric 6/ Microfacies 6	*M2d*	74.0–79.0 SM: as SMF6 (poor sample) BD: moderately humic (5.3% LOI) & moderately phosphate-rich (3130 ppm P_2O_5), with moderately low MS (108 x $10^{-8}SIkg^{-1}$), & low Pratio (1.0).	Context 718 (Roman & Saxon, some 13th C pottery): Fine fabric, coarse inclusions & chemistry comparable to samples M2a & M2b. These data testify to dumping of burned organic & phosphate-rich waste, & lengthy period of homogenisation.
	M2e	80.0–86.0 SM: as SMF 6; inc. 100 x 2 mm size coprolite of transformed bone (fine patchy grey stained, v. pale yellow to colourless with a brown stained 40–600 µm wide outermost margin, mainly isotic with v. low interference colours & form birefringence, whitish under OIL & strongly autofluorescent under Blue Light; microprobe data below). BD: moderately humic (5.2% LOI) & moderately phosphate-rich (2930 ppm P_2O_5), with moderately low MS (93 x $10^{-8}SIkg^{-1}$), & low Pratio (1.0). Probe: coprolite – (mean values n=14) e.g. 31.50% Ca & 12.8% P; margin 15.07% Ca & 6.71% P (n=2) (see Table 4.47).	Context 718 (Roman & Saxon, some 13th C pottery): Fine fabric, coarse inclusions & chemistry comparable to samples M2a and M2b. These data testify to dumping of burned organic & phosphate-rich waste (including coprolitic material), & lengthy period of homogenisation.

polarised light (XPL), oblique incident light (OIL) and blue light (BL). The combined use of these different forms of illumination permits a large number of optical tests to be made, enabling more precise identification of materials (Bullock *et al.* 1985; Stoops 1996). Archaeological microfeatures and materials were also identified from published and unpublished archaeological and reference studies, with semi-quantitative counting based upon Bullock *et al.* (1985) and (1989; 1994; Macphail and Cruise 2001; Macphail and Goldberg 2010).

A Jeol JXA8600 EPMA was used at the Institute of Archaeology, University College London (UCL) to carry out microprobe analyses of soil microfabrics, features and included materials. Areas of interest were analysed from four, uncovered thin-sections (samples M1a, M1b, M1c and M2e; Tables 4.46 and 4.47). These were first examined under the scanning electron microscope (SEM), and a number of features, were chosen for point and grid analysis, and elemental mapping. Amounts of Si, Al, Fe, Mn, Ca, K, Mg, Na, P, S and Cl were measured (reported as mean % in Table 4.47). Elemental maps were photographed from the VDU (available in archive).

Chemistry

Organic matter (LOI), low frequency magnetic susceptibility (χ; x 10^{-8} SI kg^{-1}), and phosphate (2% citric acid extractable P_2O_5 pretreated with HCl to offset the presence of any calcium carbonate) were measured on the bulk samples (Arrhenius 1934; Arrhenius 1955; Engelmark and Linderholm 1996; Macphail *et al.* 2000).

Results and Discussion

Soil micromorphology and chemistry are presented in Table 4.46, where basic interpretations are also suggested. Microprobe data are tabulated in Table 4.47. Thin section sample numbers, micro-stratigraphic units, archaeological contexts, bulk chemical data, and soil micromorphological counts are given Appendix 3. Scans of selected thin sections (x10), photomicrographs of micromorphological features (x34) and microprobe elemental maps (x20) are available in the archive. The chemistry of the 'dark earth' at Pevensey is compared with other contemporary English sites in Appendix 4 (Macphail and Linderholm 2004).

Local soils and sediments

The examination of the natural subsoil into which the piles were driven (context 510) proved to be a useful exercise, because not only did the natural sediment contain possible textural features (Bullock *et al.* 1985) of disturbance, but provided an example of the natural parent material (Table 4.46, M10), the Hastings Beds that would have supplied sands (Tunbridge Wells Sand and Ashdown Sand) and clay (Wadhurst Clay) for building purposes (Gallois 1965; see Peers 1953; Fulford and Rippon 1994). Similar sediment and soil probably formed from this geology are ubiquitous in the 'dark earth' and buried Norman soil (M9). For example, it was apparently used as a foundation material and dark earth formed over it behind the fort wall (M8). This local sediment was probably also used in the manufacturing of daub and was included as a coarse temper in mortar.

The local soils have been mapped as stagnogleyic argillic brown earths (Curtisden soil association (Jarvis *et al.* 1984). Probable fragments of these brown soils occur in the deposits and it seems likely that this soil type was extant during the Romano-British period and later. Certainly mature argillic brown earths date to the Romano-British period in London, for example, as developed in brickearth (Macphail and Cruise 2000). On the other hand, it is believed that soil formed from marine alluvium (Newchurch 2 soil association; Jarvis *et al.* 1984) is much more recent and its present exposure dates to post-Norman, artificial drainage.

Late Roman deposits

These are composed of late Roman occupation sediments that display microstratification as identified in a continuous thin section sampling sequence between 2.34–2.50 m depth (natural – context 71; fort construction – contexts 63/67 and 61; 4th century – contexts 39, 38/52? and 35/47?) (M7 and M8, Table 4.46). At the base of the studied sequence (2.46–2.50 m), upcast from the Roman fort-wall construction trench (contexts 63/67) overlies a massive, truncated natural geological layer composed of coarse silts (context 71; Hasting Beds?). These silts underwent rooting and likely earthworm burrowing from the overlying, biologically-worked occupation layer (63/67), becoming contaminated by rare anthropogenic inclusions and abundant iron-staining. Construction layers seem to be composed of three main phases. Layers 63/67; (2.45–2.46 m) are made up of an earthworm-worked deposit of wood charcoal, ash, silty to fine sandy soil, including some humic topsoil fragments, burned soil and sandstone, along with some fine bone and coprolite waste. These appear to be relic of fires, middening and site disturbance, including digging of the construction trench. Earthworm burrowing and secondary calcium-carbonate formation are evidence of a period of weathering, prior to the spread of succeeding construction debris, which also produced dusty, clay-coating features.

Context 61 commences (2.43–2.45 m) with an earthworm-worked soil composed of possible,

Table 4.47 Soil micromorphology: 'Dark earth': microprobe analysis

		%Si	*%Al*	*%Fe*	*%Mn*	*%Ca*	*%K*	*%Mg*	*%Na*	*%P*	*%S*	*%Cl*	*n*
M1a													
Impreg. Matrix (brown)	Mean	8.86	2.41	3.82	0.047	5.16	0.319	0.074	0.036	0.157	2.982	0.028	*35*
	Std. Dev.	6.82	1.84	4.04	0.051	7.42	0.290	0.059	0.030	0.134	4.628	0.019	
M1b													
Impreg. Matrix (yellow)													
	Mean	12.338	1.961	1.792	0.486	2.710	0.389	0.127	0.086	1.172	0.062	0.054	*41*
	Std. Dev.	12.017	1.555	1.842	0.600	2.111	0.220	0.092	0.064	1.231	0.064	0.024	
M1d													
'Organic' coprolite	Mean	9.69	1.87	1.89	0.61	5.24	0.30	0.11	0.05	1.82	0.10	0.04	*38*
	Std. Dev.	5.67	0.94	1.73	1.21	6.78	0.21	0.05	0.04	2.33	0.09	0.03	
M2e													
Matrix	Mean	22.3	3.33	2.20	0.173	3.02	0.649	0.176	0.061	1.00	0.332	0.069	*11*
	Std. Dev.	6.18	1.07	1.99	0.190	3.21	0.294	0.065	0.040	1.84	0.063	0.037	
Coprolite edge	Mean	6.71	1.90	1.18	0.13	15.07	0.35	0.14	0.13	6.71	0.36	0.13	*2*
Coprolite	Mean	0.171	0.373	0.456	0.114	31.50	0.113	0.103	0.104	12.8	0.369	0.097	*14*
	Std. Dev.	0.096	0.120	0.063	0.114	2.67	0.249	0.025	0.029	0.914	0.115	0.037	

dumped, pit or ditch-infill deposits that are rich in fine charcoal (such ditch silts have been described commonly from prehistoric contexts; e.g., Macphail, 1991; Macphail and Crowther 2008). This may imply that the deposits (63/67) are contemporary with the digging of the foundation trench, and that construction of the wall commenced some time after, allowing both silting of the foundation trench and biological working of the first occupation spread. Such dumping from the fill of this construction trench would account for textural pedofeatures affecting the underlying stratigraphy and the presence of latrine waste (coprolites, secondary amorphous and crystalline phosphate – vivianite). Again, this layer became biologically mixed prior to ensuing deposits of pit or ditch fills (2.42–2.43 m).

Latest Roman and earliest post-Roman 'dark earth': 4th to 5/7th century

The base of sample M7 (2.38–2.42 m) appears to be representative of late 4th century activity (contexts 39, 38/52). It is a strongly, earthworm-worked charcoal and moderately anthropogenic debris-rich pre-'dark earth' soil layer. The presence of burned soil and twig-wood charcoal could suggest small 'domestic'/camp fires as the dominant activity represented by this spread, while in addition small amounts of strongly burned and melted silty daub/slag possibly indicate 'industrial' activity alongside inclusions of ubiquitous building debris in the form of plaster and mortar, and latrine waste. The last includes phosphate-stained (*cf.* microprobe data) charcoal, possibly relic of ash employed to sweeten cess, a common finding in occupation sites ('nightsoil'). This low intensity activity may possibly mark the final character of 'formal', Roman occupation of the fort in the early 5th century.

Above (M7; 2.34–2.38 m) is the basal 'dark earth' (contexts 36/37/45), which is 'soil'-dominated and only contains 4th century pottery as dating evidence. Material, such as siliceous pseudomorphs of (burned) 'straw' are also probably relic of burned thatch as investigated through macro-botanical and soil micromorphological studies of burned-down, medieval structures elsewhere (Macphail 2001). The background presence of calcitic material (including ash), diatoms and phytoliths, which have been strongly homogenised by the action of biota such as earthworms (earthworm granules: Canti 1998), reflects broadly the pedological nature of developing 'dark earth' here, as a calcareous brown earth (Macphail 1994). Organic remains, similar to amounts measured chemically in Trench 7 (5.2–5.5% LOI), the presence of slug plates (Canti 1998), and included coprolites and staining by cess (phosphate; see M1b microprobe) indicate continued middening. The latter was recorded as a major late Roman land-use at Deansway, Worcester (Macphail 1994). This soil microfabric (SMT3b) also tends to dominate the ensuing dark earth through into the Saxon period, and is recorded from another area (Trench 7) of the site (Table 4.46).

Early medieval 'dark earth': 5/7th to 11th century

This period is studied from the base of thin section M3 down to M6, from contexts 31 (M6; 185.5–191 m), 25 (M6; 183–185.5 m) and 24 (M5, M4, M3; 1.10–1.85 m). The poorly dated contexts 714 and 718 from Trench 7 can also be employed to help characterise Saxon 'dark earth' (see Table 4.46). In addition to likely relic Roman inclusions such as building debris (fragments of mortar, Hastings Beds geology), the 'dark earth' features fine charred organic matter, phytoliths and has burrow and excremental microfabrics that testify to strong biological homogenization by soil biota. Earthworm granules and slug plates also represent the last. Inputs of coprolitic material are recorded throughout, alongside likely food waste represented by eggshell (at least two species), oyster shell and bone. The very small variation in %LOI (mean 5.3%, range 5.2–5.6%, Std. Dev. 0.133, n=9), the decreased quantity of calcitic material (low interference colours), and the presence of biogenic calcite (earthworm granules) that are partially decalcified testify to the long term oxidation and weathering of this 'dark earth', which, as argued below, seems to have developed over some six centuries (late 4th–11th century) (Appendix 3). Equally, the homogenising effect of 'dark earth' formation has influenced both phosphate (mean 2780 ppm, range 2350–3130 ppm, Std. Dev. 286.7) and χ (mean 99.8 x 10^{-8} SI kg^{-1}, range 90–110 x 10^{-8} SI kg^{-1}, Std. Dev. 7.31). These measurements are not untypical of 'dark earth' studied elsewhere, and for example reflect amounts of bone, cess, coprolite, and burned materials noted in thin section (see Tables 4.46, Appendices 3–4). Nevertheless, secondary phosphate, for example in the form of amorphous material and vivianite are indicative of localised anaerobism, relating to the decomposition of materials, which from the soil micromorphological/ microprobe evidence include weathered ash. These form Fe/Ca/P compounds (see Table 4.47, M1a; 3.84% Fe, 5.16% Ca, 0.157% P). In addition, individual bone-rich coprolites, for example that show loss of apatite from their margins, can be identified (see Table 4.47, M2d; 31.50% Ca and 12.8% P; margin 15.07% Ca and 6.71% P). Some features and inclusions can, however, be identified as reflecting microstratigraphic variation up profile.

For example, context 31 includes fragments of coprolites that are morphologically dog-like (blackish under PPL; *cf.* Macphail 2000; Macphail and Goldberg 2010) indicating scavenging of midden spreads, while context 25 above, features a major spread of eggshell (M6; including 3–4 layers of *c.* 52 fragments, 360 μm wide and up to 1.5 mm in length; also one fragment 1200 μm wide and 4 mm long). In samples M5, M4 and the base of M3, continuing weathering is recorded by the decreasing quantities of preserved ash crystals, as the 'dark earth' became increasingly decalcified upwards (context 24). Although middening rich in grass/cereal ash waste (hence high quantities of phytoliths; Macphail 1981) and coprolitic material continues to dominate, individual events can be preserved, for example at 1.56 m (M4) a dump of wood charcoal precedes midden dumping that is more rich in building debris than the underlying phase.

Unlike some sites where 'dark earth' simply forms out of building and occupation debris relic of the Romano-British period, as for example recorded at a number of London locations, the 'dark earth' at Pevensey Castle continued to accumulate and develop as a soil through continued middening, the vegetation cover likely being composed of ruderal (waste ground) plants. Unfortunately, it is not yet (archaeologically) possible to compare the details of Saxon occupation at Pevensey Castle to that recorded at Whitefriars, Canterbury (Macphail and Crowther 2007) and at Deansway, Worcester, although ash, food waste and latrine waste dumping are ubiquitous. At the last site occupation dates from the 8th century, the burh rampart of *c.* AD 890 sealing some areas of 'natural' soils formed in post-Roman 'dark earth' (Dalwood 1992).

Medieval 'dark earth': 11th to 13th century

Samples M1 (context 3) and M2 and upper M3 (context 17), and possibly samples M1a–M1d (context 717 and upper 734) record 'dark earth' formation during the Norman period up to the construction of the Keep, with sample M9 being one example of later 'dark earth' sealed by the 13th to 15th century external occupation, probably to be associated with the repairs to the Keep in the early 14th century (Table 4.46; see Chapter 2). The possible boundary (1.06 m) between the Saxon and Norman 'dark earth' is characterised by the 'dark earth' featuring marked additions of reddish brown amorphous organic matter and humified plant residues, some of which display a laminated character. Increased amounts of iron and manganese impregnation of these organic materials, sometimes also preserving rare *in situ* roots (M3), was noted. The organic remains are tentatively identified as herbivore/omnivore dung and stabling waste, as investigated in detail from ferruginised fills at Folly Lane, St Albans (diatoms, macrofossils, microprobe and pollen: (Macphail *et al.* 1999; Wiltshire 1999) and Guildhall Yard East, London (pollen: (Macphail and Cruise 1995). In addition, an example of more likely omnivore (pig?) dung, which had become partially mineralised, was also studied by microprobe (Tables 4.46 and 4.47, M1d; 1.89% Fe, 5.24% Ca and 1.82% P).

It may only be coincidental, but post-Roman 'dark earth' at both No. 1, Poultry and Guildhall Yard East, London, show an impact from domestic stock that seems to mark a new land-use of possible enclosure or stock management at the 11th/12th century interface. Perhaps, such a land-use change occurred at Pevensey Castle, the area of the excavation (and Norman enclosure of the south-east corner of the fort?) being utilised more intensively for domestic animals in Norman times.

Lastly (context 3), as recorded at other 'dark earth' sites, for example at King Edward Buildings, London, the disposal of latrine waste, perhaps into cesspits caused major contamination of local deposits (M1), which became dark, yellowish-brown coloured and includes what may be described as 'cesspit nodules' (Macphail 2000; Macphail and Cruise 1993; Watson 1998). At Pevensey Castle, microprobe analysis found these yellow stained soils to be a 'soil' (12.4% Si, 1.96% Al) impregnated by Fe/Ca/P compounds (1.79% Fe, 0.486% Ca and 1.17% P; see Table 4.47). These deposits, which may possibly have been called 'yellow clay' in the field (Rippon pers. comm.), could reflect an increased intensity of human occupation at this location and the effect of local (garderobes/cesspits) latrine outflow from the Norman Castle.

Conclusions

Soil studies were carried out on late Roman deposits and 'dark earth' that date from the late Roman to the 14th century. Despite the difficulties in dating from pottery, findings may possibly suggest that:

- Roman deposits, possibly representing occupation and digging contemporary with the fort-wall construction-trench, are present over the truncated natural geology.
- Ensuing deposits may also record cleaning out and dumping of ditch or pit fills, which had become silted and enriched in charcoal and latrine waste.
- A later spread of charcoal, soil and latrine waste, which includes small amounts of constructional, domestic (e.g., camp fires) and 'industrial' waste,

reflects the later activities of the 'Roman-period' fort into the post-Roman period.

- Initial stages of 'dark earth' formation occur in relic, late Roman deposits and continue to develop in low-intensity 5th to 7th century midden deposits.
- During the Saxon period 'dark earth' continued to form in accretionary midden spreads that contained probable, relic Roman material.
- The onset of Norman occupation may be marked by 'dark earth' formation that includes increased amounts of herbivore and omnivore dung, perhaps as stock were confined into a smaller area (south-east corner of fort). Deposits also became increasingly affected by staining from concentrations of latrine waste (garderobes/ cesspits), reflecting the presence of the Norman Castle.

Chapter 5
Discussion

Introduction

The 1993–1995 excavations of the Keep at Pevensey Castle produced important results in the following areas:

- The dating and occupation of the late Roman shore fort
- The evidence for continuity of occupation between Roman and Saxo-Norman
- Evidence for trade contact between Pevensey and the Mediterranean between the 5th and the 7th century
- The character of the occupation within the Castle between the later 11th and the later 12th century
- The date and architectural context of the original construction of the Keep
- Major repairs to the Keep
- The character of occupation between the 13th and 15th century
- Armada period re-fortification of the Keep; its post-medieval disintegration and robbing.

Roman

The presence of fragments of relief-patterned flue-tiles dated to the late 1st/early 2nd century AD along with sherds of 2nd–3rd century Central and East Gaulish samian, a sherd of a North Gaulish mortarium and of a Dressel 20 amphora provide further, limited evidence for occupation at Pevensey before the construction of the late Roman fort, complementing the earlier finds of *classis Britannica* tiles (see Chapter 1; *RIB* 2.481.7; 2481.103), as well as the small assemblages of diagnostic Roman pottery of mostly mid- to late 1st century date recovered from inside the East Gate and against the north wall (trench XIII) in the 1936–39 excavations (Lyne 2009, 102, fig. 27). The early Roman occupation is clearly extensive, but its character is unclear. Macphail's analysis of contexts associated with the construction of the shore fort wall indicates the presence of pre-fort occupation at the site of our Trench 2 (see Chapter 4).

Robust evidence for the date of the late Roman fort was provided by the dendrochronological dates derived from the oak piles used in the foundations of the fort wall. These give a date for the felling of the timber between AD 280 and 300 (see Chapter 4). Further indication of date is provided by two coins, one of Carausius, the second, and later, of Allectus (AD 293–6) found at the interface between the construction and subsequent occupation levels. Together this evidence points to the construction of the late Roman fort at the end of the 3rd century, probably after 293 during the usurpation of Allectus, the successor to Carausius (Fulford and Tyers 1995). An abraded sherd of Oxfordshire colour-coated ware (post *c.* 240) was found in a pre-fort layer, while the lowest, occupation horizon in Trench 2 contained a sherd of a late Roman shell-tempered hook-rimmed jar, usually dated after *c.* 325. Lyne has reported the earlier coin finds from Pevensey, noting that significant coin loss only starts with Reece's Period X (259–75). The representation of coins of the latter period, and their worn state, as well as of those of Period XI (276–93) are consistent, he argues, with a late 3rd century foundation date for the fort (Lyne 2009, 63–4; Reece, Chapter 3), 'establishment shortly before 300'). Lyne is also dismissive of the Constantinian coin found in a beam hole beneath interval tower 3 (see Chapter 1) as evidence for the date of the initial construction of the fort. He suggests that, if not introduced subsequently by animal activity, it might relate to the observed evidence for alteration or rebuilding of the tower in question (*ibid.*, 16–17, 63). An alternative interpretation would be to take the dating evidence from the two different locations at face value and argue that the construction of the fort was staged over 40–50 years.

Stratified Roman material in context was confined to the base of the deep Trench 2 which was cut from the present ground surface within the Keep down through the underlying sequence to the foundations of the Roman fort wall. The ceramics, including residual material, indicate wide-ranging contacts with, on the one hand, continental imports of 4th–5th century Argonne, Mayen and Mayen-type ware from northern Gaul and the Rhineland, and, on the other, regional ware from a diversity of British sources. These include Poole Harbour (BB1) and the New Forest on or close to the south coast, Alice Holt and Overwey in north-east Hampshire/north-west Surrey, Oxfordshire, late shell-tempered ware, possibly of a southern midlands origin, and a sherd of Hartshill-Mancetter mortarium from Warwickshire. Despite drawing on a wide hinterland, the relatively remote location of Pevensey provided an opportunity for local production of tableware pottery, the so-called

Pevensey Ware, imitating Oxfordshire red-colour coated vessel forms and manufactured from around the mid-4th century (see Chapter 3). Timby notes the relatively low percentage of table wares overall in the assemblage to which Pevensey Ware itself makes a significant contribution, greater than that of any of the other suppliers of the later 4th century. The establishment of an almost site-specific fineware industry (recorded finds beyond Pevensey are not numerous) is unusual and is, perhaps, indicative of the irregularity with which supplies from the major fineware producers of late Roman Britain reached Pevensey. Its development is also indicative that there was a market to be supplied, though of what size it is impossible to estimate. It would presumably have included any garrison and its followers as might have been present in the mid-4th century and later, as listed in the *Notitia Dignitatum*.

This Roman assemblage compares well both in the range of wares and their relative abundance with that reported by Lyne (2009, 96–122). The latter also notes a few sherds of a further type of late Roman imported pottery, 'céramique à l'éponge' from western Gaul, as well as sherds of the regional British ware from the kilns at Much Hadham, Hertfordshire. The 1936–39 assemblages also allowed Lyne to distinguish two patterns of supply: the earlier assigned to the first half of the 4th century, the later to the late 4th century, *c.* 370–400+. The principal difference between the two assemblages in terms of regional-traded wares is the relative increase of Alice Holt/Farnham/Overwey wares at the expense of South-East Dorset BB1.

Apart from the extensive links indicated by the pottery, the excavated area was too limited to reveal much of the nature of the occupation within the late Roman fort. While the soil micromorphology indicates that middening, including the dumping of latrine waste, accounts for the build-up of soil, small amounts of strongly burned and melted silty daub/slag possibly indicate some industrial activity alongside domestic occupation. From the perspective of the faunal assemblage, evidence for the intensive splitting and chopping of cattle bone (a characteristic of urban assemblages) and of the presence of worked antler also hints at some industrial activity. Otherwise the animal bone is indicative of food remains with the principal meat being provided by cattle, but also with significant representation of pig as well as a relatively high tenor of wild animals, mostly red deer. Although fish were not identified in the late Roman layers, there was a significant assemblage of shellfish, dominated by oyster. In conclusion, the character of the faunal assemblage is more comparable with that of a contemporary urban, rather than a rural site, though Powell and Serjeantson observe that 'the possible consumption of horse flesh, the taste for pork and for hunting' are unusual (Chapter 4). This is the only sample of animal bone from late Roman Pevensey as this type of material was not systematically retained from the earlier excavations. While it is probably premature to place much emphasis on such a small sample, the 'taste for pork and for hunting' may be explained by the local woodland environment of the south-east Weald, which could have provided an ideal context for hunting wild game and for raising pigs.

While a case has been made for associating the initial construction of the shore fort at Pevensey with the revolt of Carausius and Allectus (Fulford and Tyers 1995), there is no certainty of a continued military occupation through the 4th century and up to the time of the formulation of the *Notitia Dignitatum* at the end of the century when *Anderidos* (Pevensey) is listed as being under the command of the *Comes litoris Saxonici* (Chapter 1). The complexities of distinguishing military from civilian in late Roman Britain have been recently and carefully rehearsed by Gardner (2007) and the difficulties of interpretation are reflected in the findings from the only late Roman shore fort, that at Portchester, Hampshire, to have been excavated to any extent in modern times, i.e. post-Second World War (Cunliffe 1975). Although, on a combination of the numismatic evidence and the archaeological sequence, an argument was made for distinguishing civilian from military phases of occupation, this was not reflected in the character of the successive phases of the material culture assemblage as a whole. In the case of Pevensey the finds other than pottery and the animal bone from our excavation are too few to draw any conclusions about the identity of the occupants of the fort, but the metalwork finds from the 1936–39 excavations, which include both civilian and military items, only serve to emphasise further the ambiguities identified at Portchester and elsewhere (Lyne 2009, 78–89). While making the comparison with Portchester begs the question of a military interpretation, a major problem in contextualising the late Roman occupation of Pevensey is the latter's relative isolation in terms of neighbouring nucleated or urban communities. Until there are nearer such sites with which comparisons might be made, Pevensey will remain *sui generis*.

Roman to Saxon

The dark earth sequence recovered from Trenches 1, 2 and, to a lesser extent, from 7 does not suggest any significant break in occupation and pottery of early, mid- and late Saxon date was recovered from it. The early Anglo-Saxon material includes at least one, non-local, granite-tempered vessel from either the English midlands or Scandinavia. The soil micromorphology (see Macphail, Chapter 4) indicates that continued, low-intensive middening accounts for the gradual build-up of soil between the 5th century and the late Saxon period. A rather smaller assemblage ('only a handful of sherds') of early Anglo-Saxon pottery, whose fabric descriptions cannot be readily matched with those of Alan Vince (below, Appendix 2), was identified by Lyne from the 1936–39 excavations (2009, 122–24). This included fragments of 5th century schalenurne type, but lacked any sherds which could be certainly dated to the 6th to 7th century. However, pits from the north and north-east of the fort's interior produced some glass: a fragment of a 6th or early 7th century Kempston cone-beaker and a fragment of a late 7th to 10th century Valsgarde bowl (*ibid.*, 57–9; 90–91). These remind us of the 5th to 7th century imported 'Mediterranean' pottery discussed further below. While, given the extent of the excavated sample to date, we cannot be absolutely certain of it, the combination of the evidence of the material culture and that of the micromorphology points to a continuous occupation within the interior of the fort through the Anglo-Saxon period. The evidence of the glass and the imported pottery would argue for a high status element among the population with widespread trading contacts looking both eastwards up and across the Channel to the Rhine and westwards to the Atlantic and the Mediterranean beyond.

Post-Roman Mediterranean contacts

Notable among the material which occurred in the later contexts of the Phase 3 sequence are two sherds of a North African Red-Slipped Ware dish, Hayes 75, dated to the early-mid-5th century. Whether this sherd is to be associated with the Roman assemblage ranging in date up to the early 5th century is not certain, not least because other sherds of later North African Red-Slipped Ware were found residually in later phases. These include sherds of Hayes 91 = Bonifay (2004) 49–50, dating to the first half and middle decades of the 5th century, and of Hayes 99C = Bonifay (2004) 55 Variante C, dating from the end of the 6th to the 7th century (Appendix 2). These are the first examples of North African Red-Slipped wares with date ranges starting after *c.* AD 400 to be found in south-east England and their discovery significantly alters the perspective that such post-Roman imports from the Mediterranean are only to be found in western Britain (Campbell 2007). That some trade from the Mediterranean may have passed via the Atlantic eastwards up through the English Channel to the North Sea is also suggested by the late Roman céramique à l'éponge and the 4th to 5th century, stamped North African Red-Slipped Ware sherds from Ezinge, a settlement on the north coast of the Netherlands (Hayes 1972, 235, 241). Alternatively, the Pevensey and Ezinge finds may represent the extension of traffic down the Rhine, continuing the pattern of Roman trade, also represented in this period by a sherd of late 5th to mid-6th century, North African Red-Slipped Ware from Godorf, near Cologne (Hayes 1972, 150, form 97.6). The alternative Atlantic and Rhenish springboards from which such material may have reached Pevensey is illustrated in simplified form by Tortorella (1986, 216–18, Carta 5–6).

Possibly to be associated with these tableware imports is a body sherd of amphora of unknown type for which Williams suggests a possible east Mediterranean origin. In addition Lyne in his report on the finds from the Salzmann and the 1930s excavations at Pevensey has noted examples of late 4th–5th century southern French dérivée sigillée paléochrétienne ['D ware'] and a possible sherd of Macedonian terre sigillée grise (2009, 101). Collectively the evidence of these long-distance imports underlines the importance of Pevensey in the early medieval period, perhaps as a continuing and significant source of iron extracted from the Weald (*cf.* Cleere and Crossley 1985).

Saxo-Norman to the construction of the Keep

Pottery from the upper contexts of the sequences dug in Trenches 1 and 2 and which pre-date the construction of the Keep show that occupational material continued to accumulate in the period, broadly dated by the pottery, of the '11th to 13th centuries'. Indeed more than one metre's depth of dark earth midden deposits accumulated in the Saxo-Norman period before the building of the Keep. The micromorphology shows greater quantities of herbivore and omnivore dung and deposits were also increasingly affected by staining from concentrations of latrine waste, reflecting both a greater intensity of human occupation and of the use of the general area for penning and stabling animals. Although we cannot be certain of the start of a more intensive use of the south-eastern quarter of the Roman fort, it is likely to have followed the construction by William the Conqueror of 'a Castle with a very strong rampart' at Pevensey and the granting by him of the latter to his half-brother Robert, Count of Mortain in the late 11th century. Robert founded a small borough outside the Roman fort walls and made a Castle within it by dividing the whole eastern third of the interior of the Roman fort by a palisaded ditch and bank.

The material culture of the Saxo-Norman occupation within the Roman fort wall is dominated by pottery, the vast majority of which is cooking ware and of local, East Sussex origin, predominantly of flint and quartz gravel-tempered ware. With the possible exception of a pair of copper alloy tweezers (Chapter 3, Fig. 3.10, 20), there are very few metal finds which can confidently be attributed to this period, rather than the medieval period as a whole.

The faunal assemblage, on the other hand, is much more informative, showing a significant change from the late Romano-British period with sheep now being the predominant animal, although cattle remained the main source of meat. The sheep were relatively old at death, suggesting that they were kept for their milk and wool. While the beef and the mutton might have been brought to the site in joints, it would appear that pigs were probably slaughtered on site. The age of the domestic fowl at death suggests that they were kept for their eggs before slaughter; and eggshell was identified in the micromorphological study of the dark earth sequence. There is evidence for hunting, confirming an aristocratic element in the population of the Castle, but the percentage of hunted animals is low. In the representation of beef and pork and bacon at the expense of mutton, there are parallels with the contemporary faunal assemblages from Carisbrooke and Portchester Castles, the former also having a low percentage of hunted animals. In contrast, more mutton and less pork and bacon are to be expected in contemporary urban and rural assemblages. Fish, particularly larger fish and thus probably the product of commercial fishery, is also present in this occupation phase. In comparison with a number of medieval sites in Lewes, East Sussex, where shellfish assemblages have been reported in detail, cockles were, unusually, the most frequently consumed type of shellfish, followed by oysters and then whelks. In terms of size characteristics the oyster assemblage is comparable with that from Pevensey town, while the relatively small size of the cockles compares with the assemblage from Lydd in Kent. The small size of the cockles and also the whelks points to the possibility of over-exploitation of these species in the Pevensey area, as well as in west Kent.

This profile of the protein and fat components of the diet of the inhabitants of the Castle relates to just about a century of occupation between the late 11th and the late 12th century (below).

The date and context of the Keep

The archaeological evidence provides a broad 11th to 13th century *terminus post quem* for the construction of the Keep. This kind of evidence is hard to reconcile with the potential precision offered by dates derived from documentary sources. Not that the latter necessarily offer a more secure way forward, since a lack of specificity means it is often difficult to match a documentary reference to a particular structure or phase of construction. In fact there are no documented references to the building of the Keep, but a *terminus ante quem* is provided by the first certain mention of the Keep in relation to a record of repairs to its windows in 1284 (Table 2.1; Salzmann 1906, 8; 1910, 275). Earlier, there is a reference to a *turris de Penvesel* in 1129–30 in the first extant Pipe Roll (31 Henry I) and this has been thought to refer to the construction of the Keep in masonry. However, there can be no certainty that the tower in question was the Keep as opposed to one of the towers of the Roman circuit, or another structure altogether. But if the Keep is earlier than 1284, or 1264–5 when the Castle was besieged by Simon de Montfort, the question is by how much?

It has been noted that the remains of the Keep, the postern gate and the Gatehouse all employ similar masonry of greensand and flint and Chapman has recently advanced arguments on the grounds of architectural detail for the first phase of the Gatehouse dating from between the late 12th and early 13th century (Chapman 2007, 104). There are also clear similarities in the size and treatment of the greensand blocks used in Keep and Gatehouse to suggest a degree of contemporaneity (Chapman and Eaton 1995). This would then point to a date around 1200 for the construction of the Keep. In support of such a date, it may be noted that, although the greater part of the medieval pottery in the dark earth sequence dates to the 11th to 13th century, there were a few sherds of 12th to 14th century pottery from the uppermost layers (17 and 250).

At the time the Keep was built the ground level inside the Roman fort wall had risen by over three metres above the original surface at the beginning of the 4th century. In effect the Roman wall had become a retaining wall, which, in becoming the eastern wall of the Keep, was also to take the added weight of the new building. Contrary to Renn's view (1971, 61) that the D-plan towers (*insulae*) on the western and northern sides of the Keep were a later addition to the rectangular core, the survey of the fabric by Allen and Al Shaikley could find no evidence for the towers being secondary to the rectangular 'core' (Chapter 2, Appendix 1). The Keep in its original manifestation appears, therefore, to have been essentially of one build: three massive towers (*insulae*) projected into the interior of the Castle and a fourth (North East) tower, of which no surviving masonry survives above ground, defended the junction of the Keep and Roman curtain wall. The fifth tower at the south-east angle made use of an existing Roman bastion and was not new-build. Of the original, North East Tower, only nugatory traces survive, and insufficient to be certain of its ground plan. The dating evidence for its

Plate 5.1 Conjectural reconstruction drawing by Philip Winton of the Inner Bailey of Pevensey Castle in about 1325 (© English Heritage, NMR)

construction is the same as that from the build-up inside the Roman fort wall. Its foundations cut through layer 349 (on top of the undisturbed natural) which correlates with layers 165/167/169 in Trench 3, and the yellow clay that was dumped outside the Castle following the slumping of the creek or ditch edge immediately beyond the fort wall. All these deposits produced only 11th to 13th century pottery. The North East Tower in its initial phase would also appear to have truncated the shallow pit or hollow F803 which produced a handful of pottery of similar, 11th to 13th century date.

The Keep is an odd construction with its asymmetrical disposition of towers on the landward side and mixing new work with Roman (Pl. 5.1). The clearly secondary addition of the massive, masonry platform (Renn's (1971) Block N) on the southern side to protect the vulnerable junction of Keep and Inner Bailey wall only develops the idiosyncratic character of the Keep further. It is possible that the architects were aware of the implications of the precarious position of the Keep above the edge of the creek or ditch beyond the Roman fort-wall, and of the potential threat of collapse the topography and build-up of soil within the Roman wall posed to the retained Roman wall of the Keep. We might conjecture, therefore, that they deliberately used the massive construction of the towers, which extended well beyond the core of the Keep, as a counterweight to alleviate some of the pressure of the weight of the construction on its eastern wall and towers. At the same time the disposition of the two western towers articulates well with the orientation of the Gatehouse into the Inner Bailey (Pl. 1.2). It is hard not to believe that the Gatehouse was planned and, indeed, under construction when the Keep was being built. As Chapman's table of expenditure on Pevensey shows, after a pattern of intermittent, minor expenditure between the 1160s and the 1180s there was a significant and sustained increase during the years 1193–7, but at a level which did not approach that on Dover Castle in the 1180s (Chapman 2007, 114, table 1; Coad 1995, 23; see Table 1.1).

While the use of 'D' plan towers and their particular character at Pevensey may in part have been influenced by local conditions, a conscious attempt, perhaps, to echo the towers of the Roman wall-circuit, it is important also to see the innovations at Pevensey in the context of comparable developments in the region and beyond. At Dover there was very significant expenditure during the reign of Henry II (1184–1189) including the building of the massive, rectangular Keep and the Inner Bailey with its distinctive rectangular towers (Coad 1995, 23–37). In some sense the style of this work provides a relatively local *terminus post quem* for Pevensey's Keep and Gatehouse (*cf.* Renn 2001 on castle-building in England in the second half of the 12th century). Work on the Outer Bailey at Dover with its D-shaped towers probably started in the early 13th century, but was given great stimulus by the siege of 1216 which precipitated an intensified building campaign under Henry III, as it probably also did at Pevensey. It is unlikely that we will ever obtain a close date for the construction of the Keep and Gatehouse at Pevensey, but it is clear that the new ideas about military engineering evident at Pevensey were circulating in the years immediately before 1200 and through the first half of the 13th century.

Repairs to the Keep

Outside the Keep, the excavations of 1993–95 revealed evidence for a second phase of the North East tower which implied that the original structure had been completely taken down before re-building. Unfortunately there was no associated dating evidence, other than that for the first phase, that is pottery of 11th to 13th century date. Material of similar date provides the *terminus post quem* for the East Tower (and associated garderobe) which, on grounds of construction technique, as we have argued above, was also a secondary addition designed to shore up the leaning, east wall of the Keep. Material which belongs to our second, dated horizon of medieval ceramics, the 13th to 15th century, was found in features cut into the terrace into which the foundations of the two towers were cut. Some of this material and other associated finds might well be associated with the work on the east wall and towers of the Keep and thus might be regarded as a loose *terminus ante quem*. While the nature of the archaeological evidence cannot hope to give close precision with regard to date, there is relevant documentary evidence which gives insight into the physical state of the Castle from the late 13th century onwards.

Records show that significant costs were being incurred on repairing the Keep in the late 13th and early 14th century (see Table 1.1). The first reference specific to the Keep is the mention of repairs to the Keep's windows in 1284. If the 'Great Tower' is correctly interpreted as the Keep, then repairs totalling over £85 were undertaken on it and other parts of the Castle in 1289/90 and 1290/91. Much more modest expenditure on repairs to the Keep is recorded for 1301/02 and 1302/03, but, just a few years later, in 1306, estimates for repairs to the Keep (*turris*), four towers (*turelli*) and other works amounted to £1000. The documents give a more vivid insight into the ruinous state of the Keep a few years later when a further estimate for repairs to the Keep of £120 is recorded for 1318:

> the steps and bridge at the entrance of the Keep are entirely fallen down and broken so that they will need to be remade, and in the said Keep are many defects which cannot be clearly seen before the roofing be removed, but by estimation one hundred beams are defective and almost all the boarding, and the lead roofing on the said Keep ought to be entirely removed and recast (Salzmann 1906, 17–18).

The same survey recorded that:

> there is a breach in the corner of the Inner Bailey towards the north near the Keep and the wall from the said breach to the Keep, being 40 feet in length, is hanging over towards the town almost tottering and ought to be supported by means of a buttress or else to be entirely thrown down and rebuilt, and the said breach can be closed and the said wall underpinned for £20 but if it should be thrown down and rebuilt £40 would be required (Salzmann 1906, 18).

Further significant repairs were undertaken in 1367 and 1371 (Salzmann 1906, 20–21).

In 1405 Sir John Pelham wrote to the Privy Council that a great part of the Keep of Pevensey Castle was falling down and repairs were put in hand. Repairs continued to be regularly undertaken through the 15th century, though by the latter part of this century the Castle appears to have been largely deserted (Salzmann 1906, 23–26).

Given the lack of 15th century material from the trenches outside the east wall of the Keep, it would seem likely that the significant repairs to the east wall, including the rebuilding of the North East Tower and the building of the East Tower were undertaken during the period in which the highest figures associated with repairs are recorded – the last decade or so of the 13th and the first decade or so of the 14th century, most obviously in response to the state of the fabric reported in 1306.

Later medieval occupation: 13th to 15th century

The 13th and, to a lesser extent, the 14th century were the highwater of the Castle's life. The fabric of the Castle may have been in urgent need of repairs from the late 13th century onwards, but significant funds were found to invest in its restoration. From the small sample of finds recovered from the 1993–95 excavations, the best material indicator of the changing fortunes of the Castle and its occupants from our excavations are the imported ceramics. Alan Vince observed that very little of the imports need date before the late 12th century with the majority belonging to the 13th and somewhat less to the 14th century. The most numerous wares are of North French origin, perhaps from Rouen in the main, followed by vessels from the south west of France, of which only a minority is attributable to Saintonge itself. Rhenish wares, tentatively attributed to Pingsdorf production, are present in some quantity, as are some Flemish highly decorated, white-slipped redware. As a proportion of the entire assemblage of medieval pottery, 11th to 15th century, imports account for 3.8%. Imports are also present in the ceramic assemblages from Pevensey borough, though they account for a slightly smaller proportion (2.8%) of the assemblage. The range of wares, however, is very comparable with that from the Castle (Dulley 1967; Lyne 1999). The character of the latter assemblage in terms of quantity and range compares well with contemporary assemblages from recent excavations of other south coast castles. However, neither at Carisbrooke on the Isle of Wight (Mepham 2000), nor at Portchester Castle at the head of Portsmouth Harbour (Hampshire) from both Inner and Outer Bailey assemblages are there pottery assemblages where imports are represented to a comparable degree of diversity of origin and quantity as they are at Pevensey (Cunliffe 1977, 132–93; 1985, 210–36).

While the 13th to 15th century material culture assemblage from the Castle may be a little richer in terms of imports than those recorded from Carisbrooke and Portchester Castles, it is not distinctive when compared with assemblages from the borough. Some differences from urban and rural assemblages may be seen in the Castle's faunal assemblage, in particular through the continued representation, but lesser abundance of hunted (and thus protected) species of deer and wild boar as well as wild birds. The presence of a peacock symbolically represents the status of the occupants in this period. However, the main change from the 11th to 13th century assemblage is in the relative decrease of cattle from 30 to 23% (MNE) of the assemblage, and the increase of sheep from 40 to 50%. As Powell and Serjeantson comment (Chapter 4), the closest comparable assemblages remain those from the castles at Carisbrooke and Portchester, located to the west along the south coast.

It has to be remembered that the bulk of the 13th to 15th century material derives from the assemblage from outside the Keep. While some may derive from the interior of the Castle, a significant proportion may be associated with the teams working on the repairs to the Keep. This potential difference in the status of consumers may account for the relative decline in the representation of cattle and of wild species from the 11th to 13th century assemblage, and also of the remarkably high incidence of cockle, an incidence otherwise only paralleled in the region at Lydd in south-east Kent. Robinson postulates that some of the cereal remains from pits outside the Keep may be of animal fodder (see Chapter 4). It is also interesting to note the presence of iron slags, probably indicative of iron-making (Richards, Chapter 3), associated with this phase of extramural occupation.

Despite the poor state of the Castle and the Keep, repairs continued to be made during the 15th century (Salzmann 1906, 23–6) and the discovery of the 15th century gold ring (Chapter 3, Fig. 3.11), albeit from an unstratified context, would appear to indicate the continued presence of occupants of relatively high status.

The later history of the Keep: an improvised Armada re-fortification, disintegration and robbing

Our documentary sources show that by the 1570s the Castle was ruinous and beyond repair, and that stone, lead and other materials were being removed from it (Salzmann 1906, 27–9). Archaeologically, at least one further significant investment was made in the Keep after it became uninhabitable, when its ruins were buried under a mound, composed of yellow clay and other material. An 18th century aquatint by S. H. Grimm (Pl. 1.3) clearly shows this mound in perspective, spoil spilling down the eastern side of the Keep and the feature is also evident in Bucks' engraving of the Castle in 1737 (Pl. 1.4) which thus provides a *terminus ante quem* for its construction. This mound was investigated by Sands (1908, 26–7) and removed after Pevensey Castle was acquired by the Office of Works in 1925 but traces of it, in the form of spreads and tips of yellow clay, were recovered in our excavations, particularly in Trenches 1 and 2. From the slumped clay (context 32) in the latter trench came pottery of 16th–17th century date. Although a survey of 1587 recommended the Castle 'to be re-edified or utterlye rased' (Peers 1953, 9), the survival of fabric to the present day shows that the Castle was certainly not demolished. If some re-edification to enhance the defensive value of the site in the context of the threat posed by the Spanish Armada included making the Keep capable of supporting cannon, the dumping of clay to create a platform would be consistent with such action and the dating evidence is supportive. Such an interpretation would also help to explain the low masonry foundations built against the north tower of the Keep. Apart from being secondary to the main fabric of the Keep, there is no other independent evidence for the date of these remains. However, they would make sense as the base of a ramp for dragging cannon to the top of the Keep mound and therefore integral to the throwing up of the mound. Though the mound was once seized upon by Armitage as evidence for a Norman motte at Pevensey (Counihan 1990, 56–7), what little of it has survived and was sampled in our excavation shows this cannot have been the case.

The documentary sources give sharp insight into the robbing of the Castle from the 16th century onwards. In 1591, for example, all the best stones had been 'imbeselled and carried away' and one family had removed 677 cartloads of ashlar facing-stone (Lewis 1882, 668; Salzmann 1906, 29–30; Sands 1908, 28). As far as the Keep is concerned, however, both Bucks' engraving of 1737 and Grimm's aquatint show the eastern side of the Keep, though ruinous, still stood to some degree in the 18th century. By 1882 the eastern wall of the Keep had certainly collapsed (Clarke 1882, 425), following earlier robbing of whatever remained of the two towers. However, an engraving by S. Hooper appears to show the eastern side already in a state of collapse by 1785.

Postscript

Following the Armada fortification of the Castle, including the Keep, Pevensey, as is well known, was further utilised in Second World War and the remains of pill boxes are evident at the highest surviving point of the Keep as well as on the eastern side. Whereas the Armada work involved only an addition of soil to the structure that survived in the late 16th century, the concrete constructions of 1940 caused significant interference with the fabric, in particular obscuring relationships between the external medieval towers and the original wall of Keep.

Bibliography

Albarella, U., 1997. Size, power, wool and veal: zooarchaeological evidence for late medieval innovations, in G. D. Boe and F. Verhaeghe (eds) *Environment and Subsistence in Medieval Europe. Papers of the Medieval Europe Brugge 1997 conference* Vol. 9. 19–30, Zellik, I.A.P. Rapporten 9

Albarella, U., Beech, M. and Mulville, J., 1997. *The Saxon, Medieval and Post-Medieval Mammal and Bird Bones Excavated 1989–91 from Castle Mall, Norwich, Norfolk*, London, English Heritage Anc. Monum. Lab. Rep. 72/97

Albarella, U. and Davis, S.J.M., 1994. *Medieval and Post-Medieval Mammal and Bird Bones from Launceston Castle, Cornwall: 1961–1982 excavations*, London, English Heritage Anc. Monum. Lab. Rep. 18/94

Aldsworth, F.G. and Down, A., 1976. Medieval pottery at East Lavington, *Sussex Archaeol. Collect.* 114, 333

Arrhenius, O., 1934. Fosfathalten i skånska jordar. *Sveriges Geologiska Undersökningar*, Ser. C, 393 (Årsbok 28, no 3)

Arrhenius, O., 1955. The Iron Age settlements on Gotland and the nature of the soil. *Valhagan* II, in M. Stenberger (ed.) *Valhagan* II, 1053–64, Copenhagen, Munksgaard

Bailie, M.G.L. and Pilcher, J.R. 1973. A simple crossdating program for tree-ring research, *Tree Ring Bulletin* 33, 7–14

Barat, X., 1993. Les céramiques 'rugueuses' ou 'granuleuses' du Bas-Empire en Ile-de-France, *Trésors de terre: céramiques et potiers dans l'Ile-de-France gallo-romaine*, Musée Archéologique Dépt du Val-d'Oise-Guiry-en-Vexin, 171–7

Barber, L., 1999. The excavation of land adjacent to the Old Farmhouse, Pevensey, East Sussex, 1994, *Sussex Archaeol. Collect.* 137, 91–120

Barton, K.J., 1965. Medieval Pottery at Rouen, *Archaeol. J.* 122, 73–85

Barton, K.J., 1979. *Medieval Sussex Pottery*, Phillimore, Chichester

Becker, B., 1981. Fallungsdaten Römischer Bauhölzer, *Fundberichte aus Baden-Wurtemberg*, 6, 369–86

Bell, M., 1977. *Excavations at Bishopstone, Sussex*, *Sussex Archaeol. Collect.* 115, 1–266

Betts I., Black E.W., and Gower J., 1994. A Corpus of Relief-Patterned Tiles in Roman Britain, *J. Roman Pottery Stud.* 7

Bird, J., 1977. African Red Slip ware in Roman Britain, in J. Dore and K. Greene (eds) *Roman Pottery Studies in Britain and Beyond*, 269–77, Oxford, Brit. Archaeol. Rep. 30

Bird, J., 1982. Imports, in P. Bennett, S.S. Frere and S. Stow, *Excavations at Canterbury Castle*, 133, Maidstone, Kent Archaeol. Soc., Canterbury Archaeol. Trust, Archaeology of Canterbury 1

Boessneck, J.A., 1969. Osteological differences between sheep (*Ovis aries* Linné) and goat (*Capra hircus* Linné), in D.R. Brothwell and E.S. Higgs (eds.), *Science in Archaeology*, 331–358, London, Thames & Hudson

Boisseau, S. and Yalden, D.W., 1998. The former status of the Crane *Grus grus* in Britain. *Ibis* 140, 482–500

Bonifay, M., 2004. *Etudes sur la céramique Romaine tardive d'Afrique*, Oxford, Brit. Archaeol. Rep. 1301

Bourdillon, J., 1993. Animal bones, in A.H. Graham and S.M. Davies (eds) *Excavations in the Town Centre of Trowbridge*, 134–143, Salisbury, Wessex Archaeol. Rep. 2

Brown, D.H., 1994. Pottery and Late Saxon Southampton, *Proc. Hampshire Fld Club Archaeol. Soc.* 50, 127–152

Bullock, P., Fedoroff, N., Jongerius, A., Stoops, G. and Tursina, T., 1985. *Handbook for Soil Thin Section Description*, Wolverhampton, Waine Research Publications,

Bushe-Fox, J.P., 1932. Some notes on coast defences, *J. Roman Stud.* 22, 60–72

Campbell, E., 2007. *Continental and Mediterranean Imports to Atlantic Britain, AD 400–800*, York, Counc. Brit. Archaeol. Res. Rep. 157

Canti, M., 1998. Origin of calcium carbonate granules found in buried soils and Quaternary deposits, *Boreas* 27, 275–288

Caple, C., 1983. Pins and wires, in Mayes and Butler 1983, 269–78

Chapman, A., 2007. The gatehouse of Pevensey Castle, *Sussex Archaeol. Collect.* 145, 97–118

Chapman, A. and Eaton, T., 1995. *Pevensey Castle 1995: Report on the Standing Masonry of the Gatehouse*, Reading Univ.

Clarke, G.T., 1882. Pevensey Castle, *The Builder* 43, 424–6

Clarke, G.T., 1884. *Mediaeval Military Architecture in England,* Vol. II, London, Wyman & Son

Cleere H. and Crossley D., 1985. *The Iron Industry of the Weald*, Leicester, Univ. Press

Coad, J., 1995. *Book of Dover Castle*, London, Batsford/English Heritage

Cohen, A. and Serjeantson, D., 1996. *A Manual for the Identification of Bird Bones from Archaeological Sites*, London, Archetype Press

Cole, H.A., 1956. *Oyster Cultivation in Britain*, London, HMSO

Cool, H.E.M., 1985. Bracelets and pins, in J. Hinchliffe and C.S. Green, *Excavations at Brancaster 1974 and 1977*, 205–7, Gressenhall, E Anglian Archaeol. Rep. 23

Cool, H.E.M. and Price, J., 1987. The Glass, in G.W. Meates (ed.) *The Roman Villa at Lullingstone, Kent, Vol II: The Wall Paintings and Finds*, 110–141, Maidstone, Kent Archaeol. Soc.

Cool, H.E.M. and Price, J., 1995. *Roman Vessel Glass from Excavations in Colchester, 1971–85*, Colchester, Colchester Archaeol. Rep. 8

Cotter, J., 1997. *A Twelfth-century Pottery Kiln at Pound Lane, Canterbury: Evidence for an Immigrant Potter in the Late Norman Period*, Canterbury, Canterbury Archaeol. Trust Occ. Pap. 1

Counihan, J., 1990. Ella Armitage, castle studies pioneer, *Fortress* 6, 51–9

Courty, M.A., Goldberg, P. and Macphail, R.I., 1989. *Soils and Micromorphology in Archaeology*, Cambridge, Univ. Press

Courty, M.A., Goldberg, P. and Macphail, R.I., 1994. Ancient people – lifestyles and cultural patterns, *Transactions of the 15th World Congress of Soil Science, International Society of Soil Science, Mexico*, 250–269, Acapulco, International Society of Soil Science

Cowan, C., 2003. *Urban Development in North-West Roman Southwark Excavations 1974–90*, London, MoLAS Monogr. 16

Coy, J.P., 1985. Fish bones, in B. Cunliffe and J. Munby (eds) 1985, 256–61

Crossley D.W., 1975. *The Bewl Valley Ironworks*, London, Royal Archaeological Institute

Cunliffe, B.W., 1975. *Excavations at Portchester Castle, Vol. I: Roman*, London, Rep. Res. Comm. Soc. Antiq London 32

Cunliffe, B., 1977. *Excavations at Portchester Castle. Vol. III: Medieval, the Outer Bailey and its Defences*, Dorking, Rep. Res. Comm. Soc. Antiq. London 34

Cunliffe, B. and Munby, J. 1985. *Excavations at Portchester Castle. Vol. IV, Medieval, the Inner Bailey*. London, Rep. Res. Comm. Soc. Antiq. London 63

Dalwood, H., 1992. The use of soil micromorphology for investigating site formation processes, in K. Steane (ed.) *Interpretation of Stratigraphy: a Review of the Art*, 3–6, Lincoln, City of Lincoln Archaeology Unit

Davison, B.K., 1972. Castle Neroche: an abandoned Norman Fortress in South Somerset, *Somerset Archaeol. Natur. Hist. Soc.* 116, 16–58

Dereoux, D., Dufournier, D., and Herteig, A., 1994. French Medieval Ceramics from the Bryggen excavations in Bergen, Norway, 161–209, *The Bryggen papers Supplementary Series 5*

Driesch, A. von den, 1976. A guide to the measurement of animal bones from archaeological sites, *Peabody Museum Bulletin* 1, Peabody Museum of Archaeology and Ethnology, Harvard Univ.

Driesch, A. von den and Boessneck, J., 1974. Kritische Anmerkungen zur Widerristhöhenberechnung aus Längenmaßen vor- und frühgeschichtlicher Tierknochen, *Säugetierkundliche Mitteilungen* 4, 325–348

Driver, J., 1990. Faunal Remains, in J. C. Driver, J. Rady and M. Sparks (eds) *Excavations in the Cathedral Precincts, 2 Linacre Garden, 'Meister Omers' and St. Gabriel's Chapel*, 228–257, Maidstone, Kent Archaeol. Soc. Mongr. Ser 4

Drummond, J.C. and Wilbraham, A., 1991. *The Englishman's Food: Five Centuries of English diet.* New edn. London, Pimlico

Dufournier, D., Lecler, E. and Le Maho, J., 1998. Céramiques décorées et glaçurées des Xe et Xie siècles découvertes à Rouen (Seine-Maritime), *Proximus* 2, 151–60

Dulley, A.J.F., 1967. Excavations at Pevensey, Sussex, 1962–6, *Medieval Archaeol.* 11, 209–32

Dunning, G.C., 1958. A Norman pit at Pevensey Castle and its contents, *Antiq. J.* 38, 205–17

Dunning G.C., 1961. Medieval chimney pots, in M. Jope (ed) *Studies in Building History: Essays in Recognition of the Work of B.H. St. J. O'Neil*, 78–93, London, Odhams Press

Dunning G.C., 1967. Chimney-pots, in Dulley 1967, 229–31

Eastham, A., 1975. The bird bones, in B. Cunliffe 1975, 409–15

Eastham, A., 1985. Birds, in B. Cunliffe and J. Munby 1985, 233–23

Egan, G. and Pritchard, F., 1991. *Dress Accessories 1150–1450 AD. Medieval Finds from Excavations in London*, London, HMSO

Engelmark, R. and Linderholm, J., 1996. Prehistoric land management and cultivation. A soil chemical study. *Arkaeologiske Rapporter fra Esbjerg Museum*, 315–322

Fish, J.D. and Fish, S., 1989. *A Student's Guide to the Seashore*, London, Unwin

Fulford, M.G., 1973. A fourth-century colour-coated fabric and its types in south-east England, *Sussex Archaeol. Collect.* 111, 41–4

Fulford, M.G., 1975a. *New Forest Roman Pottery*, Oxford, Brit. Archaeol. Rep. 17

Fulford, M.G., 1975b, The pottery, in B. Cunliffe 1975, 270–367

Fulford, M., 1993. *Excavations at Pevensey Castle 1993. Interim Report*, Reading Univ.

Fulford M.G. and Bird, J., 1975. Imported pottery from Germany in late Roman Britain, *Britannia* 6, 171–81

Fulford, M. and Rippon, S., 1994. *Excavations at Pevensey Castle 1994. Interim Report*, Reading Univ.

Fulford, M. and Rippon, S., 1995. *Excavations at Pevensey Castle 1995. Interim Report*, Reading Univ.

Fulford, M.G. and Tyers, I., 1995. The date of Pevensey and the defence of an 'Imperium Britanniarum'. *Antiquity* 69, 1009–1014

Galinié, H., 2000. *Terres Noires* – 1. Documents. Sciences de la Ville, No. 6. La Maison des Sciences de la Ville, Tours

Gallois, R.W., 1965. *British Regional Geology. The Wealden District* (4th Edition), London, Institute of Geological Sciences

Gardner, A., 2007. *An Archaeology of Identity: soldiers and society in late Roman Britain*, Walnut Creek, CA: Left Coast Press

Getty, R., 1975. *Sisson and Grossman's The Anatomy of the Domestic Animals*, Philadelphia, WB Saunders Co

Goldberg, P. and Macphail, R.I., in preparation, *Color Guide to Geoarchaeological Microstratigraphy*, New York, Plenum

Grant, A., 1975. The animal bones, in Cunliffe 1975, 387–408

Grant, A., 1977. The animal bones, in Cunliffe 1977, 213–33

Grant, A., 1985. The large mammals, in Cunliffe and Munby 1985, 244–56

Grant, A., 1989. Animals in Roman Britain, in M. Todd (ed.) *Research on Roman Britain: 1960–89*, 135–46, London, Society for Promotion of Roman Studies, Britannia Monogr. Ser. 11

Green, C.M., 1977. The Roman pottery, in Bell 1977, 152–78

Grigson, C., 1982. Sex and age determination of some bones and teeth of domestic cattle: a review of the literature, in R. Wilson, C. Grigson, and S. Payne (eds), *Ageing and Sexing Animal Bones from Archaeological sites*, 7–23, Oxford, Brit. Archaeol. Rep. 109

Hancock, D. and Urquhart, A., 1966. The Fisheries for Cockles (*Cardium edule* L.) in the Burry Inlet, South Wales, *Fisheries Investigations Series 2*, 25 (3), 1–32

Hanson, W., 1982. Roman military buildings: construction and reconstruction, in S. McGrail (ed.) *Woodworking Techniques Before 1500 AD*, 169–86, Oxford, Brit. Archaeol. Rep. 129

Hare, J.N., 1985. *Battle Abbey: the Eastern Range and the Excavations of 1978–1980*, London, HBMCE Archaeol. Rep. 2

Harper, D.G.C., 1994. Some comments on the repeatability of measurements, *Ringing and Migration* 15, 84–90

Hayes, J.W., 1972. *Late Roman Pottery*, London, The British School at Rome

Hillam, J., 1983. *Dendrochronology Report. Tower of London 1976–77*, Anc. Monum. Lab. Rep. 4131 I

Hillam, J., 1990. The dendrochronology of the late Roman waterfront at Billingsgate Lorry Park and other sites in the City of London, in T. Brigham, The Roman Waterfront in London, *Britannia* 21, 164–70

Hillam, J., 1992. Tree-ring dating of oak timbers from Peter's Hill and Sunlight Wharf, in Williams T., *Public Buildings in the South-West Quarter of Roman London*, 95–99, London, Counc. Brit. Archaeol. Res. Rep. 88

Hillam, J., and Morgan, R.A., 1986. Tree-ring analysis of the Roman timbers, in L. Miller, J. Schofield, and M. Rhodes, *The Roman quay at St Magnus House, London*, London & Middlesex Archaeol. Soc. Spec. Pap. 8, 75–85

Hillam, J., Morgan, R.A., and Tyers, I., 1987. Sapwood estimates and the dating of short ring sequences, in R.G.W. Ward (ed.) *Applications of Tree-ring Studies: Current Research in Dendrochronology and Related Areas*, 165–85, Oxford, Brit. Archaeol. Rep. 333

Hinton, D.A., 1995. *The Gold, Silver and Other Non-ferrous Alloy Objects from Hamwic*. Southampton Finds Volume II, Southampton, Southampton City Council

Holbrook, N., and Bidwell, P.T., 1991. *Roman Finds from Exeter*, Exeter, Exeter City Council, Exeter Archaeol. Rep. 4

Holden, E., 1963. Excavations at the deserted Medieval village of Hangleton, Part 1. *Sussex Archaeol. Collect.* 101, 54–181

Hollstein, E., 1980. *Mitteleuropäische Eichenchronologie*, von Zabern: Mainz am Rhein

Jarvis, M.G. *et al.*, 1984. *Soils and Their Use in South-East England*, Harpenden, Soil Survey of England and Wales, Bulletin 15

Johnson, S., 1976. *The Roman forts of the Saxon Shore*, London, Elek

Keller, C., 1995. Pingsdorf-type ware – an introduction, *Medieval Ceram.* 19, 19–28

Kideys, A.E., Nash, R.D.M. and Hartnoll, R.G., 1993. Reproductive cycle and energetic cost of reproduction of the neogastropod *Buccinum undatum* in the Irish Sea, *J. Marine Biological Assoc. United Kingdom* 73, 391–403

King, A., 1978. A comparative survey of bone assemblages from Roman sites in Britain, Univ. London Inst. Archaeol. Bull. 15, 207–232

Lake R.D., Young B., Wood C.J, and Mortimore R.N., 1987. *The Geology of the Country around Lewes. Memoir for the Geological Sheet 319* (England and Wales), London, HMSO

Levine, M.A., 1982. The use of crown height measurements and tooth eruption sequences to age horse teeth, in B. Wilson, C. Grigson and S. Payne (eds.), *Ageing and Sexing Animal Bones from Archaeological Sites*, 223–50, Oxford, British Archaeol. Rep. 109

Levitan, B., 1989. The vertebrate remains from Chichester Cattlemarket, in A. Down *Chichester Excavations VI*, 242–76, Chichester, Phillimore

Lewis, W.G.B., 1882. Pevensey Castle, *The Builder* 43, 669

Locker, A., 1985. Animal and plant remains, in Hare 1985, 183–9

Lower, M.A., 1853. On Pevensey Castle and the recent excavations there, *Sussex Archaeol. Collect.* 6, 264–82

Lüdtke, H., 1985. *Die mittelalterliche Keramic von Schleswig Ausgrabung Schild 1971–1975*, Ausgrabungen in Schleswig Berichte und Studien 4

Lyne, M.A.B., 1994. *Late Roman Handmade Wares in South-East Britain*, unpubl. thesis, Reading Univ.

Lyne, M.A.B., 1999. The pottery, 105–113 in L. Barber, The Excavation of land adjacent to the Old Farmhouse, Pevensey, East Sussex, *Sussex Archaeol. Collect.* 137, 91–120

Lyne, M.A.B., 2009. *Excavations at Pevensey Castle 1936 to 1964*, Oxford, Brit. Archaeol. Rep. 503

Lyne, M.A.B. and Jefferies, R.S., 1979. *The Alice Holt/Farnham Roman Pottery Industry*, London, Counc. Brit. Archaeol. Res. Rep. 30

MacDonald, K.C., (1992). The domestic chicken *(Gallus gallus)* in sub-Saharan Africa: a background to its introduction and its osteological differentiation from indigenous fowls *(Numindinae and Francolinus* sp.*). J. Archaeol. Sci.* 19, 303–318

Macphail, R.I., 1981. Soil and botanical studies of the "Dark Earth", in M. Jones and G.W. Dimbleby (eds), *The Environment of Man: the Iron Age to the Anglo-Saxon Period*, 309–331, Oxford, Brit. Archaeol. Rep. 87

Macphail, R.I., 1991. The archaeological soils and sediments, in N.M. Sharples (ed.), *Maiden Castle: Excavations and field survey 1985–6*, 106–118, London, English Heritage

Macphail, R.I., 1994. The reworking of urban stratigraphy by human and natural processes, in A.R. Hall and H.K. Kenward (eds.), *Urban-Rural Connexions: Perspectives from environmental Archaeology*, 13–43, Oxford, Oxbow

Macphail, R.I., 2000. Soils and microstratigraphy: a soil micromorphological and micro chemical approach, in A.J. Lawson, *Potterne 1982–5: Animal Husbandry in Later Prehistoric Wiltshire*, 47–70, Salisbury, Wessex Archaeol. Rep. 17

Macphail, R.I., 2001. *Dragon Hall, King St., Norwich; soil micromorphology and chemistry*, unpubl. Rep. Norfolk Archaeological Unit, Norwich

Macphail, R.I., in prep. 'Dark earth': recent studies of 'dark earth' and 'dark earth-like' microstratigraphy in England, in L. Verslype (ed.), *Dark Earth in the Dark Ages*. Louvain, Université Catholique de Louvain

Macphail, R.I. and Crowther, J., 2007. *Whitefriars, Canterbury: soil micromorphology, chemistry and magnetic susceptibility*, unpubl. Rep. Canterbury Archaeological Trust

Macphail, R.I. and Crowther, J., 2008. Soil micromorphology and chemistry, in C. Ellis and A. Powell, *An Iron Age Settlement Outside Battlesbury Hillfort, Warminster and Sites along the Southern Range Road*, Salisbury, Wessex Archaeol. Rep. 22, Wessex Archaeology and Defence Estates

Macphail, R.I. and Cruise, G.M., 1993. *King Edward Buildings: assessment of soils and pollen (KEB92)*, unpubl. Rep. London, Museum of London

Macphail, R.I. and Cruise, G.M., 1995. *Guildhall Yard East (GYE92): brief assessment of microstratigraphy (soil micromorphology and pollen)*, unpubl. Rep. London, MoLAS

Macphail, R.I. and Cruise, G.M., 2000. Rescuing our urban archaeological soil heritage: a multidisciplinary microstratigraphical approach, in W. Burghardt and C. Dornauf (eds.) *Proceedings of the First International Conference on Soils of Urban, Industrial, Traffic and Mining Areas*, 9–14, Essen, IUSS/IBU

Macphail, R.I. and Cruise, G.M., 2001. The soil micromorphologist as team player: a multianalytical approach to the study of European microstratigraphy, in P. Goldberg, V. Holliday and R. Ferring (eds.), *Earth Science and Archaeology*, 241–267, New York, Kluwer Academic/Plenum Publishers

Macphail, R.I., Cruise, G.M., Engelmark, R. and Linderholm, J., 2000. Integrating soil micromorphology and rapid chemical survey methods: new developments in reconstructing past rural settlement and landscape organization, in S. Roskams (ed.), *Interpreting Stratigraphy*, 71–80, York Univ.

Macphail, R.I., Cruise, G.M., Gebhardt, A. and Linderholm, J., Forthcoming. West Heslerton: soil micromorphology and chemistry of the Roman and Saxon deposits, in J. Tipper (ed.), *West Heslerton Anglo-Saxon Settlement*. Landscape Research Centre, Yedingham

Macphail, R.I., Cruise, G.M. and Mellalieu, S.J., 1999. Soil micromorphological and diatom analysis of thin sections and microchemical analysis of polished blocks, in R. Niblett, *The Excavation of a Ceremonial site at Folly Lane, Verulamium*, 365–384, London, Society for Promotion of Roman Studies, Britannia Monograph 14

Macphail, R.I., Galinié, H. and Verhaeghe, F., in preparation. The end of dark earth. *Antiquity*

Mainman, A.J., 1990. *Anglo-Scandinavian Pottery from Coppergate, York*, The Archaeology of York 16/5

Maltby, J.M., 1979. *Faunal Studies on Urban Sites: The Animal Bones from Exeter 1971–1975*, Sheffield Univ.

Manning, W. H. 1985. *Catalogue of the Romano-British Iron Tools, Fittings and Weapons in the British Museum*, London: British Mus.

Mayes, P. and Butler, L.A.S., 1983. *Sandal Castle Excavations 1964–1973: A detailed Archaeological report*, Wakefield, Wakefield Historical Publications

Mepham, L., 2000. Pottery, in C.J. Young, *Excavations at Carisbrooke Castle, Isle of Wight, 1921–1996*, 98–131, Salisbury, Wessex Archaeol. Rep. 18

Mitchener, M., 1988. *Jetons, Medallions and Tokens. The Medieval Period and Nuremburg I*, London, Seaby

Morgan, R.A., 1980. The carbon 14 and dendrochronology, in C. Hill, M. Millett and T. Blagg, *The Roman Riverside Wall and Monumental Arch in London*, 88–94, London, London & Middlesex Archaeol. Soc. Spec. Pap. 3

Morris, J., 1975. The samian, in Cunliffe 1975, 276–8

Mulkeen, S. and O'Connor, T.P., 1997. Raptors in towns: Towards an ecological model, *Int. J. Osteoarchaeology* 7(4), 440–449

Munro, M.A.R., 1984. An improved algorithm for crossdating tree-ring series, *Tree Ring Bulletin* 44, 17–27

Murphy, C.P., 1986. *Thin Section Preparation of Soils and Sediments*. Berkhamsted, A B Academic Publishers

Nicholson, G.C. and Evans, S.M., 1997. Anthropogenic impacts on the stocks of the common whelk *Buccinum undatum* (L.), *Marine Environmental Research* 44, 305–314

O'Connor, T.P., 1988. *Bones from the General Accident Site, Tanner Row*, London, Archaeology of York 15/2, Counc. Brit. Archaeol.

Parker, A.J., 1988. The birds of Roman Britain, *Oxford J. Archaeol.* 7(2), 197–226

Payne, S., 1985. Morphological distinctions between the mandibular teeth of young sheep, *Ovis*, and goats, *Capra*. *J. Archaeol. Sci.* 1, 139–47

Payne, S. and Bull, G., 1988. Components of variation in measurements of pig bones and teeth, and the use of measurements to distinguish wild from domestic pig remains, *Archaeozoologia 2*, 27–66

Peacock, D.P.S., 1973. Forged brick-stamps from Pevensey, *Antiquity* 47, 138–40

Peacock, J.D., 1993. Late Quaternary marine mollusca as palaeoenvironmental proxies: a compilation and assessment of basic numerical data for NE Atlantic species found in shallow water, *Quaternary Science Reviews* 12, 263–275

Peacock, D.P.S., and Williams, D.F., 1986. *Amphorae and the Roman economy*, London

Pearce, J., 1992. *Post-Medieval Pottery in London, 1500–1700, Border Wares*, Vol 1, London, HMSO

Pearson, A., 2002. *The Roman Shore Forts: Coastal Defences of Southern Britain*, Stroud, Tempus

Peers, C., 1953. *Pevensey Castle, Sussex*. London, HMSO

Platt, C. and Coleman-Smith, R., 1975, *Excavations in Medieval Southampton 1953–1969. Vol 2: The finds*, Leicester, Univ. Press

Pollard, R.J., 1988. *The Roman Pottery of Kent*, Maidstone, Kent Archaeol. Soc. Monogr. Ser. 5

Powell, A., Serjeantson, D., and Smith, P., 2001. Food consumption and disposal: the animal remains, in M. Hicks and A. Hicks, *St Gregory's Priory, Northgate, Canterbury Excavations 1988–1991*, 289–333, Ashford, Canterbury Archaeol. Trust, Archaeology of Canterbury New Ser. Vol. 2

Reece, R., 1975. The coins, in Cunliffe 1975, 188–97

Reece, R., 1995. Site-finds in Roman Britain, *Britannia* 26, 179–206

Renn, D.F., 1971. The Turris de Penuesel: A reappraisal and a theory, *Sussex Archaeol. Collect.* 109, 55–64

Renn, D., 2001. Plantagenet castle-building in England in the second half of the twelfth century, in M.-P. Baudry (ed.), *Les fortifications Plantgenêt.* Poitiers, C.E.S.C.M., 15–21

Rippon, S., 2000. *The Transformation of Coastal Wetlands*, Oxford, Univ. Press for The British Academy

Rivet, A.L.F. and Smith, C., 1979. *The Place-Names of Roman Britain*, London, Batsford

Roach-Smith, C., 1858. *Excavations made Upon the Site of the Roman Castrum at Pevensey*, Privately Printed

Robinson, M., 1999. Charred and mineral-replaced macroscopic plant remains, in Barber 1999, fiche M 38–42

Sadler, P., 1990. Faunal remains, in J.N. Fairbrother, *Faccombe Netherton. Excavation of a Saxon and Medieval Manorial Complex I*, 462–506, London, Brit. Mus. Occ. Pap. 74

Salzmann, L.F., 1906. Documents relating to Pevensey Castle, *Sussex Archaeol. Collect.* 49, 1–30

Salzmann, L.F., 1907. Fisheries, 264–271 in W. Page (ed) *Victoria History of the Counties of England: Sussex* Vol 2. Constable

Salzmann, L.F. 1909, Excavations at Pevensey, 1907–1908, *Sussex Archaeol. Collect.* 52, 83–95

Salzmann, L.F., 1910. Pevensey documents – a correction, *Sussex Archaeol. Collect.* 53, 275

Salzmann, L.F. and Ray, J.E., 1906/7. *Excavations on the Site of the Roman Fortress at Pevensey: First Report*, Lewes, Eastbourne and East Grinstead, Farncombe and Co

Sands, H., 1908. Excavations at Pevensey Castle 1908, 20–30, in L. F. Salzmann, Excavations on the site of the Roman fortress at Pevensey, 1907–8, *Archaeol. J.* 65, 125–135

Savage, A., 1995. *The Anglo-Saxon Chronicles*, London, Tiger Books International

Schmid, E., 1972. *Atlas of Animal Bones*, Amsterdam, Elsevier

Serjeantson, D., 1996. The animal bones, in S.R. Needham and A. Spence (eds.), *Refuse and*

Disposal at Area 16 East Runnymede. Runnymede Bridge Research Excavations, Vol. 2, 194–223. London, Brit. Mus. Press

Serjeantson, D., 2000a. The bird bones, in M. Fulford and J. Timby, *Late Iron Age and Roman Silchester: Excavations on the site of the Forum Basilica, 1977, 1980–86,* 484–500, London, Society for Promotion of Roman Studies, Britannia Monogr. 15

Serjeantson, D., 2000b. Bird bones, in C.J. Young, *Excavations at Carisbrooke Castle, Isle of Wight 1921–1996,* 182–5, Salisbury, Wessex Archaeol. Rep. 18

Serjeantson, D., nd. Assessment of the animal bones: Pevensey Castle excavations 1993–96, unpubl. Rep. English Heritage

Smith, P.S., 1987. Marine mollusca, 170–172 in T. Rook, The Roman villa site at Dicket Mead, *Hertfordshire Archaeol.* 9, 79–175

Smith, P., 1994. The early Norman animal bone from Carisbrooke Castle, the Isle of Wight. Anc. Monum. Lab. Rep. 49/94

Somerville, E.M., 1996. Marine molluscs, 167–170 in M. Gardiner, M. Russell, and D. Gregory, Excavations at Lewes Friary 1985–6 and 1988–9, *Sussex Archaeol. Collect.* 134, 71–123

Somerville, E.M., 1997. Marine shells 115–117, in M. Lyne, *Lewes Priory: Excavations by Richard Lewis 1969–82,* Lewes, Lewes Priory Trust

Somerville, E. M., 1999. Marine mollusca, in Barber 1999, fiche M31–8

Spence, C., (ed.) 1990. *Archaeological Site Manual* (2nd Edition), London, Museum of London

Stoops, G., 1996. Complementary techniques for the study of thin sections of archaeological materials, in L. Castelletti and M. Cremaschi (eds), *XIII International Congress of Prehistoric and Protohistoric Sciences Forlì-Italia-8/14 September 1996,* 175–182, A.B.A.C.O., Forlì

Streeten, A.D.F., 1980. Potters, kilns and markets in medieval Sussex: a preliminary study, *Sussex Archaeol. Collect.* 118, 105–17

Streeten, A.D.F., 1985. The pottery, in Hare 1985, 103–26

Swanton, M., 1996. *The Anglo-Saxon Chronicles* [translated and edited by M. Swanton], London, Dent

Timby, J., 1988. The Middle Saxon pottery, in P. Andrews (ed) *Southampton Finds Volume 1: the coins and pottery from Hamwic,* 73–124, Gloucester, Southampton City Museums

Tomber R., and Dore, J., 1998. *The National Roman Fabric Reference Collection, A Handbook,* London, Mus. London Archaeol. Service Monogr. 2

Tortorella, S., 1986. La ceramica fine da mensa Africana dal IV al VII secolo, in A. Giardina (ed) *Societa Romana e Imperio Tardoantico. Le Merci Gli Insediamenti,* 211–25, Bari, Laterza

Tyers, I.G., 1994a. Appendix 6. Dendrochronology of Roman and early medieval ships, in P. Marsden, *Ships of the Port of London; first to eleventh centuries AD,* 201–209, English Heritage Archaeol. Rep. 3

Tyers, I.G., 1994b. *Guildhall Yard – spot-dates and sample lists,* MoLAS unpubl dendrochronology rep, 7/94

Vince, A. and Jenner, A., 1991. The Saxon and Early Medieval Pottery of London, in A. Vince (ed) *Aspects of Saxo-Norman London: II. Finds and Environmental Evidence,* 19–119, London & Middlesex Archaeol. Soc. Spec. Pap. 12

Walne, P., 1974. *The Culture of Bivalve Molluscs: 50 years' experience at Conwy,* Farnham, Fishing News (Books) Ltd

Warner, G.F., 1997. Occurrence of epifauna on the periwinkle, *Littorina littorea* (L.) and interactions with the polychaete *Polydora ciliata* (Johnston), *Hydrobiologia* 355, 41–47

Watson, B., 1998. 'Dark earth' and urban decline in late Roman London, in B. Watson (ed.), *Roman London. Recent Archaeological Work,* 100–106, Journal of Roman Archaeology Supplementary Series 24, Portsmouth, Rhode Island

White, H.J.O., 1926. *The Geology of the Country near Lewes.* Memoir for the Geological Sheet 319 (England and Wales), London, HMSO

Wiltshire, P., 1999. Palynological analysis of filling in the funerary shaft, in R. Niblett, *The Excavation of a Ceremonial Site at Folly Lane, Verulamium,* 346–365, London, Society for the Promotion of Roman Studies, Britannia Monogr. 14

Williams, A. and Martin, G.H., 1992. *Domesday Book: A Complete Translation,* London, Penguin

Williams, D.F., 1977. The Romano-British black-burnished industry: an essay on characterization by heavy mineral analysis, in D.P.S. Peacock (ed) *Pottery and Early Commerce. Characterization and Trade in Roman and Later Ceramics,* 163–220, London, Academic Press

Wilson, D.M. and Hurst, D.G., 1965. Medieval Britain in 1964, *Medieval Archaeology* 9, 192

Wilson, D.M. and Hurst, D.G., 1966. Medieval Britain in 1965, *Medieval Archaeology* 10, 200

Winder, J.M., 1992. *A Study of the Variation in Oyster Shells from Archaeological Sites and a Discussion of Oyster Exploitation,* unpubl. thesis Southampton Univ.

Ward-Perkins, J.B., 1964. *London Museum Medieval Catalogue.* London

Young, C.J., 1977. *Oxfordshire Roman Pottery,* Oxford, Brit. Archaeol. Rep. 43

Young, C.J., 1980. The Pottery, in B. Cunliffe, Excavations at the Roman Fort at Lympne, Kent, 1976–78, *Britannia* 11, 227–88

Appendices

Appendix 1: A survey of the standing masonry of the Keep and some adjacent features

by S. J. Allen and N. Al Shaikhley

Methodology

An assessment of the masonry of the Keep and part of the adjacent curtain wall at Pevensey Castle was carried out between the 7th and 11th March 1994. The aim of the survey was to provide an interpretation of the principal building phases represented, to define the stone types used in the differing phases and sub-phases of construction and repair and to characterise the masonry of these phases. An assessment of the potential for mortar analysis and tool marks was made, and areas requiring further recording were identified. The terms used to describe parts of the Keep and the locations of the rectified photographs are shown on Figure A.1.

The character of the masonry was described using a single context recording system. Each distinct area of masonry was assigned a number in a series from 4000–4067 inclusive. However, where an area of wall had a great number of individual, very small but closely similar features, such as patched repairs to eroded pointing, a single context was assigned to those of that elevation only. The recording sheets employed were those used by the Museum of London and completed following the guidelines set out in the latter's Archaeological Site Manual (Spence 1990).

The written and graphic records were then used to draw up a stratigraphic matrix to help define the building periods summarised below.

Description of the structural sequence

Unless otherwise stated, all masonry is of Greensand, probably from quarries near Eastbourne.

The Keep

First period (late Roman)

The Keep was built over and around upstanding masonry of the Saxon shore fort, incorporating in the east wall of the Keep part of the Roman curtain and in the south-east corner of the Keep, a Roman bastion. The relationship of the Keep to the Roman masonry was recorded in the area immediately adjacent to the photographed area and was sketched (Fig. A.2).

Very little of the Roman curtain, used for the east wall of the Keep, survived to the north of the bastion. Only a short stub of wall projected from the north face of the bastion above the modern ground surface and could be recorded. The outer facing of the Roman curtain (4059) consisted of regularly coursed Greensand blocks with courses of ceramic tiles at 1.2–1.7 m intervals, all bonded with *opus signinum*. The tile-coursing on the bastion and the lower, leaning, curtain to its north do not exactly match, the highest surviving course on the curtain consisting of one row of thick tiles whilst all of those on the bastion are of two rows of thinner tiles. The junction of the bastion with the curtain to the north is reinforced by tiles at more frequent intervals than the tile-coursing proper. A band of 10 courses of ironstone around the bastion was not continued in the curtain.

The core of the Roman curtain (4058) was built predominantly of flint with a smaller quantity of rough-hewn Greensand, laid in courses and bonded with a white lime mortar. The inner face was built of small Greensand blocks (*Petit Appareil*).

Second period: the Interior of the Keep

The inner (west facing) face of the Roman curtain had been robbed prior to the construction of the Keep, and was repaired with flint rubble and Greensand bonded with a white lime mortar (4057, 4064). Though similar to the Roman core, this rebuild was not as clearly coursed and had at least one bonding course of Greensand running through its thickness. This repair was faced with partially dressed blocks (4056, 4063) forming the inner face of the Keep's eastern wall. Some 3 m above the modern ground surface was a face of roughly dressed blocks (4065) running at right angles to the line of the wall, and turning south at its east end into a blocked recess in the bastion. It is matched by a similar partial refacing (4060) of the Roman bastion above the surviving height of the curtain which turns south at its west end to form the opposite side of this blocked recess.

The junction of this refacing with the rest of the Keep could not be observed, the junction with the south wall being concealed by the later thickening of the east wall of the Keep. To the north, the wall had

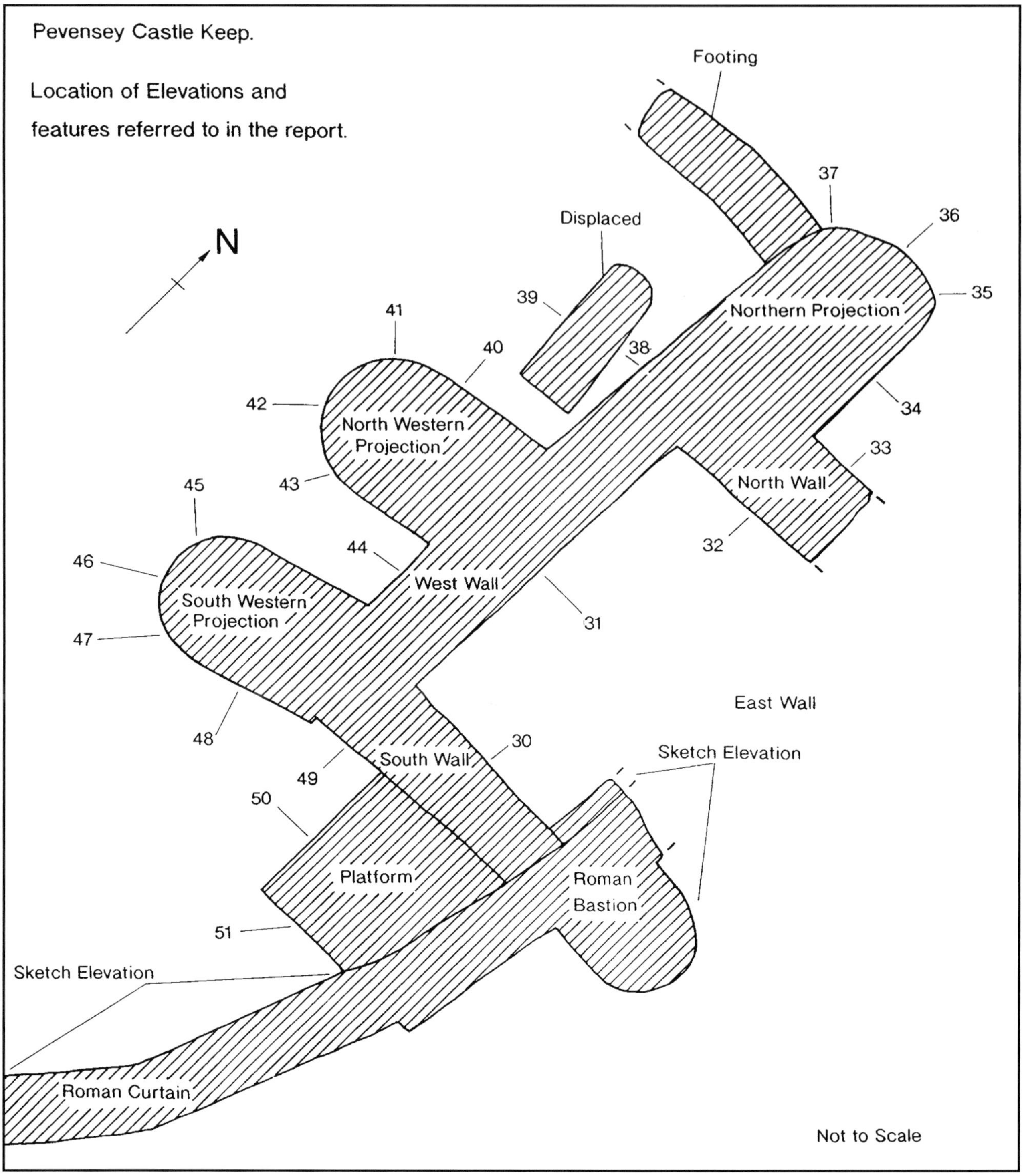

Figure A.1 Elevations and features referred to in the standing masonry report

collapsed. Its character is so similar to that of the other inner faces of the Keep that they should be considered to be of one contemporary build, allowing for the possibility that the east wall repairs may have been a strengthening of the Roman curtain in advance of the Keep's construction. The other inner faces (4029 south wall, 4023 west wall, 4020 north wall) were of irregularly coursed, partially dressed blocks bonded to each other and to the core (4005) of the Keep with white lime mortar. At each corner dressed ashlar quoins were substituted for the blocks of the bulk of the facing. One area of discrepancy was recorded at the bottom of the northern portion of (4023). This consisted of a build of pitched partially dressed blocks (4024) separated from a build of smaller blocks (4025) by a stack of ashlars (4026).

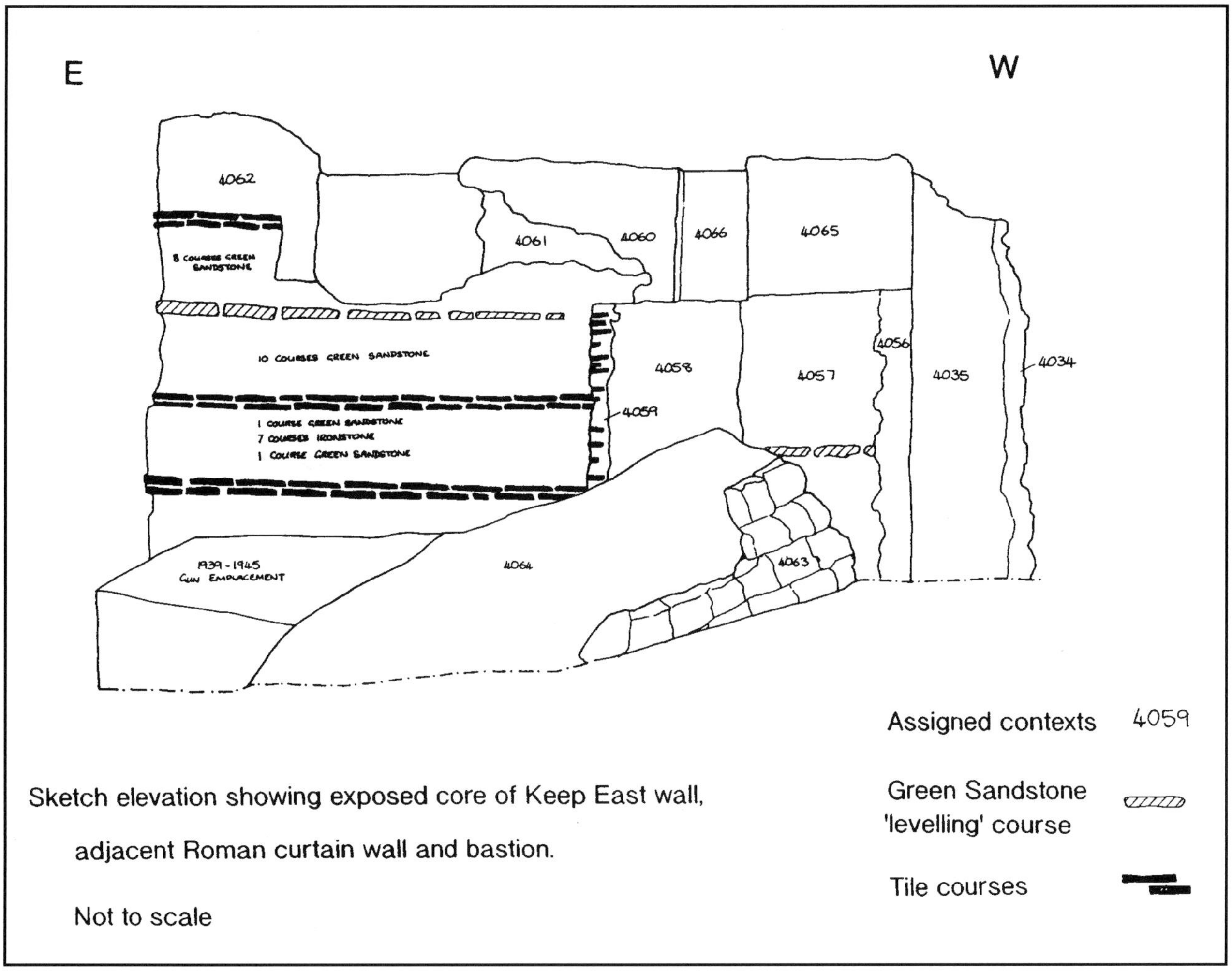

Figure A.2 Sketch elevation of exposed core of Keep East wall adjacent to Roman curtain wall and bastion

The core of the Keep (4005) consisted of coursed flint rubble with occasional pieces of stone. Some evidence was observed on the exposed southern and western faces for courses of single rows of Greensand within the rubble and for the construction of the core in 'lifts' of between 0.5 and 0.7 m.

Second period: the exterior of the Keep

The external faces of the Keep were clad in dressed ashlars. Though individual stones varied in length, the heights and that of the courses were maintained at quite uniform thickness and a uniform sequence of building was observed. This was also continued around each of the projections, whose facings were tightly bonded into the rest of the Keep. Certain discrepancies were noted, of which only one of the discrepancies in this sequence was not due to recent repair works. The standard sequence observed on the south wall and south-west projection (4008), with an isolated group of ashlars near the top of the surviving core (4007) and the west wall and north-west projection (4012) was as follows. A plinth of one course of chamfered blocks was followed by four courses of ashlars. A 5th course with some of the blocks cut for putlog holes was added. Three more courses of ashlars were added, then another course with putlog holes laid. This sequence was continued for the surviving height of the ashlar facing. Surviving holes in the rubble core suggest the horizontal spacing was continued to the top of the surviving masonry.

The one discrepancy mentioned above concerns the facing of the northern projection and north wall of the Keep (4053). A rise in the modern ground surface buries the plinth and up to three courses of the masonry above it between the north face of the north-west projection and the north end of the northern projection. The fourth course of masonry above the plinth of the north-western projection can be followed without interruption around the northern projection, but where the plinth of the latter emerges, this 'fourth' course is only the third course above this plinth. The plinth changes height at some point where it is currently buried. Though still four courses above the plinth, the putlog holes in this northern projection are

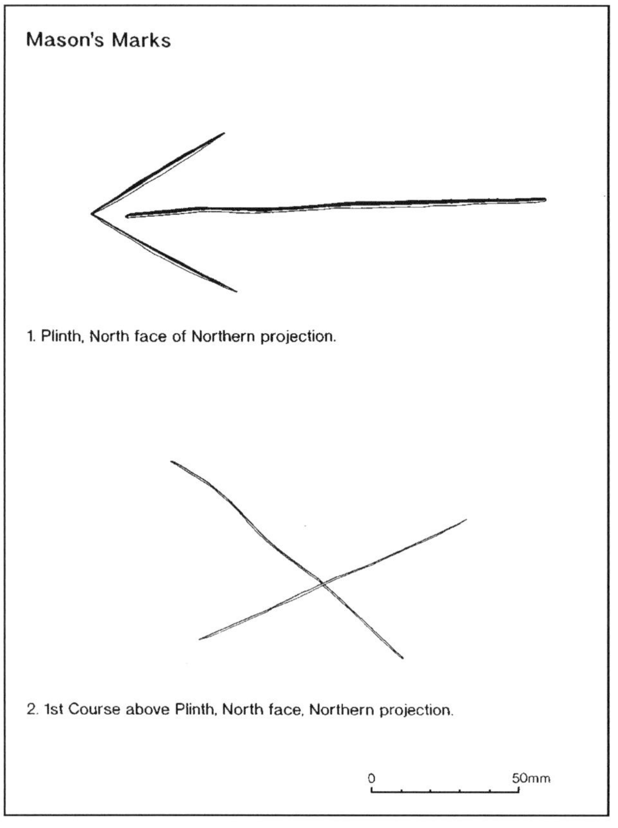

Figure A.3 Mason's marks

also therefore raised by one course relative to those elsewhere in the ashlar facing. It is quite clear that despite the statement of Renn (1971, 59), the putlog holes do *not* ascend to the north. Mason's marks are present on two adjacent stones (Fig. A.3).

Three other features of the core remain to be described. The northern projection contains a *c.* 1.0 m square vertical shaft faced with ashlars (4038) for at least 6 m depth. The highest part of the core in the north western projection has a partially surviving face of small Caen limestone and fewer Greensand ashlars (4039). The south wall is pierced by a single round headed splayed aperture faced with flints (4042). Each of these features is integral with the core and not a later insertion.

Third period

A platform was added to the south face of the Keep in the angle between the latter's south wall and the repaired Roman curtain. The platform has a solid mass of flint rubble, with some Greensand rubble and hints of coursing, bonded with a white lime mortar for its core (4000). This is faced (4002) with close fitting ashlars built with a chamfered plinth and faces battered back at 8° from the vertical, up to the 16th course above the plinth, where it becomes vertical. The three surviving stones of the 17th course, where its south face is continued above the curtain, have the remains of a continuous half-round moulded string course. The plinth itself is some 0.15 m higher than the plinth of the adjacent Keep wall.

Fourth period

The east wall of the Keep was thickened. This involved the adding of a 1.1 m thick flint rubble core (4035) faced with rough dressed Greensand (4034) against the interior face of the east wall. The elements were bonded with a white lime mortar.

Fifth period

Patched repairs were made at a number of points where the ashlars or mortaring of the Keep had been eroded or damaged. These repairs are distinctive, consisting of close packed flint nodules set in mortar with a knapped face facing out from the wall. The most extensive patching (4003) is to the south and west faces of the platform. Small areas (4009) are visible on the south wall of the Keep and (4061) on the north face of the Roman bastion. The interior of the Keep also received repairs with this material, patching being applied to the north wall (4021), west wall (4027), south wall (4030) and, to a lesser extent, the east wall (4036).

Sixth period

Collapse of the east wall and most of the upper levels of the Keep.

Seventh period: 1939–1945

A concrete chamber (4041), faced externally with random pebbles, flint nodules and stone rubble, was added to the top of the surviving rubble core. The chamber pierced by an observation slit facing north-east, and one facing south. Access to the chamber was via a small opening in its north face. This access was screened by a low parapet wall (4040) built in the same materials running along the top edge of the surviving medieval works.

Eighth period

Associated with these additions are the repair and repointing of much of the surviving masonry. Though these can be differentiated by area, they are carried out in the same hard dull orange-brown cement imitating the weathered medieval mortar. Such material (4066) also blocks the recess in the Roman bastion between the medieval refacings (4065) and (4066), though whether this is a modern blocking or the repair of a medieval blocking could not be determined by visual inspection. Where the cement is applied as repointing, it contains quantities of small pebbles. Where it is applied to patched repairs it has unknapped flint nodules pushed into it. One area

(4031) of the inner face of the south wall has been rebuilt using this mortar and is distinct from the medieval facing in incorporating machine-sawn blocks of pale Bonchurch Greensand, reset pieces of Eastbourne Greensand ashlar, roughly dressed Greensand and a piece of stone, reset upside down, front the ashlar plinth of the Keep exterior.

The repointing is especially heavy around the upper surviving ashlar courses and it must be suspected that many of these blocks have been reset or restored. A few individual blocks have been replaced throughout the ashlar facing, sometimes with machine-sawn pale Greensand from the quarries at Bonchurch, Isle of Wight. Three more extensive areas of ashlar rebuilding are of note. The first (4011) is around the south-west projection. The run of putlog holes stops some 3 m from the south face of the Keep and does not start again until the north face of this projection is reached. Between these points the character of the ashlars changes. The size of individual blocks decreases, the coursing is interrupted, the finish of adjacent stones varies widely between highly eroded and almost freshly cut blocks and several are cut to fit around their neighbours.

The second (4014) is the area of ashlars higher than the 13th course above the plinth on the west wall of the Keep. Again, the size of blocks changes, the coursing is interrupted and the putlog holes, above a single heavily restored example, disappear. The third area (4054) is around the end of the north-west projection. Although the size of blocks does not change, again the putlog holes are interrupted; the one surviving hole does not match up properly with the void in the core, and there are again marked differences in the erosion of the stones.

More recent repairs are present, usually involving no more than a repointing in pale brownish-grey mortar. One area (4033) of the inner face of the south wall of the Keep has been rebuilt with smaller dressed and undressed Greensand blocks using this mortar.

Features associated with the Keep but not integral to it

Two pieces of walling were described. One (4055) is a surviving stretch of masonry butting against the west face of the northern projection of the Keep. Nowhere higher than 0.7 m above the present ground surface it runs to the west, turning slightly south halfway along the surviving length. It appears to consist of a mass of beach pebbles, unworked flint rubble and some Greensand blocks laid in courses, but the masonry is entirely repointed and whether this is its original form cannot be determined visually.

The second is a piece of masonry standing beside but not parallel to the west face of the northern projection of the Keep. It consists of a flint rubble core (4017) incorporating Greensand rubble and several pieces of catapult ammunition faced to the west (4015) and east (4019) with roughly dressed Greensand and knapped flint. The east face has a horizontal offset 1.4 m below the highest surviving part of that face. Integral to the core at the bottom of the visible portion of the masonry is a relieving arch (4016) of undressed Greensand rubble.

The inner face of the curtain wall between the Keep and the postern gate (Fig. A4)

First period (late Roman)

This section of the curtain of the inner bailey is based on the surviving core of the Roman curtain wall. Part of this stretch was utilised in the building of the Keep where its surviving portion is recorded as (4058). This (4043, 4048) is built of coursed flint rubble set with white lime mortar. There is an horizontal offset above which the core (4044, 4052) continues, reduced in thickness by some 0.4 m. A vertical crack divides the masonry into a northern section some 11 m long and a southern section some 9 m long. No Roman inner facing was observed.

Second period

The junction of the curtain with the Keep was concealed by the addition of the platform to the south wall of the Keep. The upper part of the core above the offset was refaced with roughly dressed and very irregularly coursed stone (4045, 4049) set with white lime mortar. The relationship of this facing to the platform was concealed by later repointing but the platform was not obviously built over this facing. In contrast, at the southern end, this facing appears to butt against the ashlars of the postern gate tower.

Third period

The stone refacing was repaired and patched (4046, 4050) with knapped flint nodules set in white lime mortar with the knapped faces facing out. No repairs were made to the Roman core below the offset. Most of these repairs were to eroded mortar joints between the stones, but the southern section was more generally treated to give a crude and irregular chequerboard arrangement of alternating stone and flint repairs.

Fourth period

A hard, dull orange brown cement imitating the weathered medieval mortar was used to repoint and repair the masonry, especially towards the top where the higher stones may well have been reset and or replaced. No repairs were made to the Roman core below the offset.

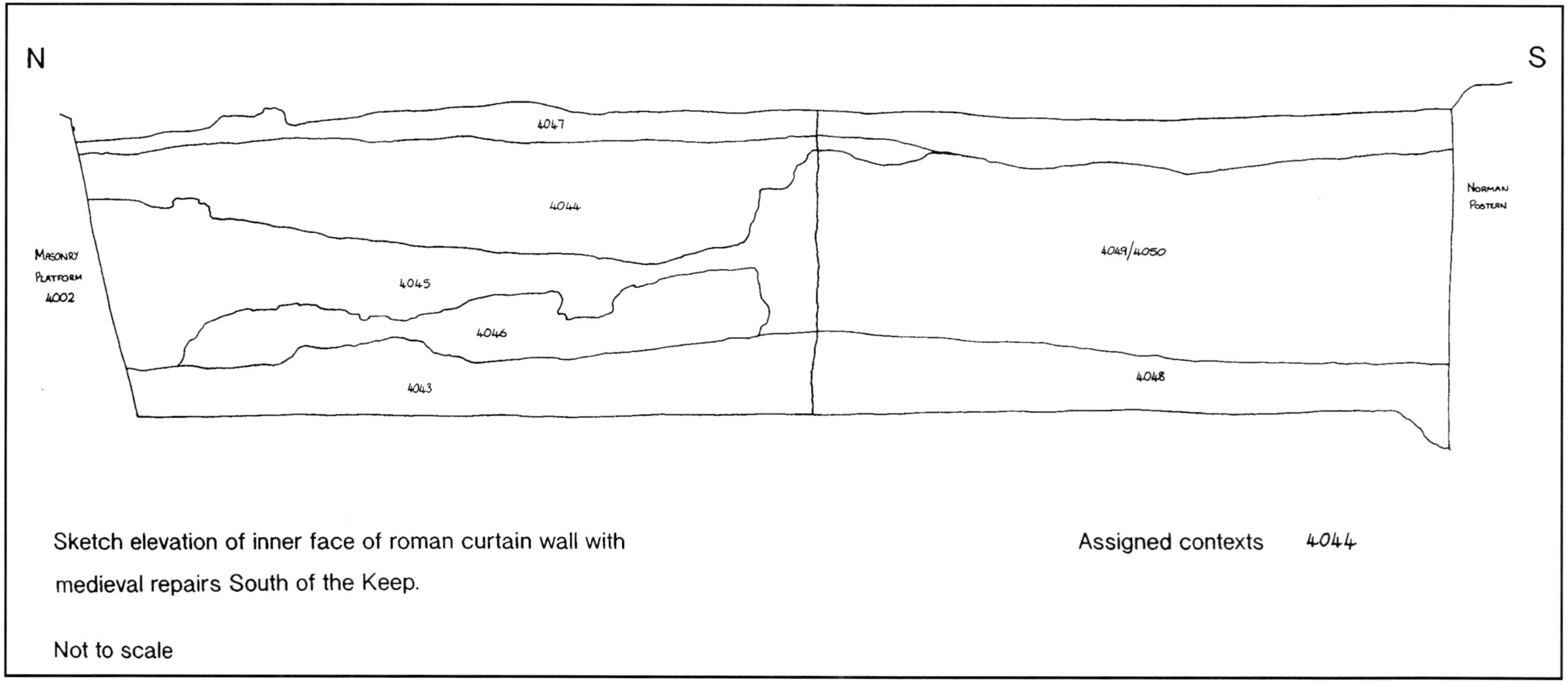

Figure A.4 Sketch of inner face of Roman curtain wall with medieval repairs

Interpretation of the structural sequence

The relationship of the Roman masonry and the medieval rebuilding

The evidence suggests that the standing Roman masonry was considered adequate and stable, even with its inner face robbed, to be incorporated into the Keep by the latter's builders. The only alterations required were a repair of the upper portion of the outer facing of the bastion and a thickening of the adjacent curtain to support the east wall of the Keep. The curtain between the Keep and the postern gate may not have been repaired until after the platform was added to the south wall of the Keep and so could have been considered adequate for its purpose in the early periods of the medieval occupation.

The Greensand repair of the inner face of the curtain to the south of the Keep may therefore be roughly contemporary with the thickening of the east wall of the Keep, rather than a primary medieval repair, and therefore perhaps part of an overall effort to reinforce the outer walls of the castle in this sector. No evidence was found to suggest the construction of buildings against the curtain after the Greensand facing was applied, or after the facing was repaired in flint, but this need not preclude the existence of an earlier range removed prior to the Greensand reinforcement. The flint repairs appear to be contemporary with those to the Keep.

A problem concerns the lack of repairs to the core below the offset. This might be taken to imply that this portion was buried during the medieval occupation and only recently cleared. An objection to this is that the plinths of both the Keep and the platform (and by implication the contemporary ground surface) are some 0.7 m below the height of the offset. Possible options are that the ground level was raised after the building of the platform but before the period of flint repairs, or that a cladding applied over this part of the core was thoroughly and completely robbed after the close of medieval occupation.

The Keep

The uniformity of the build, ashlar coursing, and putlog runs all lead to the conclusion that the Keep and the projections from it are of one build, and were planned and executed as a single entity. If the projections are later additions to an earlier rectangular Keep (Renn 1971, 61) then this suggestion requires that the entire Keep was refaced, and refaced so completely that no trace of an earlier cladding has survived or been exposed in the core.

The interior facing and the exterior ashlars were laid in courses, and the space between them made up with mortared rubble. There is *no* indication that the quoins have been shaken or fractured and that they are therefore part of an early rectangular Keep to which the projections were added and the exterior refaced. The use of an area of pitched stones and smaller stones in the inner face of the west wall can be explained as an attempt to utilise smaller and/or thinner stones in the least visible part of the Keep. The heights of the courses are maintained along the whole length of this wall, arguing for the contemporaneity of its build and in this context, the short stack of ashlars built into the wall can be seen as a strengthening of what might have been considered a weaker part of the facing.

As noted earlier, the putlog holes and plinth of the north wall and northern projection of the Keep are one course higher than the rest of the Keep. It might therefore be suggested that this part of the Keep is an addition or repair to the original plan. The short stack of ashlars may mark the intended position of the junction between the inner faces of the west and north walls but visual examination does not support this.

However the ashlar coursing around the north-west projection, the north projection and the north wall is absolutely consistent in thickness and character and thus would have demanded sufficient surplus ashlars of those respective sizes to clad the north projection even if it had not been built. The consistency exhibited would also have required an earlier north wall to have been built in such a manner that a column of alternate stones could have been removed to allow the ashlars of the north projection to have been bonded into it without any sign of recut stones, or infilling with smaller blocks to make up any discrepancy. It is simpler to regard the change in height of the plinth and the putlog holes as no more than a means of coping with a slight rise in the contemporary ground level. The modern ground surface at the north of the Keep is noticeably higher than that further south and this may reflect the medieval topography.

The inner stone facings of the Keep are not of notably high quality. No architectural features survive to indicate that the current internal space was anything but an unlit basement. If any openings were let through the walls to this space, they would need to have been in the missing east wall, which, up to the presumed height of the first floor, would have required cutting through the Roman curtain.

The principal chambers of the Keep would seem therefore to have been at first floor level or above. The opening through the south wall is a window and need not reflect the floor level. There are two possible indications of the height of the first floor. Firstly, on top of the north-western projection, the Caen limestone faced feature may represent the facing of a chamber within the projection and a passage leading to the interior of the Keep. Secondly, at a similar height above where the stub of the east wall meets the Roman bastion, the Greensand facings may represent a mural gallery leading through the length of the east wall, passing into/through the Roman bastion (subsequently blocked) with an access to the first floor of the Keep through an opening at the point where the east wall has subsequently broken away from the bastion.

The reason for the later internal thickening of the east wall is not clear, but may be associated with the Greensand refacing of the inner face of the Roman curtain south of the Keep. It would seem to be an attempt to strengthen the wall of the Keep at the point where it was most directly exposed to attack. However this also proved to be the most unstable section of the Keep, and the works may have been connected with reinforcement/repair against or following subsidence.

The flint repairs to the inside of the Keep are of some significance. Their presence implies that these faces were not only accessible for repair but that they had been exposed long enough to need repair. It suggests that this 'basement' area of the Keep was an open space and had not been filled with earth dumps after construction.

The flint repairs are of very similar character both inside and outside the Keep and this would suggest that they are contemporary.

No direct evidence was found for the function of the platform added to the south side of the Keep. The difference in plinth heights here would seem to be the result of a slight rise in ground level subsequent to the building of the Keep. No effort was made to bond the ashlars of this feature with those of the Keep, and indeed the stones are smaller and more closely fitted. The string course is not paralleled anywhere on the surviving cladding of the Keep.

Footnote

One feature was noted whilst working around the outside of the Keep which permits some speculation on the position of the south-west projection from the Keep. This projection is not perpendicular to the line of the west wall, nor does it continue the line of the south wall, but is offset *c.* 0.5 m south and angled slightly south-west. Near to the north-west face of the projection is a shallow depression 4.0 m across.

It is possible that this depression has formed as a result of subsidence into a negative feature such as a pit or well and that this feature pre-dates the Keep. If the projection had been built to continue the line of the south wall and perpendicular to the line of the west wall, the footings of the projection would have coincided with the edge of this depression, placing the footings of the masonry on the edge of a patch of unconsolidated ground. It is possible that this feature was identified at an early stage of the Keep construction, and the projection aligned so as to avoid it, with the north-west projection also being swung slightly to the south-west to conform to the alignment of the south-west projection. It must however be stressed that, at this stage, this is no more than speculation.

The medieval masonry adjacent to the Keep

The stretch of coursed rubble abutting the north projection is unlike any of the surviving Keep masonry. There are no obvious facing stones and this would tend to suggest it is a footing or foundation for a wall, rather than a wall *per se*. No evidence suggests which face was the inside or outside. The change in alignment is also difficult to understand in terms of a structure attached to the Keep. The footing is however almost parallel to the curtain of the inner bailey and changes alignment next to the junction of the curtain with the east tower. It is easier therefore to regard this feature as the footing for the south wall of a range built against the inner bailey curtain rather than part of the Keep.

The masonry shown on elevation 39 is more problematic. The putlog holes are in the west face and at a relatively low level compared to those in the nearby sections of the Keep, suggesting that this masonry is related to a different ground level. The core appears to contain more Greensand rubble than the core of the Keep, whilst the facing stones are certainly more mixed and smaller than those of the inner or outer faces of the Keep. This suggests that the wall is not part of the original build of the Keep. The core incorporates several pieces of medieval Greensand catapult ammunition and must therefore postdate their introduction to the site.

This masonry is not parallel to the adjacent Keep facing and it is hardly more than 1.0 m away from it. There are no putlog holes in the east face which would match those in the adjacent ashlars of the Keep, and thus the latter putlogs can hardly be for a wooden stair built between the Keep and this fragment (Renn 1971, 59). If there was a structure built with masonry walls so close to the Keep, it is difficult to understand why the builders did not merely utilise the wall of the Keep rather than building such a substantial piece of masonry in this position. In any case, the offset on the east face suggests that the east face should be the inner face of the wall, not the exterior. It is difficult therefore to avoid the conclusion that this piece of masonry has been displaced from an original and much higher location, perhaps a late rebuilding and raising of the Keep. The crude rubble arch casts no light on this problem.

Restoration work on the masonry

The repairs associated with the hard brown cement are attributable to the Office of Works and its successors. These repairs appear intended to blend in with the surviving masonry, and in some places have succeeded all too well. Only occasionally were newly cut stones employed; much of the stone repairs concern the resetting of medieval stone blocks, perhaps derived from the rubble removed during clearance operations. It is therefore difficult to identify with precision the line between Ministry repairs and original stonework. The clues used in the study were:

1. Significant gaps in the runs of putlog holes.
2. Areas where adjacent stones had suffered extreme differential erosion.
3. Significant irregularities in the coursing with stones cut to fit one over the other.
4. Occasional use of sawn pale Bonchurch Greensand blocks.

Significant repairs to the facings were identified using the above criteria. The use of reset medieval stones means that metrical analysis alone would be of very limited value in identifying modern restoration.

Ministry repairs were concerned with protecting the upper, most exposed courses of stone, repointing and rebuilding elsewhere where necessary. Associated with these works are the defensive works of the Second World War which are in places above Ministry cement repairs, and which themselves have later ministry cement for identification plaques and the blocking of apertures. The repair strategy also involved attention to the rubble core of the Keep which is difficult to evaluate. An effort had clearly been made to define putlog voids in the core and when compared to those visible in the ashlars, they indeed continue the runs of putlog holes. The lifts of rubble restored may therefore also reproduce the original lifts of the core. However since the structure has been so heavily repaired, it is not possible to test the accuracy of this restoration against recently exposed medieval corework.

Appendix 2: Description of pottery fabrics and associated forms

Roman pottery
by Jane Timby

The Roman pottery was subdivided into four basic groups, imported regional, local and wares of unknown source. The codes are based on those devised for the National Roman fabric reference collection (Tomber and Dore 1998) supplemented with additional site specific codes for local wares. The grey ware category in particular has been kept fairly simple to avoid repetitious descriptions which add little to our knowledge of the local industries.

1. Continental Imports

Samian

A total of 51 sherds of Central and East Gaulish samian were present presumably mainly as redeposited or curated finds. Forms include Dr 31, 33, 37 and mortaria. Several sherds are just small chips or spalls, and a few had been burnt (*cf.* Lyne 2009, 120).

Argonne red-slipped ware (ARGRS)

Fabric: (Tomber and Dore 1998, 48).

Form: Two bowl body sherds with roller-stamped decoration.

Comment: Argonne ware has been well-documented at Pevensey. Finds from previous excavations summarised by Lyne (2009, 120–21) mainly occur in forms datable to the 4th–early 5th century.

African red-slipped ware, (NAF RS)

Fabric: (Bird 1977; Hayes 1972).

Form: At least three vessels are present. Two sherds from a vessel closest to Hayes (1972) form 75 came from Phase 3. The upper rim surface is roulette decorated (Fig. 3.3, 48). A second vessel sherd, from (181), Phase 5, is part of a flange, probably from a bowl Hayes type 91 = Bonifay (2004) *sigillées* type 49–50; whilst a rim from (608), Phase 14 is from a bowl, Hayes form 99C = Bonifay (2004) *sigillées* type 55 Variante C.

Comment: African red-slipped wares have been documented from Britain in contexts dating from the late 1st to late 4th–5th century largely from sites in London, Essex and Kent (Bird 1977, fig. 20.1). These vessels are possibly the first to be documented from Pevensey. The dish (Fig. 3.3, 48) appears at present to be unique in Britain. It is a type dating from the early–mid-5th century thus placing it relatively late amongst the British finds. Bowls of Hayes type 91 are dated now by Bonifay (2004, 179) to the first half and middle decades of the 5th century, whilst bowl type 99C is probably slightly later in date, current at the end of the 6th to the 7th century (*ibid.*, 181). It has been suggested that vessels arrived with individuals, possibly artisans, rather than as part of traded cargoes (Bird 1977, 272).

Mayen ware (MAY CO)

Fabric: A hard, granular fabric, dark red-brown in colour with a slightly lighter inner core. The paste contains a moderate density of angular inclusions of mixed volcanic composition up to 2 mm in size. The fabric broadly equates with Fulford and Bird (1975), fabric 1.

Form: A single example of a lid-seated jar comparable to a vessel from Portchester (Fulford 1975b, fig. 192.151.1).

Comment: Other examples of this ware have been recorded from Pevensey (*cf.* Fulford and Bird 1975; Lyne 2009, 100–1). Occurrences in Britain range from before 330 to the end of the 4th or early 5th century.

Micaceous grey ware (RO IM1)

Fabric: A distinctive ware characterised by abundant flecks of mica, mainly muscovite but with some biotite. The matrix contains a sparse to moderate frequency of ill-sorted sub-angular to rounded quartz sand, rare linear burnt out organic inclusions and a scatter of orange-red rounded high

micaceous inclusions up to 5 mm across.
Form: Single body sherd only from (197). Could be Roman or Saxon.
Source: Unknown, probably an import.

Oxidised ware (RO IM2)
Fabric: Mid-orange ware with a darker core and slightly blackened exterior. The paste contains a scatter of fine rounded and sub-angular quartz, rare rounded ?volcanic and sparse very fine biotite mica.
Form: A lid-seated jar (Fig. 3.3, 62) typologically similar to the Mayen types. Similar lid-seated jars to the Rhineland types have also been documented from the Ile-de-France dating to the late 4th–5th centuries (Barat 1993).

North Gaulish mortaria (NOG WH4)
Fabric: (Tomber and Dore 1998, 75). A single worn body sherd from (165), Phase 4.

Dressel 20 olive oil amphora (BAT AM)
(Peacock and Williams 1986, type 25). Two small body sherds from Phases 12 and 13.

Other amphora
Two other unidentified possible amphora sherds have been reported on by D. F. Williams (below).

A note on two amphora sherds, by D.F. Williams

1. A small plain amphora body sherd in a hard, slightly rough micaceous fabric, light red (2.5YR 6/6). This sherd is quite distinctive in the hand-specimen as both surfaces contain many small flakes of mica, including the gold variety. A thin section of the sherd was examined under the petrological microscope. This showed a groundmass dominated by many small narrow flakes on mica. Also present are sparse grains of quartz and feldspar (plagioclase and potash) and several small pieces of lava which seem to have a trachytic texture.

   It is difficult to know the particular amphora form which is involved here. although the curvature of the sherd points to a fairly wide-bodied vessel. The fabric is somewhat unusual, consisting as it does of plentiful mica and inclusions of trachytic lava. Given the late date for the Roman pottery assemblage as a whole, a source close by to one of the volcanic area of the eastern Mediterranean is perhaps likely for this vessel. Context 45, Phase 3.
2. A small plain body sherd from an ?amphora, in a rough, sandy, somewhat micaceous fabric, light grey (2.5Y 7/2). Thin sectioning shows frequent grains of quartz and flecks of mica. Also present are larger inclusions of quartz-mica-schist, phyllite, and quartzite.

   It is not absolutely clear that this small sherd is from an amphora, although the thickness and the curvature of the wall suggests that it probably is, or at least from a large vessel. At all events the vessel itself must be regarded as an import to the site, for the petrology points to a source in an area dominated by metamorphic rocks. In England, the nearest source of such rocks would be in the south-west of the country. Across the channel there are large areas of metamorphic rocks in Brittany and the surrounding areas. If this sherd is from an amphora, then it opens up the possibility of a more widely travelled vessel and perhaps for an origin in a metamorphic area around the shores of the Mediterranean. Context 226, Phase 6.

2. Regional Imports

DORSET

Dorset Black Burnished ware (DOR BB1)
Fabric: (Williams 1977; Holbrook and Bidwell 1991; Tomber and Dore 1998, 127).
Forms: Largely flanged conical bowls, straight-sided dishes, jars with oblique lattice decoration.

HAMPSHIRE

Alice Holt/Farnham reduced sandy ware (ALH RE)
Fabric: (Lyne and Jefferies 1979; Tomber and Dore 1998, 138).
Forms: Flanged bowls, straight-sided dishes (Fig. 3.1, 5) and everted rim jars. Also present but less common are large greyware storage jars occasionally with white slip and combed decoration and flagons.
Comment: Distinguishing Alice Holt fabrics from other grey or black sandy fabrics is difficult and it is quite possible that some of the other sandy grey ware categories identified below belong with this group.

Overwey ware (= Portchester D) (OVW WH)
Fabric: (Fulford 1975b; Tomber and Dore 1998, 146).
Forms: Hook-rim and everted rim jars (Fig. 3.2, 22–3; 3.5, 96–7) and straight-sided dishes with plain or beaded rims (Fig. 3.2, 28; Fig. 3.5, 98).
Comment: Kilns producing this ware are known within the Alice Holt industry but other potential sources have been identified at Fareham and in East Sussex (Lyne 1994).

NEW FOREST INDUSTRY

Colour-coated ware (NFO CC; NFO RS1; NFO RS2)
Fabric: All three main New Forest colour-coated fabrics (Fulford 1975a; Tomber and Dore 1998, 141*ff*) are present in the assemblage; namely hard fired grey ware with a metallic colour-coat; whiteware with a monochrome colour-coat and pale coloured fabrics with red or brown colour-coat.
Forms: Largely beakers, flanged and other bowls and mortaria. An example of the latter (Fulford 1975a, type 104) from (31) has a paw print impressed into the inner base.

New Forest whiteware (NFO WH1–2); parchment ware (NFO PA)
A few sherds of whiteware and a single parchment ware

sherd are present. The former includes a mortarium (Fulford 1975a, type 104) dating to the mid-4th century (Fig. 3.2, 41).

NENE VALLEY INDUSTRIES

Nene Valley colour-coated ware (LNV CC)

Fabric: (Tomber and Dore 1998, 118). A single sherd from a closed form, possibly a beaker from Phase 12.

OXFORDSHIRE INDUSTRIES

Colour-coated ware (OXF RS) (Fig. 3.5, 106), (Young 1977, 123–84); **white-slipped mortaria (OXF WSM)** (Young 1977, 117–22); **white ware mortaria (OXF WHM)** (Young 1977, 56–79), and **parchment ware (OXF PA)** (Fig. 3.5, 110) (Young 1977, 80–92)

Forms: The colour-coated wares include examples of Young (1977) types C45, C50–1, C55, C61–2, C68–70, C75, C78–9, C81, C83, mortaria C99–100 and various beakers and flagon including one showing the edge of a face mask. One sherd from (31) has been fashioned into a counter. Amongst the whitewares are mortaria Young (1977) types M17, M20 and M22. The parchment wares include a possible P32 and sherds decorated with square rouletting and red paint.

WARWICKSHIRE

Mancetter-Hartshill mortaria (MAH WH)

Fabric: Tomber and Dore 1998, 189. A single sherd from a mortaria with red painted decoration on the flange from Phase 12.

SOURCE UNKNOWN

Late shell-tempered ware (ROB SH)

Fabric: (Tomber and Dore 1998, 212). Only four sherds, one a jar rim sherd (Fig. 3.1, 1) are present suggesting that Pevensey falls at the limit of the distribution of these wares which are fairly ubiquitous on sites with late 4th–5th century occupation across the southern half of the country.

3. Local Wares

GROG-TEMPERED

GROG1: East Sussex grog-tempered ware

(Green 1976; 1977)

Fabric: Dark grey, black or brown smooth soapy ware containing a moderate scatter of sub-angular buff and dark grey-coloured fine grog up to 2 mm but mainly finer.

Forms: Handmade vessels, mainly jars both curved everted and sharply everted globular types (Fig. 3.1, 8–10, 12–13; Fig. 3.3.3, 61; Fig. 3.5, 100–1). Other common forms include straight-sided bowls/dishes (Fig. 3.1, 16), and flanged bowls, one with incised wavy-line decoration (Fig. 3.1, 18–19; Fig. 3.5, 102). Less common are simple lids (Fig. 3.1, 17) and a flask. Surface coloration is patchy due to uneven firing. The exterior surfaces are frequently burnished smooth.

Comment: This is one of the commonest Roman fabrics present accounting for 11% of total assemblage, 29% of the Roman component. The ware was first identified by Green (1976; 1977) from excavations at Newhaven and Bishopstone although the chronology was not clear. At the latter site spanning the Late Iron Age to 5th century it accounted for 40–50% of the assemblage. Equivalent to Lyne (2009, 96–7) group A who observed that the ware was insignificant at Pevensey until *c.* AD 350 becoming increasingly important in the later 4th-early 5th century. From the recent excavations fabric GROG1 first appears in Phase 1 and accounts for 29% of the Phase 3, dark earth assemblage. It is not possible to establish the end of production.

GROG2: ?East Sussex variant

Fabric: A smooth soapy dark orange ware. The slightly corky texture paste contains orange-coloured sub-angular grog and a scatter of other rare inclusions such as iron, a fine-grained sandstone and rounded chalk. The clay matrix contains sparse, very fine white mica just detectable on the sherd surfaces.

Forms: Handmade jars and a flanged bowl.

Comment: Sherds are relatively sparse with only three sherds from Phase 3 and a further four sherds from the disturbed dark earth (Phase 12). Other sherds occurred in Phases 4, 5, and 10.

GROG3: East Sussex variant

Fabric: A hard, well-fired ware with a red-brown or dark grey exterior, light grey interior and very light grey core. The paste contains a sparse to moderate density, of ill-sorted, dark grey, sub-angular grog up to 2 mm in size.

Forms: Mainly handmade jars with everted rims (Fig. 3.1, 11).

Comment: Probably equivalent to Lyne (1994) fabric A4 regarded as a late variant of GROG1 occurring in post 370 groups. Sherds first occur in Phase 3 and the disturbed Phase 3 deposits.

GROG4: Thundersbarrow storage jar type

Fabric: A coarse variant of GROG1 in a dark grey or oxidised ware.

Forms: Large handmade storage jars (Fig. 3.1, 15).

GROG: miscellaneous other grog-tempered wares

A number of minor variants were present which were not distinctive enough to warrant further detailed analysis. Featured sherds Figs 3.1–3.2, 14, 21.

SANDY WARES

GREY1: Local grey sandy ware

Fabric: Mid-grey ware with lighter blue-grey core. Hard with a sandy texture but no macroscopically visible inclusions. At x20 a moderate to common frequency of very fine, well-sorted quartz sand can be seen.

Forms: Wheelmade typical late Roman forms, for example, everted rim jars with thickened or hooked rims, flanged bowls and straight-sided dishes.
Comment: A relatively large category probably distinguished more on the grade and texture of the ware rather than isolating a specific production centre. Probably from a source(s) local to Pevensey.

GREY2: grey sandy ware
Fabric: A hard, moderately fine sandy ware with mid-grey surfaces, and a grey core sometimes with red-brown margins. At x20 a sparse scatter of well-sorted, fine, rounded, quartz sand, occasional grog and rounded white calcareous nodules are visible. Occasionally vessels have a black slip. The sherds have a slightly granular pimply texture.
Forms: Vessels include handmade and wheelmade types. Common forms are flanged bowls, jars with hooked, everted or flaring rims (Fig. 3.1, 2, 6–7), bottles, straight-sided dishes and less commonly flat rim bowls/dishes.

GREY3: black sandy, slightly micaceous ware
Fabric: A hard, well-fired dark grey or black ware with a lighter grey or red-brown core. At x20 magnification the paste contains a moderate frequency of fine rounded to sub-angular clear quartz. The surfaces shows a very fine white mica presence in the clay body.
Forms: Wheelmade flanged bowls (Fig. 3.1, 3, Fig. 3.2, 24, 26; Fig. 3.5, 103), straight-sided dishes with burnished interiors imitating DOR BB1 types, other dishes (Fig. 3.3, 45; Fig. 3.5, 99) and jars (Fig. 3.3, 43).

GREY4: black sandy ware
Fabric: Red-brown ware with black surfaces. The surfaces have a fine slightly sparkling appearance from fine quartz and white mica. The paste contains a moderate scatter of well-sorted, fine, rounded, clear quartz.
Forms: Mainly occurs as everted, thickened rim jars, hook-rim jars, straight-sided dishes and flanged bowls.
Comment: Relatively common fabric mainly found in the dark earth horizons (Phases 3 and 12).

GREY5: black sandy ware
Fabric: Black sandy ware occasionally with dark brown margins. The paste contains a moderate to high density of well-sorted fine, sub-angular to rounded quartz sand (<0.25 mm) accompanied by a sparse scatter of rounded red-brown ferruginous grains up to 1.5 mm.
Forms: Straight-sided dishes with burnished interior surfaces copying Dorset Black Burnished ware.
Comment: Not a particularly common fabric with sherds first recorded from Phase 1.

GREY6: medium sandy grey ware
Fabric: Hard, grey, sandy ware with slightly granular surfaces. The paste contains a sparse to moderate frequency of ill-sorted rounded quartz (up to 1 mm) accompanied by rare fragments of flint and black iron.
Forms: Jars and flanged rim bowls (Fig. 3.5, 104).

GREY7: black-slipped grey sandy ware
Fabric: Fine grey, sandy ware with a very dense black surface slip. The paste contains a moderate to common scatter of fine, rounded, quartz sand with a sparse scatter of rounded black iron visible at x20 magnification.
Form: Wheelmade flanged bowl (Fig. 3.5, 114), everted rim jar (Fig. 3.5, 113) and flask (Fig. 3.3, 46).

GREY8: hard, grey ware
Fabric: Very well-fired, hard, dark grey ware. The paste contains a moderate to high density of ill-sorted, rounded quartz sand (up to 0.5 mm) in a semi-vitrified matrix and rounded black iron. The surfaces have a fine pimply appearance.
Forms: Wheelmade jars with everted, thickened or hooked rims (Fig. 3.3, 42). Two rim sherds from a particularly warped waster jar from the dark earth (45) might suggest relatively local production.
Comment: The ware first appears in Phase 2 with significant numbers from Phase 3 and 12.

GREY9: grey sandy ware with iron
Fabric: A mid- to light grey well-fired ware occasionally with an orange inner core or margins. The most distinctive feature of this ware is the presence of fine black iron grains (up to 2 mm across) which have left a characteristic streaking on the sherd surfaces. Occasional pale coloured fine sandstone inclusions are also present against a fine background scatter of well-sorted fine quartz sand.
Form: Dropped flanged bowls (Fig. 3.2, 25). (31).

COLOUR-COATED WARES

Pevensey colour-coated ware (PEV CC) (Fulford 1973)
Fabric: Very hard, orange semi-vitrified fabric occasionally with a blue-grey inner core. The surfaces have a glossy brownish to orange red colour-coat. The paste contains frequent iron inclusions giving a pimply surface effect and occasional calcareous inclusions, sometimes as voids with calcareous linings, sparse iron up to 2 mm in size and occasional fine linear voids. A blown kiln waster sherd is present in (68).
Forms: Mainly bowls and mortaria very similar to the examples found in the Oxfordshire repertoire (e.g., Fig. 3.2, 30–8; Fig. 3.5, 105, 107, 111–2). Various types of decoration are present including white paint, rouletting and impressed comb.

Pevensey white-slipped and colour-coated mortaria (PEV WSM, CCM) (Fig. 3.2, 39–40)
At least three types of trituration grit appear to have been used on the Pevensey ware mortaria: a rounded polished quartz sand similar to the Oxfordshire mortaria; a mixed angular flint and quartz sand and a very distinctive iron. The latter present a mixture of very metallic glossy black

rounded grains alongside matt, browner grains of ?ore.
Comment: Pevensey ware first identified by Fulford (1973) appears from around the mid-4th century and is thought to be locally produced.

4. Source unknown

OXID

Miscellaneous oxidised (orange) sandy wares.

GREY

Miscellaneous grey/black (reduced) sandy wares (Fig. 3.2, 20)

WSLIP1: white-slipped oxidised ware
Fabric: A fine orange sandy ware with no macroscopically visible inclusions. The surfaces are covered in a thick creamy-white slip.
Form: Wheelmade closed forms, probably flasks/flagons. No featured sherds.

WSLIP2: Painted white-slipped ware
Fabric: Hard, orange red sandy ware with a thick cream exterior slip. The paste contains a moderate to common frequency of moderately well-sorted, fine background quartz with a sparse scatter of larger, rounded, quartz grains up to 1–1.5 mm.
Form: A rare fabric represented by just two sherds from wheelmade closed forms, probably flagon. Possible painted orange decoration on top of the slip for one sherd.

?Local colour-coated ware (LO CC1)
Fabric: A mid-orange, fine sandy fabric, very finely micaceous. The exterior is covered in a dark chestnut brown glossy colour-coat. Probably a local colour-coated industry.
Form: Beakers (Fig. 3.1, 4, Fig. 3.2, 29).

?Local colour-coated ware (LOC CC2)
Fabric: A well fired, almost cindery very fine sandy fabric red brown in colour with a grey-brown inner core. The surfaces have a metallic silvery-black external colour-coat, matt brownish-black on the interior.
Form: Represented by a single thin walled beaker sherd from Phase 12.

Colour-coated ware (CC3)
Fabric: A very fine, orange, micaceous fabric with a dark brown colour-coat. Represented by a single sherd with unusual impressed decoration (Fig. 3.3, 47). May possibly be an import.

Mortarium (MORT2)
Fabric: A mid-salmon pink ware with a sandy texture. At x20 magnification a sparse scatter of fine, rounded quartz, occasional buff coloured clay pellets, rare red iron and very fine white mica are visible. The inner surface has angular quartzite trituration grits up to 4 mm in size.
Comment: Represented by a single body sherd from Phase 12. Source unknown.

Mortarium (MORT3)
Fabric: A very hard, orange sandy fabric with a sparse scatter of red-brown iron grains up to 1.5 mm across. The trituration grit comprises white, angular to sub-angular quartzite up to 4 mm across in size. At x20 an increased number of rounded iron grains are visible along with a sparse scatter of fine angular quartz. The clay body is slightly striated with fine linear cracks.
Comment: Represented by a single sherd from Phase 12. Source unknown.

?North French red-painted ware (NFRPT)
Fabric: A hard, pale coloured sandy ware with pimply surfaces. The ware is macroscopically quite similar to Overwey wares. It is distinguishable both typologically and by the presence of matt orange-red decoration. The technique differs from Pingsdorf where the decoration is applied by a finger dipped in slip (Keller 1995) in that it appears to have been applied with a brush.
Forms: Forms included a handled cup (Fig. 3.5, 109) and closed/jar forms (Fig. 3.3, 49–52).
Comment: The earliest incidence of this ware in the stratigraphic sequence is context (31) coinciding with the first appearance of Pevensey ware. It could thus potentially date from the later 4th century. Most of the other pieces come from the dark earth horizons suggesting if not a late Roman date a Saxon one. Lyne (1994) has recently identified other sources for Overwey type wares at Fareham and in East Sussex and it is just possible that the painted wares belong to a short-lived late Romano-British production. Slight differences between the painted wares themselves might suggest more than one source or may reflect a chronological diversity. The ware was not familiar with Roman ceramicists working in Northern France who considered it post-Roman.

Petrological analysis of red-painted ware, by Alan Vince†
A sample of the red painted ware was submitted for analysis. Possible sources for the ware were suggested to include the south-east of England, northern France, the Meuse valley and the Rhineland. These possible sources were considered in the light of the ceramic petrology.
Description: The sample was thin-sectioned and stained using Dickson's method which distinguishes carbonate inclusions (although as it happens no carbonate inclusions were present). The sample is tempered with a moderate quartzose sand composed of sub-angular and rounded grains of quartz, ranging from 0.4 mm to 0.6 mm across. With the exception of a single example of strained metamorphic polycrystalline quartz all grains are monocrystalline, although many are traversed by cracks, some filled with a thin film of brown iron-rich material. Moderate rounded dark brown to opaque grains are

present, ranging up to 0.2 mm across.

The clay matrix is composed of anisotropic clay minerals, abundant angular quartz grains (up to 0.1 mm across), and sparse muscovite up to 0.1 mm long.

Discussion: The inclusions in this sample are not particularly diagnostic. The petrological characteristics do, however, contrast with those found in products of the Rhineland which normally have little or no silt component in the clay matrix, which is usually remarkably free of inclusions. The iron-stained veins are particularly notable in quartz grains found in wares produced on the Surrey/Hampshire border where they indicate that the quartz grains were derived from an iron-cemented sandstone. However, those grains usually have a well-rounded appearance, in contrast to this sample. Samples of pottery of Carolingian and later date from the Canche valley have a similar petrology, although in these cases it seems that the dark brown/opaque grains are glauconite and altered glauconite. It is possible that the Pevensey grains too are glauconitic, but subjected to more intense heating than the northern French wares, but there are other possibilities, such as iron-replaced faecal material.

Conclusion: Thin-section analysis is inconclusive, although probably disproving a Rhenish source, and a local south-eastern English origin cannot be ruled out.

Anglo-Saxon pottery

by Alan Vince†

All pottery thought to be of early-, mid- or late-Saxon date was examined visually and using a binocular microscope. Ten fabrics were identified visually and assigned the codes CHARN, ECHAF and SX1 to SX8. Brief descriptions of each of the fabrics were made along with a quantified record of sherd count and weight. Samples of these fabrics were then chosen for analysis by thin-section (denoted by ID numbers below). As a result of the thin-section analysis the visually-identified fabric groups can be revised, since several macroscopic distinctions can be seen to have no petrological validity. The refined fabric groups are described below.

Sandstone-tempered wares (SX1, SX2 and SX3) (Fig. 3.3, 55–6; 3.6, 121)

Seventeen sherds tempered with a sandstone-derived sand are present. Nine are featureless body sherds but the remainder all have features typical of early Anglo-Saxon pottery and it is assumed that all 17 sherds are of early Anglo-Saxon date. Two have burnished outer surfaces, one is burnished inside and out, two are decorated with finger-tip impressions, two had a deliberately roughened external surface and one came from a carinated vessel with decoration applied with a round-ended tool. All five decorated sherds are of types for which a 5th century date is possible. Only one sherd had any signs of use, an internal deposit indicating either use for storing or boiling liquids.

Visually, these sandstone-tempered wares were divided into those with a micaceous but otherwise inclusion-less matrix (SX1), those with a fine sandy matrix, in which rounded glauconite could be seen as a minor component (SX2), and those with a matrix containing streaks of red, haematite-rich, clay (SX3). Unfortunately, it was not possible to sample any sherds of SX1 because of their size or decoration but the thin-sections of SX2 and SX3 show that there is glauconite in SX3, as in SX2. It is assumed that SX3 is simply a coarser, oxidised version of SX2.

Mixed flint, quartz and shell gravel-tempered wares (SX4, SX5, SX6 and SX7) (Fig. 3.3, 53–4, 58–60, 63, 68; Fig. 3.5, 92–3, 108)

A total of 133 sherds belong to this category of which 62 sherds were examined in detail. All the sherds are tempered with a mixed coarse sand/fine gravel. Thirty-nine are completely featureless. One sherd is an oval-sectioned handle (Fig. 3.3, 54), joined to the vessel at the top of the rim. Several sherds are from the rims or necks of vessels with everted rims and thickened necks, in some cases with evidence for body walls of very variable thickness. In total, 20 sherds have external sooting, suggesting that most are from cooking pots. In addition, one sherd comes from a thick-walled storage jar and another from a pedestal lamp.

In thin section it could be seen that the attempt to separate these sherds into those with predominantly flint temper (SX5), predominantly quartz sand temper (SX4), mixed temper (SX7), and predominantly shell temper (SX6) was not successful. Abundant flint is present even in sherds which, by eye, appear to be mainly quartz sand-tempered. It is likely that these fabrics are simply extremes in a continuum.

Shell-tempered ware (SX8)

A single shell-tempered sherd is present (although shell is present to a greater or lesser extent in many of the mixed gravel-tempered sherds).

Chaff-tempered ware (ECHAF)

A single sherd contains only abundant organic inclusions. Since the sherd is very small (4 g) no further analysis was possible.

Granite-tempered ware (CHARN)

A single sherd contains fragments of coarse angular rock, some of which can be identified as a biotite granite. Since the sherd is small (8 g) no further analysis was possible. The sherd comes from a vessel with an internally burnished surface.

?Saxon import (IMP WH) (JT)

A single plain whiteware body sherd with the edge of a vertical thumb strip. A hard, slightly harsh fabric. The paste contains a moderate scatter of well-sorted sub-angular clear quartz (< 0.5 mm) in a clean matrix. Rare fine grains of red iron.

Whitewares were imported from the Continent in the mid- to late Saxon period, for example Beauvais ware. This sherd may derive from the same tradition or perhaps come from a similar source as imported whiteware fabric 177 from Hamwic, probably from northern France, used for mortars and various jars/pitchers (Timby 1988, 100).

Medieval regional/local pottery

by Jane Timby

A. Local flint/quartz/shell-gritted wares: LOCMED1–3

LOCMED1

Fabric: A heavily gritted ware with grey core and brown to brownish red oxidised surface. The grit is composed of sub-angular flint and quartz, occasionally with some shell and ferruginous matter. There is considerable variation in the amount and size of the inclusions. Dulley (1967, 219) identified three grades; very copious coarse grit, fragments over 1 mm in diameter; copious grit but few particles over 1 mm; sparse grit, the particles generally finer and mixed with sand, the surface finish is smooth. These might equate with LOCMED1–3 here. The fabric equates with Lyne (2009, 125, 136) fabrics P2/P3.

Forms: Mainly cooking pots, both handmade and wheelmade (Fig. 3.3, 64, 66–7, 69; Fig. 3.4, 70, 72, 75–6, 78) and occasionally dishes/dripping pans (Fig. 3.4, 77, 79, 83, 86–91; Fig. 3.5, 94, Fig. 3.6, 116–7, 119, 124–5). Some of the hand-built bodies have wheel-turned rims. The characteristic rim is either simply everted, developing into a distinctive flange, or folded over outwards to a triangular profile. The later examples have more sharply moulded contours. Evidence from nearby excavations (Dulley 1967) shows both the less developed and more angular vessels were in use alongside late 13th-century imported French jugs. A similar fabric was used for making chimney pots. Occasionally sherds are decorated with impressed motifs or applied thumbed strips (Fig. 3.3, 57).

LOCMED2

Fabric: A hard, well-fired brown or grey ware with a slightly harsh feel. The ware generally found as jugs/pitchers appears to be a refined version of LOCMED1. The paste contains a sparse scatter of ill-sorted rounded to sub-angular quartz, angular, mainly white flint and iron. The flint is rarely larger than 1–1.5 mm. Dulley (1967, 219, fabric b) identified a similar fabric at Pevensey.

Forms: Unglazed cooking pots, glazed or partially glazed jugs and dishes (Fig. 3.5, 65, 71, 73–4, 81–2, 84; Fig. 3.6, 115, 118, 126). Featured sherds include thumbed jug bases and both strap and round section, pierced handles.

LOCMED3

Fabric: A pale brown or grey sandy ware with a grey core. The paste is quite fine, with a sandy feel, and the ware well-fired. At x20 the paste shows an even scatter of very fine quartz sand with a sparse spread of slightly larger, rounded quartz grains, sub-angular red or brown flint (0.5 mm and less) and fine red iron in a finely micaceous clay body. This presumably equates with Dulley's (1967) fabric c.

Forms: Used for handled jugs and jars (Fig. 3.4, 80; Fig 3.6, 127). The jugs are partially glazed. One partially glazed sherd from (901) has incised wavy-line decoration

B. Other flint-tempered wares: MEDFL, MEDFLG

Flint-tempered (MEDFL)

Fabric: A moderately hard ware with a grey core and brownish-orange surfaces. The finely micaceous paste has a sparse to moderate scatter of moderately well-sorted, sub-angular to rounded, quartz and flint inclusions around 1 mm in size. Source unknown but probably local.

Forms: Handmade cooking pots. One sherd has an external clear glaze.

Flint and glauconitic iron (MEDFLG)

Fabric: A fairly coarse fabric with a dark pinkish-orange core and interior and a blackened exterior. The densely sandy paste contains a moderately well-sorted scatter of sub-angular to rounded quartz sand, some iron-stained, sparse red iron, calcareous fragments and angular multi-coloured flint fragments up to 1.5 mm across. Probably a local type, not dissimilar to the Lewes material (Barber pers. comm.) which occurs in East Sussex throughout the 13th–14th century.

Forms: Cooking pots.

C. Chalk-tempered wares: MEDCH

Fabric: A very distinctive fabric with a grey core, red-brown interior and blackened exterior. The paste contains a common frequency of white sub-angular chalk inclusions up to 2–3 mm in size.

Forms: Cooking pots with fairly plain, wheel-made everted rims typologically datable to the 12th century.

D. Sand-tempered local wares

Rye-Ringmer jug tradition (RRING) (Barton 1979, 180–2; 191–254)

Fabric: Sandy wares with variously grey core with orange-red surfaces or orange-red core and surfaces, or a grey core with paler pink surfaces or grey surfaces. Quite a variety in texture is evident with some quite coarse textured pieces with abundant sand temper to sherds with abundant fine-medium sand temper. Glazes tend to be clear or green. Occasionally sherds show an internal white slip. Evidence to date might suggest that the coarser fabrics derive from the Ringmer kilns although the distinction is sometimes blurred and it has been suggested that the Rye kilns could also have been producing a coarser type (Streeten 1980, 112).

Forms: Most of the identifiable sherds come from jugs with rod handles and thumbed bases. At least three sherds show the edges of applied armorial devices which are characteristic of Rye wares. Other decoration includes square rouletting

Date: Evidence so far suggests that these wares date from the early 13th to 15th centuries. Documentary evidence suggests continued into 16th century (Streeten 1985, 103). Very similar wares have been found at a kiln at Norlington Lane, Ringmer with an associated archaeomagnetic date in the 13th century (Barber pers. comm.).

West Sussex type (WSX)
Fabric: Various fabrics, generally grey cored with grey or buff surfaces, fairly coarse with common to abundant quartz sand.
Forms: Vessels are mainly confined to glazed jugs with one example decorated with applied lozenges. Glazes are mainly slightly mottled dark greenish-brown and quite lustrous, or clear. Other decoration includes vertical combing.
Date: 13th–14th century. Included within this group are a few sherds identified as possibly from the Bohemia kilns, Hastings (Barton 1979, 184–90).

Winchelsea (WINCH) (Barton 1979, 3)
Fabric: A black fabric with a reddish core. A dense fine, sandy paste with sparse to rare fragments of shell. Similar date to the Rye kilns.

Medieval red glazed ware (MEDREW)
Fabric: A hard, dark red-orange ware with a brownish orange exterior surface. The finely sandy paste contains a sparse scatter of red and brown iron and rare calcareous inclusions. Traces of a partial external brownish-green glaze. One sherd has white slipped decoration under a clear glaze. Source unknown but probably local. Not dissimilar to Lewes fabric 8 (Barber pers. comm.)
Forms: Jugs.

E. Regional English wares

Wares not clearly of local Sussex origin and rejected as potential imports have been classified as probably English wares, source unknown.

ENG1
Various medium to fine grey or brown sandy wheelmade wares. Most of the sherds are plain although occasional splatters of glaze do occur. Most of the vessels are cooking pots but a small number of jugs/pitchers are also present. Amongst the featured sherds is a foot from a tripod pitcher (601), a sherd with an applied thumb strip (146) a sherd from context 624 with diamond-shaped roller-stamping around the girth of the vessel and a sherd decorated with horizontal grooves (129).

ENG2
Hard, well-fired sandy fabrics, largely from glazed jugs. Possibly sources include the Surrey-Hampshire kilns and possibly Laverstock, Wiltshire. A sherd from context 600 has roller-stamped decoration.

Tudor Green (TUDGR)
A single sherd of Tudor Green (15th–16th century) from Surrey was recovered from (635), Phase 13.

F. Imported medieval pottery
by Alan Vince†

One hundred and fifty-six sherds of possible medieval imports were selected for detailed study. They comprise 108 separate vessels. The sherds were recorded by context, so that there are 112 individual records. Twelve distinct wares were identified, accounting for all but 29 sherds.

RHENISH WARES (PING)

Eighteen sherds, representing no more than nine vessels, are tentatively identified as Pingsdorf ware. This ware was produced at a number of sites in the middle Rhine, to the south of Brühl and probably exported via Cologne. Earlier wares from this region, known as Badorf ware, were produced from the middle of the 8th century, through the 9th century and into the 10th century. Pingsdorf ware is first found in the later 10th century although English finds tend to be 11th century and later.

Hartwig Lüdtke, working on the late 11th-century and later pottery from Schleswig, suggested that there was a progression in the colour of Pingsdorf ware, as a result of an increase in firing temperature, from off-white, to olive to dark (Lüdtke 1985, 60–2, Taf 34–5). At St Magnus Wharf in the City of London, however, all three types were present in dendrochronologically-dated deposits of the early 11th century, earlier than the start of the Schleswig sequence (Vince and Jenner 1991, 100–2). Nevertheless, there was indeed a tendency for material from 12th-century deposits in London to be high-fired. The Pevensey examples are split evenly between dark and off-white fired sherds.

The most distinctive aspect of Pingsdorf ware is its red paint. Two standard patterns were cross-hatched lines on the upper half of the body and groups of three or four 'commas' applied with the finger tips in a circular motion. One example of the latter pattern was present at Pevensey.

A range of vessels were produced in Pingsdorf ware but none of the Pevensey sherds could be assigned to a specific form.

NORTHERN FRENCH WARES

Imports from northern France are the most numerous class found at Pevensey. In virtually no case can these wares be assigned with certainty to a production centre although it is strongly suspected that Rouen itself is the main source. All these northern French wares were produced from off-white firing silty clays to which fine sand or sparse coarser sand might be added. Examination under the binocular microscope shows that there are variations in the texture and nature of the inclusions found in northern French wares. In the absence of distinctive typological features and comparative data on the petrological composition of published wares from France it is impossible to interpret these variations.

Early Glazed ware (NFRY)
Vessels of yellow-glazed whiteware decorated with applied, stamped strips are known from a number of English sites and are thought to date to the 10th and 11th centuries. Recent excavations in Rouen have revealed a number of these vessels and chemical analysis suggests that they are locally made (Dufournier *et al.* 1998). Stratified examples are known from York (Mainman 1990, 444–62) and London (Vince and Jenner 1991, 106). One possible sherd

of this type was found in this Pevensey Castle excavation (ID53), a thick undecorated body sherd.

Unglazed vessels (NFRE)

Six sherds (four vessels) of unglazed whiteware are probably northern French cooking pots or jars. Two of these have sooted exteriors. A third is a small sherd that might be a base fragment from a glazed vessel (ID74, see below).

Pre-conquest deposits in Southampton have produced sherds of Beauvais ware jars, exported via the Ouise valley. Under the binocular microscope these vessels can be seen to have a rounded quartz sand with some probable glauconite. The Pevensey sherds, however, have a finer textured sand temper, with less evidence for rounding of the grains. The precise fabrics vary, however, with one vessel containing large muscovite flakes in a silty matrix and another containing sparse rounded quartz grains up to 3.0 mm across, also in a silty matrix. Two of the sherds have 'ribbed' surfaces, a feature of Norman pottery in the 11th and 12th centuries (discussed by Davison 1972 and more recently by Cotter 1997).

Rouen ware (ROUE, ROUL)

Two distinct groups of vessels are known in the archaeological literature. The first of these is typified by a group of vessels from Rouen museum published by Barton (1966, nos 1–3) and the two vessels from Quilter's Vault, Southampton (Platt and Coleman-Smith 1975, pl. 150). They have an off-white colour and a fine quartz sand temper and are decorated with applied, roller-stamped strips of white clay over a thin red wash. This type of jug was the model for the Rouen-style jugs made in London-type ware from the beginning of the 13th century until *c.* 1250. Vessels of this type were not common in the Pevensey Castle assemblage. Only seven sherds were found, representing no more than three vessels (ROUE). In no case could the decorative scheme be ascertained.

The second group of Rouen ware vessels (ROUL) consists of smaller, thinner-walled vessels with a slightly browner fabric with more fine sand temper. A classic example is a vessel from High Street, Southampton (Platt and Coleman-Smith 1975, fig. 189, no. 1052), a vessel associated with Saintonge polychrome ware and datable to the late 13th or early 14th century. There are 13 sherds of this type from the Pevensey Castle excavations, representing no more than 10 vessels (Fig. 3.6, 123, 131). Decorative schemes include large cone-shaped white pellets over a red wash, diagonal iron-rich strips, vertical applied white strips with small square roller-stamping and a flower modelled in white clay over a red wash with an iron-rich clay pellet at the centre.

Green-glazed ?Rouen ware (NFM)

(Figs 3.4, 85; 3.5, 95)

Jugs with a mottled green glaze, produced by the addition of copper to a lead glaze, are found alongside early Rouen ware vessels wherever the latter occur. Their fabric is very similar to those of the clear-glazed Rouen wares but there are differences in the type of decoration used. It is likely that they were produced alongside the early Rouen ware vessels but whether by a different group of potters or on the same kiln sites is unknown.

Forty-five sherds of these vessels were found at Pevensey, but representing only a maximum of 14 vessels (a single smashed vessel accounts for 28 sherds, ID48). One vessel has copper-stained glaze externally and clear glaze inside (ID109). One sherd had a pulled spout, a rare feature on these vessels, which normally have no spouts at all, and two vessels had vertical applied triangular self-coloured strips. One squared rim had an accidental smear of red clay under the glaze, perhaps an indication that it was made alongside Rouen ware vessels.

Green-glazed micaceous silty ware (NFMS)

A distinctive class of northern French import has been noted on many English and Irish sites but has yet to be given a standard name or attribution. An example from High Street A, Southampton (Platt and Coleman-Smith 1975, no. 980) will serve as a type specimen. The fabric is browner than other French whitewares, although still a light-coloured clay. The texture is siltier than other imported French whitewares and muscovite is an abundant element in the silt.

Typologically, these vessels are closer to south-western French than Rouen ware vessels. They typically have the same tall baluster form, strap handles thrown on the wheel and large parrot-beak bridge spouts. Decoration, however, is different. They can be decorated with roller-stamping and horizontal grooves.

The distribution of this type on sites in England has a western bias: Exeter, Launceston Castle, Chepstow, Bristol, and Dublin have all produced examples whereas London, Boston and Hull have not.

Direct dating is at present difficult but a case could be made for these vessels being the prototype for Ham Green B ware jugs in the later 12th and early 13th centuries, mirroring the situation with Rouen ware and London-type ware in the east. Six sherds of this type were recovered from the excavations at Pevensey Castle.

Normandy gritty ware (NORG)

Two sherds of Normandy gritty ware were present. This ware is another French whiteware, distinguished mainly by the presence of coarse rounded quartz gravel, some of which is haematite-coated. One sherd is from a standard Normandy gritty ware vessel with a wide applied band decorated with pairs of finger-tip impressions (ID64). The other sherd is a body sherd with splashes of yellow glaze.

SOUTH-WESTERN FRENCH WARES

The south-west of France was a major producer of whitewares in the medieval period. Of these, the best known is Saintonge ware. Following recent advances in characterisation of these wares it is now clear that polychrome and all-over-green vessels have a tight chemical signature, suggesting that they had a restricted source and limited period of production. Mottled-green glazed vessels have a wider spread of chemical compositions and were produced over a longer period of time and, perhaps, a wider geographic area. Following the proposal of Deroeux and Dufournier (Deroeux *et al.* 1994) the term Saintonge ware is here restricted to the polychrome and all-over-green glazed vessels and the remainder are classed as south-western French wares. It should be noted, however, that the standard practice in the British Isles and Ireland is to class both groups as Saintonge ware.

Mottled-glazed wares (SAIM)

Twenty sherds of south-western French whiteware with mottled green glaze were found in the excavations, representing no more than 18 vessels. Four of these sherds had been burnt after firing, and two of these were certainly from the same vessel. Only one featured sherd was present, the body-handle join from a strap handle.

Mottled-glazed vessels of this sort have a wide date range, being first found in early to mid-13th-century deposits and continuing throughout the 13th and 14th centuries. The earlier vessels are usually tall baluster jugs whereas squatter forms, often with less glaze, become common later on.

Saintonge polychrome and all-over green wares (SAIG, SAIP)

A single sherd from a jug coated with a homogenous copper green glaze was found in the excavation (SAIG, ID73) and one possible example of polychrome-decorated ware (SAIP, ID103).

These two decorative schemes – polychrome and all-over-green – sometimes occur together, with green glaze inside and polychrome outside and the two types have identical distributions and dates. Current thinking places the production of this ware in a very narrow band in the late 13th or early 14th century. Dendrochronologically-dated deposits in the City of London date the introduction to sometime later than 1270 and earlier than *c.* 1330.

FLEMISH HIGHLY DECORATED WARES? (AARD) (Fig. 3.6, 129)

Six sherds of white-slipped redware are tentatively identified as being Flemish imports, so-called Aardenburg ware. None of the Pevensey sherds is decorated, however, and the similarity of Flemish and English slipped wares in the 13th and 14th centuries makes this identification very tentative.

OTHER POSSIBLE IMPORTS (MISC) (Fig. 3.6, 120, 128)

Twenty-nine sherds were submitted for identification but cannot at present be assigned to any known source. They include both white-firing and red-firing vessels. Some might be of continental origin and others of non-local English origin. All are coded MISC in the archive database and are individually described there.

Post-medieval pottery

by Jane Timby

The post-medieval/modern pottery was divided up into nine classes with a tenth miscellaneous group. No work has been undertaken to trace the possible sources for the local wares.

A. English stonewares (PMESTW)

A particularly large group almost completely composed of mineral water or soft drinks bottles many carrying local trademarks (Fig. 3.6, 132, 134–5).

B. Proto-stoneware (PMPSTW)

Probably local.

C. Imported stonewares (PMISTW)

The post-medieval imported stoneware comprised single sherds of a Raeren ware flask and a Cologne/Frechen tankard and Normandy stoneware.

D. Spanish amphora (OLIVE)

Three sherds from a Spanish olive jar were present in context (600), Phase 15.

E. English earthenware (PMGRE)

A large quantity of glazed and partially glazed red earthenware were present probably from several different local sources. Amongst the identifiable forms were large bowls (Fig. 3.6, 130, 133), dishes, pipkins, chamber-pots (Fig. 3.6, 122), a spouted jug, mugs and several flower-pots.

F. Tin-glazed earthenware (PMTG)

G. Porcelain (PMPORC)

Featured sherds includes cups and a small bowl.

H. Surrey-Hampshire border wares (BORDY) (Pearce 1992)

Several sherds of post-medieval glazed ware typical of the Surrey-Hampshire border industry were present. Amongst the recognisable forms are chamber pots (Pearce 1992, type 1), bowls, cooking pots and pipkins. Date: 16th–18th century.

I. Miscellaneous white-bodied glazed earthenware (china) (PMCH)

Included within this are a few yellow-glazed sherds probably from the Graffham kilns and likely to date to the 16th–17th century (Aldsworth and Down 1976). Featured sherds include tea cups, saucers, teapots, plates and mugs.

Appendix 3. Soil micromorphology: detailed analysis

	Thin section	Bulk sample	Depth	Context	Period	%LOI	MS x 10-8 S1 Kg-1	P2O5 (HCl)	P2O5OI (HCl)	P ratio (HCl)	Microfacies
				PEV 94							
1	1		44-52	3	12th-13thC Norman/residual Roman?						SMF8
2	2		75-83	17	12th-14thC Norman						SMF8
3	3		106-110	17	12th-14thC Norman						SMF7-7a
4	3		110-114	24	7th-11thC Saxon/Roman						SMF6
5	4		134-140	24	7th-11thC Saxon/Roman						SMF6
6	5		152-160	24	7th-11thC Saxon/Roman						SMF6
7	6		183-183.5	25	7th-11thC Saxon/Roman						SMF5
8	6		185.5-191	31	7th-11thC Saxon/Roman						SMF4
9	7		234-238	36-47?	4thC Roman						SMF3b
10	7		238-242	39, 38/52?	4thC Roman						SMF3a
11	8		242-243	61	*c.*370+						SMF2c
12	8		243-245	61	*c.*370+						SMF2b
13	8		245-246	63/67	*c.*370+						SMF2a
14	8		246-250	71	*c.*370+						SMF1b
15	10		550-558	510	Geology piling substrate						SMF1a
16	9		0.5-8.5		Norman buried soil						(SMF8)
				PEV 95							
17	M1a	Mon.1 xA	24-31	717	No pottery	5.5	93	2350	2220	0.9	SMF6
18	M1b	Mon.1 xB	41-45	734	No pottery	5.3	96	2550	2550	1	SMF8
19	M1c	Mon.1 xC	46-52	734	No pottery	5.4	90	2380	2250	0.9	SMF6
20	M1d	Mon.1 xD	54-60	718	R/B & Saxon	5.2	110	3010	2880	1	SMF6 & 7
21	M1e	Mon.1	62-68	718	R/B & Saxon-some 13thC						SMF6
22	M2a	Mon.2 xA	43-50	734	No pottery	5.6	107	2950	2860	1	SMF6 & 7
23		Mon.2 xB	51-57	734	No pottery	5.3	100	2790	2690	1	SMF6
24	M2b		59-65								SMF6
25	M2c	Mon.2 xC	66-72	718	R/B & Saxon	5.4	101	2950	2860	1	SMF6
26	M2d	Mon.2 xD	74-79	718	R/B & Saxon	5.3	108	3130	3030	1	SMF6
27	M2e	Mon.2 xE	80-86	718	R/B & Saxon	5.2	93	2930	2920	1	SMF6

continued below

	Gravel (flint)	Massive silts	Chalk	"Mortar"	Shell	Brickearth/Daub	Soil inclusion/turf	Soil inclusion/silty clay, peat/reeds?	Burned organics/soil/daub	Pottery	Charcoal	Plant fragments/amorphous OM	Bone	Burned bone	Coprolite (nightsoil?)	Coprolite (herbivore?)	Coprolite (omnivore?)	Coprolite (dog)	Stabling crust	Dung mixed soil	Burned dung
	PEV 94																				
1	aaa		a	a	a	a?	aa		a	a	aa	a	a		a						
2	aa		a	aa	a	a?	a		a	a	a	a	a		a	a*				a*	
3	aa		a		a		a		a	a*	aa	aa	a		a	aaa			a?	aaaa	aa
4	aaa		a		a				a		a	a	a		a						
5	aa		a	a	a	a?	a		a		aa		a		a						
6	a		a	a	a	a?			a	a	a	a	a	a	a						
7	a-1		a		a		a		a		a	aa	a	a	a						
8			a	a-1	a	a?	a		a		aaa	a	a	a	a			a-2			
9	a		a-3	a	a		a	a-2	a		aa	aa	a	a	a						
10	a		a	a	a			a	a		aaa	a	a	a	a						
11	a	a	a		a			a	a		aa		a	a-2	a						
12	a	a	a	a	a				a	a	aa	a	a	a-1	a						
13	aa	aa	a-2		a-5		a		aa	a	aaa	a	a	a-1	a	a-1					
14	a-3	aaaaa		a-2						a-4	a-5										
15		aaaaa																			
16	*no data*																				
	PEV 95																				
17	*no data*																				
18	*no data*																				
19	a		a	a	aaa				a		a		a		a						
20	aaa		a	aa	a		a		a	a*	a	a	a		a	a?	a?			a*	
21	aaa		a	a*	a*				a	a*	a		a		a						
22	aa		a	a	a		a				a	a	a	a	a	a?				a	
23																					
24	aa		a	a	a		a				a*		a		a						
25	*no data*																				
26	*no data*																				
27	aa		a	a	a				a		a		a		aa						

continued below

	Ash	Phytoliths	Articulated phytoliths	Siliceous stem pseudomorphs	Hammerscale?/vesicular slag	Grindstone (igneous rock)	Secondary P-Vivianite (or pseudomorphs)	Phosphate stained deposit	Secondary amorphous P/Fe	Iron mottling	Secondary $CaCO_3$	Burrows	In situ roots	Massive structured	Laminated Bedding	Layered microstructure	Spongy microstructure	Packing void microstructure	Crumb/blocky/prismatic structure	Vughy microstructure	Channels and chambers
	PEV 94																				
1	a	aa			a*			a	aaa	a	a	aaaa		fff					ff		f
2	a	aa							aaaa	aa	a	aaaaa		ff					ffff		f
3	aa	aaa						a	aaa?	aaa	a	aaaaa	a	ff		ff		ff	ff		ff
4	a	aa										aaaaa		ffff					ff		
5	a	aa					a			a		aaaaa		ff					ffff		
6	a	aa	a-1		a*							aaaaa		ff					ffff		ff
7	a	a		a?	a*		a					aaaaa		ff					fff		
8	a	a		a?	a*				a	a		aaaaa		ff					fff		
9	a	a		a-3	a*		a					aaaaa		ff					ff		ff
10	a	a+			a-3				a			aaa		ff					ff	f	ff
11	a	a					a		a		a	aa		ff			f			f	ff
12	a	a					aa		aa		a	aaa		ff							ffff
13	aa	a					aa		aa		a	aaaaa		ff							ff
14										aaa		aa		ffff	f		f				
15										a				fffff	fffff			fffff			
16																					
	PEV 95																				
17																					
18																					
19	a	aa										aaa		fff					fff		
20	a	aa						a	a			aaa	a*	ff				ff	fff		f
21	a	aa										a		ffff					ff		
22	a	aa										aaa		ff				f	ff		f
23																					
24	a	aa										aaaaa		ffff				ff			
25																					
26																					
27	a	aa					a*					aaaa		fff					fff		

continued below

	Planes	Excrements (<100µm)	Textural features	Amorphous coatings	Slug plates	Earthworm granules	Excrements (<500µm)	Excrements (>500µm)
	PEV 94							
1	ff	a			a*	a	a	aaaaa
2	fff		a*		a*	a		aaaaa
3	f	a	a*		a*	a	aa	aaaaa
4					a*	a		aaaaa
5						a		aaaaa
6					a*	a*		(aaaaa)
7					a-2	a-2		(aaaa)
8						a-1		(aaa)
9			a		a-5	a-4		(aaaa)
10	f		a			a-1		(aaaa)
11			a					(aa)
12			a					(aaa)
13			a					(aaa)
14			a-2	aaa				(aa)
15			a-1	a				
16								
	PEV 95							
17								
18								
19	ff				a*	a		aaaaa
20	f	a			a*	a	a	aaaaa
21	f				a*	a		aaaaa
22	f				a*	a	aa	aaaaa
23								
24					a*	a		aaaaa
25								
26								
27					a*	a		aaaaa

Appendix 4. Soil micromorphology: the chemistry of the 'dark earth' at Pevensey compared with other contemporary English sites

Broad Context	LOI (%)					P_2O_5 (ppm)					MS (10^{-8} SI kg^{-1})				
	Mean	*Min.*	*Max.*	*Std. Dev.*	*n*	*Mean*	*Min.*	*Max.*	*Std. Dev.*	*n*	*Mean*	*Min.*	*Max.*	*Std. Dev.*	*n*
COSE DE	7.1	5.5	9.5	1.60	*7*	2100	1230	3410	737.19	*7*	140.6	91	215	41.46	*7*
COSE RB	1.5	0.9	2.1	0.85	*2*	890	510	1270	537.40	*2*	44.5	29	60	21.92	*2*
BISH DE	7.3	5.9	8.1	0.85	*5*	2130	2010	2310	114.41	*5*	157.8	150	172	9.47	*5*
BISH R	5.0	2.8	9.7	2.81	*5*	2300	840	4160	1674.27	*5*	129.2	41	269	97.03	*5*
BISH EDE	5.1	5.1	5.1	-	*1*	1780	1780	1780	-	*1*	115	115	115	-	*1*
PEP DE	5.4	5.4	5.4	-	*1*	-	-	-	-	-	75	75	75	-	*1*
PEP EDE	3.7	2.7	4.2	0.63	*5*	1380	1190	1630	179.92	*5*	73.2	39	101	24.78	*5*
PEP Bt	1.9	1.9	1.9	-	*1*	760	760	760	-	*1*	11	11	11	-	*1*
POUL N	11.9	2.3	27.4	7.52	*12*	2960	720	4330	1040.15	*12*	742.9	37	3278	1125.73	*12*
POUL DE	7.9	7.9	7.9	-	*1*	3490	3490	3490	-	*1*	210	210	210	-	*1*
POUL R	9.3	1.8	36.5	10.63	*36*	2200	660	4330	1126.98	*36*	107.9	12	948	178.15	*36*
POUL RB	5.2	3.5	9.3	2.76	*4*	500	480	520	17.02	*4*	5.7	4	7	1.50	*4*
DEAN DE	7.7	5.9	11.6	2.60	*4*	3330	2670	3670	469.11	*4*	259	212	302	20.31	*4*
CANT DE	5.4	5.4	5.4	-	*1*	2470	2470	2470	-	*1*	220	220	220	-	*1*
CANT R	3.0	1.8	4.5	1.11	*4*	1630	580	2320	741.86	*4*	68	42	97	24.72	*4*
ELM R	5.3	3.8	6.5	0.79	*15*	1300	340	2920	696.11	*15*	82.4	8	302	86.47	*15*
ELM EDE	5.4	3.7	8.1	1.41	*8*	2650	1660	3390	589.63	*8*	56.1	31	92	18.33	*8*
SCO DE	2.8	2.2	3.7	0.578	*6*	1090	760	1790	384.36	*6*	19.2	3	42	17.22	*6*
SCO R	1.0	0.4	1.5	0.472	*7*	300	100	520	180.92	*7*	4.5	0.1	24	8.65	*7*
PEV DE	5.3	5.2	5.6	0.133	*9*	2780	2350	3130	286.693	*9*	99.8	90	110	7.31	*9*
Total															***134***

COSE DE – Courage's 'dark earth'
COSE RB – Courage's Romano-British soil
BISH DE – 7–11, Bishopsgate 'dark earth'
BISH R – 7–11, Bishopsgate Roman occupation floors etc.
BISH EDE – 7–11, Bishopsgate early (2nd–4th century) 'dark earth'
PEP DE – Colchester House (PEP89) 'dark earth' formed in 4th century building rubble
PEP EDE – Colchester House (PEP89) early (2nd–4th century) 'dark earth'
PEP Bt – Colchester House (PEP89) subsoil in brickearth
POUL N – No. 1, Poultry Norman deposits
POUL DE – No. 1, Poultry 'dark earth' (contaminated by overlying Norman deposits)
POUL R – No. 1, Poultry Roman occupation deposits
POUL RB – No 1, Poultry pre-Roman/Romano-British soils
DEAN DE – Deansway, Worcester 'dark earth' ('small town')
CANT DE – Canterbury 'dark earth' (Beer Cart Lane)
CANT R – Canterbury Roman levels (Sessions House, Bradbourne House)
ELM R – Elms Farm, Heybridge Roman levels ('small town')
ELM EDE – Elms Farm, Heybridge early (Romano-British) 'dark earth' ('small town')
SCO DE – Scole/Oakley, Suffolk/Norfolk 'dark earth' ('small town/rural settlement)
SCO R – Scole/Oakley, Suffolk/Norfolk Roman podzol soils ('small town/rural settlement)
PEV DE – Pevensey Castle, Sussex 'dark earth'

Index

by Susan M. Vaughan

Illustrations are denoted by page numbers in *italics*.